Dedication

To my husband, Paul, who first challenged me to write and encourages me daily. And to my daughters Jenn and Alli, who have hopefully learned from my example that there is no shortcut to anything worth having but that a passion followed is worth the price.

—*Lynn Hogan*

"I would thank you from the bottom of my heart, but for you my heart has no bottom." To my husband Dan, whose encouragement and love helped make this endeavor possible. Thank you for taking on additional tasks so that I could focus on writing. To my mom, Connie, for her support, and for taking the time to review my chapters and give me feedback from the reader's point of view. To my dad, Mark, for his encouragement (and for Skyping with me on a moment's notice so I could take a photo and finish a chapter). To my sister-in-law, Amy, for her help with almost anything I asked of her. To my best friend, Vickie, for always being there when I needed encouragement. To all my family and friends for their love and support.

I also want to thank Lynn, Nancy, Keri, Erin, Sam, and the entire Pearson team for their help and guidance and for giving me this amazing opportunity. I have learned so much!

—*Amy Rutledge*

About the Authors

Lynn Hogan has taught in the field of Computer Information Systems for the past 30 years. She is on the authoring team of *Practical Computing* and *Your Office* and has contributed chapters for several computer applications textbooks. Specializing in microcomputer applications, she currently teaches at the University of North Alabama. She earned an M.B.A. from the University of North Alabama and a Ph.D. from the University of Alabama. Lynn resides in Alabama with her husband, Paul, and two daughters, Jenn and Alli.

Amy Rutledge is a Special Instructor of Management Information Systems at Oakland University in Rochester, Michigan. She coordinates academic programs in Microsoft Office applications and introductory Management Information Systems courses for the School of Business Administration. She is the Faculty Advisor for the Association for Information Systems (AIS) Student Chapter at Oakland University. Before joining Oakland University as an Instructor, Amy spent several years working for a music distribution company and automotive manufacturer in various corporate roles including IT Project Management. She holds a B.S. in Business Administration specializing in Management Information Systems, and a B.A. in French Modern Language and Literature. She holds an M.B.A from Oakland University. She resides in Michigan with her husband, Dan.

Acknowledgments

The authors of a textbook are but a small part of a professional team dedicated to producing high-quality educational material. Our sincere appreciation goes to Samantha McAfee, Acquisitions Editor, for directing this third edition. Erin Clark and Keri Rand kept a tight schedule, very tactfully reminding us of unwavering deadlines. Without such direction, this writing experience would not have been nearly as much fun and would certainly not have come in on time. The entire Pearson Design and Production team is to be commended for lending their talent and direction to this effort. Thanks to Nancy Lamm for coordinating the editing phase of the project and to all of the technical editors for painstakingly double-checking the content. A special note of appreciation goes to the reviewers who paid close attention to detail and who offered a wealth of practical experience in comments and suggestions that have strengthened this edition. We are proud to be included in the team effort that has produced this newest edition of Practical Computing. Our thanks to everyone involved!

Melissa Joey Bryant, Forsyth Tech
Menka Brown, Piedmont Technical College
MaryLou Wilson, Piedmont Technical College
Angel Alexander, Piedmont Technical College
Norma Marler, Catawba Valley Community College
Terry Holleman, Catawba Valley Community College
Nazih Abdallah, University of Central Florida
Lancie Affonso, College of Charleston
Gary R. Armstrong, Shippensburg University
Ita Borger-Boglin, San Antonio College
Jack Bresenham, Winthrop University
Judith C. Brown, University of Memphis
Cindy Buell, Central Oregon Community College
Debra Burhans, Canisius College
Debra Chapman, University of South Alabama
Dewey DeFalco, Jones College
Allen Dooley, Pasadena City College
Larry Dugan, Finger Lakes Community College
Mimi Duncan, University of Missouri, St. Louis
Susan Fry, Boise State University
Marta Gonzalez, Hudson County Community College
Kurt W. Kominek, Northeast State Technical Community College
Richard W. Land, International Academy of Design & Technology
Daniela Marghitu, Auburn University
Cindi A. Nadelman, New England College
Tim Pelton, University of Victoria
Jennifer Pickle, Amarillo College
Pratap P. Reddy, Raritan Valley Community College
Steven Smith, El Paso Community College
Steve St. John, Tulsa Community College
Doug Yoder, Columbus State Community College
David L. Zagorodney, Heald College
Dawn Parrish Wood, Valdosta Technical College

Preface

How and Why We Built This Book

We know the special challenges posed by the computer novice, and we are here to help you meet them! *Practical Computing* will help you ease your students into the world of computing with a user-friendly design and creative multimedia tools that make learning exciting. Designed with input from instructors who understand your needs, the lessons in *Practical Computing* address concepts in a disciplined, yet enjoyable way.

The inspiration for this book came from a computer literacy class designed for adults who had very little computer background but a real eagerness to learn. The students' questions, interests, and suggestions helped shape the content of the class and, subsequently, this book.

The result immediately sparks student interest by focusing on the tasks they want to accomplish with their PCs as well as skills that they can apply at home or in the workplace right away. The sequence of topics is carefully set up to mimic the way students typically use practical computing information both in class and at home.

Chapter 1 introduces students to computer applications in a brief overview. Chapter 2 immediately introduces the operating system, which students interact with on a daily basis in their computers. Chapter 3 discusses the Internet, one of the topics most familiar to many students, but also the quickest to evolve. Chapters 4, 5, and 6 focus on the key Microsoft applications students use inside and out of class, getting them hands-on knowledge and experience in Microsoft Office 2010. Chapter 7 describes networking and security, an extremely important topic in our highly digital world. Chapter 8 brings in social networking, online communication, and cloud computing. Chapter 9 introduces students to "the fun stuff" of multimedia applications and digital entertainment. Finally, in this edition an appendix has been added to focus on giving students starter tips and tricks in working with the most popular Learning Management Systems on campus.

With instructor feedback, we made several changes in the text for the third edition. One key change has been to focus on the practicality of content and approach, so we've pulled the hardware out of its own chapter and included it as a feature where it is relevant throughout the text. Because of the way students use the text, we have put more emphasis on boxed features to relay interesting information that will draw students deeper into the content.

This practical approach will get your students up and running in no time!

Key Learning Features:

- Content that fits the level of your students
- Case studies that make sense of the content
- Examples that demonstrate the topic in a realistic way
- Explanation of Why am I doing this?

- **Hands-On:** Projects that allow students to practice the material they have learned. Now features at least two per chapter for student activity and engagement!
- **In Depth:** Segments that go into more depth on particular issues and Technologies
- **Technology Insight:** A description of a hardware or software concept relevant to the content
- **A Look Back:** A historical look at a relevant topic to help students appreciate where technology is now versus where it came from
- **Quick Tips:** Tips and shortcuts for the practical use of the PC

For the Instructor

Instructor Resources

Your Practical Computing Instructor's Resource CD-ROM includes the tools you expect from a Pearson Computer Concepts text, such as:

- The Instructor's Manual
- Solutions to all questions and exercises from the book and website
- Online Study Guide
- PowerPoint slide presentations for each chapter
- Test Bank
- TestGen

In addition, you can find these tools on our online Instructor Resource Center at **www.pearsonhighered.com**, along with WebCT and Blackboard ePacks.

By navigating through these resources, you can collect the materials that are most relevant to your interests, edit them to create powerful class lectures, copy them to your own computer's hard drive, and/or upload them to an online course management system.

TestGen Software

TestGen is a test generator program that lets you view and easily edit testbank questions, transfer them to tests, and print them in a variety of formats suitable to your teaching situation. The program also offers many options for organizing and displaying testbanks and tests. A built-in random number and text generator makes it ideal for creating multiple versions of tests that involve calculations, providing more possible test items than testbank questions. Powerful search and sort functions let you easily locate questions and arrange them in the order you prefer. Building tests is easy with TestGen, and exams can be easily uploaded into WebCT, Blackboard, and myitlab.

Tools for Online Learning

Companion Web Site

This text is accompanied by a Companion Website for your students. You can find this at **www.pearsonhighered.com/practicalcomputing**. Features of this site include course objectives, an online study guide, supplemental chapters, end-of-chapter materials, and a glossary.

For the Student

Welcome to the exciting world of computers! *Practical Computing* was written with you, the beginner, in mind. It is carefully arranged to guide you through every step of learning how to use your computer and other digital devices, from the first plug-in to the latest upgrades. When you have completed this book, you will have the skills to get what you want out of the technology of today, including Microsoft Word, Excel, and PowerPoint.

Student Resources

Pearson's Companion Website

www.pearsonhighered.com/practicalcomputing offers expanded IT resources and downloadable supplements. Here you can find the following self-study tools for each chapter:

- Online Study Guide
- Chapter Objectives
- Glossary
- Chapter Summary
- Web Resources

Brief Contents

Contents

CHAPTER **ONE**

Understanding Computers

A PERSONAL COMPUTER CAN OFFER A WEALTH OF enjoyment to anyone who is willing to invest some time in understanding how to work with it. Perhaps friends have told you how much fun it is to explore the Internet and to keep up with family through e-mail. Others might use a computer to create family trees, monitor home finances, or maintain small business records. The people in computer commercials certainly think they need a computer! But what about you? Perhaps you have an interest, but are not certain where to start. The first thing you should do is carefully consider why you want a computer. Think about what you plan to do with it. Regardless of what you decide to use it for, owning a personal computer can open up an entire new world of activities and enjoyment.

Computer Fundamentals

The equipment that makes up a computer system is known as hardware. When you see an advertisement for a computer, you are reading about the computer's hardware. Anything related to a computer that you can pick up and hold is considered hardware. The keyboard, mouse, monitor, and printer are typical hardware components. Software is an equally

OBJECTIVES

When you complete this chapter, you will:

▶ Be able to identify types of computers and computing devices.

▶ Be aware of different computer-related careers.

▶ Identify various categories of application software and what each is used for.

▶ Become familiar with input, output, and processing components.

▶ Understand how to use and acquire software.

▶ Understand the concept of memory and how it relates to storage.

▶ Identify various forms of storage.

▶ Become familiar with the types of system software.

important component as it enables you to interact with the computer and accomplish tasks. Using software, you can write a letter, browse the Internet, and play computer games. Being aware of software and hardware that will help you accomplish your computing goals is the first step toward making sure that you have all you need to fully enjoy a computer. In this section, you will learn about hardware, software, and computer careers.

Computer Uses

You find computers everywhere in your daily life. When you use an ATM to withdraw money or purchase groceries at the store with your shopper's card, you are interacting with a computer system. So, what is a computer? A **computer** is an electronic device that can be programmed to carry out tasks. A computer receives *input* in the form of data, *processes* that data, and *outputs* the results.

Computer Careers

Careers in the computer field are very much in demand today, and will continue to be so in the foreseeable future. According to the U.S. Bureau of Labor Statistics,

> Three of the fastest growing occupations are computer specialist occupations. Network systems and data communications analysts, the occupation with the second-fastest rate of growth, will see gains across a wide range of industries. Because businesses will continue to adopt newer networking technologies and individuals and organizations will develop a growing reliance on the Internet, employment in this occupation is expected to increase by 53.4 percent. Furthermore, as new software products are needed to facilitate this reliance on technology, computer software applications engineers and systems software engineers also will grow rapidly in number. (www.bls.gov, 2011)

If you are considering a career in information technology, you should be aware of the various career paths available to you. Those careers include, but are not limited to:

- Computer software engineer—designs and develops organizational and consumer software for the personal computer. This career professional also focuses on developing applications for phones, tablets, and other devices.

- Network systems and data communications analyst (shown in Figure 1.2)—focuses on keeping a network up and running at companies and government organizations.
- Computer support specialist—provides assistance when a computer or program is not working properly.
- Database administrator—organizes and maintains data stored in databases. He or she also maintains the security and integrity of information.
- IT project manager—focuses on managing IT projects from start to finish. A project manager allocates resources to teams and is responsible for meeting the schedule and budget of the project. This career involves an understanding of IT, business, and a high degree of interpersonal skills.
- IT consultant—focuses on the processes, people, and systems needed to improve business efficiency. This career typically spans a wide range of industries and involves travel.
- Web designer and developer—designs websites and Web applications (programs that allow us to do things like bank or shop online).

Eimantas Buzas/Shutterstock

Figure 1.2 Network analysts and administrators work to maintain servers and keep the organizational network up and running.

A career in the IT field typically requires some combination of specialized training, a college degree, or professional certifications.

Types of Computers

When you think of a computer you usually envision a PC, or personal computer. However, computers can also be found in many devices you would not normally think of as computerized. For example, modern vehicles contain computers that collect information regarding a vehicle's diagnostics, which can be retrieved by a service technician at the time of repair. Moreover, many of today's mobile phones contain computer systems that enable the user to connect to the Internet, read and write e-mail, and use various software programs. In this section, you will be introduced to personal computers as well as specialty computers and supercomputers.

Microcomputers and Specialty Computers

Types of microcomputers on the market vary widely. One category of micro-computer, the **personal computer (PC)**, is typically designed for individual use, providing access to the Internet and enabling a user to work with applications such as word processing, editing photographs, and maintaining a family budget. PCs are available in many sizes, from desktop models to laptops to tablets.

When you purchase a computer, you will want to get the most capability for the lowest cost. A microcomputer system typically costs $300 to $3,000, depending on manufacturer, speed, type, and other specifications. Before considering a computer for purchase, you should think about what you plan to do with it. A popular use of home computers is to create, edit, and print documents. You can also maintain records on anything from business inventory to your

In Depth

Tablets

A tablet is a general purpose computer contained on a single panel. Perhaps the most recognizable tablet is the iPad, but the Android, HP TouchPad, BlackBerry PlayBook, and the Tablet PC are also tablet options. The most distinguishing characteristic of a tablet is its use of a touch screen as an input device. Each tablet runs apps (application software programs that are downloaded to a mobile device) designed specifically for its own operating system, which means that if you own an iPad, you can only run iPad apps. With over 65,000 iPad apps to choose from, the limitation to a single tablet platform is not a problem for most iPad users. Used primarily for Internet browsing, games, and reading, the tablet is not likely to replace the more versatile laptop for many people, but it is definitely an attractive option for portable Web browsing, entertainment, and multimedia. Those who are intent on maintaining a mobile social network will appreciate the e-mail, Twitter, Facebook, and general Web browsing facility of a tablet. E-books from Amazon, Apple, and Barnes and Noble are available for a tablet as are news apps such as Flipboard and Zite. The touchscreen and speakers make it easy to enjoy such wildly popular games as Angry Birds and Civilization Revolution, and watching videos is a breeze. Most tablets include cameras for video chatting and general photography. With up to 10 hours of battery life, a tablet might not be as easy to carry as a smartphone or iPod Touch, but it is a very versatile all-in-one entertainment and Web surfing device that is quickly gaining popularity. However it is not likely to replace more traditional computers engaged in general-purpose applications in the near future.

Figure 1.3 Desktop computers are one type of microcomputer.

book collection. It is also fun to learn to use a digital camera so you can work with digital photos on a computer, printing them in various sizes. Many people enjoy recording family data and creating a family tree. Of course, connecting to the Internet and using e-mail remain the most common reasons for purchasing a home computer.

A **desktop computer** (Figure 1.3) is a personal computer in which all the components, including the keyboard, mouse, monitor, and system unit, are not easily portable. The large rectangular component where computing takes place is either a tower, which sits upright, or a desktop, which lies flat underneath the monitor.

A **laptop computer**, also called a **notebook computer** (Figure 1.4), has just as much computing power as a desktop but comes in a much smaller package. Comprising about 40% of total PC sales, laptops integrate the display, keyboard, memory, disk storage devices, and a pointing device, such as a trackball, touch pad, or pointing stick, into a battery-operated package. A laptop is a handy tool for anyone who wants portable computer power, such as professionals who must make presentations, or instructors who wish to grade computer assignments at home. Students might take notes on laptops or use them for gathering data from lab experiments. Some people simply do not want to be tied to a desk while working with the computer and like the freedom of movement they get with a laptop. Like desktops, laptops include a microprocessor, memory, disk drives, input/output ports, and other standard components. Unlike desktops, laptops can run for several hours on some type of rechargeable battery before being plugged back into an electrical source. Even in a recharged state, a standard laptop battery seldom provides power for more than seven hours at a time, with the battery life typically becoming shorter as the laptop ages. Laptops generally cost more than desktops, in the range of $500 to $3,500.

A **tablet PC** (Figure 1.5) such as an iPad, is a wireless laptop computer model that enables a user to use either a finger or a stylus, an input device shaped much like a small pencil, to communicate through a touch screen. Combining the convenience of a laptop computer with the ease of pen and paper, a tablet PC is a perfect solution for traveling salespeople who must record transactions, or professionals who need to make appointments, annotate documents, and fill in electronic forms. iPads do not have disk drives but rather use flash storage to save data.

Another category of computer is the **netbook**. Netbooks are small, lightweight, inexpensive computers. They typically do not have all the features or as much computing power as a full notebook or desktop computer because their primary purpose is to connect to the Internet and use e-mail. They usually have a much longer battery life than a notebook. Some can go as long as nine or ten hours without charging.

Figure 1.4 Laptop computers have just as much computing power as desktops but are much smaller in size.

Mobile phones are becoming even more versatile, often including such features as Internet access, e-mail retrieval, and appointment scheduling. In fact, the dividing line between computers and mobile phones is blurring. When you consider the

Figure 1.5 Tablets and smartphones are lightweight and allow you to connect to the Internet wirelessly.

many electronic devices that people often carry, such as mobile phones, computers, and MP3 players, it makes sense to combine those features into multifunction units. **Integrated phones** are also called **smartphones** (Figure 1.5). Products such as the iPhone combine a mobile phone, e-mail, address book, task list, calendar, and Web browsing features into one convenient handheld unit. Televisions and cars with Internet connectivity and downloadable applications are likely to be the norm in the not-too-distant future.

A Look Back

Who Invented the Computer?

No simple answer exists for the question of who invented the computer, because many inventors contributed to the development of the computer in many ways. Most researchers recognize Professor John Atanasoff and graduate student Clifford Berry as the developers of the world's first electronic digital computer around 1939. John Atanasoff recorded most of the early designs for the first computer on the back of a cocktail napkin.

Scientists Presper Eckert and John Mauchly were the first to patent a digital computing device, the ENIAC computer. A subsequent patent infringement case involving Eckert, Mauchly, and Atanasoff voided the ENIAC patent and gave credit to Atanasoff. But as John Atanasoff told reporters, "I have always taken the position that there is enough credit for everyone in the invention and development of the electronic computer."

Figure 1.6 Mainframe computers handle large amounts of data. The IBM z10 BC mainframe pictured here is about the size of a large refrigerator.

Supercomputers and Mainframes

Because computer applications are not limited to personal use, specialized types of computers have been created for other purposes. Businesses and organizations use computers for specific purposes like e-mail, data storage, online commerce, or hosting Web pages. **Servers** are computers that coordinate traffic between computers and provide essential network services. They link or network other computers together, enabling them to communicate and share data. **Mainframes** (Figure 1.6), or enterprise servers, are powerful, expensive computers that handle large amounts of data. They can support hundreds or thousands of users at once. Banks and healthcare organizations use mainframes to store and retrieve records for clients and patients respectively. Specialized computers that are even more powerful than mainframes are known as **supercomputers**, which typically focus on a single, specialized task as opposed to mainframes, which are more general purpose. Supercomputers are the fastest computers available. Their first priority is to complete calculations as fast as possible, often looking for patterns in data. Supercomputers are used in areas such as weather forecasting, astrophysics, code breaking, and on the human genome project.

Supercomputer Applications – IBM's Watson Computer on *Jeopardy*!

In 2011, IBM's Watson supercomputer (Figure 1.7), named after IBM founder Thomas J. Watson, competed on the television game show *Jeopardy*! against two of the show's all-time reigning champions. IBM scientists set out "to build a computing system that rivals a human's ability to answer questions posed in natural language with speed, accuracy, and confidence. The *Jeopardy*! format provides the ultimate challenge because the game's clues involve analyzing subtle meaning, irony, riddles, and other language complexities in which humans excel and computers traditionally do not." The team of scientists uploaded a vast amount of data including the complete text of the *World Book Encyclopedia*. Watson can hold information equivalent to 100 million books, and is made up of about 90 computers. When a question is put to Watson, more than 100 algorithms analyze the question in different ways, and find many plausible answers—all at the same time. Yet another set of algorithms ranks the answers and gives them a score. For each possible answer, Watson finds evidence that may support or refute that answer. So for each of hundreds of possible answers it finds hundreds of bits of evidence, and then with hundreds of algorithms, scores the degree to which the evidence supports the answer. The answer with the best evidence assessment will earn the most confidence. The highest-ranking answer becomes the final answer. However, during this *Jeopardy*! game, if the highest-ranking possible answer was not rated high enough to give Watson solid confidence, Watson did not buzz in and risk losing money if the answer turned out to be wrong. The Watson computer does all of this in about three seconds. In the end, the Jeopardy champions were no match for Watson's speed and easy access to data. Watson outscored them by large margins.

Figure 1.7 IBM Watson Computer on *Jeopardy*! (top) and the Watson Computer Servers (bottom).

Hardware

When you purchase a computer, it is helpful to understand the function of each component and to know what to expect when you begin to work with the system. The equipment that comes with the system, including the system unit, monitor, keyboard, and mouse, is called **hardware** (Figure 1.8). At the most basic level, hardware is any part of a computer that can be touched. Hardware can be broken into four categories: input, output, processing, and storage. In this section, you will explore basic hardware components and the purpose of each.

Input

A typical microcomputer system includes **input** devices, such as a keyboard and mouse. Input devices accept commands from a user, and communicate them to the computer. Current computer systems enable you to switch input devices at will. If you are not entirely pleased with the mouse that came with

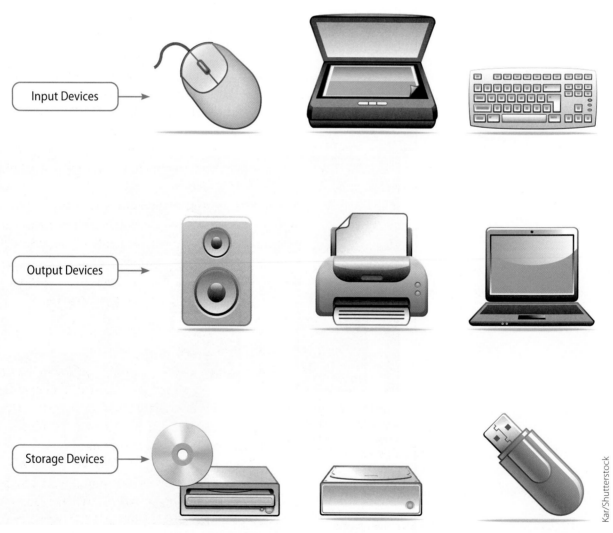

Figure 1.8 Hardware includes input, output, and storage devices.

Kar/Shutterstock

your system, you can visit a local office supply store or general-purpose retailer and select an alternative mouse. Then, you can disconnect the first mouse and connect the new one. The same flexibility applies to keyboards, scanners, and other input devices.

The **keyboard** is the primary input device for entering data into the computer. You can choose from a wide variety of keyboard models, from the most traditional to an ergonomic, possibly even cordless model, with added comfort features.

The **mouse** is the second most commonly used input device. Moving the mouse over a flat surface simultaneously moves a mouse pointer on the display screen. Pressing buttons on the mouse (called clicking) enables you to select commands or objects on-screen. Unless otherwise specified, to click means to press and release the left mouse button, whereas to right-click means to press and release the right mouse button. To double-click means to rapidly press the left mouse button twice.

You can choose from many different types of mouse devices. One of the most popular is the scroll, or wheel mouse, which is a mouse with a wheel in the center. When you spin the wheel back and forth, the mouse pointer scrolls the content of the screen (if the content is too large to display on one screen). Such a mouse is especially useful when navigating lengthy Web pages. Usually, a mouse is connected by cable to the computer. However, several popular variations are available. An attractive option is the wireless mouse, which is cordless. Such a cordless arrangement means you do not have to work around cables that can become tangled or shortened by activity. Another option is an optical mouse, which can work on almost any surface and is quickly becoming the preferred mouse option. A **light-emitting diode (LED)** transmits mouse movement, causing a corresponding shift of the mouse pointer on screen. Some ergonomic mouse units are arranged for foot movement instead of hand. Others allow you to maneuver with the thumb and fingertips instead of forcing a gripping action.

Tablets and touch screen computers employ the screen as an input device. Using your finger or a stylus, you can interact with the computer to input information. The computer responds to various commands much as it would to a mouse.

Webcams and microphones are also input devices which capture video and sound respectively.

Output

If you think about it, you only use a computer because you wish to produce some form of output, whether it is printed, displayed on-screen, or in some other form. **Output** is the information a computer produces, such as text, numbers, graphics, or sounds.

The **monitor** (Figure 1.9) is a primary output device. It is a television-like unit powered by pressing a button or flipping a switch. When searching for a monitor, you will likely find an **LCD** (liquid crystal display) monitor, which utilizes liquid crystals to project

Figure 1.9 LCD (liquid crystal display) monitors offer brilliant colors and a thin display.

Denis Tabler/Shutterstock

an image, or LCD display. Monitor screens consist of tiny dots of light called pixels (picture elements). A monitor's resolution is in part determined by the number of pixels included in a grid format on the monitor. Although you will not be able to see individual pixels, the closer the pixels are packed, the clearer the image on-screen. The more pixels, the higher the resolution, and the better the screen clarity. Within limits you can change a monitor's resolution, perhaps to adjust the screen display for particular software that calls for a certain resolution.

The **printer** (Figure 1.10) continues to be a very popular method of output for home computer users. The paperless office was once touted as a virtual certainty, given the capability to communicate and receive information electronically. However, human nature seems to suggest otherwise, as even the most sophisticated offices continue to print out many items. Especially in the home setting, you will appreciate the ease with which you can print photographs, greeting cards, correspondence, Web page information, and creative projects.

When purchasing a printer, you will probably choose among an inkjet, a laser, or a multifunction device. Another important consideration is whether a printer is networkable, either wired or wireless. With high-speed Internet connections in the home and many families using multiple computers, people are typically sharing their Internet connection and printer by putting them on a network (wired or wireless).

Most peripheral devices, including printers, require instructions (programs) that make it possible for the computer to communicate with the device. Such programs are called **drivers**, which are found on CDs that are packaged with printers and other devices. In addition, newer operating systems such as Windows 7 include drivers for various devices. To install a driver, simply insert the CD in a CD drive and follow the instructions that appear on-screen.

Inkjet printers are the most popular choice for home computer users, thanks to their affordable price and high quality. Although the initial purchase price of most inkjet printers is quite low, you should be aware that they can be rather costly to operate. Depending on how much the printer is used, both black and color cartridges may need to be replaced frequently. You can purchase print cartridges wherever computers are sold, but they are certainly not inexpensive.

Laser printers offer the highest print resolution and speed, which is measured in pages per minute. These printers, once priced out of reach for most home computer users, have become much more affordable than they once were. However, the lower-priced, low-end laser printers are usually not capable of color printing. Laser printer toner cartridges tend to last longer than inkjet cartridges, so laser printers can be cheaper to operate. Laser printer technology is similar to that of a photocopier, and, like a photocopier, laser printers are typically large, requiring more desk space than inkjet printers.

Multifunction devices are popular in homes and small offices. Multifunction printers usually have the ability to scan, print, and sometimes fax. Some multifunction

Figure 1.10 Printers are essential output devices.

stiven/Shutterstock

devices include laser printing components, while others support inkjet technology. Just as with stand-alone printers, the speed and resolution vary widely. If space is at a premium, a multifunction device may be ideal. The cost of the device, as well as the space savings, makes the purchase of a multifunction device attractive to a wide variety of users.

Processing

The **system unit** (Figure 1.11) is the rectangular case that houses hardware components, such as the processor, memory, and disk drives. It provides protection for components and usually includes space to add additional disk drives, video cards, and other components later.

The **processor**, sometimes called the brain of the computer, is the hardware unit that controls all system activity. Without a processor, there would be no computer. In computer terminology, the processor is called the **CPU** (**central processing unit**). It actually consists of electronic circuits that accept, evaluate, and act on instructions found in software programs. It also communicates with input, output, storage, and memory devices. The CPU oversees everything done by the computer.

The CPU's processing speed is measured in **megahertz (MHz)** or **gigahertz (GHz)**. CPU speeds in personal computers get faster and faster every year. At this point it is not unusual to find CPU speeds in excess of 3 GHz. Processor speed, however, is not the only factor that determines how quickly a computer processes data. Other items, such as memory and video and graphics cards also affect computer speed. The hardware unit that houses the CPU is called a **microprocessor**. AMD Phenom II and Intel Core i7 are examples of microprocessors. When you shop for a computer, you should consider both a microprocessor specification and a processor speed. Processors are manufactured by various companies, of which Intel is the most widely recognized.

Storage

When using a computer you will need to save your work so you can retrieve it later for additional editing or printing. Storage devices enable you to save such items, while also providing space for the operating system and application software programs. Storage devices are categorized as magnetic, optical, or flash.

Magnetic disk storage is composed of one or more rotating disks or platters. The surfaces of the platters are coated with metal oxide upon which data is recorded in the form of magnetic spots.

Hard drives, one form of magnetic disk storage, have considerably more storage capacity than they had in the past. The hard drive is labeled with the letter "C." Although hard drives were originally available in sizes that started at 10 megabytes (MB), today you would be hard pressed to find one smaller than 250 gigabytes (GB). When deciding what hard drive size is adequate, you must consider that this is the location of most of your software, so it is important that the disk size matches your needs. As home computers increase in storage space and power, software manufacturers

Figure 1.11 Several hardware components are included within the system unit.

Kitch Bain/Shutterstock

Spindle

Platter

Shutterstock

Figure 1.12 The interior of a hard disk drive includes a platter and a spindle.

develop software requiring ever more computer capacity. It is much like the old adage of which came first—the chicken or the egg!

An internal hard drive (Figure 1.12) is not removable. It is a storage device in which the storage medium is not removed for use on another computer. You can, however, purchase an external hard drive, which is a disk drive housed in its own case. An external hard drive is designed for portability.

Some storage media, such as CD and DVD, are categorized as **optical disc storage**. When you purchase a computer, it will probably be equipped with a CD drive or DVD drive in addition to a magnetic hard drive. A laser beam reads from, and writes to, an optical disc. A **CD (compact disc)** is a common form of optical disc storage, capable of holding data, graphics, or music.

DVD storage is very similar to a CD, but with much larger data capacity. The DVD acronym has progressed from digital video disc to digital versatile disc, but most people today simply refer to it as DVD without worrying about what the letters stand for. DVD drives are backward compatible, which means they can read CDs as well as DVDs. A typical recordable DVD can store up to 4.7 GB of data, enough to record full-length movies. Along with its cost-effective storage capacity, DVD technology facilitates very high-quality audio and video.

Flash memory is a form of storage that is neither magnetic nor optical and has no moving parts. Digital cameras, mobile phones, personal computers, and other portable computer devices also use flash memory in the form of sticks, cards, or drives. A **flash drive** (Figure 1.13)—also called a thumb drive, USB drive, or pen drive—is a small portable flash memory unit that plugs into a computer's USB port. Typically sized between 4 GB and 32 GB, a flash drive has less storage capacity than a hard drive but is smaller and more durable because it has no internal moving parts. You might think of a flash drive as a "ziploc bag" for data, allowing you to copy or move data from one computer to another.

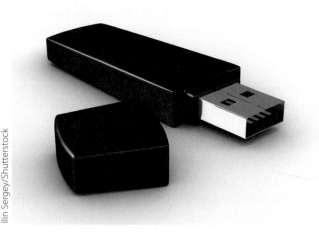

Ilin Sergey/Shutterstock

Figure 1.13 USB drives are small, so they are a convenient way to transport data.

Computer Memory: Bits and Bytes

Both memory and storage are measured in a unit called a byte. To understand the concept of bytes, think about our own numbering system. Because we have 10 fingers, our numbering system is based on powers of 10. Think back to elementary school, when you might have experimented with an abacus. The abacus demonstrated the idea of positional notation, which means that each position was actually a power of 10. For example, the decimal number 101 means that you have one "hundred," no "tens," and one "one." It makes perfect sense, given our predisposition to units of 10.

A computer, however, does not work well on decimal numbers; rather, it is naturally disposed toward a binary number system, where each digit can have only one of two electronic states: on or off. One circuit might be open, while another might be closed. A computer, then, would work much better with the binary system, in which there are only two digits, zero and one (Figure 1.14). Just as our decimal system is based on powers of 10, the binary system is based on powers of 2. Each digit in the binary system represents either a one, two, four, eight, or some power of two above that. Therefore, the number "10" in binary actually represents the decimal number 2, because the zero is in the "ones" place and the one is in the "twos" place.

The smallest binary component is the binary digit, or bit. A bit can hold one of two possible values: zero or one. It takes some combination of bits to represent what we consider a number or character on the keyboard. That combination is called a byte. As you consider bits and bytes, remember that all binary representation is internal. You will not be reading or working with data at the binary level. It is important that you understand the concept of bits and bytes, however, because that is the common measurement of memory.

Bytes are organized into larger groups as well, called kilobytes (KB), megabytes (MB), gigabytes (GB), terabytes (TB), petabytes (PB), and so on. A kilobyte consists of 1,024 bytes, whereas a megabyte is approximately 1 million bytes, and a gigabyte is 1 billion bytes. The next time you peruse an advertisement for a personal computer, note the measure of RAM as something like 4 GB (4 gigabytes). The byte is simply a measurement of capacity.

Figure 1.14 The computer uses binary code comprised of ones and zeros.

Erhan Dayi/Shutterstock

Data and programs are temporarily stored in an area called **memory** while they are being used. As you type a document, the text appears on the computer screen. This text is actually being stored in memory, which will hold it only temporarily. Memory requires a constant supply of electricity to retain its contents. If you want to recall the document later, you will need to save it to a disk or CD. Another term for this type of computer memory is **RAM (random access memory)**. RAM is volatile, which means that its contents are lost if there is an interruption of electricity.

RAM can be compared to a white board in a college classroom. After each class ends, the instructor erases the board. It only holds data or instructions pertinent to that day. It is "temporary memory." It is also limited in space; consequently, it can hold only a certain amount of information before it becomes full and must be cleared. Just as with computer memory, the white board contents change often, depending on the focus of the class.

Another type of memory is **ROM (read-only memory)**. ROM is built-in memory that can be read from, but not written to. The purpose of ROM is to perform basic system diagnostics and to provide instructions that tell your computer how to boot up. For example, ROM requires that your computer check vital system components and communications each time the computer is started up. Unlike RAM, data in ROM is permanently stored, even when the computer's power is off.

Software

Your computer is made up of hardware, which are computer components that you can touch, and **software**, the programs that provide instructions that enable a computer to function and make it possible for you to enjoy computer applications, such as the Internet, producing documents, and playing games. The two types of software are **system software** and **application software**. System software coordinates hardware so a computer can operate. Examples of system software include an **operating system**, such as Windows 7, and antivirus or security software, as well as programs that compress files and check a disk drive for errors. Application software relates to tasks and activities that you enjoy working with on a computer. For example, word processing software, image editing software—even software that enables you to create calendars or learn a foreign language—are all considered application software. In this section, you will explore system software and application software.

Application Software

Application software (Figure 1.15) can be categorized as:

- Productivity software—including word processing, spreadsheet, database, personal information management, and presentation programs.
- Entertainment and multimedia software—including image editing, video editing, media management, and gaming software.
- Educational and reference software—including reference programs such as encyclopedias and learning management programs.

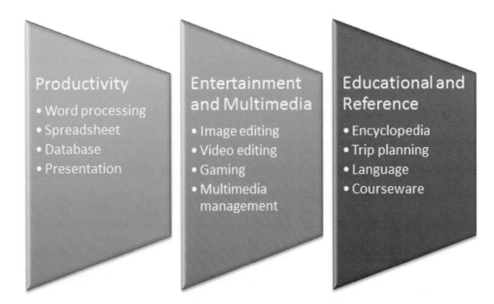

Figure 1.15 Application software is available in several categories.

Productivity Software

Productivity software typically bundles several components, including word processing, spreadsheet, database, and presentation features. One of the most recognized productivity software packages is Microsoft Office 2010, which includes Microsoft Word, Microsoft Excel, and Microsoft PowerPoint (as well as Microsoft Access in the Professional version). Depending on the version of Office 2010, other software, such as Microsoft Outlook, Microsoft Publisher, and OneNote might also be included.

Word processing software makes it easy to create, format, and edit documents such as letters, professional papers, newsletters, and brochures. Although primarily text based, word processing software often enables you to include graphics, tables, artwork, photographs, and even screen captures in a document.

Spreadsheet software enables you to organize numeric information and records in the form of an electronic worksheet. The primary advantage of a spreadsheet program is its ability to perform calculations, although it also serves as an effective database package for simple record keeping. Spreadsheets can be used to track finances, student grades, and anything else that can be represented in a grid of columns and rows.

Presentation software assists with organizing your thoughts and speaking points on a series of electronic slides. By projecting those slides to an audience, your presentation remains on track and you can effectively summarize major points in bullets, graphs, tables, or other slide elements. Rather than simply giving a lecture or presentation to an audience, you can create a slide show that incorporates graphs, photos, and video along with text, making the presentation more interesting and informative.

A database is a collection of data organized in a meaningful fashion. Businesses, schools, nonprofit groups, and even home users maintain records in database files on everything from employees, clients, and sales to collections, accounts, and schedules. An effective database enables you to ask questions, or make *queries*. For example, you might need to identify all customer accounts that are more than 90 days past due. A well-designed database would enable you to ask that question and receive an immediate answer. The goal of a database is to present data and answer your questions so you can make well-considered decisions based on data included in a database. Productivity software is shown in Figure 1.16.

Entertainment and Multimedia Software

Entertainment and multimedia software makes using the computer fun, enabling you to play games, view, edit, and organize personal photos, watch videos, and

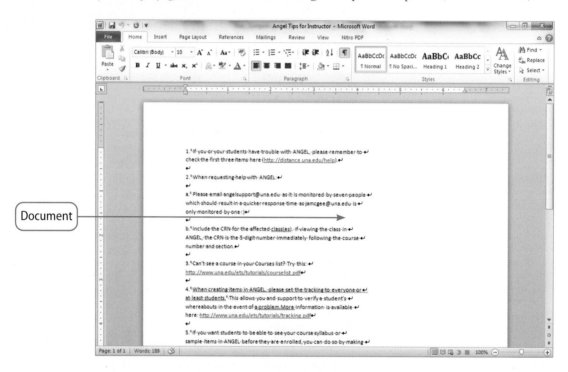

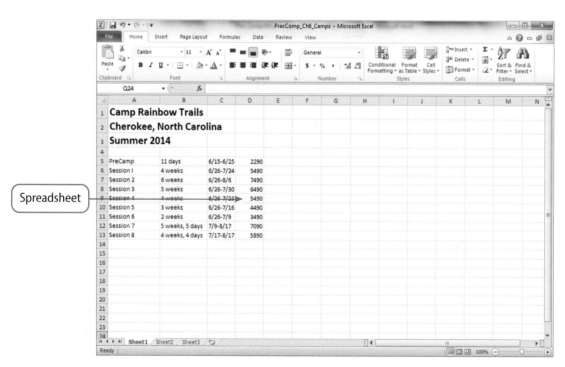

Figure 1.16 Productivity software enables you to create documents, spreadsheets, presentations, and databases.

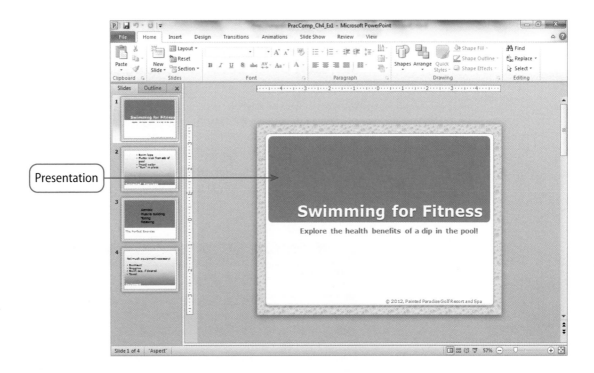

Presentation

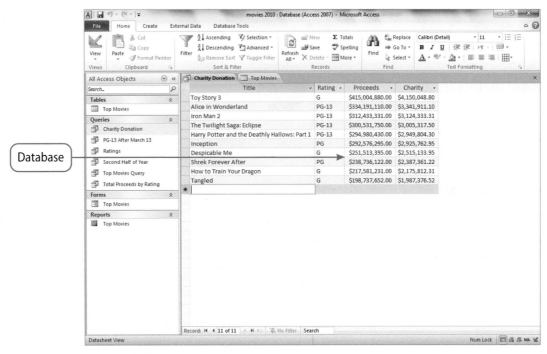

Database

Figure 1.16 (Continued)

play music. Multimedia software, including Apple iTunes and Windows Media Player, makes it possible for you to listen to music or watch a movie or video. Available free of charge, Windows Media Player is included with a Windows installation, and Apple iTunes is a free download. Although the software is free, you must purchase music that you download. Other multimedia software, such as Rhapsody and Napster, are also available, although you must subscribe to each service after a trial period.

Microsoft Office 2010: Computing on the Go

Microsoft Office 2010 integrates the concept of the "anywhere office" into the software suite. Using Web Apps (Figure 1.17), a collection of free (although limited) versions of Word, Excel, PowerPoint, and OneNote, you can work with documents, presentations, and spreadsheets online. You can also save those files online so they are available from any Internet-connected computer, even if that computer does not have Microsoft Office 2010 installed. That means you can access, view, edit, and share content from virtually anywhere, using any computer. Using Web Apps, you can collaborate on projects with other people, sharing files online. Projects can even be edited simultaneously, resulting in only a single version of the shared file.

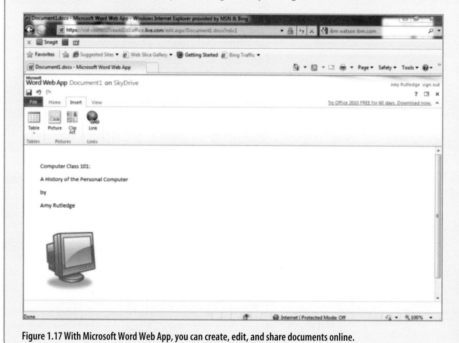

Figure 1.17 With Microsoft Word Web App, you can create, edit, and share documents online.

Image editing software focuses on organizing, cropping, recoloring, and otherwise modifying photos. With many image editing programs to choose from, a few (such as Google Picasa) are actually free. Others, such as Photoshop Elements, include a full set of picture management features but must be purchased after an optional trial period. Software packages such as Adobe Premiere, Movie Maker, and Apple iMovie, are designed to work with videos, such as those recorded with a digital camcorder. Movie Maker is actually free, available as a download with the Windows Live Essentials software package at http://explore.live.com/windows-live-essentials. With features that enable you to trim, fade, and combine movie clips, you can unleash your creativity in Movie Maker as well as other video editing software packages. Many people enjoy playing simple computer games such as Solitaire, which primarily requires the use of a mouse, or action games that often require a controller or joystick.

Educational and Reference Software

Educational and reference software includes programs that help you engage in learning activities. Such programs as children's learning software, digital

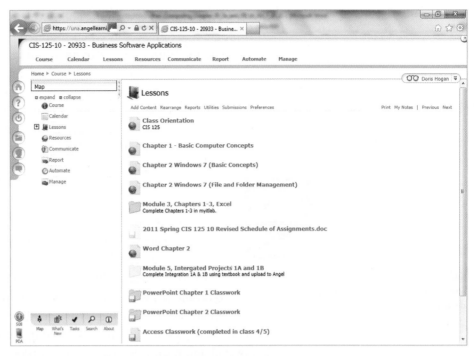

Figure 1.18 A learning platform, such as Angel, enables an instructor to post class material online.

encyclopedias, courseware, and software designed to teach a foreign language are all examples of educational software. Your school or college might use courseware and a learning platform such as Blackboard, Angel (Figure 1.18), or myitlab. Several of the most common learning platforms are discussed in the appendix to this textbook. Colleges use courseware to distribute materials, exams, and course content for both online and traditional lecture-style courses. Using a learning platform, you are able to communicate with your instructor, keep up with a class calendar, and participate in class discussions, assignments, and testing.

Using and Acquiring Software

Software can be obtained in a number of ways and at varying cost. Most software must be purchased and can only be used on a single computer, while other selections are free and can be installed on multiple computers. When you obtain software, it usually comes with a **EULA (end user license agreement)**. The agreement is a contract between you and the software maker that states what you can and cannot do with the software. You do not actually own the software, only a license to use it. It is illegal to use and copy software if you do not have a legitimate software license for the program. Violation of a copyright is a crime.

Some software is absolutely free, while other software is free for only a limited time. **Freeware** is software that is free for an unlimited period of time. Examples of freeware include Mozilla's Firefox browser and Adobe Reader. Microsoft and a number of other companies offer software on a trial basis. Software that is available at no charge on a trial basis is called **shareware**. Such programs are often available as a download. With shareware you can try the program before you decide whether to purchase it.

You can occasionally find software available as open source, which is different from freeware in that you have access to the actual lines of code for the program. With the programming code, you are free to customize and modify the program as you see fit. Open source programs are usually offered for free. Linux is an example of open source software.

Some companies are skipping the software download altogether and are offering **software-as-a-service (SaaS)**. Such programs are offered online so there is no need to download and install the software. The vendor hosts the software as an online service to companies who access the software remotely. SaaS is a type of cloud computing (Figure 1.19), which means that the software is delivered through the Internet, usually at a much lower price than would be required for a purchase of the software license.

Some online software, such as Google Docs and Microsoft Web Apps, is actually free. Intuit has delivered its popular Turbo Tax and Quick Books applications as SaaS applications; similarly salesforce.com provides a host of CRM (Customer Relationship Management) software to businesses worldwide—all hosted "in the cloud." Businesses who want access, perhaps even temporarily, to a particular program or system of software, often opt for SaaS software, thereby avoiding a complete purchase and the dedication of staff and resources to a purchased product.

You can obtain software in several different ways. You can download it directly from the Internet, or you can purchase it in a retail store on a CD-ROM or DVD. Which way is better? It depends on your preference. When you download software from the Internet, you purchase, download, and install it all in one motion. You don't have to wait in line. If you purchase the software online, you often have the choice to download the program with or without receiving a CD or DVD of the software in the mail. Ordering a CD or DVD of the downloaded program often comes at additional cost. Of course, purchasing software from a retail establishment guarantees that you have a copy of the software on storage media, along with all accompanying product literature.

When considering a software purchase, you should be aware of the software's system requirements so you can compare them to your system specifications. If your computer system does not meet the software's system requirements, the program will not run on your computer. System requirements often list the operating system, hard drive storage space, amount of RAM, and any other hardware specifications.

Windows 7 makes it easy to identify system specifications, organizing the information in an area of the Control Panel. Click **Start** and then click **Control Panel**. Click **System and Security** and then click **System**. The window shown in Figure 1.20 provides system specifications related to the processor type and speed, the operating system, and the amount of RAM. As you consider purchasing or otherwise obtaining software, you must make sure that your computer system specifications are capable of supporting the software. Being well aware of your system enables you to make well-advised decisions related to software that you are considering.

Installing and Uninstalling Software

When purchasing software from a retailer, as opposed to downloading the software, you will receive a CD-ROM or DVD on which the program files are located. To **install** the program (copy it to your hard drive so you can access it later),

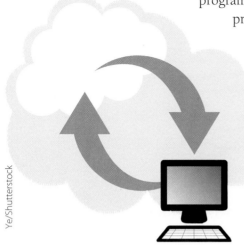

Figure 1.19 Using cloud computing, you can access data and applications from any Internet-connected computer.

Ye/Shutterstock

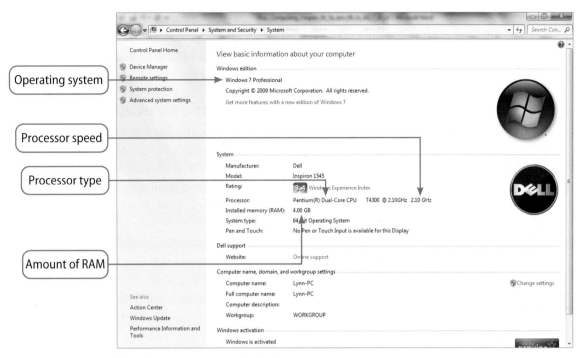

Operating system →

Processor speed →

Processor type →

Amount of RAM →

Figure 1.20 Being aware of system specifications is helpful when evaluating software for download or purchase.

simply insert the disc into the CD or DVD drive. Most often, an AutoPlay feature will guide you through a series of on-screen prompts (called a wizard) that direct the software installation. Usually, the settings the wizard suggests are the most appropriate, so unless you have some reason to change the suggested settings, you should click **Next** or otherwise make a selection that indicates your acceptance or agreement. Progress through all wizard prompts, finally selecting **Finish** or **End** to complete the installation. If AutoPlay does not present a wizard after the software disc has been in the drive for a few seconds, then you must initiate the process yourself. Click **Start** and then click **Computer**. Double-click the CD or DVD drive listed in the right pane. Most likely, you will see a filename in the right pane including either the word *setup* or *install*. If so, double-click the file to begin the installation wizard.

In Depth

Where Can I Go to Find Software?

If you are looking for a specific type of software program, the Web is a great place to search. But how do you know if you are getting a program that contains viruses or spyware? The truth is that you can never be sure. Some trusted websites, such as http://download.cnet.com/windows/ and www.tucows.com offer downloads that have been checked for viruses and other forms of destructive software, so as long as you obtain software from those or similar sites, it is unlikely that you would encounter a problem. Downloads are typically categorized by purpose, and many provide user reviews so you can check out the product before you download it. Software you can download is typically available for purchase or as freeware or shareware. If you are looking for a specific program to download, you can simply conduct a search for it through your browser.

When installing a program from an online source, you must first download and then install the program. In addition, unless the download is freeware or shareware, you will be required to purchase the product. Having located a program to download from the Internet, you will most likely see a Download button or some other indication that you should click an on-screen area to begin the download process (Figure 1.21). Click the download link and then respond to any prompts that direct the process. The Internet Explorer 9 Notification Bar will ask whether to save or run the file; always select **Save** or click the **Save arrow**. That way, the program will be saved on your computer so you can install it later or even scan it for viruses before installing it. If you click the Save arrow, shown in Figure 1.22, you can then click **Save As** and indicate a location where the file is to be saved. Otherwise, if you click **Save**, the file will be automatically saved in the Downloads folder. After the program has been downloaded, click **Open Folder** to begin the installation process. Double-click the recently downloaded file to begin the installation process. If asked whether to allow the program to make changes to the computer, click **Yes**. Then respond to any additional prompts that direct you through the installation.

Although the hard drive on your computer is probably large enough to hold quite a lot, space is not unlimited. If you find you do not have enough space for software you want to install or for other data files, you can free up hard drive space by removing, or **uninstalling**, software.

To uninstall a program:

1. Click **Start**.
2. Click **ControlPanel**.
3. Click **Uninstall a program** (under Programs). You will see a list of programs installed on your system.

Figure 1.21 Software is often available as a download.

Figure 1.22 Save a downloaded program so that you can access and install it later.

4. To remove a program, click its title in the list, and then click **Uninstall** as shown in **Figure 1.23**.
5. Click **Yes** to confirm the removal. Uninstalling a program removes all program components from a computer system.

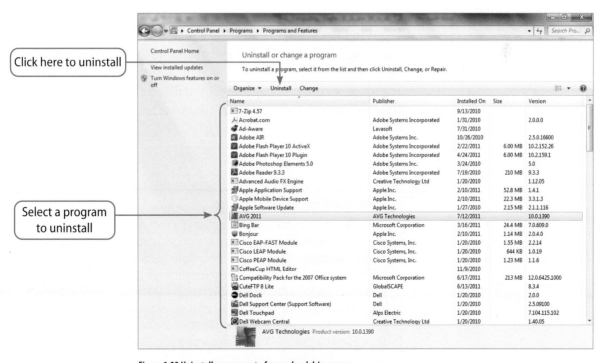

Figure 1.23 Uninstall a program to free up hard drive space.

System Software

Most likely, you do not give much thought to system software when you use a computer; however, without system software, a computer cannot function. Providing support for everything from managing hardware components to protecting a computer system from viruses, system software coordinates activities related to the way a computer functions. In this section, you will explore system software, identifying types of system software and the purposes for which various types are intended.

Operating System Software

The operating system is the most widely recognized type of system software. Primary functions of an operating system include:

- Enabling multitasking so you can engage in several tasks, or applications, simultaneously. For example, by multitasking, you can write an e-mail and browse a Web page at the same time.
- Providing a user interface, which is the display through which you communicate with the operating system. The display typically includes graphic icons representing system resources or applications that you can manage by pointing and clicking with a mouse (or another pointing device).
- Coordinating software and hardware so system resources are available to support software.
- Managing peripheral hardware such as a printer or mouse.

Although Microsoft Windows is the most common operating system in use today, other common options include Linux and Mac OS X. As you explore operating systems, you will find that one or the other best suits your needs and computer architecture. Common operating systems are discussed in this section.

Windows 7 is the newest version of Windows, the popular microcomputer operating system developed and marketed by Microsoft. With approximately 90% of the microcomputer operating system market, Windows 7 boasts improved security, enhanced help and search facility, and other performance improvements that differentiate it from earlier Windows versions.

In Depth

Uninstalling vs. Deleting

Uninstalling is not the same as deleting a program. During software installation, program files might be placed in a number of folders. The installation process might also make changes to the Windows Registry, which is a special file that keeps track of Windows and program settings. If you find what you think is the program's folder and delete it, chances are that you have removed only a small part of the complete program installation. Manually removing files can be a problem because you might remove files that are necessary for other software applications to run properly. Only a complete uninstallation will remove the program and all of its components, while ensuring that the removal does not adversely affect other software applications.

Hands-On

Activity 1.1 Exploring System Specifications

Your uncle is considering purchasing a slightly used computer for his enjoyment at home. He is interested in genealogy, writing, and digital photography. While those interests are diverse, he knows he can purchase software that will enable him to enjoy those activities more completely. For example, software is available that creates a family tree, while word processing software makes it easy to create and format documents. Using image editing software, your uncle can edit and print digital photos. He wants to be sure that the computer he is considering is capable of supporting his interests, so he has asked you to help him explore the system specifications on the computer. He also wants you to check the programs that are currently installed, identifying those he will not need if he purchases the computer.

In this exercise, you will use the Control Panel to identify system specifications and to show currently installed programs.

a. Click **Start** and then click **Control Panel**. Click **System and Security**. Click **System**.

What operating system is installed on your computer? What type of processor is in use and what is the speed? How much RAM is available?

b. Close the window.

c. Click **Start** and then click **Computer**. Right-click **drive C:** in the right pane and click **Properties**. A window opens, similar to that shown in Figure 1.24.

How much free space is available on the hard drive?

d. Click **OK** and then close the open window. Your uncle is considering installing Family Tree Maker so he can work with genealogy. The software requires Windows 7, Windows XP, or Windows Vista operating system. In addition, the computer must contain a 500 MHz processor, 512 MB RAM, and available hard disk space of 500 MB. Does the system you are testing meet or exceed those specifications? Can it support the Family Tree Maker software?

e. Click **Start** and then click **Control Panel**. Click **Uninstall a program** (under Programs).

In a few seconds, a list of installed programs displays. Click to select any of the listed programs. Note the *Uninstall* link shown at the top of the window. If you actually planned to uninstall the program, you would click the link. However, do not uninstall any program at this point.

f. Scroll through the list of programs. Can you identify any that you would uninstall if the computer were actually yours?

g. Close the window.

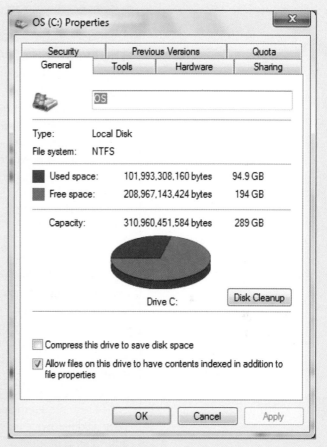

Figure 1.24 Before purchasing software, you should insure that your hard drive has enough available space.

Mac OS X is designed to support Apple microcomputers. Apple was the first company to introduce a computer with a graphical user interface (GUI)—a point and click interface as opposed to one that uses only a keyboard or commands. Mac OS X is actually similar to Windows, in that it employs a graphical user interface, windows management features, and a comprehensive search and help facility.

Linux is a family of open-source operating systems that you can freely download and install. As an open-source product, Linux is built, reviewed, and revised by anyone with an interest in contributing. Linux is available in several different distributions, or *distros*, each with unique features designed to support desktops, laptops, mainframes, or mobile devices. The graphical Linux interface is similar to Windows, Mac OS X, and Google Chrome.

Utility Software

Utility software, another type of system software, addresses system tasks such as file compression (making files smaller as they are saved) and virus protection. Along with Microsoft, vendors such as Symantec, McAfee, and Trend offer various types of virus protection and Internet security. Utility software helps keep your system running efficiently and safely.

A Look Back

The Evolution of Microsoft Windows

What we know as the Microsoft Windows operating system has its roots in a program called MS-DOS. Released in 1981, MS-DOS was a command-line interface, comprised of text commands you had to type. Unlike the multitasking Windows environment, MS-DOS could only work with one program at a time.

In 1985, Microsoft produced Windows 1.0, an operating system that included a graphical user interface through which you could point and click to make selections. A dramatic change from MS-DOS, Windows 1.0 not only presented a graphical interface, but it also enabled multitasking, so users could work with several applications at one time. In relatively quick fashion, Windows followed up with Windows 2.0 and 3.0.

In 1992, Windows 3.1 made its appearance, offering improved performance and enhanced graphics—a full 16 colors! Windows NT, introduced in 1993, was designed to address general business activities but was also capable of supporting high-end engineering and scientific applications. Windows 95 debuted in 1995, with built-in Internet support and plug-and-play capability (making it easier than ever to install hardware and software). An immensely popular Windows version, Windows 98 offered a full slate of features for home consumers. It was the first version that could read DVD discs and could connect to USB devices. Also designed for home computer users, Windows ME, introduced in 2000, offered numerous music, video, and home networking enhancements. Premiering along with Windows ME in 2000, Windows 2000 simplified hardware installation and provided support for advanced networking and wireless products.

With editions designed specifically for home or business use, Windows XP proved to be a top seller for Microsoft. Introduced in 2001, Windows XP was fast, stable, and secure. Windows Vista, released in 2007, offered enhanced security features, but was never fully accepted by the bulk of consumers and information technology professionals. They believed that Windows Vista required the dedication of too many system resources, which slowed down a computer.

In 2009, Windows 7 arrived, to the accolades of both consumers and professionals who were relieved that Windows 7 was not overly demanding of hardware. Windows 7 includes many new features such as new ways to work with windows and enhanced multimedia techniques.

Occasionally, you will want to send photographs, graphics, or large text files by e-mail. Whether you are successful sending those files depends on several variables, among them connection speed, Internet traffic, and file size. Connection speed can bring file transfer to a crawl—or stop it altogether—especially if you are working with a dial-up modem. Some files are so large that it is just not reasonable to send them as attachments, due to the time it takes to upload them to your mail server, and the time it takes the recipient to download them. You might want to consider using **file compression software**, which stores data in a format that requires much less space. It enables communication devices to transmit the same amount of data in fewer bits, thereby speeding up the file transfer.

Fortunately, file compression is not as technical as it sounds. Windows 7, Windows XP, and Windows Vista all include a file compression utility. To compress a file or folder:

1. Right-click on the file or folder in Windows Explorer and point to **Send to**.
2. Click **Compressed (zipped) folder**.

Compressing a file creates a new file with a .zip extension. For example, by compressing a file and saving it with the filename *spring_schedule*, you have actually saved the file as *spring_schedule.zip*. The *zip* extension identifies the file as a compressed version. When you send or save a compressed file it is smaller in size than the original, so the time it takes to transfer the file is shorter, and the amount of storage space required for the file is less than would have been required before compression. A recipient of a compressed file would need to decompress the file before it can be opened.

To decompress a file or folder:

1. Download and save the file or folder.
2. Open Windows Explorer, locate the file or folder, and right-click it.
3. Click **Extract All**.
4. Follow the instructions in the step-by-step wizard.

Although Windows 7 includes a file compression utility, you can also acquire other compression utilities with additional features. A popular option is WinZip, available to download at www.winzip.com. Although the product is free for a limited time, you must purchase the software after a certain number of days in order to continue using it. Other choices include PKZip, found at www.pkware .com, and StuffIt, which you can download or purchase at www.stuffit.com. All three file compression programs enable you to compress files, creating new files that are reduced in size, sometimes by as much as 95%. A search of the Internet will reveal even more choices in file compression utility software. File types that indicate compressed files include .zip, .sit, .pak, .pit, .tar, and .rar. You can also decompress, or restore files to their original size, with WinZip, StuffIt, PKZip, and other compression utilities.

To properly maintain your computer, you should regularly remove unused programs and files, and optimize (restructure for better space utilization) your hard drive. You can carry out those tasks on a set schedule, although the exact timing depends in part on the rate at which you access your hard drive. The more often the hard drive is accessed (saving or displaying files, such as documents or worksheets), the more often you should perform maintenance tasks. Some tasks can be automatically scheduled so you do not forget them.

It is quite common to accumulate unnecessary files on your hard drive. If you are not vigilant, your hard drive will become cluttered with documents and other projects that are no longer relevant. In addition, a software program that you once enjoyed might now be something you hardly ever access. A system that is bogged down with too much clutter might not access projects as quickly as it did before. One thing you can do to cut through the clutter is to run **Disk Cleanup** occasionally. Disk Cleanup is a utility that removes unnecessary files from your hard drive, effectively clearing space on the hard drive. Files that can be removed include items in the Recycle Bin (items that have been previously deleted), temporary Internet files (files containing data for every Internet site you have visited), and other items that could be considered temporary and irrelevant to the long-term operation of your computer. You do not have to wait a recommended interval of time between cleanups, but if you are very active on the Internet, thereby collecting a lot of temporary Internet files, you might run Disk Cleanup at least once each week.

Using Disk Cleanup is much like cleaning out your closets periodically. Just think how organized they would be! The same goes for your hard drive. You stand to regain a lot of room for data storage on the hard drive because Disk Cleanup can clear up many megabytes at one time. Although Disk Cleanup does not correct software problems, it might eliminate some items that could cause problems, such as a corrupted temporary file. To run Disk Cleanup, click **Start** and then click **Computer**. Right-click the hard drive (designated as **drive C:**) and click **Properties**. Click the **General tab**, if necessary, and then click **Disk Cleanup**. After calculating the amount of space that can be cleared, the operating system presents the dialog box shown in Figure 1.25. Select the categories to be removed and click **OK**.

Defragmenting a Disk

When you save files on your hard drive, you might assume that the entire file is saved in one location because when you later retrieve that same file, the operating system displays it on your screen as a single unit. However, in reality, the file might be broken apart as it is being saved, with units clearly labeled by the operating system and placed in areas called sectors. A hard drive is circular, with a series of concentric tracks on the surface. The disk is further divided by sectors, which in theory are shaped like pieces of pie on the disk surface. When a file is saved, the operating system notes the location of its pieces by the track and sector numbers. If a file is not saved in one unit, but is instead separated into a series of sectors, it is said to be **fragmented**. A file is separated into pieces (fragmented) as the operating system attempts to fill every available disk area, no matter how small. When you retrieve the file later, the operating system simply puts the pieces back together as a screen display, although the file actually remains in pieces on the disk.

Although you can run **Disk Defragmenter** (a Windows 7 system tool that basically rewrites the hard drive, reconnecting fragmented files) whenever you like, you can also develop a schedule so the defragmentation process takes place automatically. Actually, even with no instruction from you, Windows 7 will **defragment** your hard drive periodically, based on a set schedule. Usually that

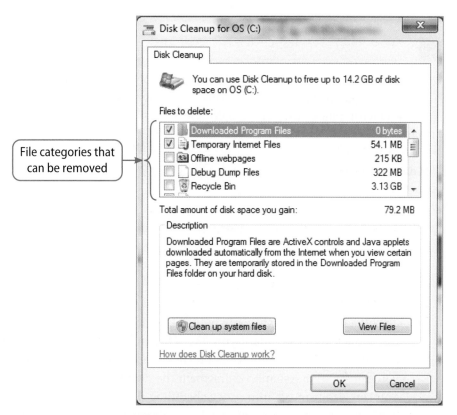

File categories that can be removed

Figure 1.25 Disk Cleanup removes unnecessary files from the hard drive.

Technology Insight

Temporary Internet Files

A temporary Internet file is a file that stores data for a Web page you visit. As you browse the Internet, a "snapshot" of each Web page is saved, so the next time you visit the same site, the page can be quickly loaded from the picture of the page that was previously collected. Loading a page in that way is called *caching*. The purpose of a temporary Internet file is to speed up the loading of a Web page. When you visit a page you have previously viewed, the browser first checks to see if the page has changed since the last visit. If there are no changes, the page is loaded from the Temporary Internet Files folder on your hard drive, which is much faster than loading the page from the Internet. Temporary Internet files also enable *offline browsing*, where you can open a Web page from the Temporary Internet Files folder, or cache, even when you are not connected to the Internet. One problem with maintaining temporary Internet files over time is the massive amount of storage space required to save the text and graphics that appear on many Web pages. Unless you initiate the process, temporary Internet files are not deleted, but remain indefinitely on your hard drive, requiring even more space as you surf the Web. Your privacy is at risk also, as anyone with access to your computer can check the Temporary Internet Files folder to see where you have been online. In fact, the evidence gathering part of cyber forensics often involves gathering data from a user's temporary Internet files. Use Disk Cleanup to remove temporary Internet files, or use the Tools menu in Internet Explorer 9 to accomplish the same thing.

Hands-On

Activity 1.2 Performing Disk Cleanup

Your uncle decided to purchase the computer and has asked you to help him set it up. One of the first things to do is to clear the hard drive of unnecessary clutter. In this exercise, you will run Disk Cleanup to assist in that task.

a. Click **Start** and then click **Computer**. Right-click the hard drive (**drive C:**) and then click **Properties**.

b. With the General tab selected, click **Disk Cleanup**.

c. Wait a few seconds for Windows to calculate the amount of space that could be freed. Deselect all categories except Temporary Internet Files. Click **OK**. If you are working on your home computer, you can click **Delete Files** to continue the cleanup process. However, if working on a computer in a college lab, click **Cancel**.

d. Close any open windows.

activity takes place in the early hours of a selected day once each week, but you can modify the schedule if you like. Of course, automatic defragmenting can only occur if your computer is on. If a scheduled defragmentation is missed, you can set your system to defragment the next time you turn the computer on. You can also turn off automatic scheduling if desired. There is no need to stop working with your computer while defragmentation is occurring, although the process might proceed more quickly if it is the only task that is running. Although fragmentation can occur on other disk media, the hard drive is of primary concern due to its large size and typically intense activity.

To run (and schedule) Disk Defragmenter in Windows 7:

1. Click **Start** and then click **Computer**.
2. Right-click the hard drive (**drive C:**).
3. Click **Properties**.
4. Click the **Tools tab**.
5. Click **Disk Defragmenter**.
6. Click **Analyze disk**, if you like, to check the disk's level of fragmentation. At that point, you can determine whether it is necessary to defragment the disk.
7. Click **Defragment disk**, as shown in Figure 1.26 (or click **Configure schedule**, if you want to adjust the scheduled time for defragmentation). The process might take quite some time, depending on how recently the last defragmentation occurred and how much activity has occurred on the hard drive since. If you choose to modify the schedule, you will indicate how often, what day, and at what time of the day you want the hard drive to be defragmented.
8. Click **OK** (or **Cancel** if no changes to the schedule were made). If asked to confirm the operation, you might have to enter your administrator password.

To modify Recycle Bin properties, right-click the **Recycle Bin icon** and then click **Properties**. You can change the maximum size reserved for the Recycle Bin and you can also choose to delete items without having them pass through the Recycle Bin. Click **OK** when done.

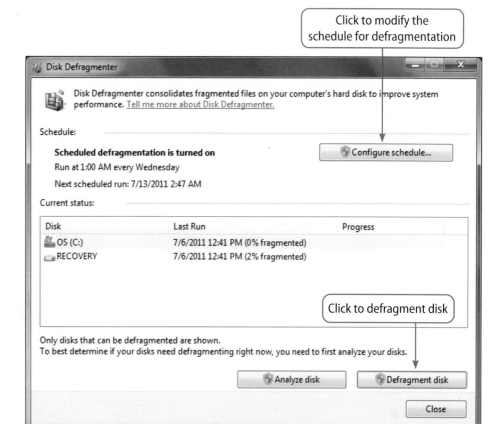

Figure 1.26 Windows 7 automatically defragments your hard drive, but you can modify the schedule.

Checking for Errors

The Windows **Error Checking utility** examines a disk for data storage errors, from physical defects on the disk surface to weakened areas that might cause that space to be unreliable. An area that cannot be used due to a physical flaw is called a bad sector and is partitioned off by the error checker so it is not available for data storage. Many identified errors can be corrected by the Error Checking utility before any data is lost. A good rule of thumb is to check your disk for errors at least once every six months.

To check a disk for errors:

1. Click **Start**.
2. Click **Computer**.
3. Right-click the **hard drive** (drive C:) and click **Properties**.
4. Click the **Tools tab**.
5. Click **Check now**. If asked to confirm the operation, you might have to enter your administrator password.
6. Select **Automatically fix file system errors** (if it is not already checked) and also select **Scan for and attempt recovery of bad sectors** (see Figure 1.27).
7. Click **Start**.
8. Click **Schedule disk check** if you want the error check to take place the next time you start Windows. Error checking cannot occur on a disk that is currently in use. Nothing will happen until you reboot the

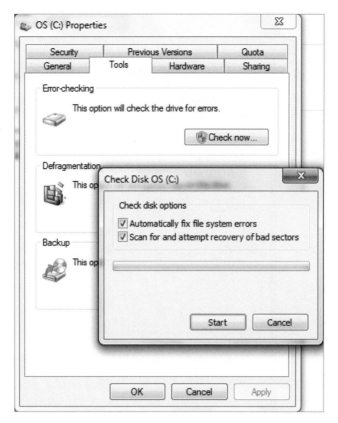

Figure 1.27 Checking your hard drive occasionally can reveal and sometimes correct errors.

computer, when the disk check will occur. At that time, you will be informed of any errors Click **OK**.

System Backup

Losing data is a frustrating and serious issue, but it can be prevented. Windows 7 provides a backup utility that can easily schedule a routine backup of your hard drive. A **backup** is simply a copy of files that is placed on another type of storage media—possibly even in another physical location as well. You can create a system image, which contains a copy of operating system files, installed software, system settings, and data files, saving the image to another storage media device, such as an external hard drive. That way, if the hard drive is damaged or becomes unusable, you can restore files and system settings to a new or repaired hard drive. You can also make a backup copy of data files on your system, so that you are able to retrieve them if they should become damaged or removed from the original location.

The Windows 7 backup utility enables you to save an entire system image, so you can recover all files and software if your system fails, or simply to create a copy of all data files. If you choose to create a system image, you must place the backup on another hard drive, or you can save the backup on a network if using either the Professional or Ultimate Windows 7 version; if you are only backing up data files, you can use any type of storage media as long as there is enough space to save all files.

Recycle Bin

The Recycle Bin is the location to which files and folders are sent when you delete them from a hard drive. Acting as a safety net, the Recycle Bin holds deleted items until you empty it (or restore any item that you find you did not mean to delete). The Recycle Bin is configured to occupy a set amount of space on your hard drive—typically 10% of the total hard drive size. If the Recycle Bin becomes full of deleted items, it will begin to remove them, starting with the oldest entries. Figure 1.28 shows a Recycle Bin.

To display the Recycle Bin, double-click the **Recycle Bin icon** on the desktop. If you do not find the Recycle Bin on the desktop, you can also open it when you click **Start** and then click **Computer**. Click **Desktop** (in the left pane) and then double-click **Recycle Bin** (in the right pane). If you have deleted any items, they will display in the Recycle Bin. To restore any file or folder, select an item and then click **Restore this item** in the bar at the top of the window (Figure 1.28). Alternatively, with no file or folder selected, you can click **Restore all items** to return everything to its original location on the hard drive. If you want to delete everything from the Recycle Bin, click **Empty the Recycle Bin**.

Click to restore items.

Click to empty the Recycle Bin

Files and folders deleted from a hard drive

Figure 1.28 Empty the Recycle Bin only if you are certain that you no longer need the files or folders that are stored there.

Backup Location

When backing up files, never place them on the same drive where Windows files are stored. Instead, save them on another storage media which is located away from the original disk, perhaps in a fireproof area. Explore online backup solutions, as well.

In Depth

Online Backup Solutions

Many people are taking advantage of online solutions when it comes to backing up files and computer systems. Even businesses that at one time depended completely on their own storage media for backups enjoy the advantages of online backup. Backing up files online is a cost-effective way to protect irreplaceable items such as documents, photos, and videos. With those copies located safely away from the original location, you can count on having access to them even if your computer is stolen or the disk drive is damaged. When you consider possible catastrophes (such as one that occurred in Japan in 2011) and the growing acceptance of cloud computing, it just makes sense to consider online backup as a viable alternative.

For a fee, many online backup services offer unlimited storage. Others, such as SkyDrive (http://skydrive.live.com), provide limited space at no charge. Some services are even adding apps for mobile devices, like iPhones, iPads, and Androids. SOS Online Backup (www.sosonlinebackup.com) and others enable you to access backed up files through an iPhone app. iDrive (www.idrive.com) even provides limited space for you to back up your phone contacts and photos at no charge. Dropbox (www.dropbox.com) and Freedrive (www.freedrive.com) are popular affordable (or free) options for consumers, while other more full-featured backup solutions are available with Mozy (www.mozy.com), Carbonite (www.carbonite.com), and CrashPlan (www.crashplan.com).

To create a system image:

1. Click **Start** and then click **Control Panel**.
2. Click **System and Security** and then click **Backup and Restore**.
3. Click **Create a system image** (in the left pane).
4. Select a location for the system image and click **Next**. Follow all steps in the wizard to complete the system image.

To back up data files:

1. Click **Start** and then click **Control Panel**.
2. Click **System and Security** and then click **Backup and Restore**.
3. If this is the first time you have used Windows Backup, click **Set up backup** and then follow the steps presented in the wizard to select backup settings. If this is not the first time you have backed up files, click **Back up Now**. Respond to all prompts to complete the backup.

Hands-On

Activity 1.3 Defragmenting and Checking for Errors

The computer you are setting up for your uncle is just about ready to go. You have installed software he will enjoy and you have removed clutter from the hard drive. Now you will defragment the hard drive and check the system for errors. In addition, you will check the Recycle Bin to make sure it is empty (or that no files there should be removed).

a. Click **Start** and then click **Computer**. Right-click the hard drive (**drive C:**) and then click **Properties**.

b. Click the **Tools tab**. Click **Defragment now**. To explore Disk Defragmenter, click **Tell me more about Disk Defragmenter** (Figure 1.29).

TROUBLESHOOTING

After a few seconds, a Help and Support window opens, but the Disk Defragmenter window is likely to be positioned in front of the Help and Support window. In that case, simply click any place on the Help and Support window to bring it to the forefront.

---

c. Click **Go to the Windows website to watch the video (1 : 03)**. If you are in a lab, connect your earphones to your computer and adjust the system volume, if necessary. Scroll down slightly and click the **large arrow** in the center of the video space. The video will begin.

d. After the video is over, close the browser window. Close the Help and Support window.

e. Click **Analyze disk**. Is the disk more than 10% fragmented? Click **Close**. You can defragment your hard drive later, if necessary.

f. Click **Check now**. Check **Scan for and attempt recovery of bad sectors**. Click **Start**. If you are working on your home computer and want to schedule the disk check to occur the next time you turn on or restart your computer, click **Schedule disk check**. Otherwise, click **Cancel**.

g. Close all open windows.

h. Click **Start** and then click **Computer**. Click **Desktop** in the left pane. Double-click **Recycle Bin** in the right pane. Are any files or folders shown? If so, they are items that have been deleted but are still available, in case you want to restore any of them. Links at the top of the window enable you to empty the Recycle Bin or restore items. If you are in a computer lab, close the Recycle Bin. If you are working with your home computer, you can either close the Recycle Bin or empty it (but only if you are sure that all items should be permanently removed).

i. Close any open windows.

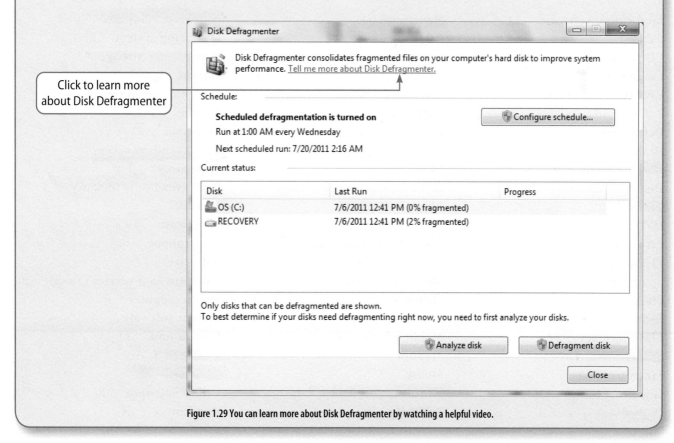

Click to learn more about Disk Defragmenter

Figure 1.29 You can learn more about Disk Defragmenter by watching a helpful video.

Chapter Summary

- A computer is an electronic device that can be programmed to carry out tasks. *2*

- A computer receives input in the form of data, processes that data, and outputs the results. *2*

- Computers can be for personal use such as the personal computer (PC), or for specialty use such as servers, mainframes, and supercomputers. *6*

- Computers can also be found in many other forms of equipment such as cell phones, cars, and even televisions. *4*

- Computers need both hardware and software to function. *14*

- Hardware is comprised of computer components that can be touched. Hardware can be divided into four categories: input, output, processing, and storage. *8*

- Software is comprised of the programs that provide instructions that enable a computer to function and that make it possible for you to enjoy computer applications, such as the Internet, producing documents, and playing games. *14*

- There are two types of software, system software and application software. *14*

- System software coordinates hardware so that a computer can operate. Examples of system software include an operating system, such as Windows 7. *14*

- Application software relates to tasks and activities that you work with on a computer such as Microsoft Word. *14*

Key Terms

Application software   *14*
Backup   *32*
CD (compact disc)   *12*
Computer   *2*
CPU (Central Processing Unit)   *11*
Defragment   *28*
Desktop computer   *5*
Disk Cleanup   *28*
Disk Defragmenter   *28*
Driver   *10*
DVD   *12*
Error Checking Utility   *31*
EULA (end user license agreement)   *19*
File compression software   *27*
Flash drive   *12*
Flash memory   *12*
Fragmented   *28*
Freeware   *19*
Gigahertz (GHz)   *11*
Hard drive   *11*

Hardware   *8*
Inkjet printer   *10*
Input   *8*
Install   *20*
Integrated phone   *6*
Keyboard   *9*
Laptop computer   *5*
Laser printer   *10*
LCD   *9*
Light-emitting diode (LED)   *9*
Linux   *26*
Mac OS X   *25*
Magnetic disk storage   *11*
Mainframe   *6*
Megahertz (MHz)   *11*
Memory   *14*
Microprocessor   *11*
Mobile phone   *5*
Monitor   *9*
Mouse   *9*
Multifunction device   *10*
Netbook   *5*

Notebook computer   *5*
Operating system   *14*
Optical disc storage   *12*
Output   *9*
Personal computer (PC)   *4*
Printer   *10*
Processor   *11*
RAM (random access memory)   *14*
ROM (read-only memory)   *14*
Server   *6*
Shareware   *19*
Smartphone   *6*
Software   *14*
Software-as-a-service (SaaS)   *20*
Supercomputer   *6*
System software   *14*
System unit   *11*
Tablet PC   *5*
Uninstall   *22*
Utility software   *26*
Windows 7   *24*

Multiple Choice

1. The primary output device for a personal computer system is a
   a. speaker.
   b. monitor.
   c. printer.
   d. multifunction device.

2. Which of the following shows numeric order from highest to lowest?
   a. Kilobyte, gigabyte, megabyte.
   b. Hertz, gigahertz, megahertz.
   c. Kilobyte, megabyte, gigabyte.
   d. Gigabyte, megabyte, kilobyte.

3. The area where data and programs are temporarily stored while they are in use is
   a. CPU.
   b. diskette.
   c. RAM.
   d. CRT.

4. Computer memory is measured in terms of
   a. bytes.
   b. inches.
   c. hertz.
   d. cycles.

5. A program that provides instructions to the computer for connecting to and operating a peripheral device, such as a printer, is a
   a. processor.
   b. driver.
   c. CPU.
   d. SaaS.

6. A hard drive on which files are physically broken apart and saved in various locations is called
   a. pieced.
   b. fragmented.
   c. recycled.
   d. formatted.

7. Which of the following storage devices is typically very large in capacity and is the location where software is installed?
   a. CD
   b. Flash drive
   c. DVD
   d. Hard drive

8. Which of the following is NOT considered system software?
   a. Error Checking utility
   b. Windows 7
   c. Microsoft Word
   d. Disk Defragmenter

9. _____ is an open-source operating system.
   a. Mac OS X
   b. Windows 7
   c. Google Chrome
   d. Linux

10. A(n) _____ is technology that incorporates several tools into one single piece of hardware.
    a. driver
    b. integrated system
    c. supercomputer
    d. spreadsheet

11. A(n) _____ manages system resources like the processor and memory, making it possible to write an e-mail and browse a Web page at the same time.
    a. operating system
    b. file compression utility
    c. system maintenance utility
    d. hard drive

12. Which of the following is not recommended as a location for a backup of files from your computer or a business computer?
    a. RAM
    b. External hard drive
    c. Online backup, such as Mozy
    d. DVD

13. It is especially important to be aware of your system's specifications, such as size of RAM, processor type, hard drive space available, and operating system so you can
    a. intelligently converse with computer professionals.
    b. upgrade your computer system yourself.
    c. be certain your computer system will support software you are considering.
    d. match computer peripherals, such as printers and mice, with your computer.

14. A primary function of ROM is to
    a. provide temporary storage for programs and data you are currently working with.
    b. serve as a backup location for your system and data files.
    c. perform system diagnostics and provide boot instructions.
    d. synchronize files from a mobile device to your computer.

15. A utility that removes unnecessary files from your hard drive is
    a. Disk Defragmenter.
    b. Disk Cleanup.
    c. Recycle Bin.
    d. Error Checking.

True/False

Circle **T** if the statement is true or **F** if the statement is false.

T F   1. The Error Checking utility can often repair disk errors that are identified.

T F   2. It is a good idea to keep backup copies of data files nearby so you can quickly restore them if necessary.

T F   3. The terms open-source software and freeware can be used interchangeably.

T F   4. Hardware is equipment you can touch.

T F   5. Mainframes are the most powerful computers today.

T F   6. It is possible to combine an MP3 player, a cell phone, and a calendar into a single device.

T F   7. Cloud computing requires an Internet connection.

T F   8. Software must be purchased at a retail store.

T F   9. Anything stored in RAM remains on the computer after it is shut down.

T F 10. Microsoft Excel is an example of system software.

End of Chapter Exercises

Shopping for a Computer

In this project, you will review a sample advertisement for a PC system, identifying hardware specifications. Record your responses on paper for submission to your instructor.

> **Laptop Computer with 14" Display**
> 14" LCD Display
> Intel Core i3 Processor 2.53 GHz
> DVD+RW/CD-RW Optical Drive
> 4 GB RAM
> 500-GB Hard Drive
> Windows 7 Home Premium

1. In the ad above, how much memory is available?
2. What is the processor speed?
3. How large is the hard drive?
4. Will you be able to create your own DVDs and CDs?
5. What operating system is installed on this laptop?

What Do I Want to Do?

Before selecting a computer for purchase, it is important that you evaluate your reasons for wanting a computer. What do you hope to accomplish? What do you think will be fun? Do you have any projects in mind?

Using the checklist below, select those areas you would like to explore.

_____ E-mail
_____ Internet Research
_____ Games
_____ Word Processing
_____ Genealogy
_____ Graphics/Digital Photography
_____ Financial/Investment Analysis
_____ Desktop Publishing (greeting cards, calendars, brochures)
_____ Other (specify)

Having identified your computer goals, visit an office supply store or general retailer and browse the software aisle to find products that might help you meet your goals. You can also check advertising inserts in a local newspaper. Find appropriate software and take a close look at the box to identify computer requirements. At a minimum, you should note the required operating system (OS), RAM (memory), and hard drive space. Do a little comparison shopping to find the same or similar products elsewhere.

You will not need to find any software to support the e-mail and Internet research categories, as those areas will be addressed when you contract with an Internet service provider.

In the table below, list your software selections. Which would you buy? Record your responses on paper for submission to your instructor.

Software	Store/Vendor	RAM Memory	OS	Cost

Internet Search Activity: Computer Careers

Imagine yourself working in a computer career as discussed in this chapter. Which computer career interests you the most? Why?

Research the career you discussed above. Using a search engine like Google, find out what education/certification/training is necessary for that job. Explain. Next, go to a website like www.salary.com and search for that career. What salary range can be expected for the career you have chosen?

Record your responses on paper for submission to your instructor.

Internet Search Activity: Searching for Software

You are looking for a word processing software program that is free. Are any available? Using a search engine like Google, search for at least three available programs. What are these programs? At what websites did you find them? Can you identify any differences between the programs?

Record your responses on paper for submission to your instructor.

CHAPTER **TWO**

Understanding the Operating System and File Management

EVERY COMPUTER, NO MATTER HOW LARGE OR SMALL, must have an **operating system** to coordinate system activities, including communication between the user and application software, or computer programs. From such basic tasks as recognizing input from the keyboard and sending output to the monitor, to more advanced traffic control, ensuring that programs running simultaneously do not conflict with each other, an operating system organizes and controls every piece of hardware and software on a computer system. Although **Microsoft Windows** is an easily recognizable and very popular microcomputer operating system, you can choose from others as well. Apple desktop computers use the **Mac OS** system, which has been redesigned in the new **Mac OS X Lion** version. **Linux**, a Windows-like operating system, is an open source software development that is becoming increasingly popular. Because it is open source, which means that users can contribute to its development, the Linux operating system is continually undergoing revision and improvement. Linux is not limited to microcomputers but is also found in applications ranging from wristwatches to supercomputers. Regardless of the operating system you use, you do not have to read lengthy operating system manuals or spend days becoming familiar with the operating system software.

OBJECTIVES

When you complete this chapter, you will:

- ▶ Be familiar with the basics of an operating system.
- ▶ Explore the desktop.
- ▶ Be able to manage windows.
- ▶ Identify ways to customize a computer system.
- ▶ Manage files and folders.
- ▶ Be familiar with Windows Search.
- ▶ Explore Windows Help.

41

All you need to do is master a few basic skills that will enable you to manage your computer efficiently and get the most enjoyment from the time you spend with software activities.

Microsoft Windows is the operating system of choice for many computer users. The newest Windows version is **Windows 7**, which is available in three editions—**Home Premium**, **Professional**, and **Ultimate**. Each edition includes features that are appropriate for different settings. You will most likely work with Home Premium on your personal computer, while your workplace might depend on the Professional or Ultimate edition. You can compare features and select the edition that is right for you at http://windows.microsoft.com/en-us/windows7/products/compare. Although it is not available for retail purchase, **Windows Starter** is a very limited Windows edition that is often preinstalled on netbooks. Designed to be simple and easy to use, Windows Starter comes with **Windows Anytime Upgrade** (as do other Windows 7 versions), which enables you to acquire a more advanced Windows edition through a simple Internet download and purchase. Windows 7 boasts improvements over earlier Windows versions in the areas of security, multimedia and entertainment, power management, and networking.

Exploring the Windows 7 Desktop

The **desktop** is the screen you see after you turn on the computer and log onto your user account (if required). The desktop is your "virtual" work environment, closely paralleling a typical office. Your desk is the place where you put paperwork and complete tasks. Similarly, the Windows desktop is the location of projects, files, and folders you are currently working with. An open software application, such as a computer game you are playing or a document you are creating, is typically shown as a window (boxed area) on the desktop.

You often have several pieces of paper or projects on your desk at the same time. If you are not extremely organized, some of the paperwork can overlap or obscure other papers. Similarly, the Windows desktop arranges and displays your projects and other system activities. You can have several windows open on your Windows desktop at one time, and they can overlap or obscure one another. However, the Windows desktop makes it easy to access all open windows, even if some are hidden from view by others. In this section, you will explore the desktop, identifying such elements as the graphical user interface, icons, the taskbar, and gadgets.

Understanding the Graphical User Interface (GUI)

A **graphical user interface**, or **GUI** (pronounced "gooey"), is a visual environment where you use a mouse to make selections and give commands. A GUI uses visual cues and pictures to interact with a computer user. Those pictures are called **icons**, representing programs, files, system resources, or folders. You can make selections and move among applications by double-clicking an icon with a mouse. When Windows 7 is installed, the desktop is almost empty (Figure 2.1). As you begin to work with your computer, you can indicate preferences and create icons so that the desktop provides access to those items you use most often.

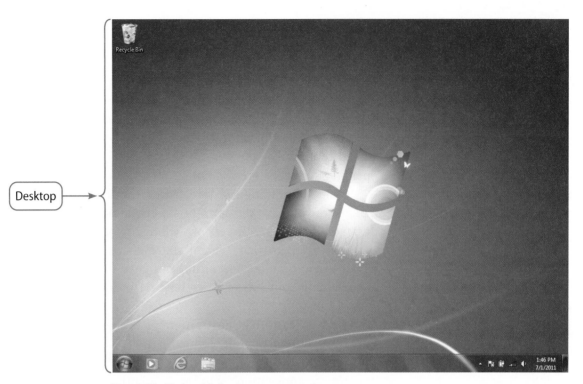

Desktop

Figure 2.1 The Windows 7 desktop is your computer work area.

Windows 7 is known as a **windowing environment**, because open applications, folders, and certain system resources are each shown in a boxed area called a **window**. Operating systems designed for use with microcomputers use a GUI interface, so resources are visually available on-screen. As a GUI, Windows 7 relies heavily on visual desktop elements to enable access to programs and system resources.

Technology Insight

32-bit and 64-bit Systems

As you shop for a new computer or consider upgrading your existing Windows operating system to Windows 7, you will select either a 32-bit or a 64-bit version of the operating system. While an appropriate version will already be installed on the computer you purchase, you will want to be aware of the difference between the two selections when upgrading from an existing Windows version on a computer you already own or when selecting software designed for a particular version. The basic difference between the 32-bit and 64-bit versions is the amount of computer memory (RAM) that can be accessed. If your computer has more than 3.5 GB of memory (the maximum that can be accessed by a 32-bit Windows 7 version), then you can select a 64-bit version. However, unless you are a power user (someone who typically works with several applications such as games, music, videos, and other applications at one time), it is unlikely that you will require a computer with more than 3.5 GB of RAM. In that case, you can easily work with the 32-bit Windows version. Ultimately, the amount of memory on your computer will determine whether you should select a 32-bit or 64-bit version. If your computer has 3.5 GB of RAM or less, you can choose a 32-bit version (although a 64-bit version can also work with that amount of memory); otherwise, select a 64-bit version. To see which version your computer is running, click **Start**, right-click **Computer**, and then click **Properties**. In the System group, you will see the System type listed as either a 32-bit or 64-bit Operating System.

All application software is designed to run in conjunction with a certain operating system. Some software is available in several versions, with each version compatible with a particular operating system. For example, you can purchase the version of Microsoft Word that coordinates with the Windows operating system, or you can purchase a different version of Microsoft Word if you work with an Apple computer. The point is that you must match application software with the operating system for which it is designed. For that reason, you should confirm that any software you consider is capable of working with your operating system before you buy it.

When considering software, check the software system specifications to make sure you have the appropriate operating system version. Most software designed for the 32-bit version will also work with the 64-bit version. The only exception to that general statement is many antivirus programs and device drivers that are specifically designed for either a 32-bit or 64-bit operating system. Software designed for a 64-bit system will not run with a 32-bit system.

You will learn that most programs designed to run under the Windows operating system include common screen elements and behave similarly. For example, the way you open a word processing program and the way you manage the application's window is identical to the way you open an image editing program and manage its window. Although particular program functions might differ, the way you access those functions will be consistent. The most important thing is that you become comfortable with the Windows environment so that learning and using any Windows application comes easily.

Quick Tip

Adding a Shortcut

If you use a program often, you might want to create a shortcut to the program on your desktop so you can access the program quickly at any time. Click **Start** on the taskbar, click **All Programs**, and identify the program that you want to add. Press and hold the right mouse button while dragging the program to the desktop. Release the mouse button and click **Create shortcuts here**.

Technology Insight

The Boot Process and ROM

Booting (or booting up) a computer refers to the process that occurs when you turn on a computer. Short for bootstrapping, which is a term related to starting from nothing (pulling yourself up by your bootstraps), the boot process results in loading the operating system into memory. When you turn on your computer, the computer goes through an initial set of activities that inventories equipment and performs a self-test. It checks to see if all equipment is connected and functioning, does a simple memory test, and loads the operating system. The instructions that control the self-check (also called a POST, or Power-On Self Test) are housed in ROM (Read-Only Memory), which is a section of hard-wired memory that can be read from but cannot typically be changed. Technically, the program containing the boot instructions is called BIOS software. BIOS is short for Basic Input/Output System. Because the BIOS software is built into the computer system, it is also referred to as ROM-BIOS. The software is actually stored on a ROM chip, which is connected to the motherboard (the main circuit board located in the system unit). Although historically a ROM chip was considered non-volatile, suggesting that its contents could not be changed, in some cases the contents actually can be rewritten, allowing BIOS software to be upgraded.

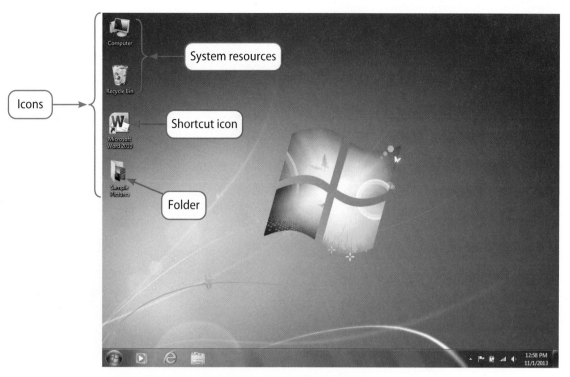

Figure 2.2 An icon represents a program, file, system resource, or folder.

Quick Tip

Arranging Icons

To arrange the icons on your desktop so that they are neatly aligned in columns, right-click an **empty area of the desktop**, point to **View**, and click **Auto arrange icons** (unless a check already appears beside the selection). Icons will be rearranged, if necessary. As more icons are added, they will be neatly arranged in columns and cannot be moved to an unoccupied area of the desktop; however, you can rearrange icons by dragging them within the existing grid of icons on the desktop. Reverse the process if you want to move icons. At that point, you can drag an icon to an unoccupied desktop position, if you like.

Using Icons and Gadgets

Icons are small graphics that can be displayed on the desktop, as shown in Figure 2.2. Although by default, icons are not displayed, you will most likely find them helpful in navigating to programs, files, folders, or system resources. You will learn to manage icons in this chapter, adding, deleting, and moving them to suit your needs. Icons that represent system resources, such as Computer, Recycle Bin, and Network, enable you to adjust settings, customize the system configuration, or access standard features. Double-click a folder icon to open a folder or subfolder containing files, such as documents or digital pictures. A **shortcut** icon is a pointer to a program. For example, you might have a shortcut icon on your desktop for Microsoft Word, as shown in Figure 2.2. Double-click the icon to open Microsoft Word. You can identify a shortcut icon because it will have a small arrow in the lower-left corner.

A desktop **gadget** represents data that is constantly changing, or a game or puzzle. Desktop gadgets can be both informative and fun. However, by default, gadgets are not shown on the desktop. If you find them useful, you can add gadgets when you right-click the desktop and click **Gadgets**. From the gallery shown in Figure 2.3, double-click a gadget. The number of gadgets shown in the gallery might vary, depending upon the configuration of software on your computer. Gadgets shown in the gallery are developed and supported by Microsoft. For even more choice, click **Get more gadgets online** to select from gadgets developed by Microsoft and others provided by third parties. Figure 2.4 shows selections that are available online. Occasionally, a gadget will relate to a program that is installed on your system (see the AVG gadget in Figure 2.3). Such a gadget is not included in a typical Windows 7

Gadgets

Click to get more gadgets online

Figure 2.3 A gadget often represents an item that is constantly changing, like the weather or stock prices.

installation. If you select a gadget that is available from a third party, you must agree to a disclaimer from Microsoft. Gadgets you select are grouped together on the right side of the desktop, as shown in Figure 2.5. When you right-click a gadget, you can change gadget settings, resize the gadget, adjust the opacity level, and close the gadget.

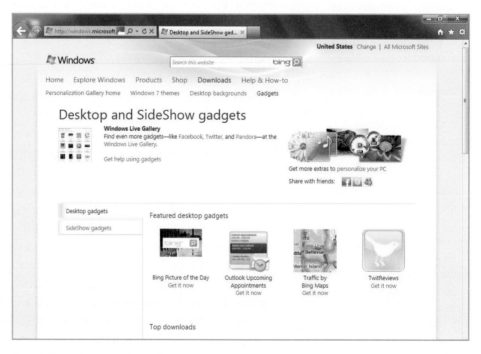

Figure 2.4 Many gadgets are available online.

Understanding the Operating System and File Management

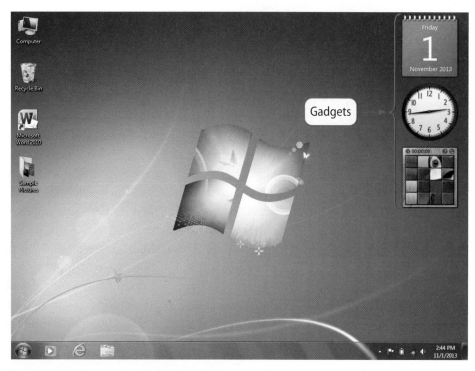

Figure 2.5 Gadgets line up on the right side of the desktop.

A Look Back

The Development of MS-DOS

The software giant, Microsoft, began as a project shared by two friends, Bill Gates and Paul Allen. A little good luck and an operating system launched the company into the powerhouse it is today. In 1980, as IBM prepared to debut the immensely successful IBM PC, the company made the fateful decision to contract with another company to develop an operating system for the new computer. IBM first discussed the incorporation of BASIC (a programming language) into the ROM chip for the IBM PC, a task gladly accepted by Microsoft. However, because Microsoft had no experience in developing an operating system, Bill Gates suggested that IBM explore the CP/M operating system, developed by Gary Kildall, of Digital Research. After a disagreement over contract terms with Kildall, however, IBM returned to Bill Gates and Microsoft, who accepted the challenge to write a new operating system. The result was MS-DOS (Microsoft Disk Operating System), which was based on QDOS (the Quick and Dirty Operating System), written by Tim Paterson of Seattle Computer Products. Microsoft paid Paterson $50,000 for the right to license the operating system—probably the best money ever spent! IBM agreed to let Microsoft market the operating system separately from the IBM PC, which Microsoft did, calling it MS-DOS. The version of the operating system used on the IBM PC was titled PC-DOS. As the personal computer market skyrocketed, so did Microsoft, which made a fortune selling MS-DOS. After eight major versions of MS-DOS, Microsoft discontinued the operating system in 2000. However, a DOS-like command interface and a subset of DOS commands is still available in Windows versions (accessible when you type cmd.exe in the Search box on the Start menu). Since that time, the Windows operating system has proven immensely successful for Microsoft, comprising approximately 90 percent of the market worldwide for all operating systems.

Understanding the Taskbar

Windows is a multitasking environment, which means that you can work with several projects at one time. The operating system was given the name Windows because each open application appears in its own boxed area, or window. Although it is not difficult for the operating system to keep track of multiple open projects, you might find it a bit more challenging. Imagine a desk, on which you have scattered papers as you worked with several projects. Imagine your frustration as you search for one particular note within the desktop clutter. Managing multiple open windows on a computer desktop could theoretically be just as frustrating! As you open a new window, or application, it is placed over a previous project so that it overlaps or completely obscures the previously viewed window. Not to worry, however; Windows makes it easy to keep up with open applications. The **taskbar** serves several purposes, but its primary function is providing a simple way to manage multiple windows.

The taskbar is the long horizontal bar located at the bottom of the Windows desktop (Figure 2.6). It includes a Start button, pinned icons, icons representing open windows, and a Notification area. Each of those items is described in this section.

Each open window is represented by a large icon on the taskbar. Although the icons are not labeled with words, they graphically represent the open program or resource. For example, the icon in Figure 2.6 that indicates one or more open Word documents displays the Microsoft Word logo. Similarly, the Microsoft Excel icon contains that product's logo. As you become familiar with programs on your system, you will learn to easily identify respective icons on the taskbar. If several programs are open, each will be shown as an icon on the taskbar. To move from one to the other, much as you would shift paper on a desk, simply click an icon on the taskbar.

It is possible to have several Word documents open at one time. You could also work with several digital pictures at one time. In fact, most applications enable you to work with several files within the application. Even so, you will see only one application icon on the taskbar, regardless of how many associated files are open. However, the icon will appear stacked, as shown in Figure 2.7, if multiple files are open within the application. In that way, the Windows 7 taskbar remains clean and uncluttered. When you place the pointer over an icon, any open files within that application display as small boxed **thumbnails**, or miniature pictures of the file's contents. As shown in Figure 2.7, you have two Word documents open, with each displayed as a thumbnail when you place the mouse pointer over the Word icon. The thumbnail preview of open files is part of the Windows 7 **Aero Peek** feature. Point to a thumbnail to temporarily view the contents in a larger size on the screen. Move the pointer away to return to the previous view. Click a thumbnail to switch to the window.

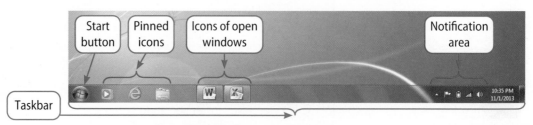

Figure 2.6 The taskbar enables you to manage multiple open windows.

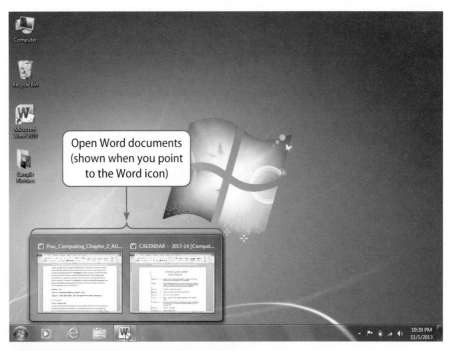

Open Word documents
(shown when you point
to the Word icon)

Figure 2.7 With Aero Peek, you can preview window contents.

Start menu

Start button

Figure 2.8 The Start menu is the gateway
to your computer.

Start Menu

Click the Start button to see the Start menu, shown in Figure 2.8. The Start menu, as its name implies, is a place to begin when opening programs, accessing system resources, and managing files. On the left side of the menu are commonly accessed programs, as well as those that are pinned (affixed to the Start menu and available until you unpin them). The following In-Depth section discusses the concept of pinning items. Click **All Programs** to select from a more complete list of programs installed on your computer system. The right side of the menu provides access to user folders—Documents, Pictures, and Music. In addition, the Computer selection enables you to view and manage disk drives on the system. Through the Control Panel (described

In Depth

Pinning Icons to the Start Menu and Taskbar

Icons pinned to the Start menu are always available, regardless of the frequency of use. Pinned items are shown at the top of the Start menu's left pane. To pin an icon to the Start menu, you must first locate it, either on the All Programs list (shown when you click Start and then All Programs) or on the desktop. Right-click the icon and then click **Pin to Start Menu**. To remove a pinned item, right-click it in the Start Menu and then click **Unpin from Start Menu**.

If you work with an application often, you might find it useful to include a permanent icon on the taskbar. That way, you can simply click the icon to open the application. Drag an icon of a program that is not currently open from the desktop to the taskbar, or right-click a program on the Start menu, and then click **Pin to Taskbar**. If the program that you want to pin is already open, click its icon on the taskbar and then click **Pin this program to taskbar**. To remove a pinned icon from the taskbar, right-click the icon, and then click **Unpin this program from taskbar**.

later in this chapter) you can customize your system. Other selections enable you to manage peripheral devices, such as printers, as well as to get answers to questions. Finally, the Start menu provides a way to shut down your computer properly. One of the most useful functions of the Start menu is the Search area, which is described later in this chapter.

In Depth

Using a Jump List

A Jump List (Figure 2.9) is a list of options that displays when you right-click the icon of an open program on the taskbar or one that is pinned to the taskbar. The options on the Jump List vary, depending on the program. For example, the Jump List of an Internet browser shows frequently viewed websites. The Jump List for a media player lists commonly played music. A Jump List might also provide access to commands related to the program, such as composing a new e-mail message or adjusting settings. Invariably, an option on the Jump List is used to pin or unpin the program to or from the taskbar.

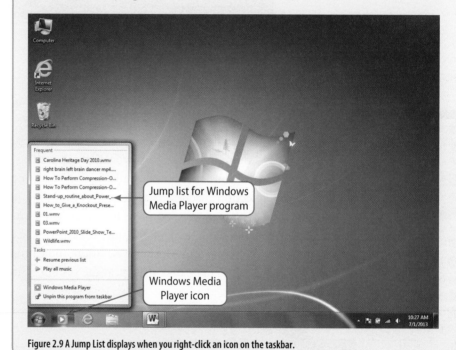

Figure 2.9 A Jump List displays when you right-click an icon on the taskbar.

Notification Area

The Notification area is located on the right side of the taskbar. In earlier Windows versions, the area was the location of icons representing system settings and utility programs, which means that it could quickly become cluttered. Windows 7 has cleaned up the area, providing fewer notifications, while still enabling you to view a more complete list upon demand. In fact, you can customize the Notification area so that it displays only those icons that you specify. By default, the Notification area provides icons related to network connections, volume, battery life or power source, the current date and time, and the Action Center (if any alerts require your attention). In addition, you can temporarily display a collection of icons that are hidden by default. Those icons represent programs that run in the background, such as antivirus and webcam software. A program that runs in the

Power Management and Shut Down Options

Shutting down a computer properly means much more than simply pressing the power button. In fact, pressing the power button to turn off a computer is not at all recommended. The developers of Windows 7 incorporated effective power management features that make it easy to power down a computer system, while providing options to save energy in the process.

To begin the Shut down process, click **Start** (on the taskbar). Click **Shut down** to power off the computer. When you shut down a computer you actually turn it off. When power is restored, the computer goes through a POST (Power-On Self Test) which checks the system's connections, memory, and other vital functions. Shutting down a computer also saves energy, as none is required. If you do not plan to use a computer for a lengthy period, you can shut it down. Otherwise, click **Start**, click the **Shut down arrow**, and select from several options, as follows:

- Restart – powers off the computer for a moment, then turns it on again. Most often, a restart (also called a reboot) is recommended after correcting a problem or making a change in configuration, a software update, or the uninstallation of software.
- Sleep – places the computer in a low-power state without turning it off. Use Sleep so that you can get back to your work quickly, without having to wait for the computer to completely restart. Sleep mode saves power during those times when you will only be away for a short time; however, it does slowly drain the battery of a laptop.
- Hibernate – if available, this option remembers the current state of the desktop and fully powers off a computer. When the computer is powered back on, any applications and files that were open before hibernation are redisplayed. Powering back on from hibernation is quicker than from a shut down, but hibernation uses no power. Use hibernation for longer intervals between computer use, but for a quicker power up than would occur with a complete reboot.

To save even more energy, you can consider several power management options, some of which might be preset on your computer. To check power management options, click **Start**, and then click **Control Panel**. Click **System and Security**. Click **Power Options**. Several options in the left pane enable you to manage a battery (especially important if you are a laptop user) and to create a power plan. The right pane shows the current plan that is in place, which is usually appropriate for your system. If necessary, click **Show additional plans** (in the right pane) to review options of your power management plan. The Balanced plan, which is most likely the default, turns off the display after 10 minutes of inactivity and puts your computer into sleep mode after 30 minutes. The Power saver plan turns off the display in 5 minutes and goes into sleep mode after 15 minutes. If neither of those plans is right for you, click **Create a power plan** and progress through the series of prompts to define custom settings. For quick power plan adjustment, click the battery icon in the Notification area of the taskbar (if using a laptop), and select from the options presented.

background is opened when you power on a computer and remains open until you shut down the computer. Often providing critical system support, those programs are unobtrusive and require little or no interaction with you. Figure 2.10 shows a typical Notification area, along with the hidden icons that are shown when you click **Show hidden icons**.

Click here to
show hidden icons

Hidden icons

Action
Center icon

Notification area

Figure 2.10 The Windows 7 Notification area is uncluttered.

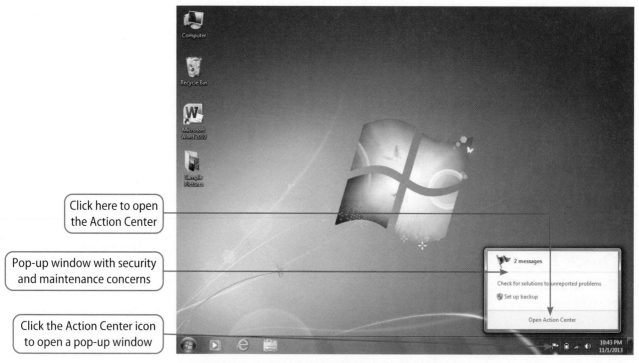

Click here to open
the Action Center

Pop-up window with security
and maintenance concerns

Click the Action Center icon
to open a pop-up window

Figure 2.11 The Action Center keeps you aware of maintenance and security concerns.

The Action Center provides notification of security and maintenance concerns. Click the Action Center icon, shown in Figure 2.11, to open a pop-up window and view any messages. Click an alert message to address the problem. For more complete information and to customize the Action Center, click **Open Action Center** in the pop-up window. Alternatively, open the

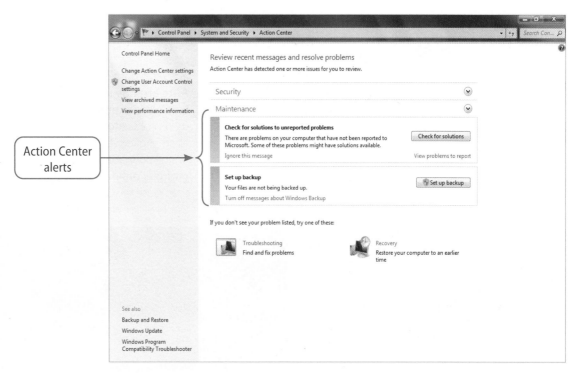

Action Center alerts

Figure 2.12 Color-coded alerts provide information on the severity of a problem.

Action Center by clicking **Start**, **Control Panel**, **System and Security**, and then **Action Center**. If necessary, click the arrow to the right of the Security or Maintenance headings to expand the view, showing more detail. Alerts are color coded, as shown in Figure 2.12, with yellow suggesting tasks that you should consider in the near future, while red indicates problems that require immediate action.

Managing Windows

Windows is a multitasking environment, which means that you can work with several projects at one time. Suppose that you are finishing up a research paper, using Microsoft Word, while conducting some Internet research for the paper. You would most likely have Microsoft Word open, while also working with an Internet browser. Both of those applications would be open in separate windows. You might even have an annotated bibliography document open while you work with the research paper. In that case, both Word documents would occupy separate windows. With that scenario in mind, you will understand the need to manage multiple windows so that projects move along smoothly. Windows 7 simplifies that management task. In this section, you will work with windows, learning to open, close, minimize, maximize, and restore them. In addition, you will explore methods of managing multiple windows.

Opening, Closing, Maximizing, and Restoring Windows

In the previous section, you learned that you can open a window by selecting a program from the Start menu (if the item that you are opening is a program). You can also open a window when you click a pinned icon on the taskbar. To

Quick Tip
Maximize and Restore a Window

If a window is not already maximized, double-click the title bar (or the bar located above the Address bar, if the window contains no title bar) to display it in full size. You can also drag the title bar to the top of the desktop to quickly maximize a window. To restore down a maximized window, drag the title bar down, or double-click the title bar of a maximized window.

Hands-On

As a graduate assistant at a university, you have been asked to review some teaching material your professor has prepared for his computer concepts course. You should pretend you are a beginning student, going through all material, and making suggestions for additional coverage where necessary.

In this exercise, you will review material related to working with the desktop and the taskbar. Although the icons on your desktop will not be identical to those shown in Figure 2.13, you will be able to recognize the basic components described in this exercise.

a. Check the icons on your desktop. As shown in Figure 2.13 some icons might represent shortcuts, while others indicate system resources or folders. Can you identify any similar icons on your desktop?

TROUBLESHOOTING

It is unlikely, but entirely possible, that your desktop includes no icons. In that case, proceed to Step C.

b. Right-click an **empty area of the desktop** and then point to **View**. Click **Auto arrange icons** (unless a check already appears beside the selection). If the setting was not already on, your icons should immediately rearrange into a more attractive position. Reverse the process to deselect **Auto arrange icons**.

c. Right-click an **empty area of the desktop** and then click **Gadgets**. Double-click **Clock** (or select another gadget if the clock gadget already appears on the right side of the desktop). Click **Get more gadgets online**. Review the online options, and then close the browser without selecting a gadget. Double-click **Weather**. Close the Gadgets window.

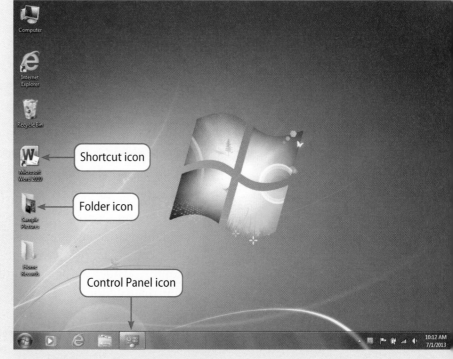

Figure 2.13 The Windows 7 desktop is simple to manage.

open an item represented by an icon on the desktop, simply double-click the icon. Later in this chapter, you will learn to open files, such as documents or pictures. Each application, file, or system resource that you open displays in its own window; each window includes common components that enable you to minimize, maximize, close, and restore the window.

The upper-right corner of a window typically includes three buttons, as shown in Figure 2.14. The **Minimize** button reduces the window to an icon on the taskbar, without removing the window from memory. That means that you can quickly redisplay the item when you click its icon on the taskbar (or point to the icon and select a thumbnail if it is one of several files open in the same application). You will minimize an application or project if you intend to return to it relatively quickly. Otherwise, you will close the item so that that both the taskbar and memory remain uncluttered.

Click **Options** (displayed as a wrench on the right of the Weather gadget when you point to the Weather gadget). Type your city and state (or the nearest metropolitan area), making sure to use the two-character state abbreviation. Click **OK**. Click **OK** again. Weather information related to your location displays in the gadget.

d. If you are using a computer in a lab, you should remove the gadgets. Right-click a gadget and then click **Close gadget**. Similarly, remove the remaining gadget.

e. Click **Start** on the taskbar. Click **All Programs**. Scroll through the programs, familiarizing yourself with the programs on your system. Click **Back** at the bottom of the list. Click **Control Panel** on the right pane to open the Control Panel. An icon should appear on the taskbar as shown in Figure 2.13. Point to the icon to see a thumbnail of the open window. If the window happened to be obscured by another open window (which is not the case here), viewing the thumbnail would provide a preview of the open window; you could click the thumbnail to bring the window to the desktop foreground.

f. Click the **thumbnail** that appears when you point to the Control Panel icon. Click **System and Security**. Click **Action Center**. Do you see any alerts? If necessary, click the arrow to the right of Maintenance or Security to expand the display, showing any alerts. Close the Action Center window.

g. Click **Start** and then click **All Programs**. Scroll through the program list, if necessary, and click **Accessories**. Right-click **Calculator** and then

click **Pin to Taskbar**. Click an **empty area of the desktop** outside the Start menu to close the menu. Click the **Calculator icon** that appears on the taskbar. Can you determine how to use the calculator? What is the result of 89+524-2? Close the calculator.

h. Right-click the **Calculator icon** on the taskbar and then click **Unpin this program from taskbar**.

i. Click **Start** and then click **All Programs**. Click **Accessories**. Right-click **Paint** and then click **Pin to Start Menu**. Click **Back**. Is Paint pinned to the Start menu? Right-click **Paint** and then click **Unpin from Start Menu**. Click **Start** to close the Start menu.

ON YOUR OWN

Pin WordPad (located on the Start menu under All Programs, Accessories) to the taskbar. Pin the same program to the Start menu. Unpin WordPad from the taskbar and the Start menu.

---

j. Click **Start** and then click **All Programs**. Click **Accessories**. Right-click and drag Calculator to the desktop. Click **Create shortcuts here**. Double-click the **Calculator icon** to open the program. Close Calculator. Right-click **Calculator** and then click **Delete**. Click **Yes** to confirm the deletion. When you move a shortcut to the Recycle Bin, the desktop shortcut is removed, but the software remains intact. You can still access Calculator through the Start menu.

k. Keep your computer on for the next exercise.

You can display a window so that it occupies the entire desktop (with the exception of the taskbar) or so that the window is sized smaller. If a window that you open displays in less than full size, the middle button at the upper-right corner of the window enables you to **maximize** the window. However, if the window opens in full size, you can use the middle button to restore (or **restore down**) the window to a smaller size.

When you **close** a window, you remove it from memory. You can always open it later, as described earlier in this section. The Close button is represented by an X, found in the upper-right corner of an open window.

Resizing and Moving Windows

With several windows open, you run the risk of one window obscuring part or all of another window. Just as papers on a desk can be placed on top of one

---

Quick Tip

Minimize a Window

To quickly minimize an open window, click its icon on the taskbar. Click the icon again to restore the window to the desktop.

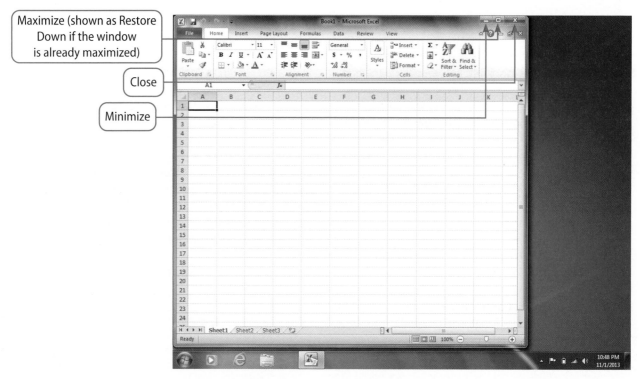

Maximize (shown as Restore Down if the window is already maximized)

Close

Minimize

Figure 2.14 You can minimize, maximize, close, or restore a window.

another so that you can only see the topmost paper, windows on a computer desktop can be similarly arranged. You have learned that the taskbar displays icons of all open windows so that you can simply click an icon to bring a window to the front. You can also manage open windows by moving or resizing them so that you can see necessary parts of several open windows. You can arrange them on-screen to support work on several projects simultaneously, viewing changes in each window as those changes are made.

Maximized windows cannot be moved or resized. However, if a window is not maximized, you can move it by dragging the title bar. To resize a window, place the pointer on a border of the window so that the pointer resembles a two-headed arrow. At that point, drag the window border to resize the window, making the window larger or smaller. If you drag a corner of a window, you can resize adjacent sides of a window at the same time.

Working with Multiple Windows

Windows 7 makes it easy to work with multiple windows. Even so, working with several windows, or projects, at the same time can be distracting for you, so only open those files or applications that are necessary. If only one window is open, it is the **active window**. If several windows are open, the active window displays on top of the other windows. The active window in Figure 2.15 is a Word document. With several windows open, you will need to know how to manage them so that you can easily switch from one to the other.

By moving and resizing windows, you can arrange multiple windows on the desktop so you can work with several at the same time. However, Windows 7 also includes features that simplify the arrangement of multiple windows. Right-click an **empty area of the taskbar** to display the shortcut menu shown in

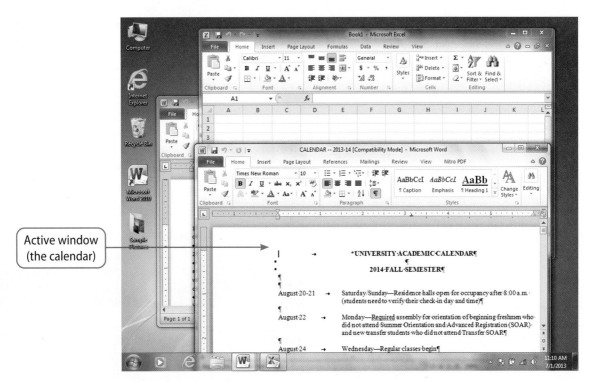

Active window (the calendar)

Figure 2.15 The active window is the topmost window in which you are working.

Figure 2.16. The Cascade windows menu selection arranges open windows in an overlapping fashion as shown in Figure 2.17. To move from one window to the next, simply click a visible part of the window to which you want to move. From the shortcut menu, you can also arrange open windows side by side, or stacked (Figure 2.17).

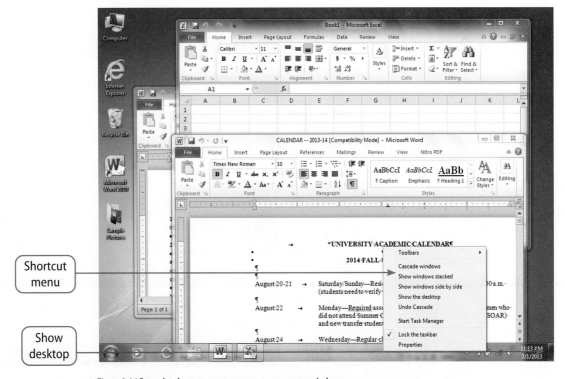

Shortcut menu

Show desktop

Figure 2.16 From the shortcut menu, you can arrange open windows.

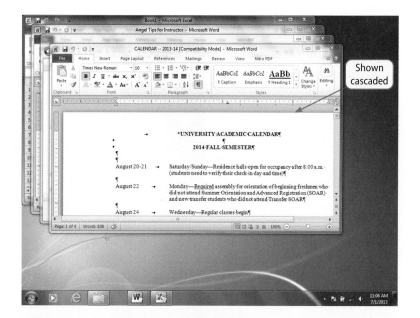

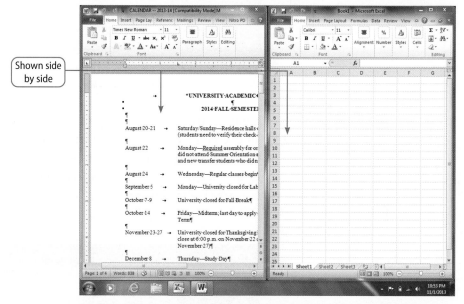

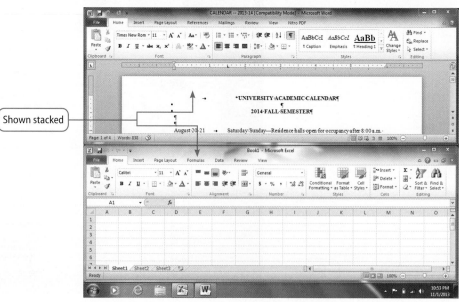

Figure 2.17 Arrange open windows cascaded, side by side, or stacked.

In Depth

Show the Desktop

With several windows open on the desktop, accessing an item on the desktop (which is hidden by the open windows) can be a challenge. Windows 7 provides a quick fix, though. Simply point to **Show desktop** (Figure 2.16) to temporarily view the desktop. When you move the pointer away, open windows reappear. Click **Show desktop** if you want to temporarily minimize open windows so that you can access a desktop item. Click **Show desktop** again to return all open windows to their original placement on the desktop. You can also access the desktop when you right-click an **empty area of the taskbar** and then click **Show the desktop**. Reverse the process, clicking **Show open windows**, to return all open windows.

Aero Peek

As its name implies, Aero Peek offers a way to *peek* at something before selecting it. Each open application or resource is shown as an icon on the taskbar. Regardless of the number of open files in the application, there is only one taskbar icon for each application. For example, if you are using Microsoft Word to edit a couple of documents—perhaps your resumé and your letter of application for a job search—there will be only one Word icon on the taskbar, although with both documents open, the icon will be stacked. Of course, you will still need to manage those two windows so that you can work in each. Aero Peek provides a way to do that.

Point to an icon to preview its contents in a thumbnail, which is actually a mini-window. As in the case described in the preceding paragraph, you might actually be working with multiple files (or documents, in this case) within one application. In that case, Aero Peek displays a thumbnail for each file, as shown in Figure 2.18. Point to a thumbnail (without clicking) to display the window

Thumbnail previews of open Word documents

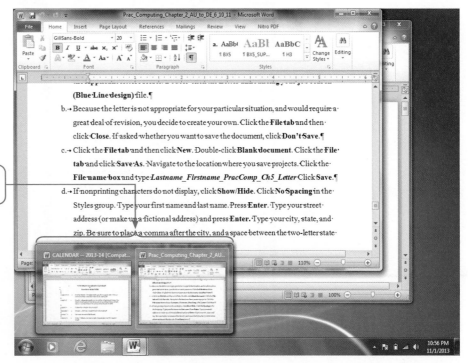

Figure 2.18 Aero Peek shows a preview of an open window.

in full size while temporarily hiding all other open windows. In that way, you can quickly preview the contents of a window without actually selecting it as the active window. If your intention is to work with the file, however, click the thumbnail to bring it to the front of the desktop, making it the active window. Note that the thumbnail also includes a Close button (visible only when you point to the thumbnail), so you can actually close a window from its Aero Peek thumbnail.

Snap and Aero Flip 3D

Snap enables you to position two windows (that are not already maximized) in an orderly arrangement on opposite sides of the desktop. Drag the title bar of one of the windows to one side of the desktop, continuing to drag until you see a transparent outline of a window that indicates placement of the window. Release the mouse button. Do the same with the second window. The result is shown in Figure 2.19.

One of the flashier new Windows 7 features, **Aero Flip 3D** displays a continuous cascade of open windows, enabling you to select any one as the active window. With several windows open, press and hold the Windows logo key while repeatedly pressing Tab. Each time you press Tab, a new window cascades to the front. Release the Windows logo key when the desired window displays. You can also click any window in the stack, regardless of its placement, to display it. An example of Aero Flip 3D is shown in Figure 2.20.

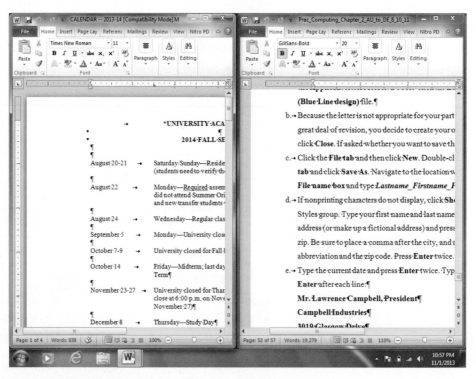

Figure 2.19 Quickly arrange two open windows with Snap.

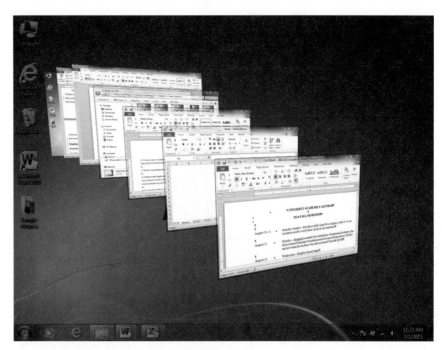

Figure 2.20 Aero Flip 3D continually cascades open windows.

Windows Update and Windows Upgrade

Perhaps because the two terms sound so similar, many people confuse Windows Update with Windows Upgrade. The two are actually very different, with each serving a unique purpose in keeping your computer up to date. *Windows Update* helps keep your computer safe and your software current. It does so by periodically downloading the latest security and feature updates from the Microsoft website. You can configure your computer so that updates occur with minimal, if any, interaction with you. *Windows Upgrade* occurs when you upgrade your operating system to a new version. With Windows 7's emphasis on anywhere (and anytime) computing, you can initiate an upgrade for your operating system without leaving your home.

Windows Update is part of the Windows 7 Action Center. Click **Start**, **All Programs**, and **Windows Update** to quickly get to the Action Center's Update page. Updates are typically configured to occur automatically, but you can adjust those settings by clicking **Change settings** in the left pane. Confirm or change the update day and time and click **OK**. Click **Check for updates** to initiate an immediate check, selecting any that are identified. Because Microsoft only supplies updates to address concerns or to improve performance, it is safer to install updates than to risk the repercussions of not installing any that you are unsure of.

Windows 7 is available in three versions—Home Premium, Professional, and Ultimate. You can upgrade from the first two to the next step by using Windows Anytime Upgrade. For example, a Home Premium user can upgrade to Professional, while a Professional user can upgrade to Ultimate. To make sure your computer is capable of supporting the Windows 7 version you are considering, visit http://windows.microsoft.com/upgradeadvisor for an online check of your system. To begin the upgrade process, click **Start**, **All Programs**, and **Windows Update**. At the bottom of the left pane, click **Windows Anytime Upgrade**. The Upgrade link is only available if you are actually able to upgrade; for example, a Windows Ultimate user cannot upgrade further, so there will be no Upgrade link. By responding to prompts, you can select an upgrade, purchase an upgrade code, and complete the process. In as few as 10 minutes, you can upgrade your computer with a new version of Windows 7.

Hands-On

As you continue to evaluate the class material on Windows 7 for your professor, you will work through the following practice on managing windows.

a. Click **Start** and then click **Help and Support** (on the right side of the Start menu). If the window is not already maximized, click **Maximize** (the middle button in the upper-right corner of the Windows Help and Support window). If the window is already maximized, skip to Step B.

b. Click **Restore Down** (the middle button on the upper-right side of the Windows Help and Support window). Drag the title bar to move the window to another location on the desktop. Double-click the **title bar** to maximize the window.

c. Click **Start** and then click **Control Panel**. If the window is maximized, click **Restore Down**. Point to a border of the Control Panel window so that the pointer resembles a two-headed arrow. Drag to make the window slightly larger. Click **Minimize** (the first button on the upper-right side of the Control Panel window).

TROUBLESHOOTING

If you minimized the Help and Support window instead of Control Panel, click the Help and Support icon on the taskbar and then click the Control Panel icon on the taskbar. Click Minimize in the Control Panel.

d. Click the **Control Panel icon** on the taskbar. Right-click an **empty area of the taskbar** and then click

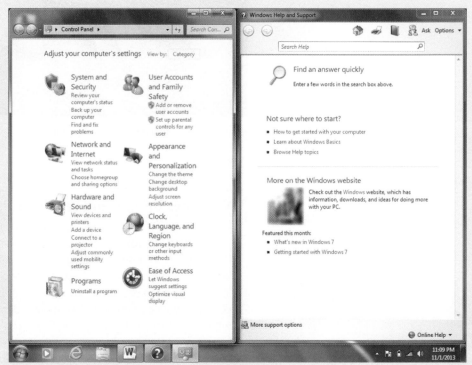

Figure 2.21 Windows 7 provides assistance with managing multiple windows.

Customizing a Computer System

If you work in an office or have a desk at home, you might have some photos, a lamp, or perhaps a clock on your desk. Adding a personal touch to the desk provides some variety and makes you more comfortable as you work. Similarly, you can personalize your computer desktop with a colorful **background** or perhaps a **screen saver** comprised of digital photos from your camera. A screen saver is a moving series of pictures or images that appears when your computer has been idle for a specified period of time. Occasionally, you might find it necessary to change the screen **resolution**, which is a measure of the sharpness and clarity of images, so that you can accommodate various software requirements. By adding **user accounts**, you can ensure that several people can use the same computer, each with personal settings and permissions. In this section, you will

Cascade windows. Click the **title bar of the Help and Support window** (or any visible part of the window) to make the Help and Support window the active window. Drag the **title bar of the Help and Support window** to the right side of the desktop, continuing to drag until a window outline displays. Release the mouse button. Similarly, drag the Control Panel to the left side of the desktop. Your desktop should appear as shown in Figure 2.21. Click **Close** (the last button on the right side of the title bar) in the Control Panel window. Close the Help and Support window.

e. Click **Start**, **All Programs**, **Microsoft Office**, and **Microsoft Word 2010**. Type your first and last names and press **Enter**. Click the **File tab**, click **New**, and double-click **Blank document**. Type your college or school name and press **Enter**. Minimize both Word windows.

TROUBLESHOOTING

If you make a mistake typing, press Backspace to remove characters and retype.

---

f. Point to the Word icon on the taskbar without clicking. Two thumbnails display, one titled Document1 and one titled Document2. Point to Document1 to see the document in its original size. Point to Document2 to view that document. Click the Document2 thumbnail to open the document

so that you can work with it. Close Document2. When asked whether to save the document, click **Don't Save**. Point to the Word icon and then point to the Document1 thumbnail. Click **Close** in the thumbnail to close the document. Do not save the document.

TROUBLESHOOTING

If you clicked the Document1 thumbnail, displaying the document instead of closing it, click Minimize (the first button on the upper-right side of the Document1 window). Then point to the Word icon on the taskbar and click Close in the thumbnail to close the document.

ON YOUR OWN

Open the Control Panel. Open Microsoft Word. Show both windows cascaded. Snap each window to an opposite side of the desktop. Close both windows.

---

g. Open the Help and Support window from the Start menu. Open the Control Panel. Hold down the Windows logo key and press Tab repeatedly to cycle through the desktop and all open windows. Release the mouse button so that the Control Panel is the active window. Close all windows.

h. Keep the computer on for the next exercise.

learn to personalize a computer with a desktop background and a screen saver. In addition, you will work with screen resolution, user accounts, and managing peripheral devices, such as a printer.

Changing the Background and Screen Saver

By changing the desktop background, you can add a personal touch or a little excitement to the desktop. Windows 7 provides a library of backgrounds to choose from, or you can identify a favorite digital picture to serve as a background. You might even locate a website that will change your desktop periodically. Because it is so easy to change the desktop background, you can do so often.

To select a desktop background, right-click an **empty area of the desktop** and then click **Personalize**. From the window shown in Figure 2.22, you can

Quick Tip

Downloading Backgrounds

Desktop backgrounds are available at various online sites, but you should use caution in downloading a background so that you do not acquire a computer virus or accept spyware onto your system. You can download free software at http://www .wallpaperdownloader.com that changes your desktop periodically, using images from Bing or National Geographic.

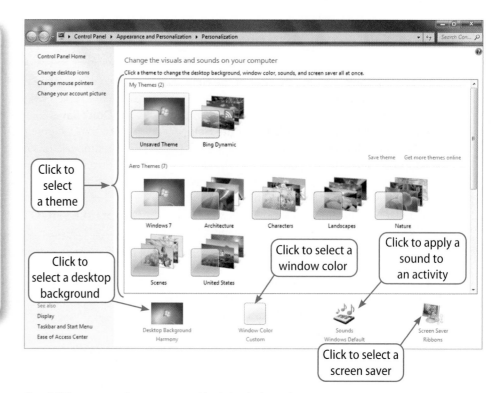

Figure 2.22 You can personalize your computer with a desktop background or screen saver.

select a theme, which changes the background, color scheme, sounds, and screen saver at one time so that all of those elements are coordinated. To change the background only, click **Desktop Background**. The Picture Location is most likely Windows Desktop Backgrounds, but you can also select from the Pictures Library or other locations on your computer. If a picture that you want to use is in another location, perhaps your hard drive, click **Browse** and then navigate to and click the picture. Click **Save changes**. If the background is in a predefined group, such as Windows Desktop Backgrounds, simply click a background thumbnail, and then click **Save changes**.

The Window Color selection changes the color of window borders, the Start menu, and the taskbar. The Sounds selection enables you to select a sound to play when a certain event happens on your computer. For example, to select a sound to hear when you exit Windows, click **Sounds**, scroll through Program Events, and select **Exit Windows**. Then click **Sounds** and select a sound—for example, Chimes. Click **Test** to hear the sound, and then click **OK**. The next time you exit Windows, you will hear chimes.

Click **Screen Saver** to select a screen saver or to identify your own pictures or images to use. Click the **Screen saver arrow** that appears in the Screen Saver Settings dialog box (Figure 2.23) and select a screen saver (or click **Photos** to include pictures from your hard drive). Some screen savers include adjustment settings that you can access when you click Settings. One such setting is the identification of a folder in which to find personal pictures for your screen saver. Adjust the wait time, which is the amount of time the computer must be idle before the screen saver begins.

At one time a screen saver was necessary to prevent static images from "burning" into the monitor, but that is no longer necessary with most monitors, given technological improvements. Instead, screen savers are often used for security or for entertainment. You can configure the screen saver so that you

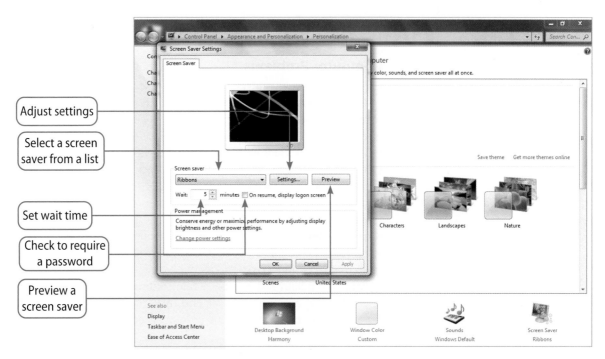

Figure 2.23 Windows 7 provides a variety of screen savers.

must enter your Windows logon password to remove the screen saver from view. That way, your desktop is hidden from view, unavailable until someone enters the correct password. Check **On resume, display logon screen** (Figure 2.23) to require a password. Finally, a screen saver can be entertaining, especially if it is composed of personal pictures.

Understanding Screen Resolution

A computer screen is comprised of a grid of dots, also called **pixels** (picture elements). A pixel is the smallest addressable screen element in which color can be displayed. The more pixels there are on-screen, the closer together they are packed, increasing the clarity of the resulting image or text. In its simplest terms, screen resolution is expressed as a grid of pixels. For example, a resolution of 1366 × 768 is a higher resolution than 1024 × 768. The higher the resolution, the better the sharpness and clarity of the screen display, but the smaller the on-screen images. You can change the resolution if you find it necessary—usually to accommodate specific software requirements. Even so, for most computer tasks, you will seldom find it necessary to adjust the resolution.

To adjust screen resolution, right-click an **empty area of the desktop** and then click **Screen resolution**. Click the **Resolution arrow** and drag a slider to adjust the resolution to another setting. Click **OK**.

Managing Peripherals

A **peripheral** is a device that can be connected to your computer. A mouse, printer, webcam, camera, cell phone, and portable media player are all examples of peripherals. The **Device Stage** is a Windows 7 feature that simplifies the management of peripherals.

When you connect a peripheral for the first time, Windows 7 will search for the particular device **driver**, which is software that enables your computer to recognize and communicate with the peripheral device. Without a driver, the peripheral device will not work properly. If the device is fairly current, Windows 7 most likely already includes the driver in the operating system's files. In that case, the driver is automatically installed on your system so you can begin to work with the peripheral. If the driver is not found, you can check for updates on Windows Update (click **Start**, **All Programs**, **Windows Update**) or you can visit the device manufacturer's website and search for a driver to download. It is also likely that a driver for the device is included with a disc that might have been packaged with the peripheral equipment.

To manage peripherals, click **Start** and then click **Devices and Printers**. Device Stage displays a large photo of your computer and each peripheral for which you have installed a driver, as shown in Figure 2.24. Double-click a

Figure 2.24 Device Stage enables you to manage peripheral devices.

In Depth

The Snipping Tool

You might occasionally find it necessary to include a screen shot within a document. For example, when describing a website in a report, you could include a picture of the website that you captured from your screen display. Windows 7 provides a tool that makes it easy to capture screen images—the Snipping Tool. Click **Start**, **All Programs**, **Accessories**, and **Snipping Tool** to open the program. Click the **New snip arrow** and then select a region to capture (e.g., Full-screen Snip, Rectangular Snip). Click **File**, **Save As**, and provide a filename. Click **Save**. You can later place the snip in a document, inserting it as a picture object.

device for information and links that are relevant to the device. If the device is connected to your computer, you can manage tasks that are currently ongoing. For example, you can pause printing or cancel printing activities for a printer currently in use. You can also use Device Stage to preset common tasks, such as synchronization (keeping two or more versions of the same file matched with each other), as in the case of coordinating files between your computer and a portable music player or mobile phone.

Working with User Accounts

By definition, a user account is actually a collection of information that prescribes a level of access and that enables an authorized user to indicate such personal preferences as a desktop background and screen saver. It also provides a separate area for the user's files, such as documents and pictures. Windows 7 provides three types of user accounts—standard (for those in your household who frequently use your computer), administrator (for the most control over a computer), and guest (for anyone who needs only temporary access to your computer).

When you purchase a computer with Windows 7, you will be required to create a user account for yourself. Although it is not required, it is highly recommended that you provide a password for your account. One reason for that is your account is considered an *administrator* account, which means that you are allowed to make sweeping changes to the computer system, installing new software and changing system settings. If an unauthorized person stumbles into your account either on purpose or accidentally, your computer system could be modified in ways that you do not want. A secure password would prevent that. For other users of your computer system, you can set up one or more *standard* accounts. In addition, a *guest* account, which you can set on or off, is available. Each account can be password protected and each account can be managed and even deleted by the administrator.

To create a user account, click **Start** and then click **Control Panel**. Click **Add or remove user accounts** (under User Accounts and Family Safety). Click **Create a new account**, provide an account name and type (standard or administrator), and click **Create Account**. To change an account name or type, click **Add or remove user accounts** from the Control Panel, click the account name and choose from the options presented, as shown in Figure 2.25. Similarly, click an account name and then click **Delete the account** to remove a user account.

Figure 2.25 You can change such items as your user account picture and your password.

Hands-On

Activity 2.3 Customizing the Desktop

The class for which you are evaluating Windows 7 material will be held in a college computer lab. You are not sure how the computers are configured with respect to settings that can be changed, so the discussion of customizing a computer system will be general. Even so, you want to make sure the material explores changing the desktop background, selecting a screen saver, and creating user accounts—even if those changes are not actually made to a computer in the lab. You will continue reviewing the material in this exercise.

a. Right-click an **empty area of the desktop** and then click **Personalize**. Click **Desktop Background** (Figure 2.26). If the Picture Location is not Windows Desktop Backgrounds, click the **Picture location arrow** and select **Windows Desktop Backgrounds**. Scroll through the choices and click a background. If you are in a computer lab, click **Cancel** so the change is not actually made to the computer. Otherwise, click **Save changes**. If you changed the desktop, minimize the window to see the effect of the background choice.

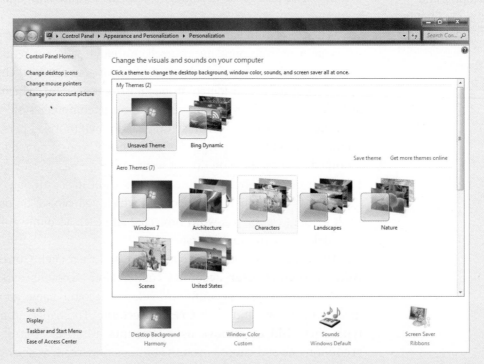

Figure 2.26 Changing the desktop background and creating a user account are among options for customizing a computer system.

If you are finished working with an account, and want to close the account without shutting down the computer, you can simply log off. Click **Start** and then click the **Shut down arrow**. Click **Log off**. If, instead, you want to simply switch to another user account, click **Switch user** and then select the account to switch to.

Managing Files and Folders

Consider an empty filing cabinet in which you plan to organize your personal records. What is the first thing you would do to prepare the filing cabinet to hold your household records? You would probably design a filing system so that similar records are grouped appropriately in named folders. For example,

b. Click the **Personalization icon** on the taskbar to return the window to view.

TROUBLESHOOTING

If you do not see the Personalization icon, you closed the window instead of minimizing it. Right-click an **empty area** of the desktop and click **Personalize**.

---

c. Click **Screen Saver**. Click the **Screen saver arrow** and then click **Ribbons**. Click **Preview**. Press **Esc**. Note the Wait time. Click the **spin arrow** to adjust the time to three minutes. If you are in a computer lab, click **Cancel** so changes are not actually made to the computer. Otherwise, click **OK**. Close all windows.

The dialog box in the preceding step includes three control buttons—OK, Cancel, and Apply. To close the dialog box without making any changes, click **Cancel**. To close the dialog box after first making all indicated changes, click **OK**. To make all indicated changes and leave the dialog box open, click **Apply**.

d. Right-click an **empty area of the desktop** and then click **Screen resolution**. What is the current resolution? Click **Cancel** so that you do not change the resolution.

e. Click **Start** and then click **Devices and Printers**. What peripheral devices, if any, are associated with the computer? Double-click a device to view its information and relevant links. Close the window.

f. Click **Start** and then click **Control Panel**. Click **Add or remove user accounts** (under User Accounts and Family Safety).

TROUBLESHOOTING

If working on a computer in a lab, you might not have access to user accounts. In that case, end this exercise now, keeping the computer on for the next exercise.

---

g. If a Guest account is shown, even if it is designated as off, click the **account name**. Note that you can then either turn the account on or off. Click **Cancel**. Click **Create a new account**. Note that you can supply an account name and indicate its type. Click **Cancel**.

h. Click **Go to the main User Accounts page**, which is an area where you can make changes to your account. Note the options that enable you to change or remove your password and to change your picture. Close the window.

i. Keep your computer on for the next exercise.

The Contributions of Apple, Inc.

Apple is a well-recognized name in the mobile device market. It is also an established company in the business of producing high-quality microcomputers. For much of its existence, Apple has been overshadowed by the software giant Microsoft, which even today places its Windows operating system on approximately 90 percent of all computers sold in the United States. Apple's move into the mobile device market has positioned it as a dominant force, albeit in a market slightly removed from its origins as a computer manufacturer.

Begun in 1976 by Steve Jobs, Steve Wozniak, and Ronald Wayne, the company first marketed the Apple I personal computer kit. The computer was sold as a motherboard, with a CPU, RAM, and additional components. Its price was $666, which would be worth approximately $2,572 today. In 1977, Apple was incorporated, but without Ronald Wayne, who sold his share of the company to Wozniak and Jobs for $800.

The Apple II computer was introduced in 1977, quickly becoming a sales success. Part of that success was due to the fact that the Apple II was selected as the platform for the immensely popular spreadsheet program, VisiCalc. Following the poorly received follow-up, the Apple III, the company focused on the development of the Apple Lisa and the Macintosh. While Apple sought to deliver richly engineered, but expensive, computers, Microsoft quickly dominated the personal computer software market with its Windows operating system that supported more affordable personal computers.

Today, the Macintosh continues to be recognized as one of the best personal computers on the market, preferred by many graphic artists and computer enthusiasts. Yet Apple's strides in the mobile device market far outdistance its success in the personal computer area. In fact, in 2007, Apple Computers, Inc. was renamed Apple, Inc. to reflect its ongoing expansion into the consumer electronics market. A culmination of its success was Fortune magazine's naming of Apple as the most admired company in the United States in 2008.

The development of the iPhone and the iPod solidified Apple's involvement in consumer electronics. Launching the App Store, Apple began to sell third-party applications for the iPhone and the iPod Touch. Within one month of its beginning, the App Store sold 60 million applications and earned on average $1 million daily. In January, 2010, Apple introduced the iPad, which is a large-screen, tablet device. Using the same touch-based operating system that the iPhone includes, the iPad is actually able to use many iPhone apps. The iPad sold more than 300,000 units on the first day of availability, reaching 500,000 by the end of the first month. Apple recently updated its iPod line of MP3 players with the inclusion of a multi-touch iPod Nano, iPod Touch with FaceTime (a video chat app), and iPod Shuffle (a somewhat limited, but inexpensive, MP4 player). One of the more recent Apple initiatives was the development of iCloud, an online storage and syncing service for music, photos, files, and software.

you might label one folder "Insurance," in which you would place insurance policies, statements, and related paperwork. If you are very organized, you might even create Insurance subfolders, labeled "Life Insurance," "Disability Insurance," and "Car Insurance." Developing computer folders requires the same thought process—the only difference is that you do not work with actual folders, but computer storage space instead. A computer **folder** is simply a labeled storage location in which you store **data files**, such as documents or digital photographs. **Program files** are software files, such as a word processor or computer game. Program files are stored in computer folders that are automatically created when you install software. In this section, you will learn to create, rename, delete, move, and copy folders. In addition, you will explore ways to select multiple files and folders.

Understanding User Folders and Libraries

Each user account on a computer is assigned a personal folder that contains several **subfolders** (a folder contained within another folder), accessible only to the logged in user or to the administrator. Those subfolders are available when a user clicks the account name shown at the upper-right side of the Start menu. Unless you specify otherwise, documents, music, pictures, and videos that you save are automatically saved to the personal folders that are associated with your user account. Those folders are accessible only by someone who is logged into the user account or to the administrator of the computer system.

Similar to a folder, a **library** is actually a collection of folders and subfolders that share a common purpose. For example, the Music library provides access to both your personal music files as well as those music files that are publicly accessible by all users of the computer. A library gathers files and folders from various locations, displaying them as a single collection, without physically moving them from their original location. In that way, you are given quick access to items that are grouped according to purpose. Windows 7 provides four libraries—Documents, Pictures, Music, and Videos. From those libraries, you can access your personal user account folders, as well as any items that are accessible by all users of the computer. Access any of those libraries when you click **Start** and then either **Documents**, **Pictures**, or **Music** (Figure 2.27).

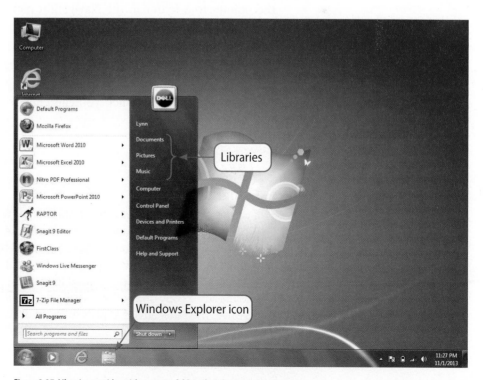

Figure 2.27 Libraries provide quick access to folders that share a similar purpose.

Working with Folders and Files

Depending on how you choose to organize files, such as documents, spreadsheets, and presentations, you will most likely create folders on your hard drive or on a USB drive. You might even use an external hard drive for data storage. An external hard drive connects to a computer through a USB port, providing a large amount of portable storage. Regardless of storage media, the process of creating folders is almost identical. You can access folders on your computer when you click the Windows Explorer icon (Figure 2.27) on the taskbar. The libraries will display, from which you can navigate to other areas by making selections in the left pane. The Start menu also provides a direct path to libraries and user folders (Documents, Pictures, and Music). The Computer selection on the Start menu provides a direct link to every disk drive associated with your computer. Figure 2.27 shows the Start menu selections that enable you to access any of those locations or libraries.

Creating Folders

Creating folders is a simple process, but one that can become frustrating if you are not careful about the placement of those folders. If you do not notice or specify the location of a folder, it can become lost in a hurry. It will be housed somewhere on your system, but probably not at all where you intended it to be. The use of libraries and user folders makes it less likely that you will misplace folders, but if you use a USB drive or external hard drive to save folders, you should carefully plan the folder structure so that it is well organized and accessible.

Click the Windows Explorer icon on the taskbar (Figure 2.28) to begin the process of creating a folder. As shown in Figure 2.28, the resulting window consists of several areas. Using the **Navigation pane**, you can select the library, disk drive, or folder in which you want to create the new folder. When you move the pointer to a folder in the Navigation pane, you will most likely see a clear or colored arrow before several of the libraries or folders. A clear arrow is an indicator that the item has additional folders beneath it in the folder structure. Click the arrow to expand the detail to another level. If any folders at the newly displayed level contain subfolders, you will see a clear arrow beside each (when you point to a folder), which you can click to display contents. As each folder

In Depth

Folder Locations

If you save a file in a folder within a library, the file is saved on the hard drive. While that may be convenient for later access, keep in mind that the hard drive is susceptible to failure or damage caused by a computer virus. Should that happen, you are likely to lose important files that you saved on the hard drive. Do not save a file that you cannot afford to lose in a folder on the hard drive, without also making a copy on another storage device or to an online account such as SkyDrive. The same advice applies to files that you save to folders on a USB drive or an external hard drive. If you cannot afford to lose the file, be sure to make a copy on another device. You will learn to make copies (also called backups) later in this chapter.

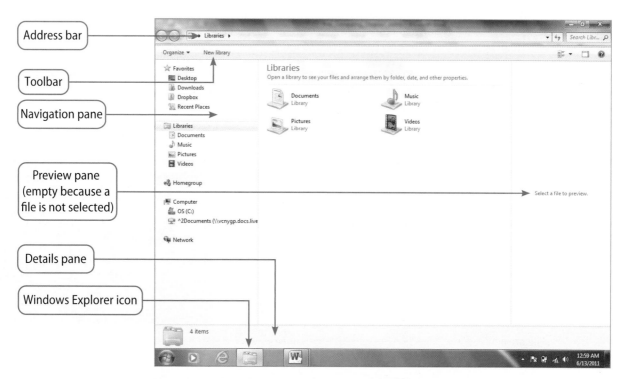

Figure 2.28 From this window, you can expand or collapse folders in the Navigation pane.

level is expanded, the display indents, so that you can easily determine which folders are on the same level and which are actually subfolders of others. After a folder is fully expanded, it will display a colored arrow to its left. Clicking a colored arrow removes the folder level's detail from the display. Note that expanding and collapsing folders only affects your *view* of the folder structure, not the *physical arrangement* of folders on the disk.

The **Address bar** appears at the top of the Windows Explorer window, displaying a hierarchical path to the current folder or window contents. In Figure 2.29, the currently selected folder is 2010 UNA Football, which is a sub-folder of the user folder Pictures, accessed through the Pictures library. You can navigate to any level of the address displayed in the Address bar by clicking the folder name on the Address bar. You can also move to a subfolder of any folder listed on the Address bar by clicking the arrow to the right of the folder in the Address bar and making a subsequent selection from the displayed subfolders. The Address bar also contains Back and Forward buttons that enable you to visit previously viewed windows.

To the right of the Address bar is the **Search box**. Using the Search box, you can quickly search for files within the selected folder. To conduct a search, all you need to do is type a word or phrase into the Search box, and Windows 7 instantly filters folder contents to show only files with names or contents that match the search criteria. You will explore the Search feature in more detail later in this chapter.

Immediately beneath the Address bar is the **Toolbar**, shown in Figure 2.29. The buttons on the Toolbar vary, according to the open folder or application, but the Toolbar's purpose is consistent—providing easy access to common tasks, such as changing the view and displaying or hiding screen elements. The Toolbar almost always includes an Organize button that, when clicked, displays a menu that includes options for basic file tasks. In most cases, the Toolbar also includes a New folder button, which is what you would click to create a new folder in the

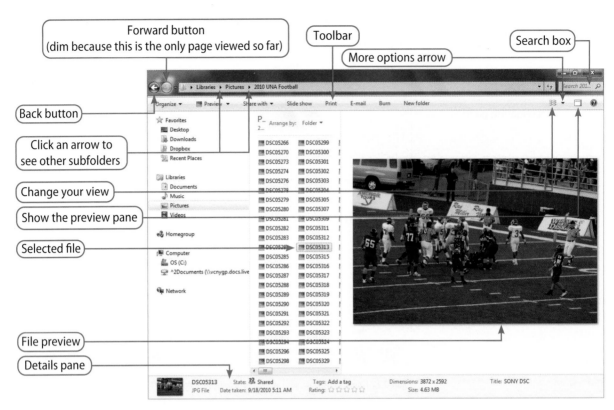

Forward button (dim because this is the only page viewed so far)

Toolbar

More options arrow

Search box

Back button

Click an arrow to see other subfolders

Change your view

Show the preview pane

Selected file

File preview

Details pane

Figure 2.29 The Address bar always shows the hierarchical path to the currently selected folder.

current location. The process of creating a folder is more fully described later in this section. Using the Toolbar, you can click **Change your view** to change the way you view file and folder icons. Repeatedly clicking Change your view cycles through available views, including Extra Large Icons, Large Icons, Medium Icons, Small Icons, List, Details, Tiles, and Content. If, instead, you click the **More options arrow**, you can drag a slider to indicate your choice of view.

The **Preview pane** displays the contents of a selected file. Although the Preview pane does not show by default, you can display it when you click **Show the preview pane** (Figure 2.29). If the selected item is a folder, no preview is available. In Figure 2.29, the selected file is a photograph, which is displayed in the Preview

Quick Tip
Shortcut Menu

You will often find it necessary to delete or rename a folder. You might even want to move or copy it to another location. Although you can accomplish those tasks in several ways, you will want to remember that you can always right-click the folder and then make a selection from a shortcut menu. On the shortcut menu, you will find options to rename, delete, cut, and copy the selected folder.

In Depth

Renaming and Deleting Folders

Managing folders involves renaming and deleting, as well as creating them. Right-click a folder and then select either **Rename** or **Delete** from the shortcut menu. If renaming a folder, simply type the new folder name and press **Enter**. The folder is renamed. You can also rename a folder if you click the folder name once, wait a second, and then click it again. Clicking the folder twice is not the same as a double-click, because the action is done much more slowly. Type the new folder name and then press **Enter**. To delete a folder, select **Delete** from the shortcut menu, and then affirm the deletion. If you are removing the folder from the hard drive, it will be placed in the Recycle Bin, from which you can retrieve it later, if necessary (unless the Recycle Bin becomes full and the items in the Recycle Bin begin to be removed). If you are deleting a folder from a USB drive, the folder and all its contents are deleted and cannot be retrieved. You can also delete a folder when you select it (click the folder once) and then press **Delete**.

pane on the right. The **Details pane** shows a thumbnail (small picture of the image, or graphic) of the item, along with any identifying **tags** (a custom file property that you can create to help identify and organize files).

To create a new folder in the currently selected location (shown on the Address bar), click **New folder** on the Toolbar. Type a folder name and press **Enter**. The folder you create is analogous to an empty folder in a filing cabinet. You have created and labeled a folder, but you have not yet placed any files (documents, pictures, etc.) in the newly created folder.

Saving Files to Folders

Files are created using application software. You might create a brochure, using Microsoft Word, or you could use Microsoft Excel to create a spreadsheet showing household expenses. Windows 7 enables you to create folders in which to place related files, as described in the previous section, but you must use an application program to create a file.

Windows 7 manages resources on your computer. It identifies available storage space for files and makes it possible to retrieve those files later. Regardless of the application software used to create a file, the process of saving a file is

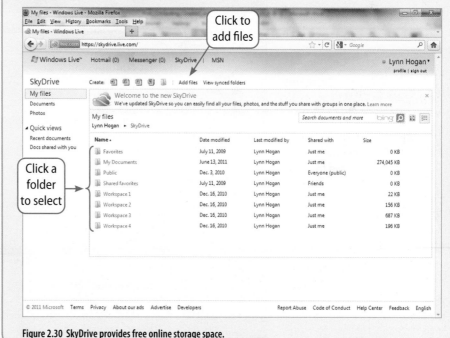

In Depth

Save or Save As

As you begin to work with application software, you will notice that when you begin the process of saving a file, you are often presented with two "save" selections—Save and Save As. What is the difference? The first time you save a file there is no difference. Either option causes a dialog box to appear so that you can indicate a location to save to and a filename. However, when you open the same file later, and then save it again, there is a difference between the two options. Choosing the Save option from the File menu will place or update the file in the same folder in which it was previously saved, with the same filename. The Save selection is a quick way to save the file if you do not want to change any of the settings. However, if you want to change the save location, effectively creating a backup, or copy, of the original file, choose the "Save As" selection on the File menu. Of course, you will also need to save the edited file in the original location, as well, to ensure a current backup copy. Until you develop a preference between the two options, the safest route is to choose the Save As option. That way, the dialog box will always appear, giving you the opportunity to make any changes in location or name, or at least to allow you to confirm that the settings should remain the same.

consistent. A typical Save As dialog box is shown in Figure 2.31. Such a dialog box is displayed when you initiate a save process. For example, having used Microsoft Excel to create a budget spreadsheet, you would have clicked the File tab and then clicked **Save** (or **Save As**). Select the disk drive and folder, as shown in Figure 2.31, in which to save the spreadsheet, provide a filename, and click **Save**. The file is saved in a folder that you selected.

Selecting Multiple Files and Folders

You will undoubtedly find occasions when you want to move, copy, or delete several files or folders at once. Although you could deal with each item individually, it is much more efficient to treat them as a group. Imagine deleting 50 files

Figure 2.31 After indicating a location to save to, and a filename, you can save a file.

If items to be selected are consecutive, you can drag to draw an outline around the items. If you want to select all files or subfolders within a folder, press **Ctrl+A** or click **Organize** and then click **Select all**.

In Depth

Drag to Copy or Move

When you right-click and drag a selection to be cut or copied, you must then specify whether the preferred action is a *cut* or a *copy*. In doing so, you are forced to confirm the action and are probably less likely to make the mistake of copying when you meant to cut, or vice versa. However, you can also simply drag a selection from one location to another. If you drag an item from one folder to another area on the *same* disk drive, the item will be moved. However, if you drag an item from one folder to another area on a *different* disk drive, the item will be copied. So that you do not have to remember the difference in results, it is probably simpler to right-click and drag a file or folder and then make a selection from a shortcut menu.

individually. For each deletion, you would click to select the file, press **Delete** (or right-click a file and then click **Delete**), and agree to the deletion. Fifty times! On the other hand, if you knew how to select all 50 files at once, you could select all of the files and delete them simultaneously.

If the files or folders for selection are consecutively listed, you can click the first file, press and hold **Shift**, and click the last item in the list. If the list covers more than one screen, you will have to scroll the display down, while holding **Shift**, to find and click the last item in the list. On the other hand, if you are selecting several nonconsecutive files or folders, click any item in the list and then press and hold **Ctrl** while you click on every other item to be included. Continue holding **Ctrl** until you have selected all items. At that point, you can proceed with the intended move, copy, or delete.

In Depth

Moving and Copying Folders and Files From One Location to Another

You will occasionally find it necessary to copy or move files and folders. For example, suppose you have saved files related to your college classes on your hard drive, and realize that you need another copy (a backup copy) of those files on another storage medium so that if your hard drive fails, you will not lose your work. You will need to know how to make a copy of the files, perhaps on a USB drive or an external hard drive. In some cases, you might want to move a file instead of copying it, a process that removes a file from its original location and places it in another. You can move files and folders from one folder to another or from one disk to another.

Before attempting a move or copy, you must first select the items to be affected. In the previous section, you learned to select one or more files or folders. When you move or copy such items, all subfolders and all files within any selected folder are moved or copied at one time. If you plan to drag a selection from one area to another, you must be able to see both the sending area and the receiving area. At that point, with one or more items selected, simply right-click and drag from the original location to the receiving folder or disk drive in the Navigation pane. From the subsequent shortcut menu, indicate whether you want to move or to copy the item.

You can also move or copy selected items by right-clicking a selected item (or an item within a selection of several files or folders), and then clicking **Cut** or **Copy**. If you select Cut, the selected item(s) will be removed from the original location. If you select Copy, the selected item(s) will be duplicated to another location, but will also remain in the original place. Then right-click the folder or disk drive into which the selection should be placed, and click **Paste**.

Hands-On

Activity 2.4 Managing Files and Folders

The class material you are reviewing is designed for several sections of a computer concepts class. Your professor has asked that you develop a folder for each class in which he can save the class material along with attendance and grading records. As you consider a folder structure, you know that multiple sections of the class will be taught during the fall and spring semesters of the upcoming year. Therefore, you should consider organizing folders by class section and by semester.

You will use a USB drive for this exercise, so **you should connect a USB drive before beginning this exercise**. In the event that you do not have a USB, ask your instructor if you can use the desktop. You will remove any folders that you create before ending the exercise. After connecting a USB drive, close any subsequent dialog box that might open.

a. Click **Start** and then click **Pictures**. If the Libraries folder is not already expanded, showing folders beneath, click the **clear arrow at the right of Libraries**. *Note: The clear arrow will only display when you point to the folder.* Click the **clear arrow at the right of Pictures**. Click **Public Pictures** (the folder name, not the clear arrow at the right). If a Sample Pictures folder is shown in the right pane, double-click the **Sample Pictures folder**. Typically, a Windows 7 installation includes sample pictures.

TROUBLESHOOTING

If you do not find a Sample Pictures folder, click **Documents** in the left pane.

b. Click the **More options arrow** beside Change your view, and click **List**. Click **Show the preview pane**. If, instead, you see **Hide the preview pane** when you point to the icon, do not click the icon. Click one of the pictures (single-click, do not double-click). A preview of the picture displays in the Preview pane.

TROUBLESHOOTING

If you double-click the picture, it will open in a default program. In that case, close the window. Then *single-click* the picture.

c. Click **Hide the preview pane**. If the Computer icon in the Navigation pane is not already expanded, click the **clear arrow at the left of the folder name**. (If the arrow is colored, the folder is already expanded.) Click **drive C:**. Depending on your system's configuration, drive C might be labeled Local

Disk (C:) or perhaps OS (C:). Whatever the name, the letter C: should be included, indicating that it is the hard drive.

TROUBLESHOOTING

If you click the clear arrow at the right of the hard drive instead of drive C:, the drive will be expanded, but not selected. Click **drive C:**.

In the right pane, you see the contents (folders and files) of the hard drive.

ON YOUR OWN

Change the view to Small Icons.

d. Click the **removable drive** shown under Computer in the Navigation pane. You have selected the USB drive, which might include the manufacturer's name as part of the drive name. If you are using the desktop instead, click **Desktop** in the Navigation pane.

e. Check the Address bar. You should see your removable drive (USB) shown as the current location (or Desktop, if you are not using a USB drive). Click **New folder** in the Toolbar. *Without clicking anywhere*, type **Fall 2013** and press **Enter**. The Address bar should still show that the current location is the USB drive (or Desktop). Click **New folder** and type **Spring 2014** Press **Enter**. Your screen should appear as shown in Figure 2.32.

f. Double-click **Fall 2013** in the right pane. The folder opens, showing that it is currently empty because you have not yet placed any files in the folder. The Address bar shows that the current folder is Fall 2013.

g. Click **New folder**, type **Computer Concepts 100** and then press **Enter**. Click **New folder**, type **Computer Concepts 101** and then press **Enter**. You have created two subfolders of the Fall 2013 folder, one for section 100 and one for section 101.

h. If the removable drive is not already expanded in the Navigation pane, click the **clear arrow at the left of the folder name** to expand the folder. Then click **Spring 2014** in the Navigation pane. Check the Address bar to make sure the currently selected folder is Spring 2014. *Note: If you are using the desktop instead of a USB, click **Desktop** in the Navigation pane and then double-click **Spring 2014** in the right pane. The current folder on the Address bar should be Spring 2014.*

ON YOUR OWN

Create two subfolders of Spring 2014, named *Computer Concepts 100* and *Computer Concepts 101*.

---

i. On the Address bar, click the **arrow at the left of Spring 2014**. From the subsequent list of locations, click **Fall 2013**. Because the professor has learned that he will only be teaching one Computer Concepts section in the Fall, you will remove section 101. Right-click **Computer Concepts 101** in the right pane and select **Delete** from the shortcut menu. Click **Yes** to confirm the deletion.

ON YOUR OWN

Delete the Computer Concepts 101 folder from the Spring 2014 folder.

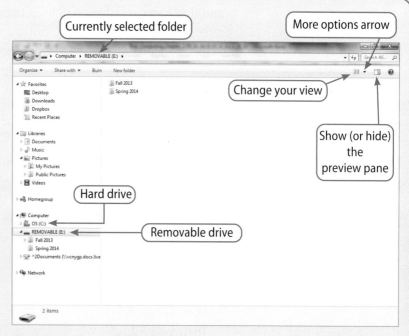

Figure 2.32 Windows Explorer shows files and folders.

---

j. Close the window. Click **Start**, **All Programs**, **Microsoft Office**, and **Microsoft Excel 2010**. Type **Last Name** in cell A1 and then press →. Type **First Name** and then press→. Type **Student No.** and then press **Enter**. You have begun an attendance worksheet that you will save in the Computer Concepts 100 subfolder of Fall 2013.

k. Click the **File tab** and click **Save As**. Scroll through the left pane, if necessary, to locate the removable drive (or Desktop, if that is the location that you are using for this exercise). If necessary, expand the Computer icon to show its contents. Click the **removable drive** (or **Desktop**). Double-click **Fall 2013** in the right pane to open the folder. Double-click **Computer Concepts 100**. Click the **File name box**, type **Attendance Worksheet** and then click **Save**. Close Excel.

l. Click **Start** and then click **Computer**. Expand the removable drive in the left pane, if necessary, by clicking the **clear arrow at the left of the drive name**. Click the **removable drive** (or **Desktop**) in the Navigation pane. Double-click **Fall 2013** in the right pane. Double-click **Computer Concepts 100**. Double-click **Attendance Worksheet** to open the file. Close Excel.

m. Right-click **Attendance Worksheet** in the Computer window and then click **Copy**. Because the same

attendance worksheet pattern will be used in the Spring 2014 section, you will copy it there. Click the **removable drive** (or **Desktop**) in the Navigation pane. Right-click **Spring 2014** in the right pane. Click **Paste**. Double-click **Spring 2014** in the right pane. You should see that the Attendance Worksheet file has been placed in that folder. However, you realize that you made a mistake; the Attendance Worksheet file should have been placed in the Computer Concepts 100 *subfolder* of Spring 2014.

n. Drag the Attendance Worksheet file onto the Computer Concepts 100 folder that displays just above the file in the right pane. Release the mouse button when the Computer Concepts 100 folder is shaded. Double-click **Computer Concepts 100**. Is the Attendance Worksheet file located in the folder?

ON YOUR OWN

Create a folder called *Summer 2014* at the same level as the other semester folders. (Hint: Select the **removable drive** (or **Desktop**) before creating the folder.) Then create a subfolder of the Summer 2014 folder, named *Computer Concepts 100*. Finally, copy Attendance Worksheet from Spring 2014 to Summer 2014.

---

o. Close the window and keep the computer on for the next exercise.

Using Windows Search

Regardless of how carefully you plan a folder structure so that you can organize and find files later, there will undoubtedly be an occasion when you cannot find a file, folder, or software that you are sure is located on a particular disk drive. Windows 7 provides a way to search for files or folders if you know any part of a file or folder name, content, or other identifying information, such as the author. Perhaps the most convenient place to begin a search is the Start menu. Click **Start** and then type whatever you can remember about the name or content in the Search programs and files box. The Search programs and files box on the Start menu is also handy if you want to locate software. Figure 2.33 illustrates a search for files, folders, or software containing the word *school* in the file or folder name, content, or other identifying information associated with a file. A search is not case sensitive, so capitalization is not considered. In this case, at least one of the results includes the word *school* as part of the name, while others apparently include the term within the file content. As you type, items that match the content will appear on the Start menu. Click an item to open it.

In Depth

Indexed Files

When you search from the Start menu, only files that have been indexed (included in an area to be searched) will appear in the search results. Indexed locations include all folders included in libraries. You can add more files to indexed locations by clicking **Start** and then **Control Panel**. In the search box (in this case, called Search Control Panel) at the top right, type *Indexing Options* and press **Enter**. Click **Indexing Options**. Click **Modify** and check only those areas that you want to index. Click **OK** and then click **Close**.

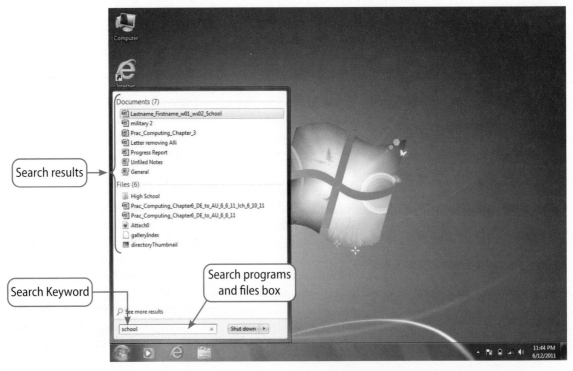

Figure 2.33 The Start menu enables you to search for a file or folder if you know any part of the name or contents.

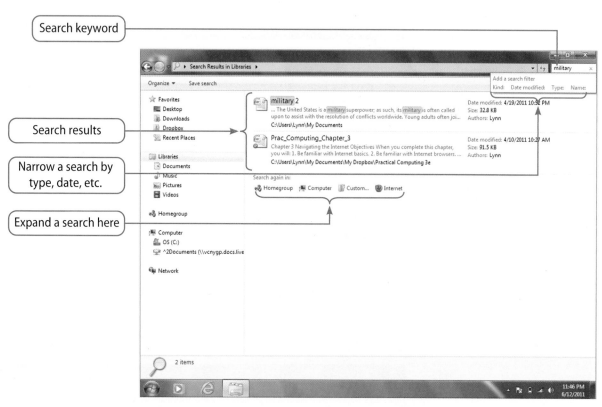

Search keyword

Search results

Narrow a search by type, date, etc.

Expand a search here

Figure 2.34 Search a particular folder by typing a search term in the search box.

To search a folder or library, use Windows Explorer (on the taskbar) to navigate to the folder. Then type the name or any identifying information related to the item that you seek in the search box. As you type, the search term is highlighted in yellow along with any results. Because libraries are indexed, a library search occurs very quickly. Searching other folders is usually a bit more time consuming. Figure 2.34 shows a typical search.

If you do not find the results you seek in a particular folder, you can expand the search to other locations. Type a search term in the search box and then scroll to the bottom of the list of search results (if any). Under **Search again in**, click **Libraries** to search each library, or click **Computer** to search the entire computer. Click **Custom** to search specific locations, or click **Internet** to search online.

Using Windows Help

Occasionally, you will need assistance with a feature of Windows or an activity of your computer. Windows Help and Support is a Windows 7 feature that

In Depth

Using Wildcards

You can narrow a search by using a wildcard. The * wildcard represents one or more characters, while the ? wildcard represents only one character. For example, suppose that you are searching for all CIS class documents, regardless of the course number. Because it does not matter what characters follow the CIS designation, you could type the search term *CIS** in the search box. Results might include a file named *CIS 150* as well as a file named *CIS 191A*. When searching for a file including a street name that is variously spelled Ganz and Gans, the search term could be *gan?*. That way, either spelling would be accepted.

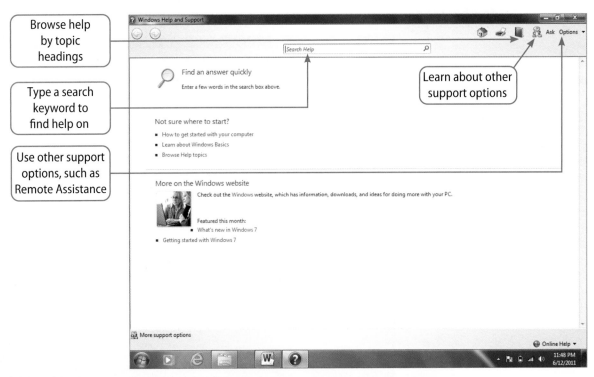

Browse help by topic headings

Type a search keyword to find help on

Use other support options, such as Remote Assistance

Learn about other support options

Figure 2.35 Windows Help and Support provides assistance with many Windows topics.

provides quick answers to questions about the Windows environment. Be aware, however, that Help and Support is not designed to help with a program that is not part of Windows—an application bought separately, such as a word processor or database program. Those programs have their own built-in support that is usually very helpful and easy to access.

Hands-On

Activity 2.5 Searching and Using Windows Help

In your haste to evaluate class material and to prepare folders for the various classes, you have forgotten where you placed some items. You will search for those items using Windows 7 search features. In addition, you have a few questions about saving and printing items; you will seek answers through Windows Help and Support.

a. Click the Windows Explorer icon on the taskbar. Expand the Computer icon, if necessary, in the Navigation pane. Click the drive or location where you saved the folders that you created in the previous exercise. Click the **search box** and type **computer concepts** (search terms are not case sensitive). All files and folders with either or both of the terms *computer* and *concepts* are identified, with the keywords highlighted. You should see the three folders you created in the previous exercise (with names including the terms *computer concepts*) identified. Double-click the **Computer Concepts 100 subfolder** of the Fall 2013 folder.

b. Close the window. You are going to prepare a PowerPoint presentation before classes begin, but you are not sure whether PowerPoint is installed on your computer. Click **Start** and then type **PowerPoint** in the Search programs and files box. If PowerPoint is installed on your computer, PowerPoint will be shown as a program in the results on the Start menu.

c. Click **Microsoft PowerPoint 2010** in the Start menu results. If you do not see the program in the results, check your spelling, correcting text in the search box, if necessary. Skip to Step D if you do not see the PowerPoint program. Close all open windows.

d. Click **Start** and then click **Help and Support**. Click **Learn about Windows Basics** and then click **The Start menu (overview)** (Figure 2.37). Read about the Start menu, click any links that look interesting. Click the **Search Help box** and type **copy a file** because you want to make sure you understand how to copy a file and that you identify any

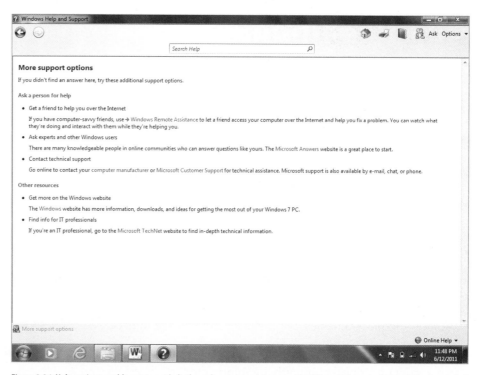

Figure 2.36 Help options enable you to get help through remote assistance, on the Microsoft Answers site, or through technical support.

To get assistance with a Windows feature, click **Start**, then **Help and Support**. As shown in Figure 2.35, you can browse help topics for an answer to your question, or you can enter search keywords. In addition, when you click **Learn about other support options**, you can get help from a friend through Windows Remote Assistance, find an answer at the Microsoft Answers site, or get technical support from Microsoft or a computer manufacturer (Figure 2.36).

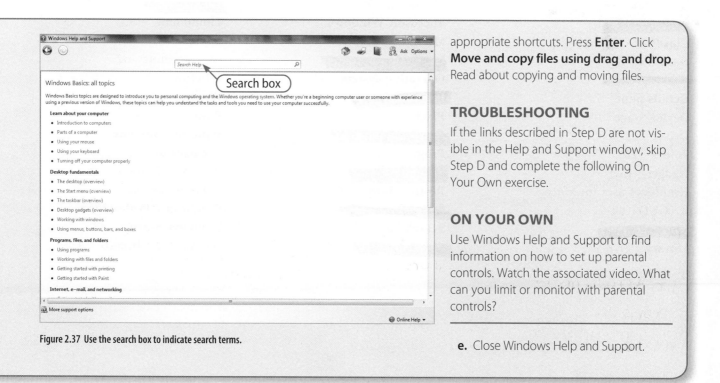

Figure 2.37 Use the search box to indicate search terms.

appropriate shortcuts. Press **Enter**. Click **Move and copy files using drag and drop**. Read about copying and moving files.

TROUBLESHOOTING

If the links described in Step D are not visible in the Help and Support window, skip Step D and complete the following On Your Own exercise.

ON YOUR OWN

Use Windows Help and Support to find information on how to set up parental controls. Watch the associated video. What can you limit or monitor with parental controls?

e. Close Windows Help and Support.

Chapter Summary

- A windowing environment includes a GUI (graphical user interface). *43*

- The desktop, Start menu, taskbar, and icons are basic elements of the Windows operating system. *45*

- The background of the Windows display that appears when a computer is first started is the desktop. *42*

- Open windows can be moved and resized. *55*

- Several windows can be open at one time, and they can be cascaded, stacked, or arranged side by side. *57*

- Windows Snap, Aero Flip 3D, and Aero Peek are features that make it easy to manage and move among open windows. *59*

- Windows 7 enables you to create multiple user accounts, at varying levels of permission. *67*

- You can personalize the desktop by selecting a background and screen saver. You can also change the screen resolution. *62*

- Windows Explorer enables you to create and manage folders. *72*

- Windows 7 includes a search facility whereby you can locate files and folders if you know any part of the name, contents, or other identifying information. *80*

- Use Help and Support to get information and assistance with Windows 7. *81*

Step to remove a file in windows

Key Terms

Active window 56	**Linux** 41	**Snap** 60
Address bar 73	**Mac OS** 41	**Subfolder** 71
Aero Flip 3D 60	**Mac OS X Lion** 41	**Tag** 75
Aero Peek 48	**Maximize** 55	**Taskbar** 48 *what is on*
Background 62	**Microsoft Windows** 41	**Thumbnail** 48
Close 55	**Minimize** 54	**Toolbar** 73
Data file 70	**Navigation pane** 72	**User account** 62
Desktop 42	**Operating system** 41	**Window** 43
Details pane 75	**Peripheral** 65	**Windowing environment** 43
Device Stage 65	**Pixel** 65	**Windows 7** 42
Driver 65	**Preview pane** 74	**Windows Anytime**
Folder 70	**Program file** 71	**Upgrade** 42
Gadget 45	**Resolution** 62	**Windows 7 Home**
Graphical user interface	**Restore down** 55	**Premium** 42
(GUI) 42	**Screen saver** 62	**Windows 7 Professional** 42
Icon 42	**Search box** 73	**Windows Starter** 42
Library 71	**Shortcut** 45	**Windows 7 Ultimate** 42

icon

- Know window control buttons

- Pinned

(handwritten at top: Know what the windows Control buttons are -)
(handwritten: ✱ Items is pinned?)

Multiple Choice

1. The Action Center
   a. scans your computer for viruses and other malicious software.
   b. provides an easy way to upgrade your version of Windows 7.
   c. warns you if a program is running in the background.
   d. notifies you of security and maintenance concerns.

2. If you have several files open in a single application, as would be the case if you had several Word documents open at once,
   a. each file is represented by an icon in the Notification area.
   b. there is only one icon for the application, but each file displays in a thumbnail when you point to the icon.
   c. each file is represented by an icon on the desktop.
   d. each file is pinned to the taskbar.

3. With Windows Explorer open, the contents of a selected file are shown in the
   a. Preview pane.
   b. Navigation pane.
   c. Details pane.
   d. Toolbar.

4. To select multiple files that are not consecutive, while you select each file press *(handwritten: are + are not consecutive)*
   a. Alt.
   b. Shift.
   c. Ctrl.
   d. Windows logo.

5. To get help on a specific Windows topic, you would access this Windows 7 feature:
   a. Help and Support.
   b. Action Center.
   c. Remote Assistance.
   d. Search box.

6. The active window is identified as the window that is
   a. bordered in red.
   b. larger than all other windows.
   c. located in the upper-right corner of the desktop.
   d. positioned on top of all other open windows.

7. This Windows 7 feature makes it easy to position two windows on opposite sides of the desktop.
   a. Aero Peek
   b. Aero Flip 3D
   c. Snap
   d. Windows Explorer

8. An item that is pinned to the Start menu is
   a. always available on the Start menu.
   b. a user folder.
   c. temporarily available on the Start menu.
   d. only available if it is a frequently accessed item.

9. The difference in maximizing and restoring a window is that
   a. a maximized window is not shown on the taskbar, whereas a restored window is represented by an icon on the taskbar.
   b. a maximized window is retained in memory, whereas a restored window is not.
   c. a maximized window is shown in high resolution, whereas a restored window is less than maximum resolution.
   d. a maximized window occupies the entire desktop whereas a restored window is less than full size.

10. The screen you see after you turn on your computer and log on to your user account is the
    a. desktop.
    b. Toolbar.
    c. Navigation pane.
    d. browser.

11. Which of the following is not a Windows 7 version?
    a. Home Standard
    b. Ultimate
    c. Home Premium
    d. Professional

12. The visual environment where you use the mouse to make selections and give commands is a(n)
    a. sidebar.
    b. Control Panel.
    c. Action Center.
    d. Graphical User Interface (GUI).

13. In addition to being entertaining, a screen saver is also useful for
    a. alerting you to possible problems with the screen resolution.
    b. providing a level of security, as a password can be required before a screen saver is removed from view.
    c. increasing the clarity and sharpness of a screen display.
    d. providing access to system settings.

14. A clear arrow beside a folder shown in Windows Explorer indicates that the folder
    a. has no subfolders.
    b. is fully expanded.
    c. contains subfolders.
    d. is a subfolder of another.

15. A miniature image of a file is called a
    a. preview.
    b. user interface.
    c. tag.
    d. thumbnail.

True/False

Circle **T** if the statement is true or **F** if the statement is false.

T F 1. The Preview pane provides a preview of a selected folder.

T F 2. Aero Peek enables you to temporarily view the desktop, even if multiple windows are open.

T F 3. The higher the screen resolution, the less the sharpness and clarity of on-screen items.

T F 4. The Address bar shows a hierarchical path to the currently selected folder.

T F 5. A search using the Windows Explorer search box is limited to the current folder, with no way to expand the search.

T F 6. A gadget represents data that is constantly changing, or a game or puzzle.

T F 7. Linux is an open source operating system.

T F 8. To remove a window from memory, minimize it.

T F 9. When creating user accounts, you cannot create additional administrator accounts.

T F 10. Windows Help and Support provides assistance with Windows features as well as application software that is configured to run on Windows.

End of Chapter Exercises

Guided Exercises

1. To earn a little extra money, you have started a business providing support for home computer users. Called Super Solutions, your company markets computer solutions primarily to new computer users who are over 60 years old. Although some requests for assistance are hardware related, most involve helping a user learn to work with Windows and software applications. You have prepared the following list of common Windows activities that you will use when helping a customer become comfortable with a computer. Before using the list of activities in a home, you will go through the activities to make sure everything is in order. You will be asked questions throughout the exercise. Record your answers in a Word document; you will save and print the document as directed in Step J. *Connect your USB drive and close any dialog box that might open.*

   a. Click **Start**, **All Programs**, **Microsoft Office**, and **Microsoft Word 2010**. Type your first name and last name and press **Enter**. As you complete Steps C–I of this exercise, type your responses in the Word document, pressing **Enter** where appropriate. If the Word document is obscured by other windows when you are ready to type a response, click the Word icon on the taskbar, type your response, and then click the **Minimize** button to temporarily remove the document from view.

   b. Click the Windows Explorer icon on the taskbar. Click the **removable drive** in the left pane (point to **Computer** and click the clear arrow at the left, if necessary, to expand the Computer folder). Click **New folder** on the Toolbar, type *PracComp_Chapter2_Project1* and then press **Enter**. Close Windows Explorer.

   c. Click **Start** and then click **Devices and Printers**. List two device(s) that you see. If a printer is listed, double-click the printer icon to see related information. If a printer is not listed, double-click another hardware device. Close the window. Close the Devices and Printers window, if necessary.

   d. Right-click an **empty area of the desktop**. Point to **View**. Are desktop icons already auto arranged? Click outside the shortcut menu to remove it from view. List up to five shortcut icons that you see on the desktop.

   e. Right-click an **empty area of the desktop** and then click **Personalize**. Maximize the window, if necessary. Click **Desktop Background**. Scroll through the selections and identify a background that you would like to choose. Point to the background thumbnail. A ScreenTip displays, providing information about the background. What is the name of the desktop background that you would choose (shown on the first line of the ScreenTip)? Click **Cancel**.

   f. Click **Screen Saver**. Click the **Screen saver arrow** and preview several screen savers. Which one would you select? Click **Cancel**. Close the Personalization window.

   g. Right-click an **empty area of the desktop**. Click **Screen resolution**. What is the current resolution? Click **Cancel**.

   h. Click **Start** and then click **Help and Support**. Type **shut down** in the Search Help box. Press **Enter**. Click a link that tells you how to shut down a computer properly. In one or two sentences, describe the process.

   i. Identify the flagged areas in Figure 2.38.

   j. Click the **File tab** (in the Word document) and then click **Save As**. Scroll down and click the **removable drive** in the left pane. Double-click **PracComp_Chapter2_Project1** in the right pane. Click the **File name box**, type **Lastname_Firstname_PracComp_Chapter2_Project1_Responses** and then click **Save**. (Type your last name and first name in place of Lastname_Firstname in the filename.) If your computer is connected or networked to a printer, click the **File tab** and then click **Print**. Close the Word document.

   k. Click **Start**. Click **Devices and Printers**. If the window is already maximized, click **Restore Down**. Drag the title bar of each open window to an opposite side of the desktop to "snap" each window into place.

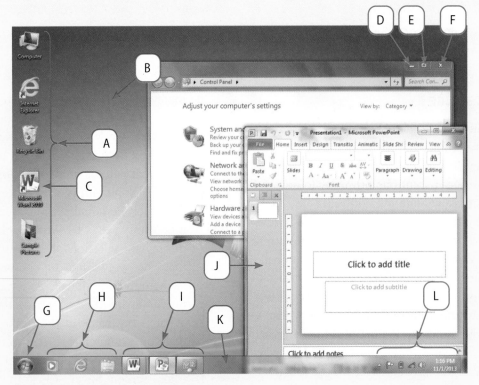

Figure 2.38 Identify the flagged areas of this figure.

l. Right-click an **empty area of the taskbar**. Click **Cascade windows**. Right-click an **empty area of the taskbar** and click **Show windows stacked**.
m. Close both windows.

2. As a volunteer for the Road Runners, a local running club, you are preparing computer folders to organize several upcoming charity runs. The folders will be used to hold spreadsheets of runner statistics and participation, as well as flyers announcing the events. *You will create folders on a USB drive, so connect the drive before beginning this exercise, and close any dialog box that might open.*

a. Click **Windows Explorer** on the taskbar. Click the **removable drive** in the Navigation pane (click the clear arrow beside Computer, if necessary, to expand the folder so that you can see the removable drive).
b. Click **New folder** in the Toolbar. Type **Rabbit Creek Fun Run** and then press **Enter**. Click **New folder**, type **Point Hope Charity Run** and then press **Enter**. The currently selected area, shown on the Address bar, is the removable drive.
c. Double-click **Rabbit Creek Fun Run** in the right pane. Click **New folder**, type **Marketing**, and then press **Enter**. Click **the arrow to the left of Rabbit Creek Fun Run** on the Address bar and click **Point Hope Charity Run**.
d. Click **New folder**, type **Promotional Material** and then press **Enter**. Click the **removable drive** on the Address bar to select it. Both Point Hope Charity Run and Rabbit Creek Fun Run should display as subfolders in the right pane.
e. Close Windows Explorer. Click **Start**, **All Programs**, **Microsoft Office**, and **Microsoft Word 2010**. Type **Rabbit Creek Fun Run** and press **Enter**. Type **April 20, 2013** Click the **File tab** and click **Save As**. Scroll through the left pane and click the **removable drive**. Double-click **Rabbit Creek Fun Run** in the right pane. Double-click **Marketing**. Click the **File name box**, type **Run Flyer** and click **Save**. Close Word.
f. Click **Windows Explorer** on the taskbar. Click the **removable drive** in the Navigation pane. Double-click **Rabbit Creek Fun Run** in the right pane. Double-click **Marketing**. Right-click **Run Flyer**, and then click **Copy**.
g. Click the **removable drive** on the Address bar to select it. Right-click **Point Hope Charity Run** in the right pane and click **Paste**. Double-click

Point Hope Charity Run in the right pane. Drag Run Flyer to the Promotional Material folder, releasing the mouse button when the folder is shaded.

h. Double-click Promotional Material and then double-click Run Flyer. Press Delete 20 times to remove the title. Type Point Hope Charity Run and press Enter. Type May 15, 2013. Click immediately after *April 20, 2013* and press Backspace to remove the entire date. Click the File tab and then click Save. The document is saved in the location from which it was opened. Close Word.

i. Click the removable drive in the Navigation pane. Right-click Rabbit Creek Fun Run and click Rename. Click after the word *Fun* and press Backspace to remove the word. Press Enter.

j. Click New folder, type PracComp_Chapter2_Project2 and press Enter. You will see both the folder that you created if you completed Project 1 and the folder that you created in this step.

k. Point to the removable drive in the left pane and click the clear arrow on the left. Similarly, expand Rabbit Creek Run and Point Hope Charity Run.

l. Click Start, All Programs, Accessories, and Snipping Tool. Click the New arrow and click Full-screen Snip. Click Save Snip in the upper-left corner, click the removable drive, and double-click PracComp_Chapter2_Project2 in the right pane. Click the File name box and type PracComp_Chapter2_Run. Click Save. Close the Snipping Tool.

m. Close Windows Explorer.

Unguided Project

A local utilities company has asked you to develop a series of exams covering Windows 7 and Office 2010. They will use the exams as screening instruments for job applicants, as well as to determine raises and promotions for current employees. You have prepared the first section of a Windows 7 exam, covering Windows and file management basics. You will now "test" the exam as if you were a student. *You will use a USB drive when you work with file and folder management, so connect the USB drive and close any dialog box that might open.*

a. Create a new folder on the USB drive named *Lakeland Utilities*. Create a subfolder of Lakeland Utilities named *Windows Exam*. Create another subfolder of Lakeland Utilities named *Office 2010 Exam*.

b. Click Start, All Programs, Microsoft Office, and Microsoft Excel 2010. Type Employee No in cell A1, and then press Enter. Save the Excel workbook in the Windows Exam subfolder of Lakeland Utilities with the filename *Employee Grades*. Close Excel.

c. Copy the Employee Grades workbook and paste it in the Office 2010 Exam subfolder of Lakeland Utilities.

d. Rename the Windows Exam folder to *Windows 7 Exam*. Open Microsoft Word, type Lakeland Utilities and then press Enter. Save the document in the Windows 7 Exam folder with the

filename *Company Info*. Close Word. Because the document should have been placed in the Office 2010 folder, cut and paste Company Info from the Windows 7 Exam folder to the Office 2010 Exam folder.

e. Rename Employee Grades in the Office 2010 Exam folder to *Employee Grades Office 2010* Similarly, rename Employee Grades in the Windows 7 Exam folder to *Employee Grades Windows 7*

f. Close Windows Explorer.

g. Create a folder on the removable drive named *PracComp_Chapter2_Unguided_Project*. For each of the following activities, provide a short description of how to accomplish the task. Record your responses in a Word document, saving it in the PracComp_Chapter2_Unguided_Project folder with the filename *PracComp_Chapter2_Unguided_Project*

1. Pin Microsoft Word to the Start menu.
2. Check the Action Center for any current alerts.
3. Select a desktop background and screen saver.
4. Check the screen resolution.
5. Maximize or restore down a window.
6. Identify an active window.
7. Snap two windows to opposing sides of the desktop.

8. Temporarily view the desktop.

9. Get information on user libraries.

10. Display an icon's Jump List.

h. Open Windows Explorer and expand the removable drive to show the entire subfolder structure. Click **Start**, **All Programs**, **Accessories**, and **Snipping Tool**. Click the **New snip arrow** and click **Full-screen Snip**. Click **Save Snip** and save the screen capture in the PracComp_Chapter2_Unguided_Project folder. Close the Snipping Tool.

i. Close Windows Explorer.

CHAPTER **THREE**

Navigating the Internet

BY CONNECTING TO THE INTERNET, YOU CAN ACCESS a wealth of information and entertainment. You can plan a vacation, get news and weather updates, take a college class, search family records, pay bills, and research almost any topic. Using an Internet-connected computer, smartphone, or tablet, you can watch TV shows, listen to music, and play games. You can even keep up with friends through social networking and e-mail. Stores that at one time offered goods only to walk-in customers have found the Internet to be a very effective and relatively cheap way to sell those same items. To say the least, the Internet has revolutionized the way we access information and conduct business, and has yielded almost unimaginable benefits for people of all ages.

Although it might at first glance appear to be rather complicated, the Internet is easy to work with and can be inexpensive to access. With a computer, smartphone, or tablet, and a contract with an Internet service provider or cellular phone service, you can enjoy all that the Internet has to offer. As you work with the Internet, you should be aware that it is not owned or regulated by any one organization, so anyone who has access to an Internet host server (a computer that is used to display pages of information on the Internet) can post anything, regardless of whether the information is true or in good taste.

OBJECTIVES
When you complete this chapter, you will:

▶ Be familiar with Internet basics.

▶ Be familiar with Internet browsers.

▶ Understand how to use Favorites and History.

▶ Understand the concept of Web addresses.

▶ Identify methods of connecting to the Internet.

▶ Be able to search the Internet for information.

▶ Understand how to download programs.

▶ Be aware of societal issues related to the Internet.

Understanding the Internet

The **Internet** is actually a group of interconnected networks that spans the world. The collection of networks is configured so that any computer can communicate with any other computer as long as they are both connected to the Internet. The physical network that provides a connection between other computers and networks on the Internet is called the **Internet backbone**. Large corporations that provide the routers (network devices that coordinate communication between networks) and cable that make up the Internet backbone are called **Internet Service Providers (ISPs)**. With orbiting satellites and millions of miles of cable crisscrossing countries, this network of networks is truly a global system that is capable of linking some of the most remote locations with other more populated areas. Estimates place the number of people using the Internet at billions.

The Internet is one gigantic system comprised of many smaller networks. If the Internet is considered a single entity, you might think that it must be owned by someone or some company. Actually, the Internet is not owned by anyone. The small interconnecting networks that are part of the Internet are owned and regulated by individuals, organizations, and countries. Although the owners of those networks can control the quality and level of access for those particular systems, they do not own or manage the Internet as a whole.

If no one owns the Internet, how is it regulated? The fact is that it is only minimally regulated. Illegal activities are prohibited and some countries do regulate content and monitor traffic, but for the most part, the Internet is open access. That means that occasionally you are likely to find offensive or incorrect content. At the same time, you will enjoy a world of informative and entertaining sites that are designed and managed well. As you navigate the Internet, you will learn to rely more heavily on sites sponsored by reputable organizations. For example, you will most likely put more stock in medical information obtained from the American Medical Association than what you might find at a site with an unknown or unqualified sponsor, such as a Web page titled Ed's Health Tips.

Even though the Internet is not regulated, it does operate based on certain rules of communication and standards. Several organizations from various countries coordinate standards for global operation of the Internet and develop technical aspects of the network. The **World Wide Web Consortium (W3C)** is the leading organization that creates Web standards and develops specifications, guidelines, software, and tools. A private nonprofit corporation, the **Internet Corporation for Assigned Names and Numbers (ICANN)** manages the Internet's **Domain Name System (DNS)**, making sure that every **domain name** (a name that identifies a particular website, also known as a Web address) links to the correct Web page provider. The **Internet Engineering Task Force (IETF)** is an international organization composed of several working groups with the goal of maintaining the Internet's architecture and stability. Each IETF working group focuses on a specific topic, such as Internet security.

Identifying Internet Protocols

With so many interconnected networks comprising the Internet, each system must somehow communicate with others so that data can be exchanged. Much as languages facilitate communication among people in various countries and world regions, computer **protocols** facilitate communication and data transfer between networks and computers along the Internet. **TCP/IP (Transmission Control Protocol/Internet Protocol)** is the set of communication protocols used by the Internet, coordinating the transfer of data in units that are recognizable by both the sending and receiving device. Protocols that operate within the TCP/IP framework include **HTTP (Hypertext Transfer Protocol)**, **HTTPS (Hypertext Transfer Protocol over Secure Sockets Layer)**, and **FTP (File Transfer Protocol)**, among others.

HTTP is the standard protocol for transferring Web page content along the **World Wide Web**. As you begin to work with the Web, you will find that Web page addresses most often begin with the letters "HTTP," indicating that HTTP protocol is in use. For example, the address for this publisher's website is http://www.pearsoned.com. The first part of the Web page address (http://) indicates that the page is based on the HTTP protocol. In a later section of this chapter, you will learn how to interpret the remainder of the Web page address.

HTTPS is a secure version of HTTP. When purchasing an item **online** (on the Internet) or when banking online, you will want to be sure that the information you provide (credit card details, banking password, and any other personally identifying text) remains private. You can rest assured if the characters *https* precede the Web address of the page to which you are directed as you complete the transaction. For example, perhaps you are purchasing an item from Target online. Upon selecting a product to purchase, you will be asked to indicate a method of payment. At that point, check the Web address. If the information is protected by **Secure Sockets Layer (SSL)**, the characters *https* will be the first letters in the address. Used by millions of websites worldwide to protect online transactions, SSL is an industry standard protocol that encrypts (converts data into a coded form) the transfer of private or sensitive information. It guards against interception, protects data integrity, and ensures clean data transmission and authentication.

FTP is a protocol designed to transfer files across the Internet. Whereas HTTP is used to display a Web page, FTP is used to transfer a file from one computer to a specified location on another computer. Your instructor might use an FTP site to transfer files from his computer to a computer server (a computer that connects several computers or serves as an entry to the Internet). Similarly, you might visit an FTP site to transfer a copy of a file from a remote computer to your laptop.

Exploring the History of the Internet

The history of the Internet can be traced to 1957, when Russia launched Sputnik, the first man-made satellite. At that time, the United States and Russia were extremely distrustful of each other. The Cold War was at its peak. With the launch of Sputnik, Americans realized that if Russia could launch a satellite, it could also launch a missile at the United States. In response, President Dwight Eisenhower created the Advanced Research Projects Agency (ARPA), charging the group with exploring ways to give the United States a technological edge over Russia. ARPA focused on computer science and data transfer as a means to that end. In the late 1950s, a computer was an enormous device that filled an entire room. A typical computer had a fraction of the processing power of today's personal computers, and could not communicate with other computers.

ARPA determined to create a computer network so that research and ideas could be shared from coast to coast. The first network was to connect four computers running on four different operating systems. When the network was successfully configured, it was named **ARPANET**. At the first demonstration of the network, there were no reporters, no photographs, and no records. No one remembers the first message; they remember only that it worked. The Department of Defense had an interest in the network as an installation that would withstand attack, allowing continual transmission of information and plans. With assistance from the Department of Defense, ARPANET progressed into a secure, defense-funded network to which access was limited. Computers along the network were connected in such a way as to allow communication to continue even if part of the network were disrupted, as in the case of an attack.

A forerunner of the Internet, ARPANET provided text-based screens. Although informative, the display was visually boring, intended only to distribute research and military information in text form (no graphics or multimedia). The National Science Foundation (NSF) recognized the need for universities to communicate research findings and to collaborate on projects, so it created CSNET in 1981. With a link to ARPANET, CSNET facilitated even more communication among networks nationwide. Other institutions and companies began to form their own networks, using the TCP/IP communication protocol shared by ARPANET and CSNET. The term Internet began to be used to refer to all of the connected networks. In 1986, the National Science Foundation sponsored the creation of NSFNET, a computer **backbone** (a network core composed of high capacity communication devices) that connected five supercomputer centers located throughout the United States. Smaller community and educational networks were allowed access to the backbone, creating a true "network of networks." It became the focal point of nationwide networking, laying the groundwork for today's Internet. In 1990, NSFNET replaced ARPANET, which was officially retired. From that point, the Internet continued to progress into what we know it as today, complete with the World Wide Web component.

Working with the World Wide Web

The World Wide Web (WWW or the Web) is a subset of the Internet that displays pages of information in a way that is easy to navigate and understand. The World

A Look Back

Did Al Gore Create the Internet?

You might have heard the claim that Vice President Al Gore created the Internet. The origin of that idea is a 1999 interview in which Gore stated, "During my service in the United States Congress, I took the initiative in creating the Internet." Although he didn't exactly claim that he "invented" the Internet, his words were used to portray him as an out-of-touch politician during the presidential election of 2000. The truth is that in 1989, then-Senator Gore introduced the National High Performance Computer Technology Act, a five-year, $1.7 billion program to expand the capacity of the "information superhighway," connecting government, commercial, and academic entities. The support for an improved national computer system that assisted in research, development, and commercial interests, is a testament to Gore's foresight and awareness of the benefits that improved information technology would bring to the nation. Al Gore gave political support to a funding drive to expand NSFNET, resulting in today's Internet, but he certainly did not invent the Internet. It is also likely that he never intended to imply such.

Mobile Computing and Apps

Mobile computing and the use of apps is an emerging force that appears to be changing the face of online computing. Anyone with a smartphone or an iPad is familiar with the availability of apps, which are small programs that extend the functionality of the device or provide information or entertainment. With more than 60,000 apps designed specifically for the iPad, and over 300,000 offerings available for the iPhone, Apple is a leader in the apps market. Google's Android is a force in the mobile apps area, and other companies such as Verizon and AT&T are competing with similar offerings. You can even download apps for some versions of the Apple iPod. Clearly a phenomenon that is taking flight, mobile computing and the use of apps, is changing the way we work and play.

Wide Web is to the Internet much as one room is to the rest of a house. It is not the whole, but it is a significant part. It was designed to be a graphical (point-and-click) medium, so you can make most choices and move from page to page by clicking areas on the screen known as **hyperlinks**—more commonly referred to as **links**. Because it is so visual and user friendly, the World Wide Web is typically the most accessible and interesting part of the Internet for a computer user. It actually contains billions of documents, or pages, with thousands of new pages appearing every day. The number of people using the Web around the globe is multiplying rapidly. In fact, the Web is so much a part of our lives that it has become a defining element of human culture. It is easily the fastest-growing component of the Internet.

Web Browser

A **browser** is a software tool that enables you to view and interact with the Internet. An identifying characteristic of the World Wide Web, a browser is your window to the Internet. As shown in Figure 3.1, a typical browser includes

Figure 3.1 A browser is your window to the Web.

features that allow you to customize your view of the Internet and to enhance your Internet experience through tabbed browsing (having more than one Web page open at a time, with a tab representing each). In addition, most browsers provide protection against safety concerns such as phishing attempts and spyware. Specific safety concerns are addressed in Chapter 7. The browser shown in Figure 3.1 is Internet Explorer 9.

Although the most commonly used browsers are Internet Explorer and Mozilla Firefox, others are also available, including Google Chrome, Opera, and Safari. Examples of various browsers are shown in Figure 3.2. Most browsers are available as free downloads from the Internet. When you purchase a

Firefox

Internet Explorer

Figure 3.2 You can select from several browsers.

Windows-based computer, the system will most likely include a version of Internet Explorer. You can choose to use the pre-installed browser, or you can download another of your preference. Just as you might have more than one car in the garage, you can install more than one browser. And, just as one car might be best used for long-distance travel, while another is perfect for city jaunts, each browser has its own strengths. You can use one browser for certain tasks, while moving to another for other activities. However, most people have a preferred browser to which they gravitate for all Web usage. Web designers (those who develop websites and pages) tend to design content that will display well within the most commonly used browsers. If you use a browser other than Firefox or Internet Explorer, you might find that some websites lack some functionality, probably due to differences between the current browser and the one for which the site was designed.

Because your choices are many, you might be wondering how to select a browser that is appropriate for your needs. As you have learned, websites are usually designed to work well with the most popular browsers, which at this time include Firefox and Internet Explorer. Table 3.1 describes features of

Table 3.1 Each browser has features that make it unique.

Browser	Features	Download Site
Internet Explorer 9	Minimal toolbar leaves more Web page space InPrivate browsing protects privacy Tabbed browsing, with drag and drop functionality One Box feature integrates addresses and searches into one area Parental controls	http://windows.microsoft.com/en-US/internet-explorer/products/ie/home
Firefox	Tabbed browsing (with single-click option to open new tabs) Add-ons customize and enhance browsing Integrated find-on-page function facilitates quick location of a word or phrase on a Web page Awesome Bar adapts to your use and preferences	www.mozilla.com/en-US/products/download
Google Chrome	Parental controls Incognito mode insures private browsing Focus on tabs, enabling you to drag tabs to open new windows, rearrange tabs, and duplicate tabs Integrated download manager Integrated find-on-page function	www.google.com/chrome
Opera	Voice navigation Tabbed browsing, including saving and undeleting tabs Integrated search function, quick find, and customizable toolbars Thumbnails of pages as you mouse over tabs	www.opera.com/download
Safari	Tabbed browsing Top Sites, offering an at-a-glance preview of favorite websites Provides a Mac (Apple) look and feel to Internet browsing	www.apple.com/safari/download

several readily-available browsers. After exploring those features and considering the Internet activities that you enjoy, you are likely to identify a browser that is suited to your needs.

Web Addresses (URLs)

Any person, group, or organization can post a **website** on the Internet. All that is required is a little technical expertise in the use of a **Web authoring tool** or **Web scripting program**, access to a Web server, and a domain name. Much like a book, a website can contain one or more **Web pages**. For example, a local community college might sponsor a website, containing a **home page** (the top level page from which you can travel to others on the same website) as well as pages for academic services, financial aid, and library resources. A Web page is based on a set of instructions, coded in a Web scripting language or add-on application, such as Flash. Web authoring software simplifies Web page programming by allowing developers to specify design without actually writing the supporting code.

A Web page is actually a file that is created by a Web designer (using a scripting language or Web authoring software) and then placed on a Web server. The purpose of the file is to display Web page contents, including all hyperlinks, text, and graphics. The location of the file on the server and the Internet is called a **URL (Uniform Resource Locator)**. A URL is a unique Internet address, comprising a string of characters. When you type the address of a Web page into your browser, such as www.msnbc.com, you are typing a URL. Taking a closer look at a typical URL, as shown in Figure 3.3, note that there is a standard way to designate exactly where and on what server a Web page is found. The access method, or protocol (shown as *http://* in Figure 3.3), identifies the method of communication. HTTP is a type of communication that uses hyperlinks, which are images or text on a Web page that you can click to move to other Web

Quick Tip

Using StumbleUpon

Having fun with the Web is contagious. As you locate fantastic websites, you will want to share them with others. Similarly, you will want to enjoy sites that others have found. StumbleUpon is a website dedicated to just such sharing. Visit www.stumbleupon.com and click **Join for Free**. After completing the online form, click **Get Started**. Click **validate with captcha** (a test to insure that a human, not a computer, is requesting entry). After responding to the captcha and selecting your categories of interest, click **Start Stumbling**. Although you can also install a StumbleUpon toolbar, you can simply visit www.stumbleupon.com and login to occasionally check interesting sites and share others.

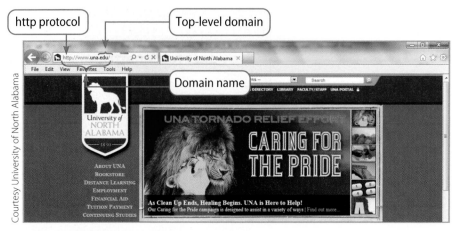

http protocol

Top-level domain

Domain name

Figure 3.3 A URL includes several components.

locations. When typing a URL, you usually do not have to type the *http://* part of the address. Unless you specify otherwise, the browser will automatically assume that the page is an HTTP page.

The domain name, which follows the double slashes, is a less complicated version of the **Internet Protocol (IP) Address** (which is typically a string of digits). Instead of a numeric string of digits, a domain name is more descriptive and readable. The domain name will always have at least two parts, separated by a period, or "dot," as it is often called. In the United States, the last part of the domain name describes the purpose of the organization hosting the Web page. For example, www.irs.gov is a government website. Similarly, www.ebay.com is a commercial entity. The final part of the domain name, usually indicating the organization's purpose, is called the **top-level domain**. Many URLs include a two-letter, top-level domain name that indicates the country of origin, such as *uk* (United Kingdom) or *ca* (Canada). Table 3.2 describes a few of the most common top-level domains.

Most Web pages include links to other Web pages or locations within the current page or site. Those links, or hyperlinks, enable you to move to various areas without typing the entire URL of a specific file. For example, from the White House home page (www.whitehouse.gov), you can click the White House link, followed by First Ladies. In that manner, you can move to other Web

Table 3.2 The top-level domain can identify a website's purpose or origin.	
Top-Level Domain	Purpose or Organization
.com	Commercial institution
.net	Internet Service Provider or network
.org	Nonprofit organization
.edu	Educational institution
.gov	Government
.mil	Military
.info	Unrestricted (for any purpose)
.tv	Video, animation, and user-generated content

Hyperlink (indicated by a pointing hand, in this case)

Figure 3.4 A hyperlink can be text or graphic.

pages within the White House website. Hyperlinks are unique to World Wide Web pages and make moving among sites no more difficult than pointing and clicking. You can usually identify a hyperlink on a Web page when the mouse pointer changes into an arrow or hand with a pointing finger, as shown in Figure 3.4.

Following the domain name, a URL often includes additional directory and file information. A slash in a URL indicates a page or resource that is located within the preceding area. You might think of those "sublevels" as folders within other folders, or pages within chapters. Unless you are well aware of a particular URL, perhaps having identified it in a magazine article or research paper, you will most likely begin at the home page of an area and then click links to narrow the focus to a particular topic.

A key element of the browser, enabling you to enter a URL, is the Address bar, shown in Figure 3.5. Internet Explorer 9 refers to the Address bar as **One Box**, because the area is actually used for two activities—entering a URL and entering keywords during a Web search. Searching the Web is discussed later in this chapter. To move to a website, simply type the site's URL in the Address bar, or One Box, and press **Enter**. As you type a URL, you can choose to turn on suggestions, resulting in a list of URLs, all of which begin with the same letters that you just typed, from which you can select (instead of continuing to type). Figure 3.6 illustrates the process of turning on suggestions.

A Look Back

Origin of the World Wide Web

Before the World Wide Web, the Internet was used primarily by educators, researchers, and government personnel for communication and exchange of information. Not at all inviting to most people, the Internet was text-based and command driven (managed by typing commands). That all changed in 1989 when Tim Berners-Lee, a computer scientist at the European Organization for Nuclear Research (CERN) in Geneva, Switzerland, wrote a proposal suggesting managing information by linking documents together over a network, using remote access, hyperlinks, graphics, and unlimited access to existing data. The subsequent World Wide Web evolved into the most traveled subset of the Internet—actually the one that most people refer to, even if they use the word *Internet* instead.

Address bar or One Box

Figure 3.5 Type a URL in the Address bar, or One Box.

Turn on suggestions

Figure 3.6 Turn on suggestions to show a list of similar URLs.

Most browsers use **tabbed browsing** to simplify movement among websites. Internet Explorer 9 places tabs at the top of the browser window (Figure 3.7). The current website is indicated by a tab, as shown in Figure 3.7. To move to another website, you can simply type the URL in the Address bar. However, if

Technology Insight

File Names and Directories in URLs

URLs often include slashes between parts of the address, sometimes even ending in a slash. Additionally, a URL might end with an abbreviation such as htm or aspx. Although such addressing schemes are not all that significant to you as an end user, you might want to understand a little more about what those designations mean. A *directory* is a Web page located within the current website, as a sublevel. For example, in the URL http://www.lincolncollege.edu/ personnel/ the personnel directory is a page located on the Lincoln College website. Because it is a directory, and not a file, the personnel directory is followed with a slash in the URL. By including the slash, you are letting the Web server know there is no need to search for a file—the final item in the URL is definitely a directory so the Web server can save time by instantaneously directing the display to the correct directory. A file is a set of commands that causes the Web server to take some action, such as obtaining parts of a page from a database or performing computations. Such commands are known as *dynamic pages*. When a URL ends in a page extension such as asp or php, the final component in the URL is a file.

Quick Tip

No Web Page Found

When you type a URL and press Enter, you expect to be directed to the Web page. If, instead, you receive a message that the Web page cannot be displayed, it is likely that you typed the address incorrectly or that the Web page is no longer available. Check the URL to see if you made a typing error. If so, click in the Address bar and retype the address, or simply make any necessary corrections. If the Web page is no longer available, retyping the address will not help. The Web page is simply not there anymore. Your alternative is to use the search tools you will learn later in this chapter to locate a similar Web page.

In Depth

Web Generations

Since its inception, the Web has evolved from a static presence to what we know today as an interactive, collaborative medium. Some have suggested that the Web has actually progressed through two iterations, Web 1.0 and Web 2.0. The Web was first designed to present information in a "read-only" format. Interaction and content contribution was not possible during Web 1.0. With the emergence of Web 2.0, many websites promoted sharing and collaboration. Blogs, wikis, and RSS feeds, along with sites like Facebook, YouTube and Flickr, encourage interaction and content sharing. Some experts believe that the next Web iteration—Web 3.0—will occur around 2015. Your browser will become your personal assistant, actually learning your interests as you browse so that it can intuitively direct you to areas of interest. Tim Berners-Lee, the founder of the World Wide Web, coined the term *Semantic Web* to describe Web 3.0 as an era in which search engines innately peruse the Web, narrowing results based on learned preferences. More buzzwords than well-defined progressions, Web 1.0, Web 2.0, and Web 3.0 are ways to express the continuing evolution of the Web toward more user interaction and guided information retrieval.

you want to move to another site while keeping the current site available, you can click the **New Tab button**. You can choose from suggested sites or you can type (or copy and paste) a URL in the Address bar to proceed to a website, which then displays on a new tab (Figure 3.7). To return to the previously viewed website, click the corresponding tab. To close a tab, click **Close** on the tab.

You can quickly rearrange or disassemble tabs within Internet Explorer 9 by simply dragging a tab to a new location. When you drag a tab down, you can remove it from the tabbed arrangement, making it available in a separate browser window (Figure 3.8). To reattach the tab, drag it back to the original location. Similarly, you can rearrange the order of tabs on the tab bar by dragging a tab to place it in a new location.

Figure 3.7 Each website displays on a separate tab in Internet Explorer 9.

Activity 3.1 Surf the Web

You are preparing a research report and plan to collect some information from the Library of Congress. You will visit the Library of Congress site, exploring various links.

a. Connect to the Internet. If you are in a computer lab, you can probably click the Internet Explorer icon on the taskbar. Alternatively, you might see an Internet Explorer icon on the Desktop that you can click. Or click **Start**, point to **All Programs**, and click **Internet Explorer**. If the lab uses a browser other than Internet Explorer, select that browser or otherwise connect through your Internet Service Provider.

b. Click in the **Address bar (One Box)**, selecting existing text (it should be shaded). Type **www.loc.gov** Press **Enter**.

c. Move the pointer over elements of the page. A hyperlink is any area where the pointer becomes a pointing hand. Some hyperlinks are pictures, which are graphic hyperlinks, whereas others are words. Click **any hyperlink** to proceed to a new page of the website.

d. Click **Back** (Figure 3.9) to return to the Web page viewed immediately before the currently displayed page. The Back button is normally found at the top left of the browser. It is often represented by a large left-facing arrow.

TROUBLESHOOTING

Occasionally, when you click a link from a Web page, the new page will open on a separate tab. In that case, clicking the Back button on the new tab will not return you to the previously visited Web page. Instead, you will have to close the new tab or click the previous tab.

ON YOUR OWN

Visit your school's Web page and navigate through some of the links displayed. Ask your instructor for the school URL, if necessary.

e. Keep the browser open for the next exercise.

Quick Tip

Showing Tabs Below the Address Bar

To provide the most space possible for the display of Web pages, Internet Explorer 9 displays tabs immediately to the right of the Address bar. If you want tabs to display on their own row beneath the Address bar, right-click the open area to the right of New Tab. Click **Show tabs on a separate row**.

Detached tabbed window

Figure 3.8 You can cause a tabbed website to appear as a separate window.

Courtesy University of North Alabama

Favorites and History

As you travel the Internet, you will no doubt find favorite sites to which you want to return often. Typing the URL each time you want to access a particular page, however, can get tiring and is time consuming. **Favorites**, or **bookmarks**, tag selected sites so that you can easily return to those sites. The process of

Figure 3.9 Use the Back button to return to a previously visited website.

setting a favorite varies, depending upon the browser in use. Because Internet Explorer is a very popular browser, it will be the focus of this discussion. With slight variations, you will be able to adapt the discussion to other browsers you might use.

When you are viewing a Web page you want to mark for later reference, click **Favorites**, as shown in Figure 3.10. Click **Add to favorites**. It is a good idea to organize your favorites so they are logically ordered. For example, if you are conducting some research for an English paper, and you have identified a

Figure 3.10 Use Favorites to keep track of favorite websites.

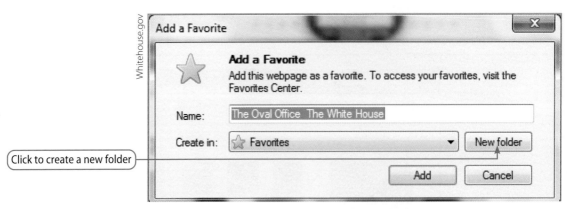

Click to create a new folder

Figure 3.11 Create folders to organize your favorites.

relevant Web page to support your topic, you could create a folder, titled *English Report*, in your Favorites list to include the website as well as any others that you might want to keep track of. Click **New folder** (Figure 3.11) and type a name for the folder. Click **Create** and then click **Add**. The Web page reference will be placed in the new folder.

The next time you want to visit a page you have listed as a Favorite, you will not have to type the URL in the Address bar. Simply click **Favorites** (Figure 3.10), click the **Favorites** tab, and then navigate through any folder structure to locate the page link. Click the link to open the page.

To delete a Favorite, click **Favorites**, click the Favorites tab, and then navigate to the link for the page reference you want to remove. Right-click the link and click **Delete**, as shown in Figure 3.12. Similarly, you can rename a Favorite when you right-click the link and click **Rename**.

Your browser also keeps a list of Web pages you have visited, called **History** (Figure 3.13). Locate the History list when you click **Favorites** and then click the **History** tab. The History list is handy if you want to revisit a page but cannot remember the URL. To revisit a page, click the date range in which you last visited the page (e.g., Today, Last week) and then click the page link in the History list. Of course, clicking the Back button (Figure 3.13) is the quickest way to get to a recent page from your current online session, but perhaps you want to find one that you saw yesterday or last week. Depending on the browser settings, the History list can keep a list of visited sites going back a month or more.

Although viewing the History list and clicking the Back button are similar methods of displaying previously visited Web pages, the Back button will only display websites visited during the current online session—not those that were accessed last week or even yesterday. Also, some Web page links are configured so that when you click a link, a separate browser window opens, obscuring the original site. Clicking the Back button from the new window does not return to the original website because it is actually only hidden by the current browser window. To return, you must first close the new window.

Browser Security

When you are online, you are susceptible to a variety of security and privacy threats. As you visit certain Web pages, especially if you download a

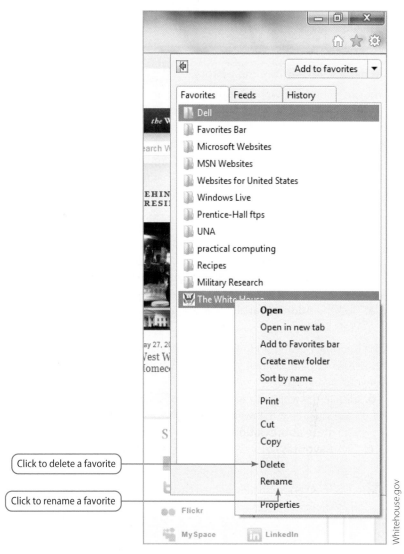

Click to delete a favorite

Click to rename a favorite

Whitehouse.gov

Figure 3.12 Right-click a favorite to delete or rename it.

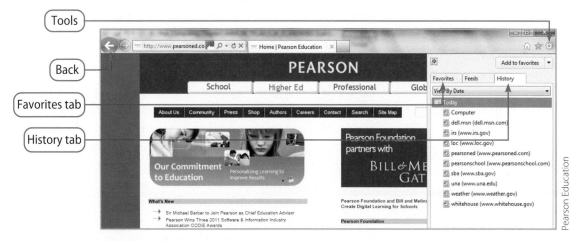

Tools

Back

Favorites tab

History tab

Pearson Education

Figure 3.13 Use History to revisit Web pages.

Understanding the Internet   **107**

Hands-On

Activity 3.2 Favorites and History

You are a volunteer with Special Olympics, an organization that works with people with intellectual disabilities. As a coach, you assist those athletes who are competing as runners. Each day, weather permitting, you and your team run at a local park. Because it is important that you remain aware of weather conditions that might affect the running schedule, you check an online weather site daily. In addition, you often access the Special Olympics website for access to schedules, forms, and guidelines. You will create a folder to maintain websites related to Special Olympics that you frequent. You will also use the History list to return to a recently viewed website.

a. Click the **Address bar** and type **www.weather.gov**. Press **Enter**.

The National Oceanic and Atmospheric Administration's (NOAA) Web page enables you to find a weather forecast for your area.

b. Click in the white box under *Local Forecast by "City, St"*. Type **your city**, followed by a **comma**, a **space**, and your **state abbreviation**. Click **Go**.

c. Click **Favorites** ⭐ and click **Add to favorites**.

You plan to organize all links associated with the Special Olympics in an appropriately named Favorites folder.

d. Click **New folder** (Figure 3.14). Type **Special Olympics** in the Folder Name box. Click **Create**. Note the text in the *Name* box. Because the text is so long, you will change it. Click in the **Name box** and delete the existing text (using **Delete** or **Backspace** as appropriate). Type **Weather** and then click **Add**.

e. Now to test the favorite, move to another page—perhaps www.msn.com. To do so, click the Address bar and type **www.msn.com** Press **Enter**.

f. Click **Favorites**. Click the **Favorites tab** and scroll down the Favorites list, if necessary, to locate Special Olympics. Click **Special Olympics**. Click the weather link under the Special Olympics heading. You should move directly to the weather forecast for your area.

ON YOUR OWN

Visit **www.specialolympics.org**. Add the page as a favorite in the Special Olympics Favorites folder.

So that other students who work at your computer are able to complete this exercise, you will remove the Special Olympics Favorites folder along with its contents.

g. Click **Favorites**. Scroll through the list, and right-click **Special Olympics** (the folder). Click **Delete**. Click

program or click a link, you might be unwittingly inviting **spyware** or **socially engineered malware** to infiltrate your computer. A combination of the words *malicious* and *software*, malware is software designed to do harm to a computer system. Viruses, Trojan horses, worms, and spyware are all examples of malware. Such threats are described more completely in Chapter 7. Spyware is a type of malware that is sometimes downloaded along with what appears to be a legitimate program or game. It is automatically installed on a user's computer system and then begins to collect information about the user's browsing habits. In some cases, spyware can even collect items that are typed, such as credit card numbers or passwords. Obviously, identity theft is a major concern as related to spyware and other forms of socially engineered malware. Because a browser is your window to the Web, it is the first line of defense against such threats. As you evaluate browsers, be sure to explore security features. In the development of Internet Explorer 9, Microsoft sought to produce a browser with more built-in security than any other browser. Although Internet Explorer 9 is designed to combat malware and to enable you to customize its security settings, you should not depend on it for total computer security. Your computer should also be protected by antivirus software and a firewall (see Chapter 7).

Figure 3.14 Identifying a website as a favorite makes it easy to locate the site later.

Yes when asked whether to remove the folder to the Recycle Bin.

h. Click **Favorites**, and check to make sure the Special Olympics folder is removed.

i. Click the **History tab**. Click **Today**. Click **weather** (**www.weather.gov**) and then click **NOAA's**

National Weather Service to return to NOAA's home page.

j. Click **Home** (Figure 3.14) to return to your browser's home page. Keep the browser open for the next exercise.

Cookies are small text files that websites place on your computer to store information about you and your preferences. Although some cookies might threaten your privacy by tracking sites that you visit, most are more helpful than harmful. For example, a cookie might identify you as a legitimately registered student when you log in to an online class. In that case, you would not want to limit the cookie or delete it. Others might "remember" login information so that you are not burdened with that task. Internet Explorer 9 enables you to adjust privacy settings, especially where cookies are concerned. With Internet Explorer open, click **Tools** (Figure 3.15), and then **Internet options**. Click the **Privacy tab** (Figure 3.16). Drag the slider to adjust the privacy setting, blocking certain types of cookies in the process. Click **OK** to accept any changes. To remove cookies from your system, click **Tools** and then point to **Safety**. Click **Delete browsing history**. Select **Cookies** (and any other items that you want to delete, such as History) and click **Delete**.

Internet Explorer 9 includes a filter that screens sites, informing you of dangers associated with Web locations that you attempt to access. Called **SmartScreen Filter**, the feature helps detect **phishing** websites (containing false claims that attempt to scam you into surrendering private information) and protects you from downloading or installing malware. Internet Explorer 9

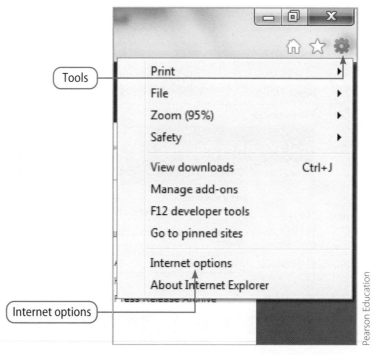

Figure 3.15 Use the Tools menu to customize Internet options.

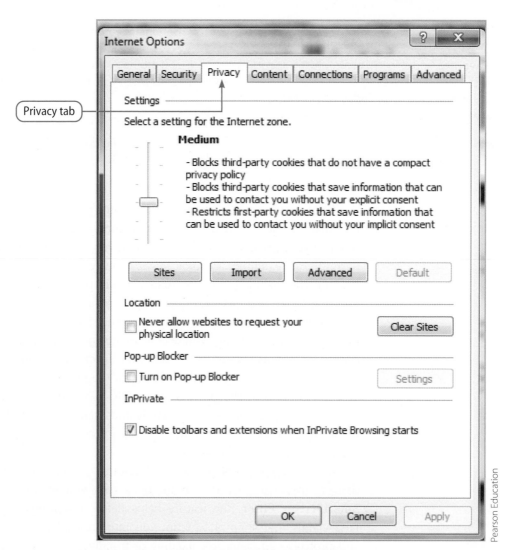

Figure 3.16 Internet Explorer 9 enables you to select a privacy setting.

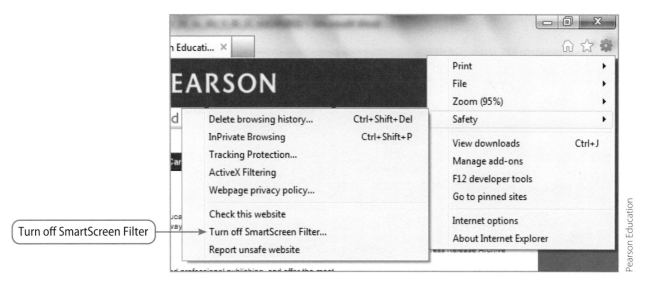

Turn off SmartScreen Filter

Pearson Education

Figure 3.17 SmartScreen Filter adds another level of security.

will block a download from a reported malicious site or will inform you that the download appears to be safe. SmartScreen Filter is turned on by default, but if you ever want to turn it off, you can do so when you click **Tools**, and then point to **Safety**. Click **Turn off SmartScreen Filter**, as shown in Figure 3.17. Click **OK**. Reverse the procedure to turn on SmartScreen Filter.

A website typically contains a wealth of content—images, advertisements, and other code—some of which is provided by third-party websites. By definition, a *third party* is an organization that is not owned by the owner of the website. Postings by some third parties are legitimate marketing devices, but others are considered **malvertisements**, or malicious advertisements. Malicious advertisements are marketing ploys that actually deliver malicious content to visitors' systems through links on what appear to be legitimate websites. The malicious content is often designed to track your browser, collecting information on your online activities. In some cases, the page links are misrepresented as belonging to a legitimate company. In others, attackers are able to replace legitimate advertisements with versions that have malicious content. The **Tracking Protection** feature of Internet Explorer 9 limits the browser's communication with certain websites, effectively blocking most malicious third-party links. Tracking Protection is not enabled by default, but you can turn the feature on. Click **Tools**, and then point to **Safety**. Click **Tracking Protection**. In the dialog box shown in Figure 3.18, click **Your Personalized List**. Click **Enable**. From that point forward, any time a site or in-page element tracks your movement across 10 or more sites, it is added to the automatic tracking list and blocked in the future.

Internet Explorer 9 automatically maintains a history list, which is a collection of links to previously visited pages. As you learned earlier, the history list is helpful if you want to revisit a Web page but do not remember the URL. In some cases, however, you will not want your browsing session to be documented. For example, when shopping for a gift on a shared computer, or when checking an account while in a public computer lab, you will want no trace of your browsing history to be recorded. **InPrivate Browsing** prevents your browsing history, form data, cookies, and user names and passwords from being retained by the browser. InPrivate Browsing opens a new browser window (Figure 3.19), from

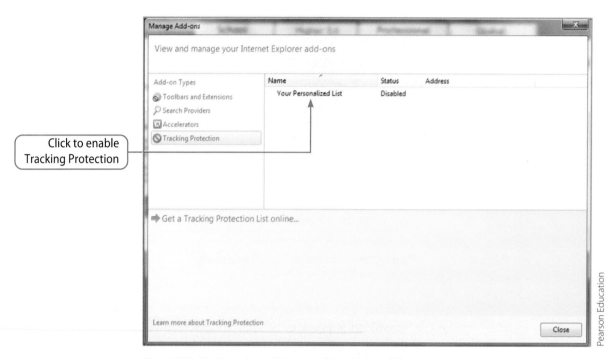

Click to enable Tracking Protection

Figure 3.18 Tracking Protection prohibits most malicious third party links.

which no data is recorded. Begin InPrivate Browsing by clicking **Tools** and then pointing to **Safety**. Click **InPrivate Browsing**. Closing the browser window will end your InPrivate browsing session.

As you browse the Web, you might find sites that do not display properly until you install an ActiveX control. If such an action is required, you will be instructed to click a link to install the control. An ActiveX control is actually a browser **plugin** (an add-on program that adds functionality, such as enhanced

Figure 3.19 InPrivate browsing prevents your browsing session from being recorded.

Hands-On

Activity 3.3 Browser Security

You have recently purchased a new laptop computer for use in your job as a marketing representative. Because you will be using your computer in various locations for online access, you want to make sure that your browser is as secure and private as it can be. You will explore various browser security settings in this exercise.

a. Click **Favorites** and then click the **History tab**. If you see no links in the History list, click **Today**. If your browser is configured to keep a history of sites visited, you should see several page links. You will delete the history.

b. Click **Tools**. Point to **Safety** and then click **Delete browsing history**. Deselect all areas except History, by clicking any check boxes that are checked (leaving History checked). Click **Delete**, as shown in Figure 3.20.

c. If a Notification bar displays at the bottom of the browser window, informing you that the deletion task is complete, click **X** in the top-right corner of the bar to close it.

You will open an InPrivate browsing session so that no history is recorded.

d. Click **Tools**. Point to **Safety**, and then click **InPrivate Browsing**. A separate browser page opens with information about InPrivate browsing.

e. Type www.cnn.com in the Address bar. Press **Enter**. Catch up on some top news stories of the day, clicking any interesting links.

f. Click **Favorites**. Click **Today**. Are any of the pages related to www.cnn.com listed? Because you were engaged in InPrivate browsing, no history should be recorded.

g. Close the InPrivate browsing window tab. Keep the remaining browser window open for the next exercise.

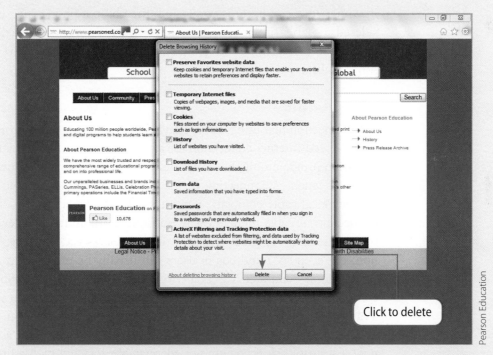

Figure 3.20 You will want to delete your history if you are using a public computer lab.

audio or video). The only problem with it is that once activated, the ActiveX control is also available for use on other websites, as well. Occasionally, that produces content you do not want to see, or it might even prevent content from displaying properly in other areas. With **ActiveX Filtering**, you are in charge of the ActiveX controls running in your browser. Only sites you have approved can run selected ActiveX controls. To enable filtering, click **Tools**, and then point to **Safety**. Click **ActiveX Filtering**. Reverse the process to turn off the filtering.

Connecting to the Internet

Most home computers sold today are configured for Internet access. You can even connect to the Internet through your cell phone, if it is designed for such access, which is usually fairly expensive. For Internet access from your computer, you will need to contract with an Internet Service Provider (ISP), most likely paying a monthly access fee. Invariably, all new computers include browser software, such as Internet Explorer, which is necessary to view the Web. You should be aware that a browser does not guarantee Internet access. It only displays Web pages if you have a connection with an ISP. Web pages often include rich multimedia content. Interaction is a common feature of many Web pages; you can even place phone calls through your Internet connection. To enjoy the various multimedia and interactive possibilities of the Web, your system should include speakers, a microphone, and a webcam. In addition, plugins such as Macromedia Flash Player, Windows Media Player, Adobe Reader, and Apple QuickTime ensure that you are able to access online resources.

One of the first things to consider when connecting to the Internet is the connection type. **Cable**, **DSL**, **wireless**, and **satellite** are all considered **broadband** types of Internet connection. They are characterized by "always on" connections, which means that your computer is always connected to the Internet, even when you are not actively working online. A **dial-up** connection, in which your computer is connected directly to a phone jack, is seldom considered a viable option due to the relatively slow speed when compared to broadband connections and its inability to stream video effectively or to access some multimedia resources.

Using Cable

The connection that brings cable television to homes can also be used to provide a high-speed Internet connection for an additional fee. A television cable carries television programming, but it has more than enough extra bandwidth for other purposes, such as connecting to the Internet. With a cable modem, installed by your local cable company, you are ready to take advantage of a high-speed connection. A cable modem easily transmits at more than 1 Mega-bps (million bits per second). A small cluster of homes shares each Internet cable connection, but even so, hundreds of users can usually be online without any loss of speed. Home computers can be networked with a cable connection so that each computer can be online at the same time, even visiting different websites. With a cable modem, you are always online when your computer is on. Although that "always on" access is attractive from the standpoint of quick access, it might pose a security risk if you are not adequately protected with a firewall to block out unauthorized access to your computer. Firewalls are discussed in Chapter 7.

Using DSL (Digital Subscriber Line)

DSL (Digital Subscriber Line) is a high-speed telephone connection that enables you to be online without tying up your phone line. Asymmetric DSL (ADSL) is a type of DSL that uses existing phone lines. It reserves more **bandwidth** for downloading (copying a file from another computer to yours) files than for uploading (sending files to a remote computer). Bandwidth is the rate at which signals can travel through a medium, such as cable or DSL. The disparity between the upload speed and download speed is evident in all connection technologies; typically downloading takes place with greater speed than uploading. Using a router that is available at most office supply stores, you can network several home computers so that they can all be online at the same time through the DSL connection.

Many telephone companies offer DSL and can install the service in your home; however, you must be within 18,000 feet (approximately 3.5 miles) of a phone company's switching station to be eligible for a DSL connection. As part of the installation, the telephone company usually provides a DSL modem. In most cases, you can install your own DSL service by using a kit provided by the DSL company. You must also pay a monthly subscription fee for the service. To determine whether you are eligible for DSL service, call your local phone company or another DSL provider.

Using Wireless Connection

A wireless service is a popular option for computer users who travel about and still need to be online. With a wireless card in a laptop computer, you can communicate through a wireless access point. Many public areas such as libraries, hotel lobbies, airports, and neighborhood coffee shops offer wireless access points, called **wi-fi hotspots** (or just hotspots), where mobile computer users can access the Internet, usually free of charge. Offices and workplaces often provide wireless access, although such access is most often protected so that only those who are authorized are able to connect wirelessly. You can locate wi-fi hotspots in your area through a website such as www.wi-fihotspotlist.com.

While a hotspot connection is ideal if you can count on being in one location for a period of time, it is not at all convenient for those who must move around and want to remain on the Internet. Those mobile users might consider a **wireless air card**, which is a device that uses cell phone frequencies, providing Internet access wherever a cellular signal can be obtained. You can most likely obtain a wireless air card from your cell phone provider for a monthly subscription fee.

Using Satellite

If you live outside the service area of DSL or cable, you might consider satellite Internet service, an option that can be combined with satellite TV. Although the speed of satellite Internet is comparable to other high-speed connections, the cost can be quite high. Satellite Internet does not use telephone or cable connections, but instead uses a two-way dish for communication. Although an attractive broadband connection in terms of speed and availability, satellite connection is relatively costly and is prone to weather-related interference. Although rain does not disrupt signals, it can cause "rain fade," which results in slowed upload and download speed and erratic Internet connection. Another disadvantage, especially when using a satellite connection to make Internet phone calls (called VoIP, or Voice over Internet Protocol), is latency. Latency is the amount of delay, measured in milliseconds, that occurs when data is bounced off of a satellite and returned.

Connecting a Home Wirelessly

When you contract with an Internet Service Provider for broadband access (cable, DSL, or satellite), the provider will assist you with connecting one or more computers to the Internet. A wired connection is a physical connection between a computer and a modem (a device that enables connection to the Internet). Because many families own several computers, connecting only one of those computers to the Internet is not practical. Connecting all of the household computers in a wired arrangement to the modem is also not feasible. Instead, most families opt to connect multiple computers wirelessly to one device that can then provide Internet access to them all. In such an arrangement, each computer on the home network can enjoy online activities, independently of other computers on the network. While one computer user is checking the weather or working with his social networking account, another might be playing a game or conducting online research for an English assignment.

Depending upon the broadband connection in use, your Internet Service Provider might be able to configure your Internet connection so that multiple computers can connect wirelessly through a modem that is designed to integrate wireless networking capability. Such a modem is called a **wireless router**. It is a device that coordinates signals from your Internet connection into a wireless broadcast, enabling multiple computers to use the same Internet connection. Connecting and configuring the wireless router is not a difficult task. By following the directions included with the router, most people are able to configure the wireless connection with ease. Be sure to follow any directions related to securing the router, as well, so that it is protected from unauthorized access. Every computer connecting wirelessly to a home network must be equipped with a **wireless network adapter**, which is a hardware device that connects a computer to a network wirelessly. Most laptop computers, and many desktop units, are equipped with a wireless network adapter at the time of purchase. If you are considering purchasing a new computer, you would be well advised to make sure the computer includes a wireless network adapter, just in case you decide to connect it wirelessly at a later time.

Selecting an Internet Service Provider

After you settle on a connection type, you must consider an ISP, which is a company that allows you to connect to the Internet through its host server. Some ISPs are full featured, meaning they provide specialized services. Others simply provide an Internet connection, without any special content. The cost for ISP service varies and is dependent on the level of service provided. Providers can include local phone companies, long-distance carriers, locally owned firms, and national providers, such as America Online.

Often, the connection and the ISP are one and the same. For example, if you are interested in cable connection, you could consider working with the cable carrier in your area. In that case, the cable hookup is owned and managed by the cable company with which you contract. The cable company would be your ISP. Similarly, DSL is often coordinated by a telephone company, which becomes your ISP when you select DSL. You might find it cost effective to bundle services so that your television, Internet, and phone are included for one affordable price. Your cell phone provider can even provide Internet access along with cell phone services. With the blending of communication technologies, you have a great deal of choice for your Internet connection and ISP. However, if you are somewhat geographically isolated, your choices might be limited to dial-up or satellite.

Select an Internet Service Provider

When selecting an ISP, you should give careful consideration to how you plan to use the Internet and the level of service you will require. The following tips should help you narrow the field of ISPs.

1. High-quality service and support. Be sure the company uses current technology, is receptive to your questions, is knowledgeable, and offers timely technical support.
2. Contract terms. Examine the total cost, including the contract duration, any penalty for terminating the contract, and the cost increase if the current offer is a promotional rate.
3. Security. Be familiar with included security features such as a spam (unsolicited e-mail) filter and antivirus protection.
4. Privacy. Understand the provider's privacy policy so that you know what personal information the company might collect and distribute.
5. E-mail. Be sure the provider supports you with one or more e-mail accounts. Many families require multiple e-mail accounts so that family members can have their own.
6. Parental controls. Ensure that the service provides security settings appropriate for your family situation. If you have children in the house, you might want to limit or monitor Internet activity.
7. Download and upload speed. Be aware of the speed with which downloading and uploading will occur.
8. Terms of service and access policies. Be aware of any service limitations or access policies that might restrict the amount of data that you can download or upload at certain times of the day.

Searching the Internet

Browsing, sometimes called **surfing**, is fun and easy, but it is not the most efficient method for finding specific information. When you browse, you visit websites without direction, following interesting links as you find them. Just as you would not flip aimlessly through a book to find specific information, neither would you leisurely browse the Web to find what you are looking for. When working with a book, you would more likely move to the index or table of contents to determine the location of information. When dealing with the Web, you would more likely use a search tool.

The Web includes major portals, or websites, that offer a broad array of services. Some portals provide resource discovery tools, called **search engines** or **subject directories**. In most cases, a search site can locate information for you once you have typed in one or more **keywords**, which identify your search topic. For example, if you want to find information on diabetes, you might use that term as your keyword to initiate the search for corresponding websites. A subject directory searches broad categories of information, from a limited number of websites. Perhaps you are looking for information on car insurance. You can use the keywords *car insurance* to begin your search. The more specific you are in your choice of keywords, the more focused the search, and the more likely that you will quickly find the information you desire. Once your search has returned a list of websites, you can visit any of them, following hyperlinks to find the information that you seek. Expect to be disappointed with your first query, because it often takes several tries to express exactly what you are searching for with keywords. It is not unusual for an initial search to return thousands of matching sites.

Using Search Engines and Subject Directories

Think carefully about your search topic before attempting a search. With experience, you will learn to analyze your information needs, select concise search terms, and evaluate search engines so that you can take full advantage of Internet information resources. Searching can be a complex process, one that is as scientific and thorough as you want to make it. It can also be simple and rewarding.

You can use either a search engine or a subject directory when performing an online search. Both offer similar services, with the dividing line between them often blurring. Both services enable you to locate information related to a topic or keywords you provide; however, they differ in that a subject directory is more attuned to broad categories of information, whereas a search engine is better suited for narrow or obscure topics. Most people who search for information online use a search engine, such as Google. If you are engaged in academic research, you are more likely to gravitate to a subject directory.

A subject directory offers links that are organized into subject categories. An excellent example of a subject directory is Infomine (http://infomine.ucr.edu), compiled by academic librarians from the University of California. Editors of that subject directory select only those sources that are considered useful to the research community. Other subject directories are managed by commercial portals. For example, Yahoo! (www.yahoo.com) is considered a subject directory because it organizes information in broad categories. It is more attractive to the general public rather than to academic researchers. Although beneficial for research, subject directories are not nearly as numerous as search engines.

Subject Directory or Search Engine?

When conducting Internet research, how do you know whether to use a search engine or a subject directory? The following suggestions might help you decide.

- The more specific and narrow your topic, the more likely it is that a search engine would be your best choice. Because some subject directories do not have search capabilities, you might find yourself browsing through categories and subcategories instead of quickly obtaining results.
- If you are just beginning to research a topic, you might use a subject directory to obtain lists of words that might narrow the search—words you can later use in a search engine to retrieve specific results.
- A search engine is likely to provide the most current information on a popular topic. Because computers update search engines whereas humans update subject directories, a search engine's database is likely to be more current than a subject directory's.
- If you are not certain of exactly what you are looking for, but have a broad topic in mind, a subject directory is a good place to start.

Search engines are useful when you have a narrow or obscure topic to research or when you want to search the full text of pages. Using a search engine, such as www.bing.com, you will likely retrieve a large number of documents, not all of which will be directly related to your topic. A search engine actually consults a database of Internet files collected by a computer program sometimes called a **spider** or **web crawler**. Results of a search engine query are indexed by title, full text, size, and URL. Although the results might be prioritized in order of relevance, the returned sites often contain few references to the searched keywords. Understanding that, it is important to be as specific as possible in your choice of keywords, so the resulting list is narrowed to those pages that are more relevant to your search.

General search engine sites include Google (www.google.com), Bing (www.bing.com), AltaVista (www.altavista.com), Dogpile (www.dogpile.com), and Ask (www.ask.com), as shown in Figure 3.21. Google is the preferred choice for many people because it provides fast, accurate, and comprehensive search results in order of keyword frequency. As you become comfortable with a particular search engine, you will tend to gravitate to it each time you conduct a search and may even want to make it your home page. Your browser will most likely include a search bar, powered by a search engine of your choice, so you can enter keywords without first navigating to a search engine page.

In your list of search results, you are likely to find a mix of at least two categories. Some results might be those of advertisers who have paid the site sponsor. Others are simply links to websites for additional information on the subject. Each search engine displays search results a bit differently; some search engines clearly label paid links, whereas others are less open. Most

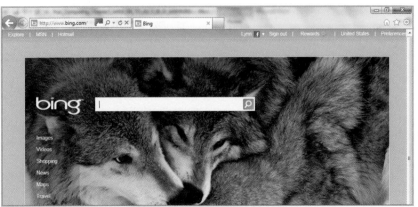

Figure 3.21 You have a great deal of choice in search engines.

search engines also enable you to narrow the search by content type, such as images or video.

If you do not get the results you need with one search, or if you get too many sites, do not be discouraged. Either narrow your search, or try another search site. Choose your search keywords carefully, because they are critical to the success of your search. Try to be as specific as possible when wording your search terms.

Identifying Search Techniques

Perhaps the simplest method to search for information online is to type keywords in the Search bar (or Address bar, in Internet Explorer 9). Choose keywords carefully. The more specific you can be, the more likely you are to get relevant results. To narrow a search, you might plan to use several keywords. Using only one keyword is probably not enough to obtain the results you seek. Using more than eight is probably too many. Your challenge is to define your topic as completely and succinctly as possible so that you do not end up with too many or too few search results. You might write down all of the information you are looking for and then identify the best keywords for your search. For example, if looking for information on a scholarship in biology, you would not want to simply specify *scholarship* as your keyword. Imagine the number of sites that search would return! Instead, you might begin with *biology scholarship* and work to narrow your search, if necessary, from there. Figure 3.22 shows the results of a search for *biology scholarship*.

Entering keywords as a phrase is often the best way to obtain meaningful results. A phrase is a combination of two or more words that must be found in the exact order shown. When searching for scholarships in biology, you could type **"biology scholarship"**, including the quotation marks, in the Address bar as your keyword phrase. The quotation marks indicate that all results must include the keywords in the exact order shown.

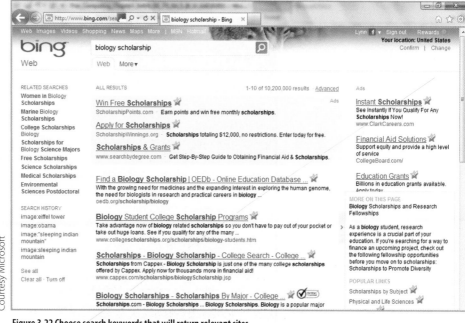

Courtesy Microsoft

Figure 3.22 Choose search keywords that will return relevant sites.

Selecting a Search Engine

You do not have to navigate to a particular search engine site to conduct a search. Instead, you can type one or more keywords in the Address bar or search bar of your browser. If you use Internet Explorer 9, Bing is most likely the search engine that powers your searches. However, you can specify another search engine as the default search provider if you prefer. The following steps enable you to change search providers.

1. Open Internet Explorer 9.
2. Click the small black arrow to the right of the magnifying glass icon beside the Address bar.
3. Click **Add**, located at the bottom-right side of the suggestion box that displays.
4. A page of add-on search sites will display. Click a preferred search provider and then click **Click to Install**.
5. Check **Make this my default search provider** if you want the search engine to conduct your searches, or make sure **Use search suggestions from this provider** is checked so that the search engine will be included in a search engine list from which you can select a default search engine later. (To select the search engine at a later time, click the small black arrow to the right of the Address bar and click the search engine.)

If you do not include quotation marks in your search phrase, search results can include one or more of the keywords. For example, suppose you are looking for information on *monarch butterflies*. If you type the words **monarch butterflies** in the Address bar and press **Enter**, the results can include information on *monarchs* (people who have served as kings or queens) or *butterflies* (all types, even those that are not monarch butterflies). While it is true that the most relevant sites (those including both search terms) are likely to be shown first, the results will also include many that are not relevant. Results would have been more closely related to the topic if you had typed **"monarch butterflies"** (including the quotation marks) as the search terms.

Yahoo!

Yahoo! is a widely used subject directory with an odd name. The name actually stands for *Yet Another Hierarchical Officious Oracle*. Two Stanford University graduate students, David Filo and Jerry Yang, coined the term in 1994 for their index of favorite websites. Originally called *David's and Jerry's Guide to the World Wide Web*, the indexing system was quickly relabeled *Yahoo!*. Developed as a hierarchical list of Web subject categories and subcategories, Yahoo! was one of the first context-based subject directories on the Web. Incorporated in 1995, Yahoo! is now a leading global communications, commerce, and media company. David Filo and Jerry Yang are now young billionaires. Neither of them ever went back to finish their doctoral studies, but they are each ranked as one of the 400 wealthiest men in America. By the way, Google is actually a misspelling of the word *googol*, which means one to the hundredth power. Its name was an attempt to enumerate the number of websites that were seemingly available to be itemized.

In Depth

Bing and Google

Google is most likely the first name that comes to mind when you think of searching the Web. With approximately 66% of the search market, Google is definitely a leader in that area. In fact, the word *google* is now considered a verb. When you *google* a topic, you search for it online. Microsoft is now making inroads into the search market with its Bing search engine. Aggressively going after Google's market share, the developers of Bing (which, according to a popular joke, is short for *But It's Not Google*) have had to answer charges that they actually watch what people search for on Google and the sites they select, and then use that information to improve Bing's search listings. Microsoft does not deny the claim, but a frustrated Google executive likens it to the digital equivalent of Microsoft cheating off of Google's exam, profiting from someone else's work. One thing is for certain—Google is still the search leader. Recently, however, Microsoft and Yahoo! signed a deal whereby Bing now powers Yahoo! searches. Even so, Bing has a lot of ground to make up if it intends to overtake Google.

Most search engines are not case sensitive. Typing search terms in uppercase, lowercase, or a mix of the two will yield identical results. Be careful with punctuation, however. Various search engines have different rules concerning punctuation. You can usually find a Help area on the search engine's home page for assistance with specific search rules that are unique to the site.

If your search is more advanced, you should check the rules for advanced searches found at the search engine site. Perhaps you are looking for information on all countries in Asia except Japan. How would you exclude Japan from the search? Depending on the rules of the search sites, you can include the NOT or OR operators. Called **Boolean searching**, the use of AND, OR, and NOT operators can significantly narrow a search by excluding or including additional variables. To exclude Japan from the search for countries in Asia, you could type *Asia NOT Japan* as your search terms. In some cases, it is even easier to phrase such searches—use the Advanced Search link, or its equivalent, to complete a form giving your preferences, without concern to exact phrasing. Check the search engine site for assistance with advanced searching. Figure 3.23 shows such a form provided by Google through its Advanced Search link.

As a further example, suppose you are searching for sites related to Paris and the Eiffel Tower and the Louvre Museum. Using the Boolean operator AND, you can indicate that results should contain all of the search terms. Type *"Paris" AND "Eiffel Tower" AND "Louvre Museum"* to require all three search terms in any resulting sites. The OR operator means that any of the terms should be included in search results, but all of the terms are not necessarily required. Type *"Paris" OR "Eiffel Tower" OR "Louvre Museum"* to return sites related to either Paris, or the Eiffel Tower, or the Louvre Museum. Resulting sites do not have to reference all of the search terms, but any one of them. Finally, the AND NOT operator (sometimes used as BUT NOT) indicates that results should include sites that contain one or more keywords (but not if the site also includes another keyword). For example, the search phrase *"Paris" AND "Eiffel Tower" AND NOT "Louvre Museum"* indicates that results should be those that include the words *Paris* and *Eiffel Tower*, but not those that also include the words

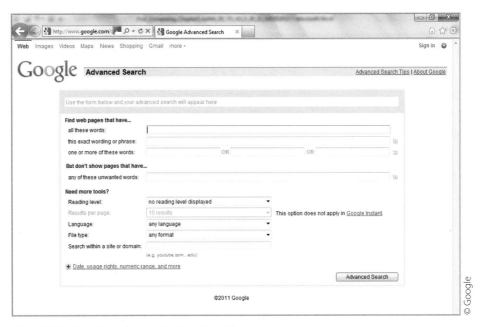

Figure 3.23 Google provides assistance with advanced searching.

Louvre Museum. Keep in mind that you will seldom need to use such advanced search techniques. Most of your searches will be simple and can be achieved through simple phrasing, using quotation marks or simply indicating relevant search keywords.

Searching the Internet methodically yields a wealth of information on most topics. Consequently, it is important to remember that the Web is not regulated and there is no guarantee that posted information is accurate. Critically evaluating sites, with regard to purpose, accuracy, objectivity, author, and currency of the subject, will help you determine whether a document is relevant.

In Depth

Search Suggestions

When selecting keywords that will return the most relevant results, keep the following suggestions in mind.

- Check your spelling. Be careful to make no mistakes and also consider alternate spellings. If you want to return results that include both the word *color* and *colour*, use both spellings as keywords.
- Use no more than eight keywords as search terms. Remember that although it is sometimes all you have to work with, the use of only one keyword is likely to return many more results than you need. Be as specific as possible.
- If possible, combine keywords into phrases, using quotation marks to force results to be in the exact order as your phrasing.
- If looking for a particular media type, such as an image or video, you can include the media type as a search term. For example, the search terms *video:cpr* will locate sites with a video on cardiopulmonary resuscitation. Similarly, *image:eiffel tower* returns pictures of the Eiffel Tower.
- Avoid the use of pronouns (*she, he*), articles (*the, a*), prepositions (*of, in*), and conjunctions (*and, or*) in your search terms.

Hands-On

Activity 3.4 Search the Web

You have the opportunity to travel with your photography class to Wyoming. If you choose to participate, you will be assigned the task of photographing the Sleeping Indian mountain formation for inclusion in a class photography portfolio. Because you are completely unfamiliar with the mountain formation, you will conduct some Internet research on the topic.

a. Click the **Address bar** and type **www.google.com** to get to the Google search engine. Press **Enter**.

b. Type **sleeping indian** in the Search bar beneath the word *Google*. Press **Enter**.

Although several of the resulting sites might relate to the Sleeping Indian mountain formation, you are likely to see others related to clothing designs, condominiums, and racehorses. You will narrow your search. Because a search is not case sensitive, you do not need to capitalize search keywords. In fact, it might be easier to type in all lowercase.

c. Change the search terms in the Search bar to **"sleeping indian mountain"**. Press **Enter**.

By enclosing search keywords in quotation marks, you are requiring resulting sites to include all words, in that order. The resulting sites, similar to those shown in Figure 3.24, should all relate to Sleeping Indian Mountain. You can learn much more about the mountain formation by consulting some of those sites, but you want to narrow the results to only show pictures of the formation.

d. Click **Images** on the left side of the browser window (Figure 3.24).

The results should all be pictures, arranged so that the Sleeping Indian Mountain pictures are shown first. Can you tell why the mountain formation is called the Sleeping Indian?

e. Click **Everything** (Figure 3.24). Click **Advanced search**.

To experiment, you will find all sites that contain the words *sleeping indian*, but none that also include the word *mountain*.

f. Click the box beside *this exact wording or phrase* and type **sleeping indian** Click the box beside *any of these unwanted words* and type **mountain** Click **Advanced Search**. Do any of the resulting sites include the word *mountain*?

ON YOUR OWN

You are preparing a research paper for your English class in which you take a position for or against the involvement in the military of very young adults (those aged 18–20 years). As part of your research, you will explore public opinion, some of which might be expressed in the poem *Dulce et Decorum Est*. Conduct an Internet search to locate the poem's text. Then narrow the focus to locate only sites that provide an analysis of the poem.

g. Close the browser.

Figure 3.24 Use relevant keywords to narrow a search.

Quick Tip

Exploring Download Sites

When possible, only download programs from reputable sites on the Internet. Among the most favored download sites are www.download.com, www.tucows.com, and www.pcmag.com (click **Downloads** link).

Downloading

The Internet contains a wealth of information and resources. As you work with it, you are likely to identify software, games, and other items you would like to use on your computer. Software manufacturers now offer versions of software for **downloading**, enabling you to purchase it online or acquire the software for a trial period before making a purchase decision. You can download screen savers, clip art, games, antivirus software, productivity software, and all sorts of handy gadgets. Although some downloads are available only by purchase, others are free for personal use.

By definition, downloading is the process of getting a file or software application from another computer or storage medium and placing it on your computer's hard disk or a USB. Instead of simply viewing a file on a Web page, you are able to keep a copy of the file on your computer system for later use. For example, you might want to have a copy of a lengthy worksheet, prepared by a colleague and included as an e-mail attachment. Friends or family might want to send you a photo of a new baby, or you might identify some computer games you would like to try that are available as a download from the Web. Those are all examples of items you can download and keep on your computer.

Uploading is the process of copying a file from your computer to another computer or server. An instructor might prepare a learning unit at home and then upload it to the campus server for class access. A special type of Internet site, called an FTP (File Transfer Protocol) site, makes it easy to transfer files from your computer to an online computer server. Although it is important to understand the concept of uploading, you are much more likely to be involved with downloading files.

Basically, two types of items are available for download—programs and data files. Many sites offer programs, such as a trial version of an antivirus scanner, as a download. After you download the program, you must install it to make it functional. A data file might be your colleague's worksheet or a photograph attached to an e-mail message. You do not have to install data files, but you do need to have appropriate software to open a data file. For example, if the colleague's worksheet you just downloaded was created with Microsoft Excel, you must have the correct version of Microsoft Excel on your system to view the worksheet. Likewise, you must have appropriate software loaded before you are able to view graphic files, such as photographs.

Before downloading anything, you must consider the potential risk to your computer. Downloading programs and files is one of the most common avenues for the transmission of viruses, spyware, and other destructive programs. A download that appears to be safe might actually be a virus in disguise. A virus can destroy data on your computer or provide open access to all of the information on your hard disk. Spyware often tags along with legitimate downloads, changing your computer's behavior—perhaps slowing it to a crawl, changing your browser settings, or even causing your computer to fail. In addition, spyware can record your passwords, monitor keystrokes, and even track your browsing habits.

Even considering the inherent risk, downloading is a great way to try out new software and to enjoy sharing files. To minimize your risk, be sure to take the following precautions.

- Make sure to activate the Windows firewall on your system or to purchase and install another firewall. Chapter 7 provides information on activating Windows Firewall.
- Schedule regular Windows Updates, or set your system to automatically download and install critical updates when they become available. See Chapter 2 for more information on Windows Update.
- Install antivirus software and make sure to keep it current. Set the antivirus program to actively scan all incoming files and e-mail attachments. Visit www.microsoft.com/security_essentials to download Microsoft's free software, Security Essentials, that protects against viruses, spyware, and other malicious software.
- Install spyware removal software and run it often. You might consider installing a version that is on constant alert for spyware activity.
- Use a spam filter to block unwanted e-mail.

To download a file from the Web:

1. Create a folder, possibly on the desktop, to hold downloaded files and programs. Although downloading is not complicated, locating the file after it has been downloaded can be time consuming if you are not careful about where the file is placed on the hard disk. To create a download folder, right-click an empty area of the desktop. Point to **New**, and click **Folder**. Type a name for your folder, and press **Enter**. Use the new folder as the location for all downloaded items so that you can easily find them.

2. Locate the item to be downloaded. It might be that you are visiting a Web page and notice an interesting item available for download. Click whatever link on the page appears to initiate the download. Figure 3.25 shows a Web page with a download link. Remember that a link is an item, either graphic or text, that you can click to proceed to another page or process. When you move the mouse pointer over a link, it usually becomes either an arrow or a pointing hand. The download link might be as obvious as a *Download Now* designation, but there is no set way for a file or program to be identified. Read the Web page carefully to find any download links.

Figure 3.25 Click a download link to initiate the download process.

3. Follow all prompts to download the item if you are working with Internet Explorer. Depending on the browser, some might automatically download to a download folder, after which you can indicate whether to save the item, and where. If asked whether to open the file in its current location or save it to your disk, click the **Save** option, as shown in Figure 3.26 That way, you can scan it for viruses before opening it. You will have to specify a location (folder) in which the file should be saved. Click **Desktop**, and double-click the download folder that you created on your desktop in Step 1. Make note of the filename. Although you can change the filename later, it will be helpful to know the name of the file, so you can identify it when you install the program later.

4. Double-click the downloaded item to install or open it. If the item is a program, you will follow the prompts to install it. If the item is a file, you must have the appropriate software on your system to open it.

5. Manage the contents of the download folder. Especially if you download a lot of files and programs, you will want to keep the download folder from becoming too cluttered. When a program file is installed, it is placed either as an item on your program list or as an icon on the desktop. At that point, you will not need to keep the download installation file in the download folder, so delete it. The installation program you downloaded and placed in the download folder is only used to install the program and is not necessary after the installation is complete. A data file is not a file that you need to install, but you do need to open it to view its contents. If the data file is something you want to keep, you should move it to a more appropriate folder on your hard disk or USB drive. You learned how to move files in Chapter 2. If you no longer need the data file, delete it from the download folder.

Figure 3.26 If given a choice, always choose to save a downloaded file.

Download Safety

Keep the following tips in mind when downloading from the Internet or when using e-mail:

- Only download from reputable sites. The website to which you were referred by e-mail might not be safe. Also, be cautious about accepting offers that appear too good to be true. Avoid sites that contain objectionable content.
- Never open attachments in an e-mail or instant message that you receive from strangers. Even if you know the sender, but the correspondence appears suspicious, do not open an attachment.
- Do not click links in e-mail, instant messages, or pop-up windows and banner ads.
- Do not click *OK*, *I agree*, or *I accept* to close a pop-up ad or an unexpected warning. Even if the warning concerns your computer's safety settings, do not click links. Instead, close the window by clicking **Close** or by pressing **Alt+F4**.
- Never download copyrighted material. If you are unsure of whether the item is copyrighted, do not download it. Stiff legal penalties accompany copyright infringement. To make matters worse, if you download copyrighted material to your company's computer, the company could be held liable.

Understanding Societal Issues of the Internet

Although the Internet is a wonderful informational tool, you should consider some inherent concerns. The very fact that it is so widely accessible leaves the Web open to misuse and hacking. Computer hackers welcome the chance to explore and possibly modify files on other computers, sometimes just for a challenge, but often to gather information that can be used for profit. Viruses, attached to e-mail messages or downloaded with files, are always a possibility. Viruses infect computers, often destroying files and entire hard disks. Of even more concern to many people is the risk to personal privacy that results from traveling and conducting business on the Internet. It is a good idea to be aware of security and privacy risks; however, most people agree that the benefits of using the Internet far outweigh any possible problems.

Being aware of privacy and security concerns is a first step toward protecting yourself as much as possible. Antivirus software and firewalls (discussed in Chapter 7) are necessary to prevent damaging viruses that cause you to lose data and to prohibit unauthorized access to your computer. Identify theft, where a third party profits from illegally collecting your private information, is also a common concern. You might worry that businesses keep too much information about you in computer databases, with not enough control over how the information is used. All of those concerns are valid but should not discourage you from using the Internet—simply remain aware of the risks and informed of solutions.

The Internet is full of possibilities and is a revolutionary approach to daily activities, business, and information retrieval. Through your home personal computer, you can easily begin your Internet experience.

Chapter Summary

- The Internet comprises millions of computers connected globally and in communication with one another. *92*

- The World Wide Web is a subset of the Internet that enables you to move among pages by clicking hyperlinks. *94*

- A browser, such as Internet Explorer or Mozilla Firefox, is software that displays Web pages. *95*

- The Internet was established as a network for national information and defense, called ARPANET. Later, it progressed into NSFNet, a network facilitating the exchange of educational research information. *94*

- An Internet protocol facilitates communication and data transfer between networks and computers on the Internet. *93*

- Methods of connecting to the Internet include cable, DSL, wireless, and satellite. *114*

- An Internet Service Provider enables you to connect to the Internet, usually charging a monthly access fee. *114*

- A URL uniquely identifies a Web page. *99*

- A typical URL, such as http://www.sciquest.org/activities, contains several components, including protocol, domain name, and a directory. *100*

- An analytical approach is used to search the Web and quickly find information, using search engines and subject directories. *117*

- Using Favorites, you can tag a Web page so that you can visit it later without having to remember the URL. *104*

- The History list displays recently visited sites, enabling you to quickly access them. *106*

- Downloading is the process of copying files to your computer from another computer. *126*

- Societal issues related to the Internet include privacy, security, and identity theft. *129*

Key Terms

Know dif. b/t Sub. directory + search engine

Multiple Choice

1. The Web generation characterized by "read-only" pages with little or no user interaction is
   a. Web 1.0.
   b. Web 2.0.
   c. Web 3.0.
   d. Web 4.0.

2. A disadvantage of DSL is that
   a. the connection can be shared by your neighbors, resulting in slower Internet travel.
   b. the telephone line is tied up when you are online so that you cannot send or receive calls.
   c. the DSL modem requires professional installation.
   d. you are always online, so security is a concern.

3. The Internet traces its earliest beginnings to
   a. NSFNET.
   b. ARPANET.
   c. CSNET.
   d. the World Wide Web.

4. An Internet protocol is
   a. a type of spyware.
   b. a method of communication, enabling networks to share data.
   c. another term for the Internet backbone.
   d. a set of rules for Web design.

5. Which of the following browsers is a Microsoft product, included with versions of the Windows operating system?
   a. Chrome
   b. Safari
   c. Firefox
   d. Internet Explorer

6. When searching online for information on a broad topic, such as World War II, the most effective tool would be a
   a. search engine.
   b. Web crawler.
   c. subject directory.
   d. Internet browser.

7. Tabbed browsing refers to
   a. placing each open Web page on its own tab.
   b. using more than one browser, with each located on its own tab.
   c. indenting open Web pages so that each one appears as a subset of another.
   d. using multiple search engines so that results from each appear on a separate tab.

8. Cable, DSL, and satellite are examples of what type of Internet connection?
   a. Broadband
   b. Wideband
   c. Wireless
   d. Wi-Fi hotspot

9. During a search, you can insure that resulting websites recognize your keywords as a phrase by
   a. enclosing search keywords within parentheses.
   b. separating search keywords with a dash.
   c. leaving no space between search keywords.
   d. enclosing search keywords within quotation marks.

10. The process of copying a file from a remote computer to your computer is
    a. Uploading.
    b. Downgrading.
    c. Downloading.
    d. Copying.

11. Surfing the Internet refers to
    a. a precise search, based on keywords you suggest.
    b. communicating with friends and family through social networking sites.
    c. exploring sites of interest, with no particular goal in mind.
    d. using one or more search engines to locate information on a particular topic.

12. A software tool that enables you to view websites is a
    a. subject directory.
    b. browser.
    c. favorite.
    d. search engine.

13. Another term for the Address bar in Internet Explorer 9 is
    a. One Box.
    b. New Tab.
    c. Browser bar.
    d. Status bar.

14. Which of the following is not a safety feature of Internet Explorer 9?
    a. Tracking Protection.
    b. SmartScreen Filter.
    c. InPrivate Browsing.
    d. Cookie Disable.

15. The World Wide Web is characterized by
    a. the use of text-based commands.
    b. text-based pages, with very few graphics or multimedia features.
    c. browsers and hyperlinks.
    d. a high degree of regulation and censorship.

True/False

Circle **T** if the statement is true or **F** if the statement is false.

T F 1. You can only have one browser at a time installed on your computer.

T F 2. Uploading is the process of copying a file from your computer to a remote computer.

T F 3. Boolean operators that can be used in a Web search include AND, OR, and NOT.

T F 4. The event that led to the development of the Internet was China's invasion of Korea.

T F 5. To return to a recently viewed Web page, you can use the History list.

T F 6. A disadvantage of creating Favorites is that you cannot categorize your favorites into folders.

T F 7. A DSL connection uses existing telephone lines in such a way that you can make and receive phone calls even when you are online.

T F 8. A possible problem with downloading files is the transmission of viruses.

T F 9. Secure Sockets Layer is a technology that encrypts online transmission to make financial transactions more secure.

T F 10. The Internet is highly regulated, so there are no incorrect or offensive sites online.

End of Chapter Exercises

Searching the Web

1. Use a Web search engine to answer the following questions. In your response, provide the answer to each question as well as the website at which you found the information.
   a. What U.S. president was born in a town called Stonewall? *Lyndon B Johnson*
   b. Why was Legionnaires' Disease given such an odd name? When and where was the disease first identified?
   c. Who played in the 1976 World Series? *Cincinnati reds + New y yankees*
   d. Where is the tallest building in the world located? *Burj Khalifa in the United Arab Emirates) 2,717 feet*
   e. What is Rhode Island's state bird? *RhodeI Red chicken*
   f. Who invented the paper clip? *Johann*
   g. Give one retired hurricane name. *Carol - Hazel*
   h. What country had the largest recorded earthquake, and when? *may 22,1960 9.5 Valdivia, Chile*
   i. What was Jacqueline Kennedy's maiden name? *Bouvier*
   j. What is the significance of potato latkes? Find a recipe.
   k. In the original Dr. Seuss book, *How the Grinch Stole Christmas*, what color was the Grinch? *b+w with some red & pink splotches*
   l. How did the kangaroo get its name? *when 1st ex saw*

Internet Scavenger Hunt

2. Assume you are completing a graduate degree in education, with an emphasis in information technology. As a student teacher in a 9th grade computer literacy class, you are responsible for a lesson on basics of the Internet. Using this chapter as a resource, develop an Internet scavenger hunt to be completed by students in your class. The purpose of the scavenger hunt is to reinforce concepts related to Internet basics, similar to those that you have studied in this chapter. The scavenger hunt should include at least 10 items that students must search for online. For example, you might ask them to locate the name of the person commonly given credit for first suggesting the World Wide Web. As you develop the scavenger hunt, test it to make sure students will be able to find answers online. Type or handwrite your scavenger hunt for submission to your instructor.

Internet Timeline

3. Your Business Communication instructor has assigned you to a group of students charged with creating a presentation on the development of the Internet. Your task for the group is to develop a timeline, showing the progression of the Internet from its inception to the present. Prepare the timeline as a sketch, showing contributors, years, and a short summary of each event. Provide enough detail to fully describe the history of the Internet.

Internet Connections

4. As you consider choices related to broadband Internet connection, you will find that the most popular selections are cable and DSL. Both are widely available high-speed connections, with specific strengths and weaknesses. Develop a one- to two-page typed report comparing cable and DSL Internet connections. In the report, include specific advantages and disadvantages of each, along with specifications related to upload and download speed and required equipment.

Independent Study

5. You are enrolled in an Independent Study course in which you will develop a teaching unit for a local elementary school. The topic is cyberbullying. Through national news, you are aware of several tragedies in which young people have actually committed suicide after having been bullied online. The goal of your teaching unit is to present information on the topic, suggest strategies for addressing the problem, and include learning resources for the elementary school children. In your online research, you might identify free resources such as handouts, activities, and videos suitable for students. Be sure to explore government websites that provide statistics, information, and resources. Your teaching unit should be a typed document with sufficient detail to support a lesson on deterring cyberbullying. Include links to information and resources online.

Photos by Andresr/Shutterstock; arikamadov/Shutterstock

CHAPTER **FOUR**

Working with PowerPoint

IF YOU HAVE EVER TAKEN A BUSINESS COMMUNICATION or Speech class, it is a safe bet that you have been introduced to the concept of speaking before a group. Whether you enjoy that task or not, you are well aware that presentation skills can be vital to your success in school and in a career. One of the most difficult aspects of preparing a presentation is organizing your thoughts and staying on track as you interact with your audience. Even a small degree of stage fright can spell disaster for your effectiveness as a speaker if it distracts you from your purpose. Above all, you want to be as prepared as possible, with your speaking points well ordered and attractively presented. That is where presentation software comes in handy. **Presentation software** enables you to deliver information using text, charts, sound, animation, and color. Although presentation software does not replace a speaker and is actually not appropriate in all cases, it might be exactly what you need to organize your rambling thoughts into a well-structured flow of ideas.

Using **Microsoft PowerPoint 2010**, you can easily develop and present a series of **slides** (single pages of a presentation) that makes your points in an effective manner. The computer presentation not only keeps your audience informed of your intentions but also keeps you on the right track. Although it is most often used as a tool in making presentations to groups, PowerPoint is also used to display self-running informational slides in kiosks and on billboards.

OBJECTIVES

When you complete this chapter, you will:

▶ Become familiar with PowerPoint basics.

▶ Understand how to modify a presentation.

▶ Preview and print a presentation.

▶ Insert objects into a presentation.

▶ Understand how to use multimedia in a presentation.

▶ Enhance a presentation by adding transitions and animation.

Learning to use PowerPoint as an effective visual aid requires more than simply learning the mechanics of working with the software. Making a presentation before a group requires that you are center stage—not the software—and requires that you understand your audience and address their needs. It requires that you convey enthusiasm for the topic and that your energy is contagious. Always remember that PowerPoint is simply a way to encourage understanding of the points you include in your presentation. As a tool for organization and synthesis, PowerPoint can assist you in presenting complete coverage of your topic. It can even be entertaining if you effectively include sound, video, and slide transition effects (the way that one slide progresses to another). However, it is not a cure-all—it does not relieve you of the responsibility of having to organize your thoughts and it will not magically design colorful, data-rich sides. In fact, it will only be a distraction that buries your message if you do not use good design principles.

In this chapter, you will be introduced to concepts of presentation design as well as PowerPoint basics, so you can use words, color, charts, and animation in ways that will appeal to an audience and deliver information effectively. When used correctly, presentation software can help audiences follow your message with at-a-glance comprehension, while also allowing you to provide details and supporting thoughts. Learning to use PowerPoint as a visual aid can give you the freedom to explore new ways to excite and involve your audience.

Understanding PowerPoint

Presentation software is used to boost the clarity, communication, and retention of ideas you present to an audience. Used primarily in business, presentations are also effective for communicating ideas to any group, such as a civic club, church committee, or class. The leader in the field of presentation software is Microsoft PowerPoint 2010, a component of Microsoft Office. PowerPoint includes a wide variety of tools for designing slides, including color choices, fonts, formats, animation, and styles. PowerPoint's range and flexibility enables you to quickly assemble impressive visuals to support any speech.

In this section, you will learn to identify an audience, tailoring a presentation to its needs. In addition, you will explore PowerPoint's interface, identifying various components that enable you to open and save a PowerPoint presentation and to view it in various ways.

Identifying an Audience

As soon as you know you are to give a presentation to a group, you should do two things. First, you should define the audience by asking yourself several questions. Why is the audience interested in your topic? What do you think they want to hear? How informed are they on your topic already and how can you support their need for more information? How many people do you expect to be in attendance?

After you define the group to which you will be speaking, you must begin planning your presentation. Note that defining the audience and planning the presentation are activities that take place before you even open PowerPoint. Technical skill is secondary to mastering the organization of your thoughts and purpose. As you think about your purpose, consider the outcome you expect

Delivering an Effective Presentation

When considering whether (or how) to develop a PowerPoint slide show to support a presentation, consider the following points:

1. Delivering an effective presentation does not necessarily require that you develop a PowerPoint slide show. One of the most important things to remember is that you are the key element in an effective presentation, not a PowerPoint slide show. PowerPoint should supplement your points but should never be the main attraction. In fact, in some cases, using a PowerPoint slide show could even detract from your message. Most often, however, a slide show is an effective supplemental visual aid if used in the proper context.

2. Humans retain facts that are presented visually much longer than lengthy text or statistics. Wherever possible, portray main points graphically or in pictures. For example, to drive home the point that the Windows operating system is the dominant OS sold, develop a slide with a pie chart showing a large piece of pie that is designated *Windows*. Other operating systems could be identified as smaller pieces of the pie. No matter what statistics are involved, your listeners will retain the image of the pie chart and will leave with the understanding you intended to convey.

3. Do not simply read from your slides. And above all, do not turn your back to your audience while you read from a PowerPoint slide. If your presentation is simply the slide content, there is no need for your presence. Remember, slide content should help you drive your point home, but you are the presenter. Draw from your understanding of the subject, using your notes if necessary, to convey your message. The slide show is only there for reinforcement and to draw emphasis to major points.

4. PowerPoint presentations are usually developed to help you inform or persuade an audience. With that in mind, make sure that your comments and slides inform an audience of where they are now, where they need to go, and how they are going to get there. Develop slides with simple text, informative images, and easy-to-read graphs.

5. Keep your presentation as short as possible, while at the same time addressing all the points you intend. A concise delivery will inform or persuade an audience but will not leave them bored or resentful of what they might see as a waste of time.

from your audience. Perhaps your presentation is intended to inform the audience of an organizational change, in which case your goal is for them to become aware of how the change will affect their environment. Or maybe you are attempting to persuade them to take action or to better understand a position. With your goals and objectives clearly defined, and with an understanding of your audience, you can then use PowerPoint to develop an effective presentation to support your purpose.

Beginning and Opening a PowerPoint Presentation

A presentation consists of a series of slides, each containing some items of information. Individual pages in a presentation are referred to as slides. The entire series of slides is a **slide show**, which can be published in several formats, including in print, on the Web, in a kiosk, or as an electronic presentation projected on a screen. The latter format is the focus of this chapter.

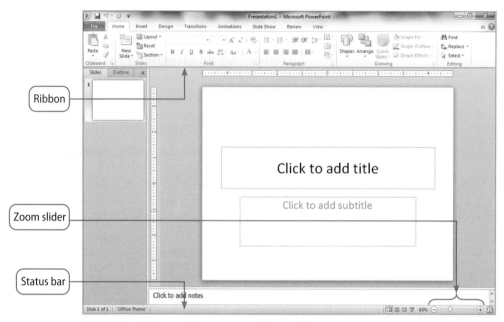

Figure 4.1 PowerPoint makes it easy to create a slide presentation.

To open PowerPoint, click **Start**, **All Programs**, **Microsoft Office**, and **Microsoft PowerPoint 2010**. PowerPoint opens as shown in Figure 4.1.

Figure 4.1 shows PowerPoint in **Normal view**, which is the view you will most often use. Other views are described in the next section. A **view** is simply the way a slide, or series of slides, is shown. In Normal view, the current slide is displayed in a large format. Because the presentation shown in Figure 4.1 has not yet been designed, the current slide is empty. To add content to the slide, simply click in a designated area and type.

The **Notes pane**, located beneath the current slide (in Normal view), is where you can type your presentation notes. The notes you type will not display when you are presenting the slide show, but you can print them so you can refer to them during your presentation. As certain as you may be that you are well prepared, it never hurts to have notes handy so you do not forget to make any pertinent points. Some speakers like to print presentation notes as handouts for the audience. Although you are not required to use the Notes pane, it is definitely an option.

In Normal view, the left pane includes two tabs—Outline and Slides. By default (unless you specify otherwise), the Slides tab is selected. The Slides tab displays **thumbnails** (small versions of slides). If you want to select one of the slides so you can modify or delete it, simply click its thumbnail. You can also change the order of slides by dragging to reposition them. The Slides tab is selected in Figure 4.1. In some cases, it might be easier to work with slide elements in a hierarchical, text-based, fashion (using the Outline tab), rather than the visual perspective afforded by the Slides tab. The Outline tab presents the text for each slide in outline format (major heading, subheadings, and so forth). By modifying or adding text in the outline, you can create or modify slides. The Outline tab is selected in Figure 4.2. To select a slide on the Outline tab, click the icon to the left of the slide title. To move slides, drag the slide icon to another location in the outline.

The **Ribbon** is located at the top of the PowerPoint window. Using a tab structure, the Ribbon organizes commands into groups. The Home tab, shown

Quick Tip

Using Key Tips

As you create PowerPoint slides, you will spend a great deal of time typing. However, you must move a hand from the keyboard to the mouse when selecting commands on the Ribbon. To save a little time by keeping your hands on the keyboard, you can use key tips to select Ribbon commands. Press **Alt** (on the keyboard) to display key tips, as shown in Figure 4.3. You can then select a Ribbon tab or command by pressing the corresponding key. For example, to select the **Insert** tab, press **N**. Press **Alt** again to remove key tips from view.

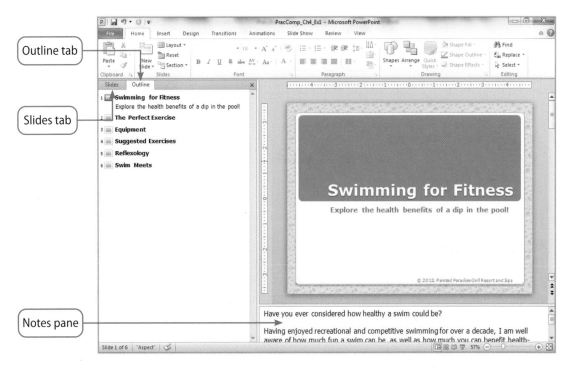

Figure 4.2 Use the Outline tab to manage slides in hierarchical a fashion.

selected in Figure 4.1, includes the Clipboard, Slides, Font, Paragraph, Drawing, and Editing groups. Each of those groups includes related commands. Other tabs are similarly grouped by category. You will explore each of those tabs and related commands later in this chapter.

The **status bar**, located at the bottom of the PowerPoint window (Figure 4.1) provides information about the current presentation, including the number of slides included, the current **theme** (set of formatting choices including colors, fonts, and effects), easy access to various presentation views, and a **Zoom Slider**, which enables you to view the current slide in different sizes. In Normal view (described later in this chapter), drag the Zoom Slider to the left or right to view the slide in a larger or smaller size. The Fit slide to current window option resizes a slide, if necessary, so that it displays well in the PowerPoint window.

The Title bar, located at the top of the PowerPoint window, includes the **Quick Access Toolbar** and the filename of the current slide presentation. If you have not yet saved the presentation, it will be titled Presentation1. Otherwise, the filename is the name you assigned when you saved the presentation. You will learn to save a presentation later in this chapter. The Quick Access Toolbar enables you to save a presentation or undo or redo recent commands, as shown in Figure 4.4. You can even customize the Quick Access Toolbar to include more commands. The purpose of the Quick Access Toolbar is, as its name suggests,

Figure 4.3 Key tips enable you to select Ribbon commands while keeping your hands on the keyboard.

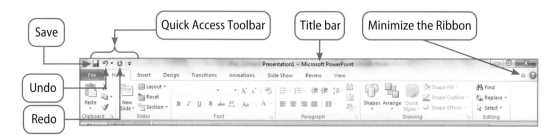

Figure 4.4 The Title bar and the Quick Access Toolbar are located above the Ribbon.

Quick Tip

Minimizing the Ribbon

As you become familiar with PowerPoint, you might rely less on the Ribbon and more on shortcut key combinations (some of which you will learn in this chapter). If you do not need the Ribbon, or simply need more working space, you can minimize the Ribbon by clicking **Minimize the Ribbon** (Figure 4.4). You can also press **Ctrl+F1** to minimize the Ribbon. Finally, you can double-click a selected tab to minimize the Ribbon. Reverse the procedure (click **Minimize the Ribbon**, press **Ctrl+F1**, or double-click a selected tab) to return the Ribbon to full size.

Quick Tip

Opening a Template

A template is a predesigned presentation consisting of one or more slides. Depending on the purpose of your presentation, a template might be available with content you can easily modify. To explore templates, click the **File tab** and click **New**. Navigate through the template categories and double-click to open a template. You can then modify and add to the content, saving the presentation to your computer.

to provide easy access to commonly executed commands. Therefore, if you use a command often, it is possible to customize the Quick Access Toolbar to include often-used commands.

When you open PowerPoint, you open a new blank presentation. At that time, you can create slides and save the presentation for later reference. Instead of working with a new presentation, however, you might want to open and modify a previously created presentation.

To open a previously saved presentation, click the **File tab** and then click **Open**, navigate through your folder structure to locate the PowerPoint presentation, and double-click the file to open it. When you click the File tab, **Backstage view** opens, which is a collection of common actions and settings related to the current presentation. It is also the location where you can define global settings, such as whether to check spelling automatically or on demand. Backstage view is shown in Figure 4.5. You can view document properties, such as file size and author, and you can set security permissions. Backstage view provides a quick

Figure 4.5 Backstage view includes options related to the current presentation.

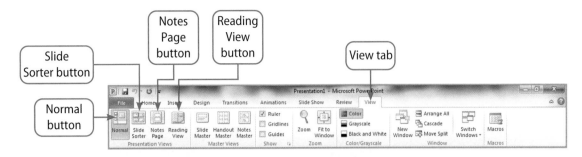

Figure 4.6 The View tab enables you to change the view of a presentation.

Quick Tip

Resizing Panes

If the Notes pane or the left pane is too large or too small when you are creating a slide, you can resize them. Simply drag the bar dividing the left pane from the Slide pane (called a splitter bar) to change the size of the left pane. Similarly, you can drag the splitter bar between the Notes pane and the Slide pane to resize Notes. You can close the left pane (and the Notes pane) by clicking the **Close** button at the upper-right corner of the pane. To return to the three-paned Normal view, click the **View tab** and click **Normal**.

way to open recently accessed PowerPoint files, to print slides and handouts, and to save files to a disk drive or to share them online. You can also use Backstage to close a file and exit PowerPoint. Best defined as a collection of common actions, properties, and settings related to an open file, Backstage view is unique to Office 2010 and is found in Word and Excel, in addition to PowerPoint.

Identifying PowerPoint Views

As you work with a PowerPoint presentation, you can display the slides in various views. Depending on the task in which you are involved, you will select an appropriate view. The View tab (Figure 4.6) enables you to select from several views, including Normal, **Slide Sorter**, **Notes Page,** and **Reading View**. You can also select a view by clicking a View button on the status bar, as shown in Figure 4.7. Status bar buttons include Normal, Slide Sorter, Reading View, and Slide Show.

As you learned earlier, Normal view is the view that first displays when you begin a new presentation. It shows the current slide in a large view (Figure 4.1). Normal view includes a Notes pane, in which you can type your speaker notes. If you prefer more typing space in the Notes pane, you can drag the splitter bar to expand the space. As an alternative, you can display the presentation in Notes Page view, which enables you to enter and edit large amounts of text to which you can refer when making your presentation. You can even print the notes as handouts for your audience, which is very effective because each Notes Page prints along with a picture of the associated slide. You will learn to print a presentation later in this chapter. The Notes page view is shown in Figure 4.8.

Slide Sorter view is a very effective way to manage multiple slides. As you can see in Figure 4.9, slides in Slide Sorter view are lined up as thumbnails, where each thumbnail represents a slide. To quickly enlarge a slide and work with it in Normal view, you can double-click a thumbnail. Slide Sorter view is handy

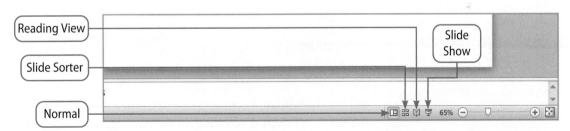

Figure 4.7 View buttons are located on the status bar.

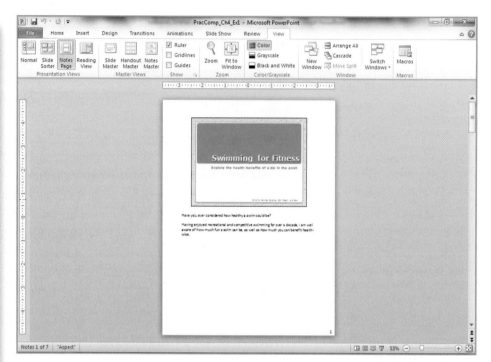

Figure 4.8 Notes Page view provides space for you to include presentation notes.

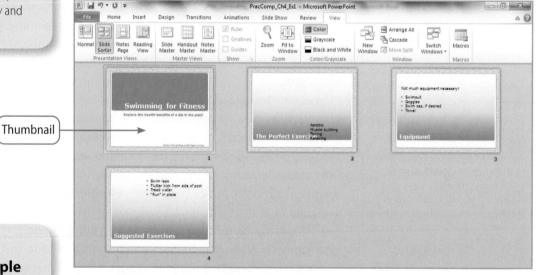

Figure 4.9 Slides appear as thumbnails in Slide Sorter view.

if you want to rearrange or delete slides. By selecting a group of slides in Slide Sorter view, you can manage them as a group, perhaps adding special effects to the selected slides or deleting the group.

Most often, you develop a PowerPoint presentation for display as a slide show to a group of people. A slide show is a collection of slides, shown one after the other, occupying a full screen. Slide shows are often shown in large view on a projection screen, so an audience can view the presentation. New to PowerPoint 2010, Reading View is similar to viewing slides as a slide show, but with a few notable differences. Although a slide shown in Reading View occupies the full screen, you will still see the Title bar as well as the status bar and the Windows taskbar. In Reading View, you can navigate a slide show but still access items on the status bar such as selecting an alternate view or zooming. Figure 4.10 shows a slide in Reading View. Note that the Ribbon is not displayed.

Title bar

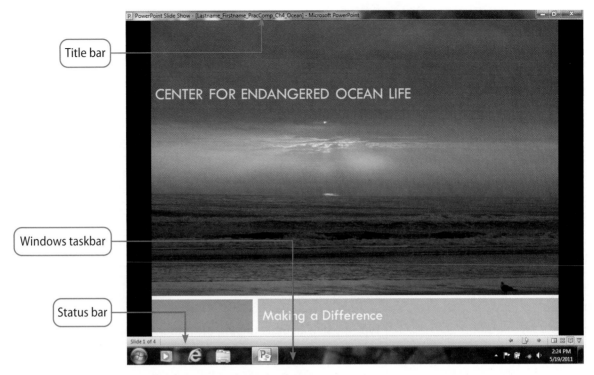

CENTER FOR ENDANGERED OCEAN LIFE

Windows taskbar

Status bar

Making a Difference

Slide 1 of 4

Figure 4.10 Reading View does not display the Ribbon.

Working with a Slide Show

Often, the end result of a presentation is displaying it on a large screen as you address an audience. If well-organized, the slide show will convey your points in an effective and easily understandable way. It will also help you keep your comments on track. Displaying the slide show is as simple as clicking the **Slide Show tab** and then selecting either **From Beginning** or **From Current Slide**. You can also use the status bar to begin a slide show. The Slide Show button is shown in Figure 4.11. Click **Slide Show** on the status bar to begin a slide show from the current slide.

You can also create a custom slide show that displays some, but not all, of your slides. To do so, click the **Slide Show tab** and then click **Custom Slide Show**. Click **Custom Shows** and respond to prompts to create a custom presentation.

If your audience is not together in one location, you might decide to **broadcast** your slide show online, so audience members can access a URL to view your slide show as you present it. With a PowerPoint presentation open, click the **Slide Show tab** and then click **Broadcast Slide Show** in the Start Slide Show group. Click **Start Broadcast** and follow all prompts to begin the online slide show, sending a URL to attendees so they can access the slide show in real time (at the same time you are presenting).

Slide Show

Slide 1 of 4   "Aspect"   57%

Figure 4.11 You can begin a slide show from the status bar.

Table 4.1 Use any of these methods to advance through a slide show.

Result	Action
Display the next slide	Click the left mouse button.
	Press the right arrow. →
	Right-click and select **Next** from the menu that displays.
	Place the pointer on the lower-left corner of the displayed slide. Click the right arrow that displays. →
Display the previous slide	Press the left arrow. ←
	Right-click and select **Previous** from the menu that displays.
	Place the pointer on the lower-left corner of the displayed slide. Click the left arrow that displays. ←
Go to a specific slide	Type the slide number (during the presentation) and press **Enter**.
	Place the pointer on the lower-left corner of the displayed slide. Click the menu options icon. Click **Go to Slide**, click the slide to view, and press **Enter**.

As you present the slide show, you will need to know how to navigate among the slides. Although you can configure a slide show to advance automatically from one slide to another, it is more common to control the advancement of slides (usually with a mouse click). Often, you will use a remote mouse during a presentation, in which case a mouse click would be the easiest way to advance. However, you can also press the right arrow on the keyboard → to move from one slide to the next. Similarly, to return to a previous slide, press the left arrow. ← These and other methods of moving among slides are presented in Table 4.1.

To end a slide show at any point during the presentation, simply press **Esc** on the keyboard. You can also place the pointer on the bottom left corner of the displayed slide, click the menu options icon, and select **End Show** (or more simply right-click a displayed slide and click **End Show** on the shortcut menu).

PowerPoint provides convenient tools you can use while displaying a slide show. To draw attention to specific elements on a slide, you can use a pen or highlighter to emphasize areas. Afterward, you can erase the drawings or save them along with the presentation. During a slide show, place the pointer over the lower-left corner of a slide and click the pen icon. From the menu that displays, select a pen or highlighter. Then draw on the slide or highlight items. Press **Esc** to return to the mouse pointer.

Saving a Presentation

As you develop a PowerPoint presentation, you will want to save it often so you do not lose your work. Although there is no absolute rule, it is a good idea to save at least every 10 minutes and to make a backup copy on another disk when the slides are complete. If you plan to collaborate with others, you can use online storage such as SkyDrive. That way, collaborators can access the slide show project, contributing to it and saving it back to SkyDrive.

To save a presentation, click the **File tab**. Click **Save** or **Save As** to save a presentation to a storage device. The first time you save a presentation, there is no difference in the two Save commands. Both will direct you to a Save As dialog box (Figure 4.12) so you can enter a filename and a location to save to. However, the next time you open the slide show, perhaps to modify it or to add slides, the two commands behave differently. If you click Save, the presentation is saved in the same location with the same filename as the last time it was saved. If, however, you click Save As, you are presented with the same dialog box you saw the first time you saved the file. You can accept the filename and location

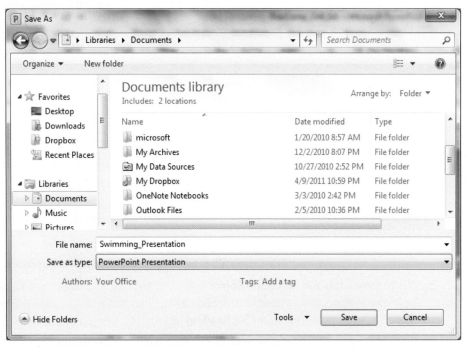

Figure 4.12 When saving a presentation, you must provide a filename and a location to save to.

by clicking Save, or you can navigate to a new folder or drive and/or change the filename to create another copy of the slide show. Obviously, Save As is a handy way to make a backup copy of the presentation.

If you plan to share a presentation with other collaborators, or perhaps you simply want to make an online copy of a presentation for easy retrieval later, you can save to a SkyDrive account. **SkyDrive** is storage space that Microsoft makes available to you at no charge. With up to 25 GB of free online storage space, you can upload presentations, documents, photographs, and any other files. You can then access those files from any location or share them with friends or coworkers. If you do not have a SkyDrive account, you can create an account at http://skydrive.live.com. You can also create a SkyDrive account as you are saving the PowerPoint presentation. Click the **File tab** and then click **Save & Send**, as shown in Figure 4.14. Click **Save to Web**. Sign in to your SkyDrive account (or create an account) and click **Save**.

Creating and Modifying a Presentation

To create a PowerPoint presentation, you will design a series of slides. Learning to design slides requires more than simple technical skill; you should also become familiar with accepted practices related to slide content, presentation

Hands-On

Activity 4.1 Explore PowerPoint, Open and Save a Presentation, and View a Slide Show

You are enrolled in a Speech class and have been assigned the task of developing an informative speech. To give you an idea of how to design a PowerPoint presentation, your instructor has provided a sample presentation. You will open and view the presentation, explore the PowerPoint interface, and save the presentation to your flash drive. If you have not already done so, you should connect the USB drive or prepare to save the presentation to a disk drive or folder as directed by your instructor.

a. Click **Start**, **All Programs**, **Microsoft Office**, and **Microsoft PowerPoint 2010**. Click the **File tab** and click **Open**. Navigate to the location of your student data files and double-click **PracComp_Ch4_Ex1**.

b. Click the **View tab** and click **Slide Sorter** in the Presentation Views group. Double-click **Slide 1** to open the slide in Normal view. Click **Reading View** on the status bar (Figure 4.13). Press → (on

Figure 4.13 You can select a view from the status bar.

the keyboard) to move to the next slide. Continue pressing → to view all slides and return to Normal view. Click **Notes Page** in the Presentation Views group on the View tab to view notes pages (including both the slide and your notes). Press → to progress through all notes pages. At the last notes

Save to Web

Save & Send

Figure 4.14 Save a presentation to SkyDrive so that you can access the presentation from anywhere.

page, click **Normal** in the Presentation Views group to return to Normal view.

c. Click **Slide Sorter** in the Presentation Views group to change the view to Slide Sorter. Click to select **Slide 3**. You plan to move Slides 3 and 4 so that they become the second and third slides in the presentation. Press and hold **Ctrl** and click **Slide 4**. Both slides 3 and 4 are selected, as you see by the colored border surrounding each slide. Place the pointer on either of the selected slides and drag to the space between Slides 1 and 2. You will see a vertical bar between the two slides. At that point, release the mouse button. Slides 3 and 4 are repositioned as new slides 2 and 3.

TROUBLESHOOTING

If the slides are positioned incorrectly, click **Undo** on the Quick Access Toolbar and repeat Step c.

d. Click the **File tab** and click **Save As**. Navigate to the location where you will save your student files. Click **New folder**, type a name for the folder (for example, PowerPoint Projects), and press **Enter**. Double-click the new folder. Click in the File name box and change the filename to Lastname_Firstname_PracComp_Ch4_Ex1, replacing Lastname with your last name and Firstname with your first name. Click **Save**.

e. Click the **Slide Show tab**. Click **From Beginning** in the Start Slide Show group. Click to progress through each slide in the slide show. Click at the end of the slide show to exit and return to Slide Sorter view.

f. Click to select **Slide 1**. Click **Slide Show** on the status bar. Click to progress to the next slide. Press ← to return to the previous slide. Press → to move to the next slide. Press → again.

g. Right-click the current slide. Click **Pointer Options** and click **Pen** on the displayed menu. Using the mouse, drag to circle the word **Equipment**. Press → to progress through the rest of the slide show. At the end of the show, press → once more. Click **Discard** when asked whether to keep the pen annotations.

h. Click **Slide 4**. Press **Delete** to remove the slide from the presentation. Click **Save** on the Quick Access Toolbar to save changes to the presentation.

ON YOUR OWN

Change the view to Normal view. Select Slide 2. Drag Slide 2 to position it beneath Slide 3. View the Slide Show, beginning at the first slide. Save the presentation.

i. Click the **File tab**. Click **Exit** to close the presentation and PowerPoint.

Technology Insight

Microsoft Web Apps

With the release of Office 2010, Microsoft introduced Web Apps, a feature that not only lets you store Office 2010 files (such as PowerPoint presentations) online, but also enables you to open those files in a Web version of PowerPoint, Word, or Excel. That means you can open and work with Microsoft Office documents, worksheets, and presentations, even if your computer does not have Office 2010 installed. Although much more limited in functionality than their desktop counterparts (versions that are installed on your computer), the Web Apps versions of PowerPoint, Word, and Excel do include core editing and formatting elements. Begin working with Microsoft Office Web Apps at www.officelive.com.

length, and color choice for slide background and font. A simple Web search will identify multiple sites dedicated to the practice of preparing excellent presentations. You will find that PowerPoint is only one component of a well-done presentation. You, as the presenter, are the main focal point. However, as a supporting player, a well-designed PowerPoint presentation can certainly contribute to a successful presentation.

Whether creating a new presentation or modifying one created earlier, you will need to know how to navigate among slides, create new slides, remove slides, format text, manage themes (coordinated font and color schemes), and select a slide layout. All those activities are presented in this section.

Creating Slides

When you open PowerPoint, you are able to begin a new presentation or open one you previously created. If your goal is to create a series of slides, you can immediately begin to design slide content. The first slide in a presentation, shown in Figure 4.13, is the **Title slide**, which introduces the presentation to the audience. Each of the remaining slides focuses on a particular topic and can include items such as bulleted lists, charts, and graphics. A **subtitle** expands on the slide's main topic. If a subtitle is included on a slide, it appears in smaller text just beneath or above the **title**.

Creating a slide in Normal view (the view shown in Figure 4.15) can be as simple as clicking in a designated area, called a **placeholder**, and typing. For example, simply click the area labeled *Click to add title* and type a slide title. A placeholder provides a space for slide content and also determines the position and format of placeholder contents. A placeholder can hold text or **objects**. An object is an item, such as a picture, table, or chart. You will learn more about objects later in this chapter.

Each slide you create is based on a particular **slide layout**. You can either specify a slide layout or build the slide around a slide layout that PowerPoint automatically presents. A slide layout is a slide format designed to contain specific content or objects. For example, when you begin a slide show, PowerPoint assumes your first slide will contain a title and perhaps a subtitle. Therefore, the first slide presented, shown in Figure 4.15, includes placeholders for the title elements.

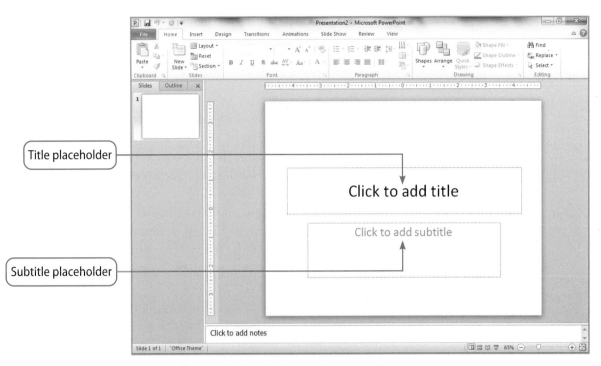

Title placeholder

Subtitle placeholder

Figure 4.15 A Title slide provides space for a title and subtitle.

To create a new slide, click the **New Slide arrow** on the Home tab (Figure 4.16) and then select a slide layout from the **gallery**. A gallery, shown in Figure 4.16, is a collection of visual options from which you can choose. The slide layout you select depends on the content planned for the new slide.

To enter text in a slide, simply click in a placeholder and type. Using options on the Home tab, you can format the text before or after you type. You will learn to format text later in this chapter. If a slide contains elements you do not plan to use, such as a subtitle, just leave the placeholder as is, without typing any text;

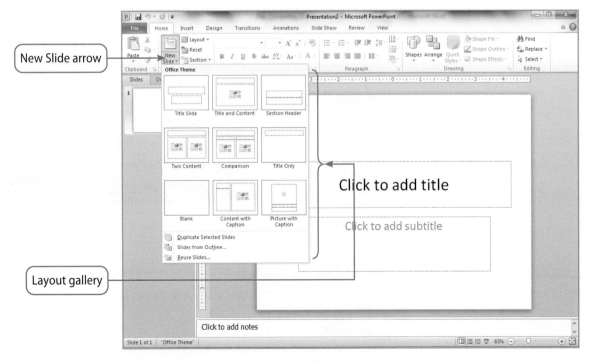

New Slide arrow

Layout gallery

Figure 4.16 Select from several slide layouts in the gallery.

Creating and Modifying a Presentation

the placeholder will not show when you run the slide show. You can even delete a placeholder along with all included text by clicking the **placeholder border** to select the placeholder and then pressing **Delete**.

Managing Slides

If a slide presentation includes several slides, you will want to move among the slides, checking content and readability. In Normal view, only one slide displays in the Slide pane. To display another slide, drag the vertical scroll bar (Figure 4.17). As you drag the bar up or down, a ScreenTip appears letting you know which slide will be current if you release the mouse button. Another way to change the current slide is to use the Slides pane. Click the **Slides tab**, if necessary, to display a thumbnail of all slides in consecutive order. Click any slide in the left pane to move directly to it. Finally, you can view slides in Slide Sorter view, double-clicking any slide to display it in full size (Normal view).

As you work with your slides, you might want to see the text more clearly and in larger print. You can adjust the magnification level of a slide so that the text is increased in size by whatever percentage you indicate. Keep in mind that changing the zoom setting does not actually change the font size or adjust other slide elements. It just magnifies the view. A quick way to zoom in or out is to drag the Zoom Slider found on the status bar (Figure 4.18). You can also click the **View tab** and click **Zoom**. From the subsequent dialog box, indicate a zoom setting and click **OK**. Also on the View tab is a Fit to Window option, which quickly resizes the slide to display in the available space.

Editing and Formatting Slides

You will often find the need to change the content or modify the formatting of slides. When you format a slide, you work with such effects as font size, color,

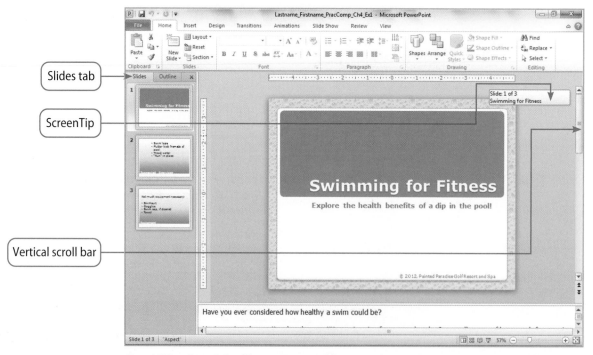

Figure 4.17 Drag the vertical scroll bar to move among slides.

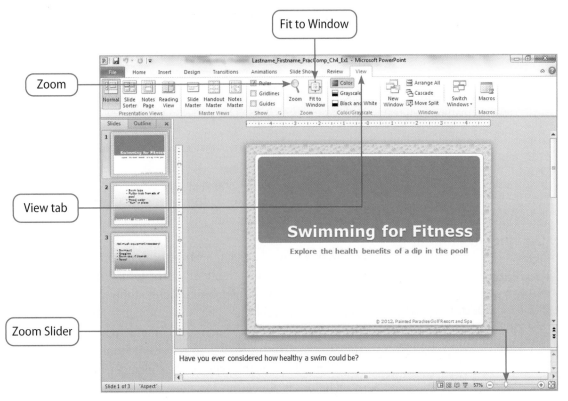

Figure 4.18 Zoom settings enable you to change the magnification of a slide.

type, and attributes (boldface, italics, and underlining), as well as alignment (left, right, or center) and spacing. A **font** is a character design, including typeface and spacing. One of the most compelling reasons to use PowerPoint is the capability to format slides to make them eye-catching and informative. Always keep in mind the need to convince or persuade your audience through your presentation. You can do that more effectively with appropriate color choice and readability.

If you know how you want a section of text to be formatted, you can choose the formatting option before typing. The most common formatting options are located on the Home tab (Figure 4.19). More often, however, you decide to format text in a certain way after you have placed text on a slide. In that case, drag to select the text or use one of the shortcut selection methods shown in Table 4.2, then apply the desired format. The Font dialog box (Figure 4.20)

Table 4.2 Select text using a shortcut method.	
To Select	**Do This**
A word	Double-click the word.
All text within a placeholder	Click in a placeholder. Then place the pointer on a border of the placeholder so the pointer becomes a four-headed arrow. Click.
A segment of text	Drag to highlight.
A full line of bulleted text	Place the pointer on a bullet so it becomes a four-headed arrow. Click.

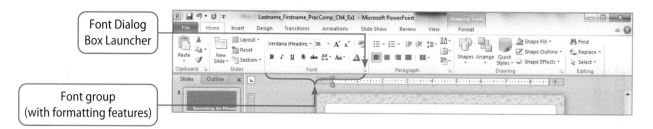

Figure 4.19 Use formatting options to change the appearance of slide text.

includes even more formatting options. Open the dialog box by clicking the Font Dialog Box Launcher (Figure 4.19) and select formatting to be applied to selected text.

When you select text, a **Mini toolbar** appears, as shown in Figure 4.21. The Mini toolbar contains frequently used formatting options, making them available near the selection so you can quickly apply a format (instead of looking for an option on the Ribbon). The Mini toolbar is almost transparent until you move the pointer close to it. Then it becomes brighter. If you prefer not to work with the Mini toolbar, press **Esc** to remove it from view.

Depending on the type of slide element (e.g., title, bulleted item), text in a placeholder is aligned in a certain way. It is most often centered or left aligned. However, you can change the **alignment** by selecting text and choosing an option in the Paragraph group on the Home tab, shown in Figure 4.22. You can also adjust **line spacing**, which is the amount of space between lines in a slide, as well as **paragraph spacing**, which is the amount of space between paragraphs. A paragraph is defined as text that ends with a hard return (when you press **Enter**). Basic line and paragraph spacing options are located in the Paragraph group on the Home tab. You will find additional selections when you click the Paragraph Dialog Box Launcher.

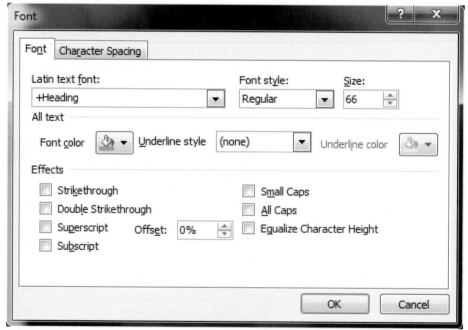

Figure 4.20 The Font dialog box provides even more formatting options.

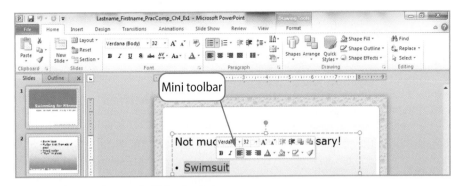

Figure 4.21 When you select text, the Mini toolbar displays.

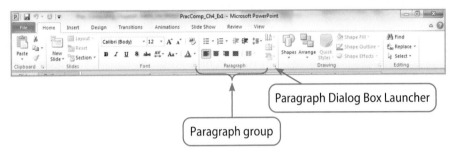

Figure 4.22 Change paragraph formatting using options in the Paragraph group.

Slides often include **bullets**, and even sub-bullets, which provide varying degrees of detail. A bullet is a small graphic, usually a dot or square, which denotes an item in a list or a speaker's point. The Title and Content slide layout, shown in Figure 4.23, is a very popular option because it provides a placeholder for bullets. For additional bullet detail, you might want to include a sub-bullet. For example, as a subcategory of a bulleted item *Desserts*, you might want to

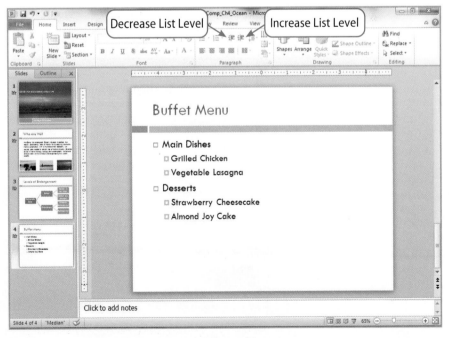

Figure 4.23 You can increase or decrease the level of a bullet on a slide.

include specific dessert items. For each dessert item listed, press **Tab** (or click **Increase List Level**). To move a bullet item back one level, press **Shift+Tab** (or click **Decrease List Level**).

Working with Themes

A theme is a presentation format that includes predetermined color, fonts, and effects such as shadowing or glows. In most cases, you will select a theme when you begin a presentation, so a uniform color scheme and background is automatically applied to all slides in the presentation. The nice thing about using a theme is that most of the work is done for you. It also saves time by helping you create a professional-looking slide show quickly. You simply add text and any other objects, such as tables or clip art.

Explore themes by clicking the **Design tab**. A series of themes is displayed in the Themes group as shown in Figure 4.24. Click **More** to see a full gallery of theme options. From there, you can even visit Microsoft's online gallery when you click **Browse for Themes**. For a quick preview, called **Live Preview**, of how a theme will look, place the pointer over a theme. Click a theme to apply it to all slides in the presentation (even those you have yet to create). You can change the design at any time by simply selecting another theme.

A theme includes not only color and a unique background, but font formatting as well. This means a theme will automatically apply orientation and font style settings to what you type. Even so, you are not locked into the predesigned color selection and font formatting. You can change the colors, font style and orientation, background style, and other effects of a theme by indicating preferences as shown in Figure 4.25. Each option—Colors, Fonts, and Effects—provides selections in a gallery. The Colors gallery is shown in Figure 4.26.

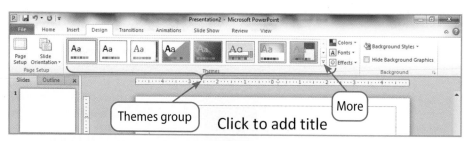

Figure 4.24 A theme includes predetermined color, fonts, and effects.

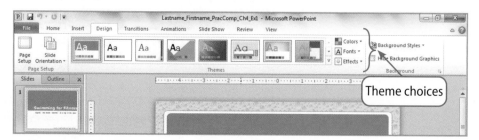

Figure 4.25 Theme options enable you to adjust a theme's effects.

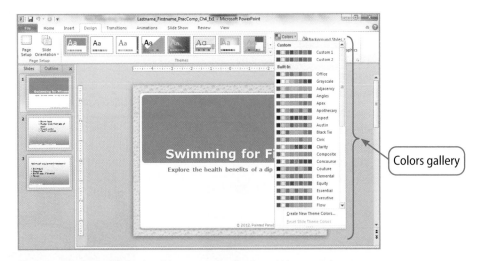

Figure 4.26 Each theme option, such as Colors, presents a gallery from which you can select.

Previewing and Printing a Presentation

For the most part, a presentation is designed to be projected on a large screen or otherwise made available for viewing on a display. You do not often think about printing a presentation, but sometimes you might want to do just that. Perhaps you want to make handouts for your audience. Or maybe you want to print your notes so you can refer to them during your presentation. You can even print the presentation outline as an audience handout or as a quick reference for yourself. Before printing anything, you should preview the printout, saving time and paper by making corrections before printing. You can adjust the page orientation, add headers and footers, and make other minor adjustments to page layout and print settings.

Including Headers and Footers

Headers and **footers** are areas of recurring information you can display on one or more slides (or only on notes and handouts). Using headers and footers, such as page or slide numbers, can help your audience keep track of the presentation's content. They can also help keep you on track during the presentation. You might even use headers and footers to keep your name, or your company's name, in front of the audience.

In Depth

Changing Background

A background style is a variation of the current theme colors. To slightly modify the current theme, without changing the heading and body text fonts or slide alignment, you can explore a set of related background styles. You can apply a background style to one or more slides within a presentation when you click the **Design tab** and then Background Styles. Place the pointer over any style to see a live preview of its effect on the current slide. Click a style to apply the style to all slides (or right-click a style and click **Apply to Selected Slides** to apply the style to only those slides you have selected). For even more options, click the **Design tab** and then Background Styles. Click **Format Background** to apply various fill effects, including gradient and texture designs. You can even select a personal photo as the background. Click **Apply to All** to apply the background design to all slides, or click **Close** to apply only to selected slides.

Hands-On

Activity 4.2 Creating and Formatting a Presentation

You decide to prepare an informative speech on the sport of show jumping, which involves riding a horse over a prescribed set of jumps in a closed arena. Having competed in the sport for the past five years, you are well versed in the intricacies of the sport and plan to develop a PowerPoint presentation to support the speech that you must give to your Speech class.

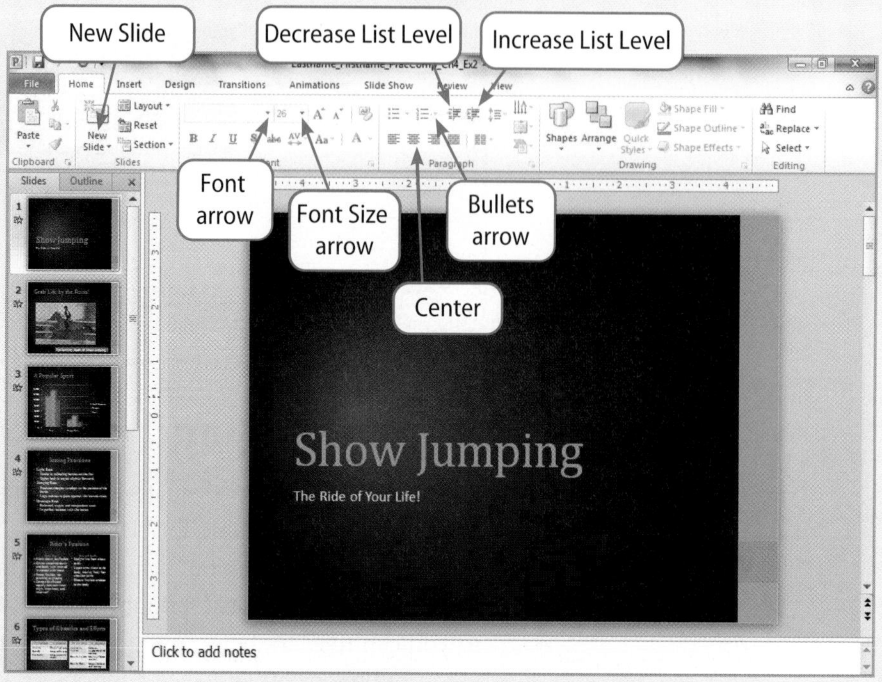

a. Open PowerPoint. A new blank presentation opens. Click the **File tab**. Click **Save As**. Navigate to the location where you will save your student files. Click the **File name box**. Type **Lastname_Firstname_ PracComp_Ch4_Ex2** Be sure to replace *Lastname* with your last name and *Firstname* with your first name. Click **Save**

b. Click the **Title placeholder** and type ***Show Jumping*** Click the **Subtitle placeholder** Type **The Ride of Your Life!**

c. Click the **Design tab**. Point to any theme in the Themes group to see a live preview of the theme on the current slide. Note that as you point to a theme, a ScreenTip provides the name of the theme. Click **Adjacency**. Click **Background Styles** in the Background group. Point to any style in the Background Styles gallery and note the ScreenTip that identifies the style. Click **Style 8**. Click **Colors** in the Themes group. Scroll through the Colors options and click **Horizon**

Figure 4.27 Use the Ribbon to format a presentation.

d. Click the **Home tab**. Click the **New Slide arrow** (Figure 4.27). Click **Title and Content** from the gallery of slide layouts. Click the **Title placeholder** and type **Correct Seating Positions** Click beside the bullet in the content placeholder. Type **The Light Seat** and press **Enter**. Type *The Jumping Seat* and press **Enter**. Type **The Dressage Seat** but do not press Enter.

TROUBLESHOOTING

If you make any mistakes throughout this exercise, click **Undo** on the Quick Access Toolbar and repeat the step in which the mistake occurred.

TROUBLESHOOTING

If you press Enter after the last bulleted item, a new bullet will display. Press **Backspace** twice to remove the bullet and return to the preceding line.

e. Double-click the word *Correct* in the Title placeholder to select it. You will delete the word because it is not necessary. Press **Delete**. Similarly, delete the word *The* that precedes each bullet item.

f. Click after the words *Light Seat* and press **Enter**. You will provide detail on the Light Seat, so the information should be indented under the major heading. Click **Increase List Level** (Figure 4.27) so the line becomes a sublevel of the preceding bullet.

g. Type **Useful in schooling horses on the flat** and press **Enter**. Type **Upper body is angled slightly forward**

h. Click after the words *Jumping Seat* and press **Enter.** Type the following two bulleted items, indenting them to become a sublevel of the Jumping Seat bullet

- **Position changes to adapt to the position of the horse**
- *Legs remain in place against the horse's sides*

i. Add the following two bullets after the *Dressage Seat* bullet, indenting each as a sublevel bullet

- **Balanced, supple, and independent seat**
- *In perfect balance with the horse*

j. Click the dashed line on the border of the bullet placeholder so it becomes solid. At that point, any formatting changes will affect all text within the placeholder. Click the **Font arrow**, scroll through the font selections, and select **Century Schoolbook**. Click the **Font Size arrow** and select **24**

k. Click the **Title placeholder**. Click **Center** in the Paragraph group.

l. Click the **New Slide arrow**. Select **Comparison** from the gallery of slide layouts.

m. Click the **Title placeholder** and type **Rider's Position** Center the title (see Step k). Click the **Title placeholder** on the left (at the top of the left column) and type **Lower Legs** Click the **Title placeholder** on the right (at the top of the right column) and type **Arms and Hands**

n. Click beside the first bullet on the left. Click the **Bullets arrow** and select a hollow round bullet. Type the following bulleted items, each at the same level

- **Heels down, but flexible**
- **Calves stretched down and back, with inner calf in contact with the horse**
- **Knees flexible, not pinching or gripping**
- **Contact distributed equally among inner thigh, inner knee, and inner calf**

o. Note the AutoFit Options icon that displays when text completely fills the placeholder. It enables you to select options related to fitting text within the placeholder.

p. Click beside the first bullet on the right. Click the **Bullets arrow** and select a hollow round bullet. Type the following bullets in the right placeholder

- **Straight line from elbow to bit**
- **Upper arms close to the body, moving freely from shoulder joints**
- **Elbows flexible and close to the body**

ON YOUR OWN

Add a new Title and Content slide after Slide 3. Type the title, **The Sport of Show Jumping** Center the title. Include two bullets at the same level. Type the first bullet, **Riding and jumping for fun** The second bullet should read **Harmony, unity, and cooperation between horse and rider** Change the font of the bulleted items to Century Schoolbook and the font size to 32.

q. Save the presentation and keep it open for the next exercise.

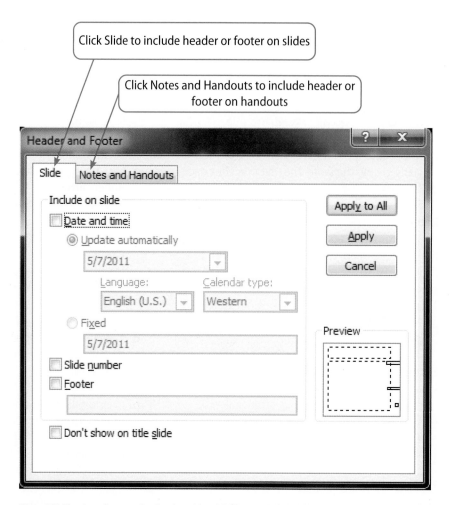

Figure 4.28 A header or footer can be placed on either slides or notes and handouts.

Although you can always change their placement later, headers and footers that are placed on slides are positioned according to the selected theme. Some themes might place a header in the top right corner, whereas others might reserve the lower left corner for headers. Similarly, the placement of footers can vary. To include a header or footer, click the **Insert tab** and then click **Header & Footer** in the Text group. From the dialog box shown in Figure 4.28, select a tab (either Slide or Notes and Handouts). Select or type the information you want to include in a header or footer. If applying the changes to slides, you can choose whether to apply them to all slides or only to selected slides. If applying the changes to your notes and handouts, you must apply them to all.

Modifying Print Properties, Previewing, and Printing

Before printing a PowerPoint presentation, you should consider exactly what you want to print. You can print slides, notes, or the presentation outline. When printing slides, you can indicate how many slides should print on each page. You might want only certain slides to print, or perhaps you want to specify that slides should print on both sides of the paper. To conserve printer ink, you can avoid color printing, opting instead for grayscale or black and white. You can even change the page orientation, printing a page in **landscape** (wider than it is tall) or **portrait** (taller than it is wide) orientation.

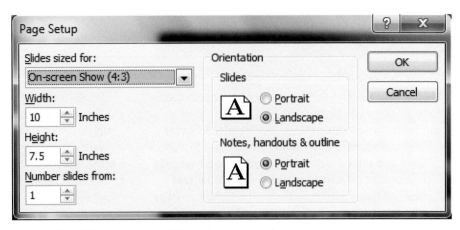

Figure 4.29 Adjust slide size and orientation before printing.

The Page Setup dialog box includes selections that enable you to adjust slide size and orientation. Click the **Design tab** and then click **Page Setup** to display the dialog box shown in Figure 4.29. Note that you can change the orientation of slides as well as notes and handouts. Other options enable you to adjust slide sizes for on-screen display as well as for various paper sizes. If you only want to change the orientation (portrait or landscape), click the **Design tab** and then click **Slide Orientation**. At that point, you can indicate the preferred orientation.

Many print settings are included in PowerPoint's Backstage view, which is available when you click the File tab. Click **Print** to access settings shown in Figure 4.30. Backstage view not only enables you to change print settings but also presents a preview to let you check the presentation before printing. As shown in Figure 4.30, you can indicate the number of copies and the printer to use. In addition, you can specify exactly what to print (slides, notes, or an outline) and you can select other print settings that will affect how a printout is to occur. After indicating all desired print settings, click **Print**.

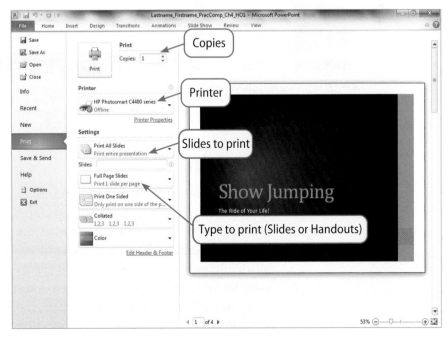

Figure 4.30 Select print options in PowerPoint's Backstage view.

Hands-On

Activity 4.3 Adjusting Print Settings and Printing

Although you are not yet ready to print your presentation, you will explore various print options.

a. Click the **Insert tab** and then click **Header & Footer**. Click the **Notes and Handouts tab** (Figure 4.31). Check **Date and time** and make sure **Update automatically** is selected. Check **Header**, click in the **Header text box** and type your first and last name. Make sure **Page number** is selected. Click **Apply to All**. The header will only appear at the top of any handouts that you print. It will not display at the top of your slides.

b. Click **Slide 1** in the Slides pane on the left. Click the **File tab** and click **Print**. A preview of the current slide shows on the right. Click **Next Page** to progress through the slides. Click **Full Page Slides** and then select **4 Slides Horizontal**. Click **Portrait Orientation** and then click **Landscape Orientation**. Note the header and footer at the top and bottom of the handout.

c. Click the **Copies up arrow** to increase the number of copies to 5. If you were going to print the handout, you could click Print. However, you will not print the handout at this time, so click the **Home tab** to leave Backstage view.

d. Click **Save** on the Quick Access Toolbar to save the presentation. Keep it open for the next exercise.

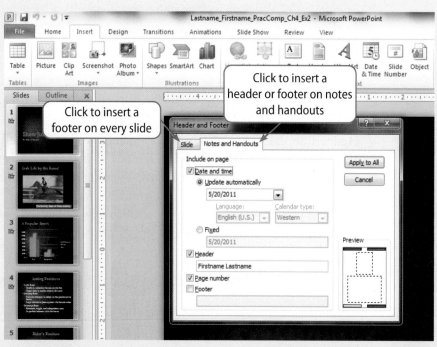

Figure 4.31 Include a header on notes and handouts.

Inserting Objects

Even for those of us who are artistically challenged, PowerPoint offers a way to stretch our creativity. By including objects such as clip art and pictures in a presentation, you can make it much more fun and informative for your audience. In addition, tables, charts, and SmartArt enable you to organize your thoughts pictorially or in a column format for better understanding. PowerPoint 2010 even includes the capability to insert screenshots (graphic images of a computer display), enabling you to prepare explanatory presentations related to a computer process or display. In this section, you will learn to include graphic objects, tables, charts, SmartArt, and text boxes.

Adding Clip Art and Pictures

When used correctly, graphics help hold audience attention by adding variety to your presentation. The challenge is to keep the inclusion of pictures and clip art to an effective level; make sure not to overuse graphics to the point of being distracting. **Clip art** is an electronic illustration (non-photographic drawing) that is available both online (in Microsoft's clip art gallery) and within a built-in library in a typical PowerPoint installation. A **picture** is any photograph or clip art image that is stored on a disk, such as a USB drive. Slightly misleading, the term *picture* is not restricted to photographs, but in fact is much broader, including any graphic housed on a disk. A picture could even be a photograph created with a digital camera. Clip art and pictures are considered objects. As such, they can be inserted on a slide, and adjusted in size, scale, and placement.

Some slide layouts include placeholders where you can insert an item of clip art, a chart, a table, or another type of non-text object. The easiest way to insert a picture or clip art is to select a slide layout containing an object placeholder. However, even if a slide layout does not include a placeholder, you can still insert an object. For example, the Title and Content layout (Figure 4.32) includes both a title and a content placeholder. Each icon in the placeholder is a link for a particular type of object. To insert clip art, click the **Clip Art icon**. To insert a picture, click the **Insert Picture from File icon**.

After clicking the Clip Art icon in the placeholder, you will see the Clip Art pane shown in Figure 4.33. Type a search term that describes the type of clip art you seek, and indicate the media sought (photographs, illustrations, videos, or audio). For more choice, be sure that the Include Office.com content box is selected. PowerPoint will display suggested matches in the form of thumbnails in the Clip Art pane. Click a thumbnail to place the clip art on the PowerPoint slide.

If you want to insert a picture (graphic saved on a disk), click the Insert Picture from File placeholder icon, and then browse to the location of the picture. Double-click the picture file to place it on the PowerPoint slide.

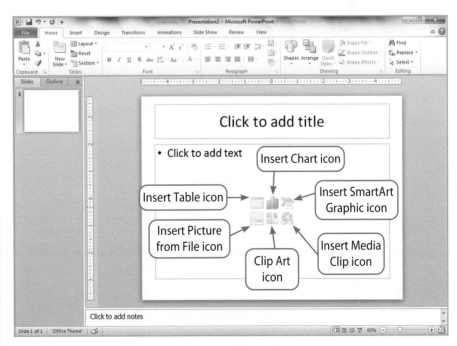

Figure 4.32 An object placeholder enables you to insert an object in a slide.

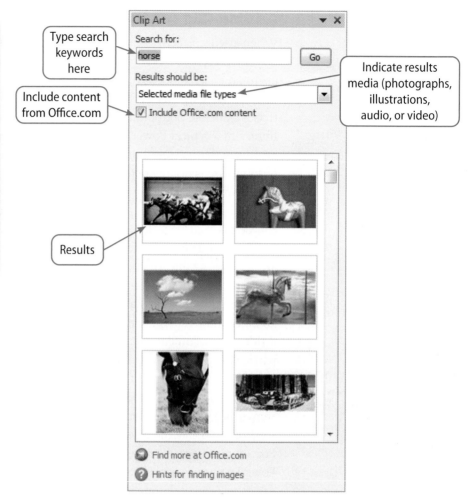

Figure 4.33 Use the Clip Art pane to locate clip art.

The inserted clip art or picture appears on the slide, surrounded by a box and **handles**, which are small squares or circles at each corner and in the middle of each side. When an object is *selected*, it is surrounded by a box and handles. As shown in Figure 4.34, a selected object causes a **contextual tab** to display on the Ribbon. A contextual tab includes one or more groups of commands related

In Depth

Including Color and Graphics

Including graphics and color in a presentation can help convey your message while holding the attention of the audience. Too much color and excitement, though, can actually be distracting. Keep these tips in mind when developing a presentation, so you hit just the right balance.

- Limit the number of graphics on each slide so the slide is clean and uncluttered.
- Use a consistent and subtle background on each slide.
- Use the same style graphics throughout the presentation. For example, if you begin with cartoon clip art, continue that theme throughout.
- Keep text on charts to a minimum. Use only enough to explain clearly.
- Limit the number of colors on a single chart to four.
- Use bright colors to make small objects and thin lines stand out. However, avoid using bright colors for text, as they are difficult to read when projected.

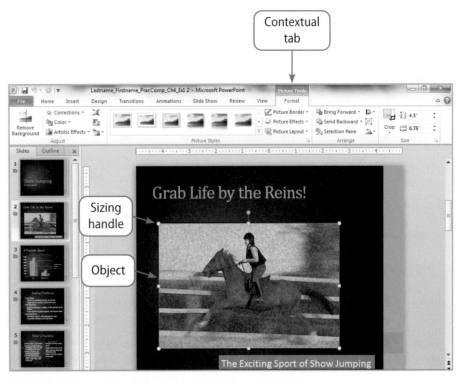

Figure 4.34 The Ribbon includes additional commands related to a selected object.

to the selected object. Using commands on a contextual tab, you can adjust the size, color, and placement of an object, among other things.

PowerPoint 2010 includes image editing functionality that enables you to adjust color, modify contrast and brightness, and add artistic effects to graphic objects. With a graphic selected, you can work with PowerPoint's image editing tools found in the Adjust group on the Format tab (Figure 4.35). Often a clip art or picture image is not the right color shade to match your presentation scheme. In that case, you can adjust the color to incorporate different shades or you can remove color altogether. Artistic effects can transform an ordinary graphic into an eye-catching and color-coordinated slide element.

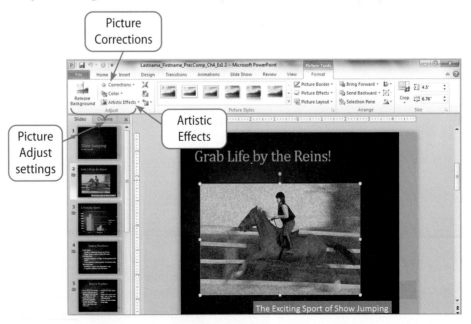

Figure 4.35 Adjust a picture's color and artistic effects.

Working with Charts

Charts are often included in presentations to convey numeric information in an understandable way. A **chart** can illustrate trends and summarize statistical data that might otherwise be presented as uninteresting columns of numbers. Experts suggest that an audience retains very little of a verbal presentation, but a much higher percentage of a combined verbal and visual presentation, including charts and diagrams.

Several slide layouts, including Title and Content, contain a placeholder with a chart icon (Figure 4.32). Click the icon to begin the process of creating a chart. If you are inserting a chart on a slide with no placeholder, click the **Insert tab** and then select **Chart**. After a chart is inserted, you can resize and move it just as you would a graphic object. With a chart selected, you can work with commands related to the chart on the Chart Tools tab.

To create a chart, you will enter data on a **datasheet** provided by Power-Point. A datasheet is similar to an Excel worksheet, in which you enter data in a series of columns and rows. The intersection of each column and row is called a cell. As you type data, PowerPoint builds a chart on the slide. Using commands on the tabs on the Chart Tools tab, you can modify the chart, adding titles and data labels, adjusting color, and working with other chart components to ensure that the chart is readable and understandable.

Working with Tables

A **table**, displaying data in columns and rows, can be effective in helping your audience understand details about your topic. Several slide layouts include a placeholder for a table, as shown in Figure 4.32. To create a table in a slide with a placeholder, click **Insert Table** and enter data in the table that displays. To move from one cell to the next, press **Tab** or simply click in the cell. You can insert a table on a slide without a placeholder when you click the **Insert tab** and click **Table.**

A table is considered an object. As you work within a table, the table is selected. A border and handles (small dotted areas in the corners and center of each side) surround the table, and a Table Tools tab displays on the Ribbon. Commands on the tab enable you to change the table size, insert and remove columns and rows, and select a table style or adjust colors and other settings. Figure 4.37 shows a PowerPoint table along with a tab on the Ribbon.

Exploring SmartArt

SmartArt is a feature that makes it easy to illustrate processes, lists, and relationships. Click **Insert SmartArt Graphic** in a slide placeholder (Figure 4.32) to select a SmartArt category, as shown in Figure 4.38. If your goal is to diagram a process or to illustrate an organizational chart, SmartArt is the tool to use. From the simplest diagrams to the most complex, SmartArt has options for all sorts of illustrations. Using the SmartArt tab, which displays on the Ribbon when a SmartArt diagram is selected, you can add, remove, and resize shapes. By selecting from SmartArt styles and color choices, you can color coordinate a SmartArt diagram with the color scheme of the presentation. SmartArt is an excellent way to graphically display relationships and processes to ensure that an audience understands your point.

Activity 4.4 Including Graphics and Charts

You will include appropriate clip art and charts to generate excitement and to further describe the sport of show jumping.

a. Click **Slide 4** in the Slides pane. Click the **New Slide arrow** Select **Title and Content** Click the **Title placeholder** Type **Grab Life by the Reins** and click **Center** in the Paragraph group on the Home tab.

b. Click the **Clip Art icon** 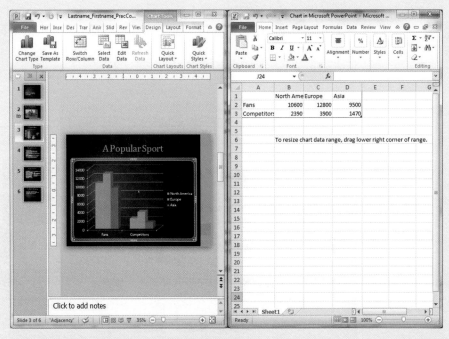 in the content place-holder. Click the **Search for box** in the Clip Art pane, remove any existing text, and type **horse** Click the **Results should be arrow** and deselect all categories except Photographs. Click **Go** Scroll through the list of results to identify the photograph shown in Figure 4.35. If the photograph is not available, identify another. Click the photograph to insert it on the slide.

c. On the Format tab, click the **Height down arrow** repeatedly in the Size group to decrease the picture height to 4.5" (or click the **Height box** and type 4.5). Point to the picture until the mouse pointer becomes a four-headed arrow. Drag to position the picture approximately as shown in Figure 4.35.

d. Click **Artistic Effects** in the Adjust group. Click **Watercolor Sponge** (row 3, column 2). Select **Soft Edge Rectangle** (sixth from left) in the Picture Styles group. Close the Clip Art pane.

e. Drag Slide 5 in the Slides pane to position it after Slide 1 (so that it becomes Slide 2). Click the **Home tab**, if necessary. Click the **New Slide arrow** Click **Title and Content** Click the **Title placeholder** and type **A Popular Sport** Center the title.

f. Click **Insert Chart** in the content placeholder. Click **3-D Clustered Column** (fourth from left) and click **OK** Click **Series 1** in the datasheet, type **North America** and press **Enter**. Click **Series 2**, type **Europe** and press **Enter**. Click **Series 3**, type **Asia** and press **Enter**. Click **Category 1**, type **Fans** and press **Enter**. Click **Category 2**, type **Competitors** and press **Enter**. Complete the datasheet as shown below, clicking or tabbing to position the pointer in each cell before typing

	North America	Europe	Asia
Fans	10600	12800	9500
Competitors	2390	3900	1470

g. To remove the unnecessary rows, click to the left of Category 3 and drag to the next row, highlighting both rows. Right-click in either of the selected rows and click **Delete**. Click any cell to deselect the rows. The slide should display as shown in Figure 4.36. Close the datasheet.

h. Save the presentation. Keep it open for the next exercise.

Figure 4.36 Using a datasheet, you can create a chart.

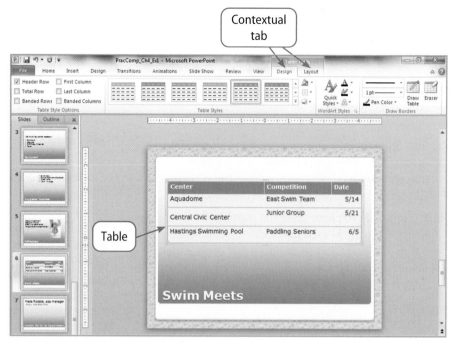

Figure 4.37 A table shows columns and rows of data.

Including Shapes and Text Boxes

A **text box** is a rectangular area on a slide, in which you can type text. For example, you might include a text box at the bottom of the current slide with your contact information or a company slogan. Resizing a text box is easy, as is adjusting font size and color and identifying text box effects such as background, shadowing, and bordering. To insert a text box, click the **Insert tab** and then select **Text Box** in the Text group. A Drawing Tools tab enables you to modify the text box, changing its size, background color, font color, and alignment. In addition, you can add interesting text effects, and you can even change the orientation of the text box so it reads vertically instead of horizontally.

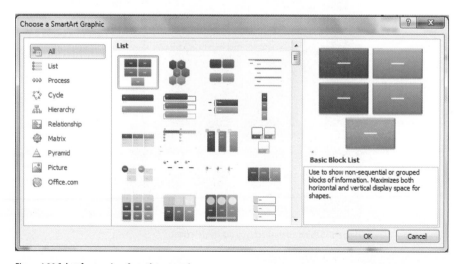

Figure 4.38 Select from various SmartArt categories.

Hands-On

Activity 4.5 Inserting Tables and Text Boxes

You will include a discussion of jump obstacles, which are easily described in a table format. For added emphasis, you will include a text box.

a. Click **Slide 5** in the Slides pane. Click the **New Slide arrow** on the Home tab and select **Comparison**. Click the **Title placeholder**, type **Types of Obstacles and Effects** and click **Center** in the Paragraph group. Click the **Title placeholder** on the left and type *Fences* Click the **Title placeholder** on the right and type *Combinations*

b. Click **Insert Table** in the content placeholder on the left and type **2** columns and **4** rows. Click **OK**. With the insertion point in the upper-left corner of the table, type **Fence** Press **Tab** and type **Effect** Pressing **Tab** between each entry, complete the table as shown below (also see Figure 4.39)

Vertical	*Short, high jump*
Spread	*Long, wide jump*
Liverpool	*Long, powerful stride*

c. Click **Insert Table** in the content placeholder on the right and type **2** columns and **4** rows. Click **OK**. Complete the table as shown below. Disregard any red wavy underlines that appear beneath possible misspellings (unless the word is actually misspelled). The underlines will not appear in a slide show

Combination	*Effect*
Vertical to Vertical	*Balance, engagement, and accuracy*
Oxer to Vertical	*Excellent balance control*
Oxer to Oxer	*Scope, balance, and accuracy*

d. Click the **table border** to select the table on the right, if necessary. Click **Medium Style 2 - Accent 4** (fifth from left) in the Table Styles group. Click the **table border** to select the table on the left and apply **Medium Style 2 – Accent 4** style.

e. Click **Slide 2** in the Slides pane. Click the **Insert tab** and click **Text Box** in the Text group. Move the pointer over the slide and note the small dashed bars on the horizontal and vertical ruler that indicate the position of the pointer. Position the pointer at -2 on the horizontal ruler and -3 on the vertical ruler, and click.

TROUBLESHOOTING

If the Ruler does not display, click the **View tab** and select **Ruler** in the Show group.

f. Type **The Exciting Sport of Show Jumping** Position the pointer on the border of the text box so it appears as a four-headed arrow and click. The dashed border should now appear as a solid line, indicating that all text within the text box is selected. Change the font size to **28**. Position the pointer on the text box so it appears as a four-headed arrow. Drag the text box to position it at the lower-right corner of the black slide background.

g. Click the **Format tab** and click **Shape Fill** in the Shape Styles group. Click **Gold Text 2, Darker 25%** (row 5, column 4).

h. Save the presentation. Keep it open for the next exercise.

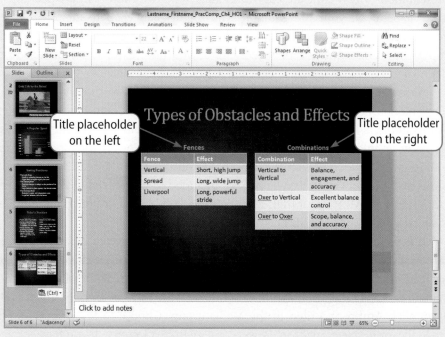

Figure 4.39 A slide can include more than one table.

Technology Insight

Converting iTunes for a PowerPoint Slide

iTunes music selections are saved in MP4 format, which is a file type that cannot be included in a PowerPoint presentation. With just a little effort, you can convert an MP4 file into MP3 format, which can then be inserted in a presentation. First select the track in your iTunes library and burn it to a CD. Then open Windows Media Player (Start, All Programs, Windows Media Player) and select the music track that you want to include. Rip the music into WMA format. Right-click the track and click **Send to Windows Audio Converter**. Choose **MP3 format** and save it to a folder. Then in the PowerPoint presentation, click the **Insert tab** and click **the Audio arrow**, Click **Audio from File**, navigate to the track, and double-click.

Occasionally, you might want to include a shape on a slide. When you click the **Insert tab** and then select **Shapes**, you can select from a gallery of shapes. Drag to place the shape on a slide. Just as with other objects, you can resize a shape by dragging a corner handle, or you can move a shape by dragging from the center of the shape. The Drawing Tools tab includes a variety of options related to the shape, such as color, size, and alignment.

Adding Multimedia

You are not limited to text and graphics when using PowerPoint 2010. You can also include **audio** and **video**. You may wish to play a track from a CD while a presentation is running. Or you might locate a music selection online you want to use. You can also include music files from your music library if you like. You can even use a microphone to record a sound or narration to support your presentation. Video clips are easy to include; you can even trim a video clip to make it better fit your presentation. You might even want to include a video you recorded with a digital camera. Remember that you should not include copyright-protected music or videos unless you have explicit permission from the owner.

Although PowerPoint's Clip Art Library includes very short video animation and sound clips, you will most often include music and video from files. For example, a CD track or a song in your iTunes library is considered a file; similarly, an informational video that you locate online or on YouTube is a video file. Sound and video files are available in various file types. PowerPoint supports most file types, but not all. A sound file included in a PowerPoint 2010 presentation must be AIFF, AU, MIDI, MP3, WAV, or WMA type. A video file must be SWF, ASF, AVI, MPG (or MPEG), or WMV.

If the slide with which you are working includes a content placeholder, you can click **Insert Media Clip** to begin the process of inserting a video file. Simply navigate to the file's location and double-click the video. If the slide does not contain a placeholder, you can insert audio or video by clicking the **Insert tab**. Then click **Audio** or **Video** in the Media group. Choose to insert an audio or video file, or to select one from PowerPoint's Clip Art Library. If you have located an online video, choose to insert a video from a website. If you plan to record

Hands-On

Activity 4.6 Inserting Audio and Video

At a recent competition, you recorded the ride of a person who was on your show jumping team. You will include the video in your presentation so your audience can see an actual show jumping round.

a. Select Slide 6 in the Slides pane. Insert a new slide with the Title and Content layout. Click the **Title placeholder** and type **A Show Jumping Round** Center the title.

b. Click **Insert Media Clip** in the content placeholder, navigate to the location of your data files, and double-click **PracComp_Ch4_Jump**. Click **Play** in the Preview group on the Format tab. Watch the video, noting that it might be a little long for your presentation and that the background noise is distracting. The video is also somewhat choppy at the end, so you will trim (remove) the final few seconds.

c. Click **Simple Frame, White** (sixth from left) in the Video Styles group on the Format tab. Click the **Video Border arrow** and select **Gold Text 2, Darker 25%** (row 5, column 4). Click the **Playback tab**. Click the **Start arrow** in the Video Options group and select **Automatically**. Click **Volume** and select **Mute** to remove the background noise. Change the **Fade In** and **Fade Out** durations in the Editing group to **1.00**. Click **Play** to preview the video.

d. Click **Trim Video** in the Editing group. Drag the red end indicator to the left so that End Time shows

approximately 39.5 seconds. Click **OK**. Click **Play** to view the shortened video.

e. Click the **Insert tab** and click the **Audio arrow** in the Media group. Click **Audio from File**. Click **Music** in the left pane of the Insert Audio dialog box, and double-click **Sample Music**. If sample music selections are displayed, double-click a selection. If no sample music selections are displayed, skip to Step H.

f. Click **Playback** on the Audio Tools tab. An audio icon displays on the slide, indicating that an audio clip is inserted, as shown in Figure 4.40. Click **Hide During Show** to hide the audio icon during the slide show. Click the **Start arrow** in the Audio Options group and select **Automatically**.

g. With the audio icon selected, click the **Animations tab** and click **Move Earlier** (under Reorder Animation in the Timing group), so the music will play along with the video, instead of after the video. Click near the video border on Slide 7 to select the video. Click the **Start arrow** in the Timing group on the Animations tab and select **With Previous**. You will explore animation in the next section of this chapter.

h. Drag Slide 7 to position it beneath Slide 8.

i. Click the **Slide Show tab** and click **From Current Slide** in the Start Slide Show group. Press **Esc** when the video ends.

j. Save the presentation. Keep it open for the next exercise.

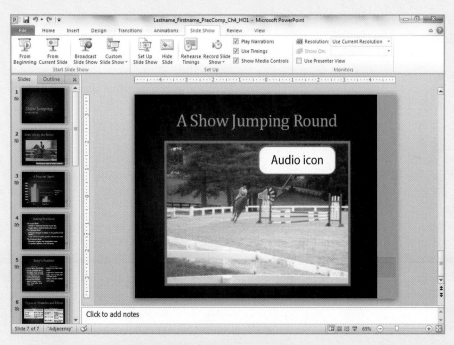

Figure 4.40 You can include both video and audio in a PowerPoint presentation.

narration for your slide show, choose the Record Audio option. After inserting an audio or video component, select options on the Video or Audio Tools tab related to the format or playback of the sound or video.

After having inserted an audio or video file, you will find options on the Audio Tools or Video Tools tab that enable you to adjust the volume, trim the video, and fade in or out. You can also modify the appearance of the video window by resizing it as you would any other object, or adding a frame or style effect. Click **Play** to preview the media.

Adding Transitions and Animation

Transitions and animation add energy to the delivery. Although you certainly do not want transitions and animation to detract from your message, a little on-screen movement could be just the thing to liven up the presentation and hold audience attention. A **transition** is the movement from one slide to another. **Animation** includes entrance, exit, and emphasis effects of slide elements such as titles, bullets, and objects. For example, a picture on a slide that slowly fades in, or a title that spins in, are examples of animated items. A transition effect can be the fading out of one slide, while another fades in. Or it could take the form of a checkerboard approach, where a slide fills the screen gradually in blocks of color. Many transition and animation effects are available in PowerPoint 2010. The choice of transition or animation, if any, is up to you. Your creativity is endless! The challenge, quite simply, is to refrain from overwhelming a presentation with too many animation and transition effects.

PowerPoint 2010 includes a Transitions tab and an Animations tab. Each tab includes groups of commands related to assigning and configuring transitions or animations. You can apply a transition to the current slide or to all slides. Click the **Transitions tab** and then select from a gallery of transitions. Click **More** for even more choice, as shown in Figure 4.41. Click to select a transition. If you want to apply the transition to all slides, click **Apply to All**. If you do not apply the effect to all slides, it will affect only the current slide. You can also adjust the transition speed and add a sound effect. New to PowerPoint 2010, you can also identify a duration for the transition.

In preparation for your slide show, you will also need to decide whether you want the slides to advance automatically after a certain number of seconds or to advance only when you click the mouse. The Advance Slide options (Figure 4.41) enable you to select either automatic or mouse-driven slide

Quick Tip

Using Animation Painter

Especially if you have applied several animation effects to an object, you will find the Animation Painter useful in applying all of those animation effects to another object. Select the object with animation effects assigned. Click the **Animations tab** and click **Animation Painter**. Then select the object that you want to copy the animation effects to. All animation effects are applied. Use the Animation Pane if you want to remove or adjust any of the newly added animations.

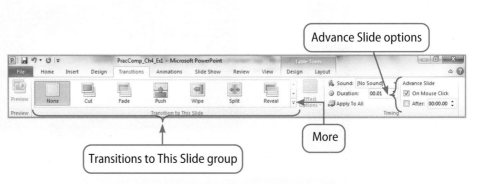

Figure 4.41 Select from transition options to control the way one slide progresses into another.

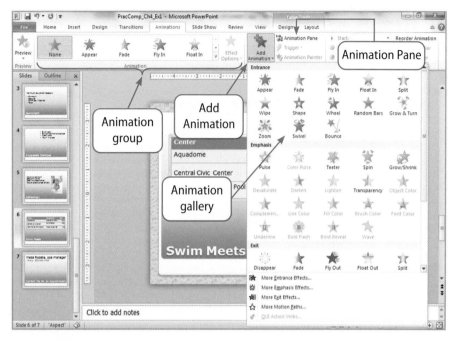

Figure 4.42 Select an animation from the Animation gallery.

advancement. If your presentation is to be shown at a trade show or in a constantly repeating format, you will probably want to make your slides advance automatically. If, however, you are presenting your topic personally, you will want to use the mouse to advance.

To add animation to an item on a slide, such as a title or an object, display the slide in Normal view and select the item. Click the **Animations tab** and point to any animation effect in the Animation gallery. Click **Add Animation** for even more choices, as shown in Figure 4.42. Having assigned an animation effect, you can click **Effect Options** to further define the manner in which the animation is to occur (from which direction it should appear, etc.). When working with several animation effects on the same slide, you might want to reorder the effects, or perhaps you want to apply several animations to one item, as is the case if you want the item to appear in one manner and depart in another. All those tasks are possible when you click Animation Pane to open a task pane dedicated to animation order, effects, and timing.

Hands-On

Activity 4.7 Adding Transitions and Animation

As you finalize the presentation, you will add transitions and animations so the slide show progresses smoothly and is as attractive as possible.

a. Click the **Slide Show tab** and click **From Beginning** in the Start Slide Show group. Click to progress from one slide to another as you view the slide show. Press **Esc** or click when the video on the last slide ends.

b. Click the **View tab** and click **Slide Sorter** in the Presentation Views group. Click **Slide 1**.

c. Click the **Transitions tab** and click **Wipe** in the Transition to This Slide group. Click **Apply To All** in the Timing group. Note the small star below each slide, indicating a transition.

d. Click **Slide Show** at the lower-right corner of the status bar. Click to progress through the slides, noting the transition effect. If you do not want to view the video in its entirety, click when the video begins and then click once more to end the slide show and return to Slide Sorter view.

TROUBLESHOOTING

If the transition effect is only active on one slide, you did not apply the effect to all slides. Select any slide and repeat Step c.

e. Double-click **Slide 2** to display it in Normal view. Click the picture to select it. Click the **Animations tab**. Place the pointer over any effect in the Animation group to see a preview of the effect on the picture. Click **Fade**. Click the **Start arrow** and select **After Previous**.

f. Select the text box at the bottom of Slide 2. Click **Fade** in the Animations group. Click the **Start arrow** and select **After Previous**.

g. Click **Slide 3**. Click near a border of the chart to select the entire chart. The border showing the selected area should surround the entire chart, as shown in Figure 4.43. If, in addition to the border, you see small dots (indicating another chart selection), click nearer an outside border of the chart. Click **Float In** in the Animations group. Click **Effect Options**. Click **By Series**.

h. Move Slide 7 between Slides 2 and 3, so it becomes Slide 3.

i. Click the **Slide Show tab**. Click **From Beginning**. View the slide show, clicking to progress between slides. Click once more at the end of the slide show to return to Normal view.

ON YOUR OWN

Click **Slide 6** and then click the left bullet placeholder. Apply a Fade animation that starts After Previous. Similarly, apply a Fade animation, starting After Previous, to the right bullet placeholder. View the slide show to see the effect of the new animation.

j. Save the presentation and exit PowerPoint.

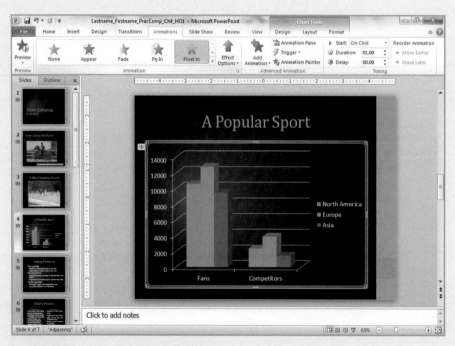

Figure 4.43 Objects, such as this chart, can be animated.

Technology Insight

Saving a Presentation as a Movie

You will often want to share presentations with others. Perhaps your presentation is a collection of photos from a recent trip and you want to make that presentation available to other family members. You can save the slide show in a format that is easily accessible by others, without the need for PowerPoint or any other specialized software. Windows-based computers typically include Windows Media Player, which is software that facilitates access to videos or music. By saving a presentation in WMV format, you can be sure that almost anyone can view the presentation. Follow the steps below to convert a PowerPoint presentation into WMV format.

1. Click the **File tab** and then click **Save As**.
2. Click **Save as type** and select **Windows Media Video**.
3. Click in the File name box and supply a filename. Navigate to the desired save location and click **Save**.

For even more options related to saving the slide show as a movie, click the **File tab** and then click **Save & Send**. Click **Create a Video** and select from available options. Click **Create Video**.

Chapter Summary

- Presentation software enables you to deliver information using text, charts, animation, and color in a series of slides. *135*

- A slide show is a series of slides displayed in full-screen view. *137*

- As you design a slide show, it is important to understand your audience. *136*

- PowerPoint 2010 is the leader in the field of presentation software. *136*

- A theme is a predesigned presentation format that includes fonts, backgrounds, and color. *154*

- PowerPoint includes four views: Normal, Slide Sorter, Notes Page, and Reading View. *141*

- You can format text in a slide much like you do in a Word document—by underlining, italicizing, and aligning text. *151*

- Clip art, pictures, SmartArt, and other images can be included in a PowerPoint presentation. *160*

- A slide can include audio and video. *169*

- Charts and tables included in a presentation help convey information in an understandable way. *164*

- You can move, edit, and delete slides. *150*

- Animation and transition effects can be applied to individual slides. *170*

- You can print slides and handouts. *155*

- Headers and footers can provide identifying information on slides and handouts. *155*

Key Terms

Multiple Choice

1. The PowerPoint view that displays slides as thumbnails so you can easily select and rearrange them is
   a. Slide Sorter.
   b. Normal.
   c. Notes Page.
   d. Slide Show.

2. A picture on a slide that slowly fades in, or a chart that floats in from the bottom are examples of
   a. transition.
   b. slide movement.
   c. progression.
   d. animation.

3. A contextual tab appears on the Ribbon when
   a. Backstage view is selected.
   b. you right-click a slide.
   c. a slide is animated.
   d. an object is selected.

4. The feature that enables you to diagram processes, lists, and relationships is
   a. WordArt.
   b. SmartArt.
   c. Charts.
   d. Text boxes.

5. A rectangular area in which you can include such items as contact information or a company slogan is a
   a. text box.
   b. table icon.
   c. tab.
   d. data box.

6. Which of the following is not considered an object?
   a. Table
   b. Bullet
   c. Chart
   d. Picture

7. You can tell that an object is selected because it
   a. will be surrounded by a black frame.
   b. will include a graphic just beneath the object.
   c. will be shaded much darker than other parts of the slide.
   d. will be surrounded by a border and sizing handles.

8. The Notes pane provides space for
   a. notes you can refer to while presenting a slide show.
   b. a footer.
   c. links to websites you can access during a presentation.
   d. footnotes.

9. A small graphic that denotes a list is a
   a. sublevel.
   b. clip art selection.
   c. graphic object.
   d. bullet.

10. A background style is
    a. a color scheme that displays during a slide transition.
    b. a variation of the theme colors.
    c. only available if you have not already selected a theme.
    d. a template downloaded from Office.com.

11. A theme includes
    a. predetermined slide color, fonts, and effects.
    b. background slide color only.
    c. slide color, graphics, and SmartArt.
    d. font and alignment settings, but no color or other special effects.

12. A collection of visual options from which you can choose is a(n)
    a. gallery.
    b. object set.
    c. menu.
    d. list.

13. To select all text within a placeholder
    a. click the Select tab and click Select All.
    b. click the dashed line surrounding the placeholder to make it solid.
    c. click Select All on the status bar.
    d. double-click the placeholder.

14. The object that best illustrates trends and summarizes statistics is
    a. SmartArt.
    b. Clip Art.
    c. a text box.
    d. a chart.

15. You can change the PowerPoint view in both of these places:
    a. The Page Layout tab and the View button above the vertical scroll bar.
    b. The View tab and the right side of the status bar.
    c. The View tab and the Home tab. .
    d. The Page Layout tab and the Zoom Slider.

True/False

Circle **T** if the statement is true or **F** if the statement is false.

T   F   1. Backstage view enables you to preview a presentation, but not to print it.

T   F   2. When developing a slide show, you can configure slides to advance automatically or only when clicked.

T   F   3. A transition adds energy and emphasis to individual slide elements, such as pictures, tables, and bullets.

T   F   4. Format Painter enables you to copy animation from one object to another.

T   F   5. Headers and footers cannot be moved.

T   F   6. The only object that cannot be animated is a chart.

T   F   7. In Normal view, the left pane includes two tabs—Outline and Slides.

T   F   8. It is always a good idea to include a PowerPoint presentation when making a speech.

T   F   9. Reading View, which shows multiple slides as thumbnails, is an effective way to manage multiple slides.

T   F   10. Undo is located on the Quick Access Toolbar.

End of Chapter Exercises

Guided Projects

1. As a volunteer for the Red Cross, you have been asked to prepare a PowerPoint presentation for an elementary school. The slide show will present CPR basics at a level that is understandable for young children. Use the following steps to design the presentation.

   a. Open PowerPoint. Click the **File tab** and click **Save As**. Navigate to the location where you save your student files and save the file as **Lastname_Firstname_PracComp_Ch4_CPR**

   b. Click the **Title placeholder** and type **Basics of CPR** Click the **Subtitle placeholder** and type **Saving a Life**

   c. Click the **Design tab** and select **Austin** in the Themes group. Click the **Home tab**, click the **New Slide arrow**, and click **Title and Content**.

   d. Click the **Title placeholder** and type **What is Cardiopulmonary Resuscitation (CPR)?** Click the **text placeholder** (beside the first bullet) and type **First-aid technique to keep a victim of cardiac arrest alive until medical help arrives** Press **Enter**. Type **CPR has two goals:** Press **Enter**.

   e. Press **Tab** to increase the indent level. Type **Keep blood flowing throughout the body** and press **Enter**. Type **Keep air flowing in and out of the lungs**

   f. Click the **dashed line surrounding the text placeholder** so it becomes solid. Click the **Paragraph Dialog Box Launcher.** Click the **Spacing After up arrow** twice to increase spacing after to 12 pt. Click **OK**.

   g. Click the **Title placeholder** and then click the **placeholder border**. Click the **Font Size arrow** on the Home tab and select **40**.

   h. Add a new slide with the Title and Content layout (see the latter part of Step c). Click the **Title placeholder** and type **Anyone Can Learn!** Click the **Clip Art icon** in the content placeholder to open the Clip Art pane. Click the **Search for: box** and remove any existing text. Type **CPR** Make sure to include Office.com content, and click the **Results should be arrow**. Select **Illustrations** and **Photographs**.

   Deselect any other media. Click **Go**. Click a photograph or illustration that depicts CPR.

   i. Adjust the picture height in the Size group to **4**. With the clip art selected, click **Reflected Rounded Rectangle** (fifth from left) in the Picture Styles group. Reposition the clip art, if necessary, so it is centered beneath the slide title (move the clip art when the pointer appears as a four-headed arrow). Close the Clip Art pane.

   j. Click the **Home tab**. Add a new slide with the Title and Content layout. Click the **Title placeholder** and type **CPR Steps** Click the **Insert Table icon** in the content placeholder. The table should include **2** columns and **4** rows. In the top left cell, type **Action** Press **Tab** and type **Result** Continue tabbing between cells, completing the table as follows.

Position victim's head back, pinch the nose, and blow into victim's mouth	Force oxygenated air into the lungs
Compress the victim's chest 30 times	Artificially recreate blood circulation
Repeat steps	Victim begins to breathe on own (hopefully!)

   k. Click the **Home tab**. Add a new slide with a Title and Content layout. Type the title **Let's Watch!** Click the **Insert Media Clip icon** in the content placeholder. Navigate to the location of your student data files and double-click **PracComp_Ch4_CPR**. Click **Center Shadow Rectangle** (second from left) in the Video Styles group. Click the **Playback tab** and click the **Start arrow** in the Video Options group. Select **Automatically**. Click **Play** (in the Preview group, or under the video on the slide) to watch the video.

   l. Drag Slide 3 to position it between Slides 1 and 2.

   m. Click the **View tab** and click **Slide Sorter** in the Presentations group. Click the **Transitions tab** and click **Push** in the Transition to This Slide group. Click **Effect Options**. Click **From Left**. Click **Apply to All** in the Timing group.

n. Double-click **Slide 3** to open it in Normal view. Click **the text placeholder** (with the bulleted items) to select it. Click the **Animations tab**. Click **Fade** in the Animation group.

o. Click the **Slide Show tab** and select **From Beginning** in the Start Slide Show group. Click to progress from one slide to another. Press **Esc** at the end of the video.

p. Save the presentation and exit PowerPoint.

2. As a recent graduate in marine biology, you are working at the Center for Endangered Ocean Life. Located on Dauphin Island in Alabama, the Center is actively involved in promoting awareness of endangered species and soliciting public and private funding. You will develop a brief PowerPoint presentation that will be placed on the Center's Web page. Use the following steps to design the presentation.

a. Open PowerPoint. Click the **File tab** and click **Save As**. Navigate to the location where you save your student files and save the file as *Lastname_Firstname_PracComp_Ch4_Ocean*

b. Click the **Design tab** and click **More** ⏷ in the Themes group. Click **Median**. Click the **Title placeholder** and type **Center for Endangered Ocean Life** Regardless of how you type the title, it will appear in all caps. Click the **Subtitle placeholder** and type **Making a Difference**

c. Click the **Home tab**. Click the **New Slide arrow** and select **Title Only**. Click the **Title placeholder** and type **Who Are We?**

d. Click the **Insert tab** and click **Text Box** in the Text group. Click just below the top left corner of the blue horizontal bar and drag to create a box the width of the bar. Remember to click **Undo** on the Quick Access Toolbar if you make a mistake. The height is irrelevant at this point, so just make sure the box encompasses the width of the bar. Type **The Center for Endangered Ocean Life seeks to address the rapidly deteriorating state of marine life by applying science to marine conservation. With a multidisciplinary approach, we provide data needed to prevent loss of marine diversity. Scientists skilled in marine biology, ecology, and oceanography collect and analyze data on the numerous challenges facing the world's oceans.**

e. Proofread the paragraph and make any corrections necessary. Click the **Format tab** and then click the **Height box** in the Size group. Type **3** Click the **Width box** and type **9** Press **Enter**. Click the dashed line surrounding the text box to make it solid. Click the **Home tab**. Click the **Font Size arrow** and select **24**.

f. Click the **Insert tab** and click **Picture** in the Images group. Navigate to the location of your student data files and double-click **PracComp_Ch4_Sunset**. Click the **Height box** in the Size group and type **2** Press **Enter**. Move the pointer to the center of the picture so the pointer appears as a four-headed arrow. Drag the picture to the lower-left corner of the slide.

g. Repeat Step f, but insert a picture titled **PracComp_Ch4_Surfer**, adjust the picture height to 2, and position the picture in the lower-center of the slide. Repeat Step f again, but insert a picture titled **PracComp_Ch4_Sunrise**, adjust its height to 2, and position the picture in the lower-right corner of the slide.

h. Click the first picture, press and hold **Ctrl**, and click each of the remaining pictures. All pictures should be bordered with handles, indicating that they are all selected. Click **Align,** 🖼 and then click **Align to Slide** (unless a check mark already appears beside Align to Slide). Click **Align** 🖼 and click **Align Bottom**. Click **Align** 🖼 and click **Distribute Horizontally**. Click **Soft Edge Rectangle** in the Picture Styles group.

i. Click the **Home tab** and insert a new slide with the Title and Content layout. Click the **Title placeholder** and type **Levels of Endangerment** Click **Insert SmartArt Graphic** 🖼 in the content placeholder. Click **Hierarchy** and select **Horizontal Hierarchy** (row 3, column 4). Click **OK**.

j. Click in the first shape on the left and type **Adequate Data** Click in the remaining shapes and complete the SmartArt diagram as follows.

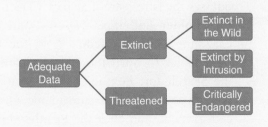

k. Right-click the **Critically Endangered shape**, point to **Add Shape**, and click **Add Shape After**. Type **Endangered**

l. Click **Change Colors** in the SmartArt Styles group. Click **Gradient Loop – Accent 2** (fourth selection under Accent 2).

m. Select **Slide 1** in the Slides pane. Click the **Design tab**. Click **Background Styles** in the Background group and click **Format Background**. Click **Picture or texture fill**. Click **File**. Navigate to the location of your student data files and double-click **PracComp_ Ch4_Beach**. Click **Close**.

n. Click the Title placeholder (containing the text *Center for Endangered Ocean Life*). Place the pointer on a border of the placeholder until the pointer appears as a four-headed arrow. Drag the placeholder to the upper-left corner of the slide.

o. Click the **Home tab**. Click the **Font Size arrow** and select **28**.

p. Select Slide 3. Insert a new slide with the Title and Content layout. Click the **Title placeholder** and type **What You Can Do** Click beside the bullet and type **Learn all you can about the**

threats facing the ocean and marine life Press **Enter**. Press **Tab** to increase the list level of the bullet and type **Read up on how to protect the ocean** Press **Enter** and type **Consult a marine biologist** Press **Enter**. Click **Decrease List Level** in the Paragraph group. Type the following three bullets:

- **Vote for candidates who support marine conservation**
- **Practice safe and clean boating**
- **Visit www.marinelifeaction.com for more information**

q. Click the **View tab** and click **Slide Sorter** in the Presentation Views group. Select **Slide 1**. Click the **Transitions tab** and select **Split** in the Transition to This Slide group. Click **Apply to All**.

r. Double-click **Slide 4** to open the slide in Normal view. Click the bullet placeholder. Click the **Animations tab** and click **Fade** in the Animation group.

s. Click the **Slide Show tab** and click **From Beginning** in the Start Slide Show group. Click to progress through all slides.

t. Save the presentation and exit PowerPoint.

Unguided Project

1. As a project for your history class, you are assigned the task of selecting a well-known disaster, such as the Titanic, and developing a series of slides to describe the event. You have chosen to explore the disaster of the Challenger, the shuttle that exploded on January 28, 1986.

   a. Open PowerPoint and save the blank presentation to the location of your student projects as *Lastname_Firstname_PracComp_ Ch4_Shuttle*.

   b. Select the **Concourse** design theme. The title of the first slide is *The Challenger Disaster* The subtitle is *January 28, 1986*

   c. Insert a new slide with Title and Content layout. The title is **The Crew** Type bullets as shown below. The graphic of your bullets might not match those shown here, but the text and the indent levels should. Disregard any red wavy underlines that indicate a possible misspelling.

The underlines will not be shown in the slide show:

- **Mission Commander**
  - **Francis Scobee**
- **Pilot**
  - **Michael Smith**
- **Mission Specialists**
  - **Ronald McNair**
  - **Ellison Onizuka**
  - **Judith Resnick**
- **Payload Specialists**
  - **Gregory Jarvis**
  - **Christa McAuliffe**

   d. Insert a clip art image on Slide 2 related to the space shuttle. Make sure to include content from Office.com. Resize and position the clip art image attractively on the slide. Adjust the color, if possible, to match the design theme. Select an appropriate picture style.

e. Insert a new slide with a Title and Content layout. The title is **The Shuttle Timeline**. Insert the following table:

Event	Time
Launch	11:38 EST
First indication of problem (puff of gray smoke)	0.678 seconds into flight
Swirling flames from the right solid rocket booster	64 seconds
Tragic explosion, claiming the crew and shuttle	73 seconds

Make sure the table is formatted attractively and positioned in the center of the slide. Change the font color of the slide title to **Turquoise, Accent 1, Darker 50%** (row 6, column 5).

f. Insert a new slide with the Title Only layout. Type the title **America Responds** Insert the video **PracComp_Ch4_Reagan**. Resize the video, if necessary, so it fits in the center of the slide, and select an attractive border. Click the **Playback tab**. Play the video. Trim the video so it begins at approximately 3 minutes and 11 seconds. Click the **Start arrow** and select **Automatically**.

g. Click the **Design tab** and click **Hide Background Graphics** in the Background group.

h. Change the Background Style to **Style 7**. The change should automatically be applied to all slides.

i. Apply the **Cut** transition to all slides. Set the Effect Options to **Through Black**. Apply the Through Black effect option to all slides.

j. Animate the table on Slide 3 so that it fades in when clicked.

k. View the slide show from the beginning.

l. Save the presentation and exit PowerPoint.

CHAPTER **FIVE**

Working with Word

IF YOU USE YOUR COMPUTER FOR ONLY ONE TASK, IT IS likely to be **word processing**. Using a word processor, such as **Microsoft Word 2010**, you can type a letter, write and edit a research paper, create a flyer, print a brochure, publish a newsletter, and print labels, among other tasks. Anyone who writes or is responsible for producing documents can take advantage of the speed and ease of use of a word processor.

Using Microsoft Word to create simple documents is not a complicated task. In fact, in a matter of a few minutes, you can be typing, editing, and printing documents. Of course, it takes a little longer to become a proficient user, but even then, most word processing activities are intuitive. With an excellent built-in Help facility, Microsoft Word makes it easy to explore options and get assistance with just about any project. This chapter introduces you to word processing basics, providing direction on how to create, format, edit, and print documents.

OBJECTIVES

When you complete this chapter, you will:

▶ Be familiar with Word basics.

▶ Format characters.

▶ Work with paragraphs.

▶ Format a document.

▶ Preview and print a document.

Understanding Word

Microsoft Word 2010 is probably the most well-recognized word processing software worldwide. Not limited simply to office tasks, Word supports students and home users with such activities as research reports, mailings, and general documents. Needless to say, very few home computer users or office workers are unfamiliar with Word.

By definition, word processing software is designed to create, edit, and print documents. It enables you to save your documents and edit, or update, them later. Word processing software also includes a full range of options for working with graphics and animation, enabling you to create vivid documents with pictures, borders, backgrounds, tables, and many other formatting features.

Not all word processing software is the same. Some, like Microsoft Word and Corel WordPerfect, include everything necessary to create just about any kind of document. In fact, both **Microsoft Office 2010** (a software suite that includes Word as a component) and Corel's **WordPerfect Office** suite each provide a comprehensive productivity package that meets the needs of most business environments. In addition, OpenOffice.org is a free productivity suite that is available for download online. Both Word and WordPerfect feature complete document formatting and production, spelling and grammar checkers, predesigned document formats, many different fonts and document styles, and even an art component, from which you can choose text designs.

Other types of word processing software are more basic, with more limited capability. **Microsoft Works** is a product that includes word processing functionality, along with other components that address specific categories of tasks, such as keeping a calendar and building worksheets. Although it is well suited for home applications, its breadth is probably not sufficient for most businesses. Microsoft Works is often found on new computer systems because it is effective, but much less costly than Microsoft Office. As you consider purchasing word processing software that will address your needs, you will find a wide variety of cost and capabilities. Although a little more costly than some, Microsoft Word is definitely a leader in any market—home, school, or business.

In this section, you will explore Microsoft Word 2010 basics, including the Word window, Word views, and entering text. You will also learn to begin and open a document, and to save a document.

Beginning and Opening a Word Document

If Word is installed on your system, you will find it by clicking **Start**, **All Programs**, **Microsoft Office**, **Microsoft Word 2010**. It might also appear as an icon on the desktop, which you can simply double-click to open. Finally, if Word is a program that you often access, it might be listed as a selection on the left side of the Start menu, accessible after you click Start.

When Word opens, you will see a new blank document as shown in Figure 5.1. A blinking vertical line at the upper-left corner of the white document area—called an **insertion point**—indicates the position where text will appear when you begin typing. As you type, the insertion point moves with you. Always remain aware of the insertion point so you will know where text will appear when you type. As you move the mouse over the document, you can see that the pointer moves. Click anywhere within existing text to reposition the insertion point.

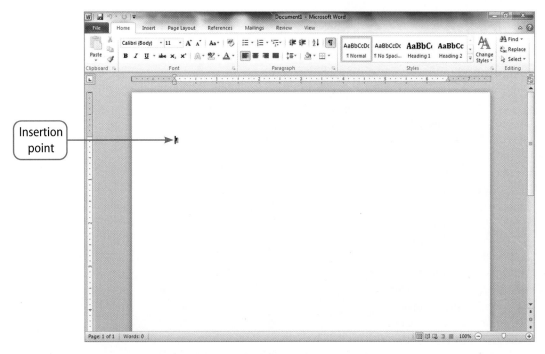

Figure 5.1 Microsoft Word is a popular word processor.

A Look Back

The First Word Processors

Word processing did not actually evolve from computer software. Instead, it began as an attempt to automate certain aspects of writing and typing, progressing from the typewriter to a dedicated word processing system, and finally to the microcomputer. Although the typewriter was in widespread use for much of the 20th century, early typewriter versions did not save a document so that it could be mass produced, nor did they make it easy to correct typing mistakes. In 1964, IBM marketed the IBM Selectric typewriter, which recorded text on tape. In its marketing campaign for the IBM Selectric, IBM coined the phrase "word processing." Then in 1969, IBM went a step further with its MagCards, which were inserted into a typewriter-like device that recorded typed text for later reprinting. Although groundbreaking at that time, MagCards were actually quite limited as only about one page of text could be recorded on each card. Similar to an IBM Selectric, the Wang 1200 (released in 1971) was able to record keystrokes and then play them back onto paper. A typist could review and correct a document repeatedly before committing it to paper. Large, bulky, and expensive dedicated word processing systems were prevalent in the 1970's and early 1980's. They were designed for only one function—word processing. Finally, the floppy disk was developed by IBM in the 1970's, bringing word processing to the desktop computer. Early disks, capable of holding 80 to 100 pages, facilitated the creation and editing of multi-page documents without having to change storage media. The first word processing program designed for the personal computer was the Electric Pencil, in 1976. Soon after, Apple brought out EasyWriter, which was later revised for inclusion on an IBM. Radio Shack even produced its own very popular word processor, Scripsit.

Quick Tip

Opening a Recent Document

Word makes it easy to open a document you recently viewed. Click the **File tab** and then click **Recent**. The 20 most recently opened documents are listed, from which you can click to open a document. As other documents are opened, recent files are bumped from the list. However, you can keep a document in the list indefinitely if you click the pushpin icon to the right of the file in the Recent Documents list. Similarly, you can "unpin" a document from the list by clicking the pushpin icon again.

Figure 5.2 Microsoft Word is open, but all documents are closed.

Occasionally, you will close all open documents without closing Word. Instead of a blank document, you will see an empty gray area, as shown in Figure 5.2. If you want to create a document, you must first open a blank document. Click the **File tab** and then click **New**. Double-click **Blank document**.

Later in this chapter, you will learn to save a document to work with later. To open a saved document, click the **File tab** and then click **Open**. From the Open dialog box (Figure 5.3), navigate to the document's location and double-click the document to open it.

Understanding Backstage

When you click the File tab, you are in **Backstage view**, which is the location of actions and settings related to an open document. All Office applications include Backstage view, with only slight differences in the information displayed.

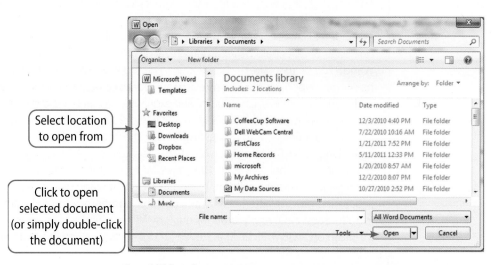

Select location to open from

Click to open selected document (or simply double-click the document)

Figure 5.3 Select a document to open.

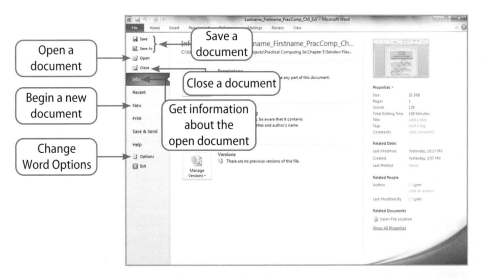

Open a document

Begin a new document

Change Word Options

Save a document

Close a document

Get information about the open document

Figure 5.4 Backstage view provides options and information related to an open document.

Figure 5.4 shows Word's Backstage view, which is where you can save, open, or print a document. You can also retrieve information related to the document, such as file size and permissions. From Backstage view, you can set global options related to Word, such as whether spell checking should occur as you type and where all documents should be saved by default.

Entering Text

The blinking insertion point shows where new text you type will begin. You have learned that you can reposition the insertion point by clicking elsewhere in the document. Of course, if you are beginning a new document, the insertion point will display at the upper-left corner of the empty document space. As you type, Word automatically returns the insertion point to the next line when it reaches the right side of the page. That action is called **word wrap**. Although you should never press Enter in the middle of a paragraph, you will do so at the end of a paragraph or a line of text that needs to stand alone. When you press Enter, you create a **hard return**. A hard return is defined as a return that is forced where

In Depth

Working with Templates

A template is a predesigned document that you can personalize to include your own content. For example, you can open an application letter template, and then modify it to include text relevant to your own job search information. A template can definitely jump start a project if you need a nudge. You can find a template when you click the **File tab** and then click **New**. Some templates are local, which means they are included with a typical Word installation, while others are available from Office.com. In both cases, templates are listed so you can select them from within Word. After selecting a template, click Download or Create to open the document. Then simply modify the document and save it. Occasionally, a template that you select is produced by a third party, so you must agree to Microsoft's disclaimer before you can download and open the template.

Using Overtype

By default, text you type is inserted between existing text. Occasionally, you might want typed text to *replace* existing text instead of being inserted. In that case, configure Word so that you can simply press Insert to toggle between insert mode and overtype mode. Click the **File tab** and then click **Options**. Click **Advanced**. Select **Use the Insert key to control overtype mode**. Click **OK**. Then, when you press **Insert**, typed text will replace existing text. Press **Insert** again to return to insert mode.

A Look Back

The History of the Typewriter

By broad definition, the first word processor was the typewriter. Patented by Christopher Sholes in 1867, the typewriter was first marketed commercially by a gun manufacturing company, E. Remington and Sons. A major drawback of the first typewriter was that it printed on the underside of the roller, so that the typist could only view his work when completely finished. Soon thereafter, improvements included the Shift key (making it possible to type uppercase and lowercase), printing on the upper side of the roller, the Tab key, and the setting of margins. Businesses, which had previously relied on written correspondence, produced documents more quickly and legibly on the typewriter. By the early 1900s, the first portable type-writers brought typed text within reach of everyone. Thomas Edison patented an electric typewriter in 1872, but it was not introduced until the 1920s. The typewriter that came closest to a true word processor was the M. Shultz Company's automatic or repetitive typewriter, which facilitated automatic storage of information for later retrieval. The machine made it possible to produce multiple typed copies of form letters. Because the type bars on a manual typewriter tended to jam if a typist typed too quickly, the keyboard was arranged so that the most commonly accessed keys were further apart, effectively slowing the typist. That keyboard arrangement became today's standard QWERTY keyboard. It is called QWERTY because those letters occupy the first few keys on the top row of the keyboard.

one would not normally occur. On the other hand, a **soft return** occurs during word wrap when text automatically continues on the next line.

As you type, you are likely to make mistakes. Of course, the ease with which you can correct errors is one of the features that makes word processors so appealing. Simply click to place the insertion point where you want to make the correction. Press **Delete** to remove characters to the right of the insertion point, or **Backspace** to remove characters to the left. Then just type the correct text to insert it in place.

Because a Word document is in insert mode by default, characters you type are placed between existing text. For example, if you have typed the word *together* as *togethr*, click to place the insertion point after the *h*. Then type the letter *e* to place it between *h* and *r*.

In Depth

Positioning the Insertion Point

When you want to begin typing in another part of a document, perhaps because you are inserting text within an existing paragraph, you can simply click to position the insertion point, and then type. However, what if the location where you want to type is far below the last paragraph on a page? For example, a page might include only one paragraph, and you want to begin typing in the lower part of the empty area on the page. Because the document actually "ends" after the last paragraph, clicking much farther down the page will only result in the insertion point positioning at the end of the paragraph, which is not where you intended. Instead, double-click in the new location—an action known as *click-and-type*. Word will automatically insert multiple hard returns between the end of the paragraph and the location of the insertion point.

Understanding the Word Window

As shown in Figure 5.5, the **Ribbon** contains tabs that relate to an open Word document. Similar to the PowerPoint Ribbon that you studied in the previous chapter, the Word Ribbon includes a few groups that are unique to the preparation of documents. Each tab contains groups of related commands. For example, the Home tab provides access to common editing tasks, such as changing the font, working with styles, and using the Clipboard. The Page Layout tab enables you to add borders, change spacing, and adjust margins.

The **title bar** is the long shaded bar at the top of the Word window that contains the name of the document and the Office program (Microsoft Word, in this case). The **Quick Access Toolbar**, located on the left side of the title bar provides easy access to the Save, Undo, and Redo commands. You can easily customize the Quick Access Toolbar by clicking the arrow to the right of the Quick Access Toolbar (called Customize Quick Access Toolbar) and selecting other items to include (Figure 5.5).

The **status bar**, found at the bottom of an open document (Figure 5.5), provides information about the document, such as the page number and word count. On the right side of the status bar are View buttons, which enable you to view the document in different ways. Word views are described in the next section of this chapter. You will also find a **Zoom Slider** on the status bar, which changes the magnification of the document. Zooming in (increasing the zoom setting) on a document enables you to get a closer view of the effect of some document changes or just makes it easier for you to see what you are typing. Drag the tab on the Zoom Slider (Figure 5.5) to the right to increase the size or to the left to decrease the size of a document. Be aware, however, that changing the magnification affects the current display only. It does not actually increase the **font** (character) size or affect the way the document will print. Another way of adjusting the Zoom is to click the View tab and then select a preset option (One Page, Two Pages, Page Width,

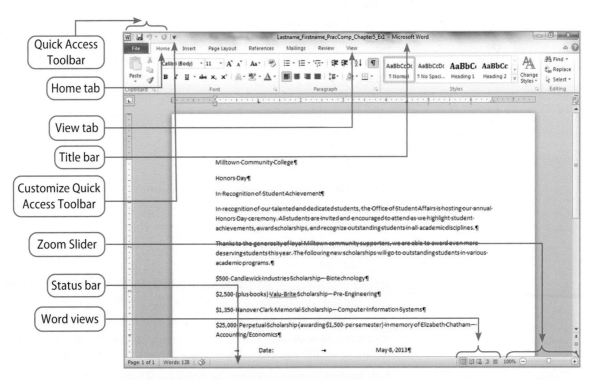

Figure 5.5 Groups on the Ribbon assist in the preparation of a document.

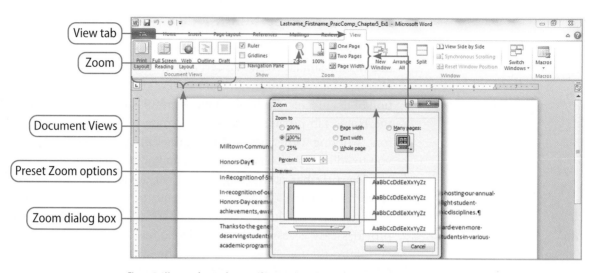

View tab

Zoom

Document Views

Preset Zoom options

Zoom dialog box

Figure 5.6 You can change the magnification of a document by using zoom options.

or 100%), or click Zoom (in the Zoom group), as shown in Figure 5.6. If you click Zoom, a dialog box similar to that shown presents several zoom options. Select a zoom option in the dialog box to adjust to a preset size, or indicate a specific percentage to more precisely control the resulting size.

Identifying Word Views

On occasion, you might want to view a document in different ways. By default (a setting that is automatically prescribed, unless you specify otherwise), new documents are shown in **Print Layout view**, which shows the document much as it would print, with all margins, headers, footers, and graphics. Similar to Print Layout view, **Full Screen Reading view** does not display the Ribbon, providing more document space on screen. **Draft view** shows the document with the most available screen space, but without margins, headers, footers, graphics, or other page features. If the document includes headings, subheadings, and other levels of detail, **Outline view** provides a hierarchical view of the document, with all headings and levels of detail. You can expand or collapse the summary to provide more or less detail. **Web Layout view** shows a document as it would appear on a Web page. All of those views are available in the Document Views group on the View tab, as shown in Figure 5.6. You can also find them at the lower-right side of the status bar (Figure 5.5). As you place the pointer on each view button on the status bar, a **ScreenTip** appears, identifying the view represented by the button.

Navigating a Document

As you learned earlier, you can click within a document to reposition the insertion point. Any text you subsequently type will be placed at the location of the insertion point. In addition, use any of the shortcuts shown in Table 5.1 to reposition the insertion point.

You can view other areas of a document with or without repositioning the insertion point. The shortcuts shown in Table 5.1 reposition the insertion point. You can also use the vertical scroll bar (Figure 5.7) to view other parts of a document without changing the position of the insertion point. Remember, though, that regardless of what is shown on screen, new text will always be inserted at the location of the insertion point, even if you do not see the insertion point when you begin to type (as would be the case if you had scrolled to another location in the document).

Showing Nonprinting Characters

Most keys on the keyboard, even those not considered text or numeric (such as the Spacebar and the Enter key) are included as characters within a document. For example, each time you press Enter within a document, a nonprinting character is inserted. Similarly, the Spacebar and the Tab key both result in the insertion of a nonprinting character. You can choose to view those nonprinting characters by clicking **Show/Hide** ¶ in the Paragraph group on the Home tab. Figure 5.7 shows a document with nonprinting characters displayed.

Why would you want to see nonprinting characters? It is actually a matter of preference, but many people like to see nonprinting characters because they assist with troubleshooting. Suppose a document in which you recently changed margins now shows awkwardly spaced lines, with some ending at the right margin while others leave a great deal of space on the right. Most likely, you pressed Enter at the end of each line within a paragraph, but you cannot be sure of that unless you display nonprinting characters (also called formatting marks). You can then delete the hard returns the same way you would remove any other character (pressing the Delete or Backspace key). Occasionally, Word will alert you to a grammatical mistake, as indicated by a wavy green underline (described later in this chapter). The "mistake" is sometimes caused by too many spaces between words within a sentence. You cannot be sure of how many spaces are between words unless you show nonprinting characters. At that point, you can simply delete any extra space. As the name suggests, nonprinting characters that display in a document on-screen are not printed. Therefore, you do not need to hide them before printing. If you prefer they do not display, however, simply click **Show/Hide** again to toggle them off. A toggle setting works much like a light switch. Click a command to invoke an action, and then click it a second time to end, or remove, it. Show/Hide is an example of a toggle.

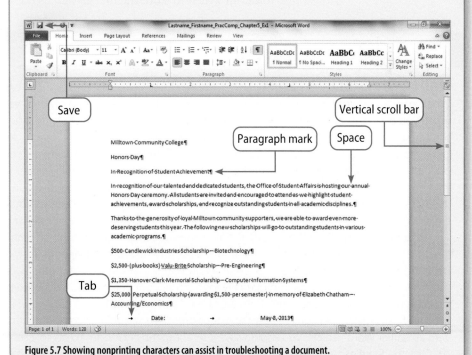

Figure 5.7 Showing nonprinting characters can assist in troubleshooting a document.

Table 5.1 Use these shortcuts to reposition the insertion point.

To Move Here	Do This
Up one page	Page Up or PgUp
Down one page	Page Dn or PgDn
Beginning of the document	Press Ctrl+Home
End of the document	Press Ctrl+End
Beginning of the current line	Home
End of the current line	End

Quick Tip

Using Arrow Keys

Computer novices often confuse Backspace and the Left Arrow ←. The function of each is actually very different. When you press Backspace, the insertion point moves one space to the left, deleting any character in its path. However, when you press the Left Arrow, the insertion point moves one space to the left, while leaving intact any character that it passes. Using the arrow keys, then, is one way to reposition the insertion point—to the left, right, up, or down—without removing any existing text.

Saving a Document

Saving a document means placing it on a USB or other storage medium for later retrieval. RAM (temporary computer memory) holds documents only while you are working with them. As you type a document, it appears on screen and is stored in RAM. However, RAM is active only when there is a constant supply of electricity. To avoid losing your document due to a power outage or power surge, you should periodically save the document on a USB or hard drive. You will also want to back up important files by saving them in several locations, so you do not risk losing a document that would be difficult to recreate. See Chapter 2 for a discussion of backing up files.

To save a document, click the **File tab** and click either **Save** or **Save As**. The first time you save a file, there is no difference between selecting Save or Save As. Both selections produce a Save As dialog box in which you specify the drive or folder in which to store the file, as well as the filename you want to assign. If you

Technology Insight

Understanding File Types

When you save a Word document, it becomes associated with the version of Word you are using. That means that when you open the document, it will be displayed as a Word document. Because Microsoft Word continues to evolve through different versions (a specific edition of software with additional or changed features from earlier releases), file types occasionally are changed to match the version. Therefore you cannot always count on being able to open a Word document, especially if you are attempting to open a document created with a later Word version than the one with which you are working. For example, you typically cannot open a document saved in Word 2010 if you are using Word 2003 or earlier. However, if you know that someone will be opening a document you are creating, but will be using an earlier Word version, you can save the document in such a way that they can open it.

When you save a file in Word 2010, the filename you assign will be followed with a dot and a *docx* designation (called a file extension). For example, if you save a document with the filename *sales_team*, the document will actually be saved as *sales_team.docx*. The docx extension indicates that the file is a standard Word 2007 or Word 2010 document, saved in XML format (an improved file format that coordinates data exchange between Office applications and provides more efficient file storage). Both Word 2007 and Word 2010 add *docx* as an extension to all filenames. Word 2003 and earlier Word versions used a *doc* extension. When saving a document that might be opened by someone with an earlier Word version, you should save it in Compatibility Mode. To do so, click the **File tab** and then click **Save As**. Click the **Save as type arrow** and select **Word 97-2003 Document**. Assign a filename and click **Save.**

Suppose you are using Word 2003 and you have received a document saved in Word 2010. All is not lost! You can download the Microsoft Office Compatibility Pack for Word, Excel, and PowerPoint 2007 from http://office.com, which enables you to open the newer file type.

have not already created or identified a folder in which to place the file, you can create one by clicking **New Folder**. Type a new folder name, press **Enter**, and then double-click the new folder to select it as the save location. After supplying or confirming a filename, click **Save**.

After saving and closing a document, you might open it later to revise or print. At that point, you can save the document in the same location with the same filename by clicking the **File tab** and then clicking **Save**. Selecting the Save option is a quick way to update a file when you do not want to make any changes to the location or filename. You can even click the **Save button**, found on the Quick Access Toolbar (Figure 5.7), which is a shortcut for clicking the File tab and selecting Save. If, instead, you click the **File tab** and select **Save As**, you are presented with the same dialog box you saw during the initial save, asking for confirmation of the save location, filename, and file type. If you want to make a backup copy of the file, possibly on another storage medium, clicking the File tab and Save As is the best way to do so, because you can then indicate another storage medium on which to save a backup copy of the file.

Technology Insight

Saving to SkyDrive

SkyDrive is free storage space that Microsoft makes available to you at no cost. In fact, you are allowed access to up to 25 GB of online storage space that you can retrieve from any location. Using SkyDrive, you can upload (send files to a remote Web server) documents, spreadsheets—even digital photographs—so you can access them from any Internet-connected computer. SkyDrive is an excellent way to make backup copies of important documents, as well. Sign up for a free SkyDrive account at http://skydrive.live.com.

As you save a Word document, you can choose SkyDrive as the save location. Even if you have previously saved the document to a disk, such as a USB or hard drive,

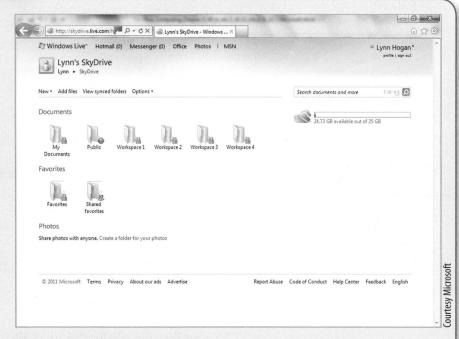

Figure 5.8 SkyDrive provides free online storage space.

you can easily create a backup copy by also saving the document to your SkyDrive account. Click the **File tab** and then click **Save & Send**. Click **Save to Web**. Sign in to your SkyDrive account, indicate a filename, and the document is saved! As it is never a good idea to save a document in only one location, you should also save the document to a USB or hard drive. That way, if you have difficulty retrieving the document from one location, you are sure to find it in the other. During the Save to Web process, you can respond to a Word prompt, providing your SkyDrive login information so you are not asked for a user name and password each time you save to SkyDrive. Having instructed Word to save the login information, you can later open a document from SkyDrive by selecting the location from the Open dialog box when you click the **File tab** and **Open**. You can upload and download files directly from SkyDrive when you visit http://skydrive.live.com and select **Add files** (to upload) or simplynavigate to a saved file and double-click to open it. Figure 5.8 shows a typical SkyDrive account.

Activity 5.1 Beginning a New Document, Exploring the Word Interface, and Saving a Document

As assistant to the Dean of Students at a local community college, you have been asked to prepare a flyer providing information on the upcoming Honors Day ceremony. Students from all disciplines will be recognized for academic achievement, and scholarships to universities will be awarded. The flyer will be posted around campus, and an electronic version of the flyer will appear on plasma screens in various buildings.

In this exercise, you will begin the document, saving it for additional editing later. If you plan to use a USB drive to save this project, you should connect it to a USB port. Close any dialog box that subsequently opens.

a. Click **Start, All Programs**, **Microsoft Office**, and **Microsoft Word 2010**. A blank document opens, with the insertion point in the upper-left corner. If nonprinting characters are not showing, click **Show/Hide** in the Paragraph group on the Home tab. You can determine whether nonprinting characters are showing by noting the presence of a paragraph mark ¶ immediately to the right of the insertion point in the blank document.

TROUBLESHOOTING

If you remove nonprinting characters instead of displaying them, click **Show/Hide** again to display nonprinting characters.

b. Type **Millwood Community College** and press **Enter**. Type **Honors Day** and press **Enter**. Type **In Recognition of Student Achievement** and press **Enter**.

TROUBLESHOOTING

If you make a mistake as you type, click either before or after the mistake and press **Delete** to remove characters to the right of the insertion point, or press **Backspace** to remove characters to the left. Then type the correct text.

c. Type **In recognition of our talented and dedicatedstudents, the Office of Student Affairs is hostingour annual Honors Day ceremony. All students areinvited and encouraged to attend as we highlightstudent achievements, award scholarships, andrecognize outstanding students in all academicdisciplines.** (Include the period.) Do not press Enter at the end of each line, but allow Word to wrap lines automatically. Press **Enter**.

d. Type **Thanks to the generosity of loyal Milltowncommunity supporters, we are able to award evenmore deserving students this year. The followingnew scholarships will go to outstanding studentsin various academic programs.** (Include the period.) Press **Enter**.

e. Click the **File tab** and then click **Save As**. Navigate to the location where you will save this project. Click the **File name box** and type **Lastname_Firstname_PracComp_Ch5_Ex1** Type your last name instead of Lastname and your first name instead of Firstname. Click **Save**.

f. Press **Ctrl+Home** to position the insertion point at the beginning of the document. Press **Enter**. Press **Ctrl+Home** to return to the top of the document. Type **INVITATION**

Modifying a Document

As you work with a document, you will want to make sure it is attractive and well received by your audience (those for whom the document is intended). Your first attempt will rarely be the final one. You will undoubtedly revisit the document, making changes and adding features that improve its readability. Your options are almost unlimited; Word enables you to create a document that is appropriate for just about any audience and any occasion. In fact, the challenge is often refraining from using so many special features that the document becomes gaudy and over-the-top with respect to color, graphics, and borders. Remember that most business documents should remain conservative, with low-key color and text selection.

When you modify a document, you change or add to it in some way. Formatting is the process of enhancing a document by changing the appearance of text, paragraphs, or the document itself. You might change the color or size of text, realign paragraphs, change the spacing between paragraphs, or change

g. Click the **View tab** and then click **Draft** (Figure 5.9) in the Document Views group. The document displays with the most document space possible. Margins and special features are not shown.

TROUBLESHOOTING

If the document displays in small size in Draft view, click **Page Width** in the Zoom group.

h. Click **Full Screen Reading** on the lower-right side of the status bar. Click **Close** in the upper-right corner of the Word display.

i. Click **Zoom** in the Zoom group. Select **200%** and then click **OK**. Click **Page Width** in the Zoom group. Click **100%** in the Zoom group.

ON YOUR OWN

Hide the display of nonprinting characters.

j. Click **Save** on the Quick Access Toolbar. The document is saved in the same location with the same filename as when you first saved it. Click the **File tab** and then click **Exit** to exit Word and close the document.

TROUBLESHOOTING

If you are asked whether to save the document, you have apparently made a change to the document since the last save. Even if you merely pressed the Spacebar, that is enough change for Word to recognize and to subsequently prompt you to save the document again. Click **Save**.

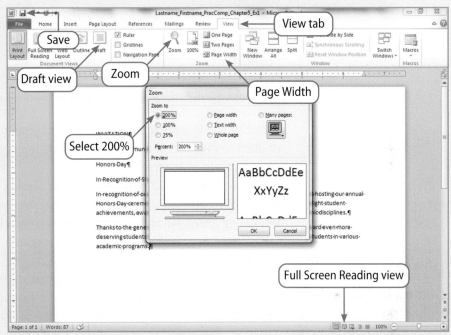

Figure 5.9 It is simple to change the view of a document.

margins. The Ribbon's Home tab includes formatting selections that simplify the task of enhancing, or modifying a document.

In this section, you will learn to format characters, paragraphs, and documents. You will also explore reviewing a document for accuracy, finding and replacing items, and moving or copying text from one area to another.

Formatting Characters

An effective way to make a document more appealing and to draw attention to specific text is to modify some character features. A different font (character design, including such qualities as **typeface**, size, and spacing) might be more appropriate or attractive for a particular document or selection. A typeface is a style of printed characters. Changing font color, italicizing text, or adding boldface can enhance text and make it more readable. Perhaps you intend to create headings of different sizes, or you want to underline a selection to emphasize it.

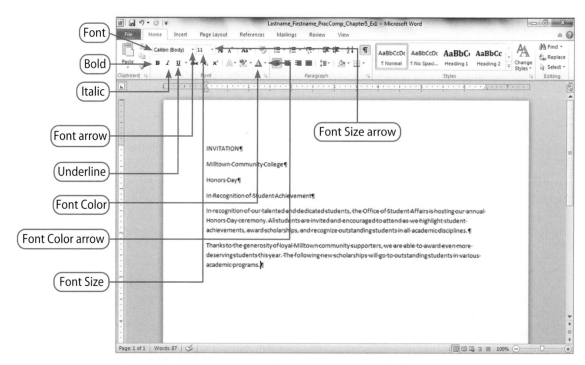

Figure 5.10 Selections in the Font group enable you to change character formatting.

Word provides numerous possibilities for changing text or for formatting before or after you type. Commonly used formatting options are available on the Home tab, as shown in Figure 5.10.

In a perfect world, you would plan ahead, selecting all formatting options *before* typing affected text. However, more often, you identify the need for different formatting *after* a paragraph or document is complete. Although you can certainly select formatting attributes before typing, you can also apply formatting afterward.

Suppose you want to boldface text that you have not yet typed. Click **Bold** in the Font group on the Home tab (Figure 5.10) to *turn on* boldfacing, type the text, and then click **Bold** a second time to *turn off* the formatting feature. Obviously, Bold is an example of a toggle, which is a setting that is activated when the option is clicked and then deactivated with a second click. If you determine that boldfacing should be applied to text that has already been typed, you must first select the text, and then click **Bold**. Other formatting features, such as underlining and italicizing, are applied in the same manner.

Before applying changes to existing text, you must first select the text. Although you can select text by simply dragging to highlight (select) it, you can also take advantage of shortcut selection methods, as shown in Table 5.2.

Table 5.2 There are several ways to select text.	
To Select	**Do This**
One word	Double-click the word
One sentence	Hold Ctrl while you click the sentence
One paragraph	Triple-click the paragraph
One line	Position the pointer in the margin to the left of the line to be selected, and click
One document	Press Ctrl+A

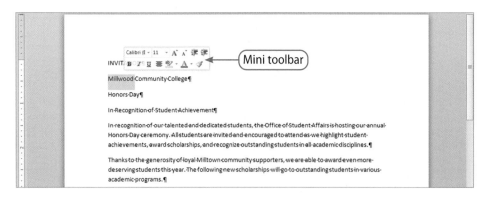

Figure 5.11 The Mini toolbar places formatting options near a selection.

Dragging to select text can be quite cumbersome, especially if the selection is very large or extremely small. Therefore, you will most likely appreciate taking a few shortcuts. Remember, however, that these shortcuts only apply to text that has not yet been selected. In fact, the purpose of a shortcut is to select text.

The Font group on the Home tab provides many formatting options, but the **Mini toolbar** can also be helpful, especially if you are applying more than one formatting attribute. As shown in Figure 5.11, the Mini toolbar groups several of the most common formatting options. It becomes available when you select text, appearing very near the selection. As you move the pointer nearer the selection, the Mini toolbar grows brighter. It becomes more transparent, or disappears altogether, when you move the pointer away from the selection. If you prefer not to use the Mini toolbar, you can just ignore it, or press **Esc** to remove it from view.

Although the Font group on the Home tab provides common formatting options, you can find even more choice in the Font dialog box (Figure 5.12). To open the Font dialog box, click the **Dialog Box Launcher** located in the lower-right corner of the Font group.

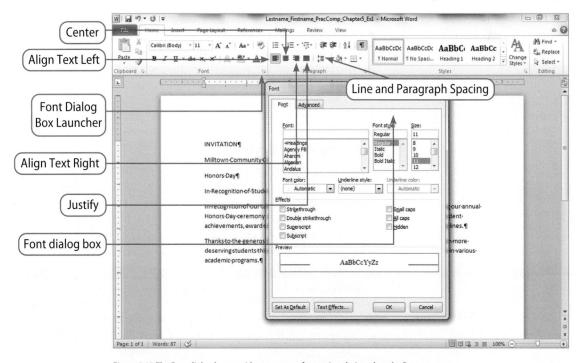

Figure 5.12 The Font dialog box provides even more formatting choices than the Font group.

Formatting Paragraphs

Word defines a paragraph differently than you do. While you might consider a paragraph a block of related text, Word considers a paragraph as anything that appears before a hard return. As you recall, a hard return is placed in a document when you press Enter. Therefore, by Word's definition, a heading, a title, a salutation—even a blank line created when you press Enter—is a paragraph. Certain formatting options, such as tabs, alignment, and spacing, apply only to paragraphs. Unlike character formatting, you do not have to select an entire paragraph in order to apply paragraph formatting. The only requirement is that the insertion point is positioned within the paragraph to be affected. Of course, if you want to apply the same formatting to multiple paragraphs, you do need to select them all.

Paragraph Alignment

By default, text is lined up on the left margin (left aligned). You can also align text on the right, center it, or fully justify it. Full Justification is an alignment where lines are evenly aligned on both the right and left margins, as you see in many newspaper articles. All those options are available in the Paragraph group on the Home tab, as shown in Figure 5.12.

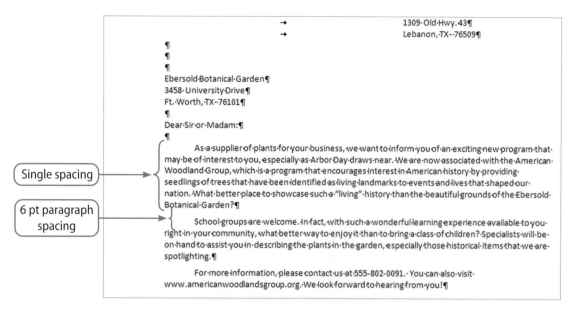

Single spacing

6 pt paragraph spacing

→ 1309·Old·Hwy.·43¶
→ Lebanon,·TX··76509¶
¶
¶
Ebersold·Botanical·Garden¶
3458··University·Drive¶
Ft.·Worth,·TX··76101¶
¶
Dear·Sir·or·Madam:¶

As·a·supplier·of·plants·for·your·business,·we·want·to·inform·you·of·an·exciting·new·program·that·may·be·of·interest·to·you,·especially·as·Arbor·Day·draws·near.·We·are·now·associated·with·the·American·Woodland·Group,·which·is·a·program·that·encourages·interest·in·American·history·by·providing·seedlings·of·trees·that·have·been·identified·as·living·landmarks·to·events·and·lives·that·shaped·our·nation.·What·better·place·to·showcase·such·a·"living"·history·than·the·beautiful·grounds·of·the·Ebersold·Botanical·Garden?¶

School·groups·are·welcome.·In·fact,·with·such·a·wonderful·learning·experience·available·to·you·right·in·your·community,·what·better·way·to·enjoy·it·than·to·bring·a·class·of·children?·Specialists·will·be·on·hand·to·assist·you·in·describing·the·plants·in·the·garden,·especially·those·historical·items·that·we·are·spotlighting.¶

For·more·information,·please·contact·us·at·555-802-0091.·You·can·also·visit·www.americanwoodlandsgroup.org.·We·look·forward·to·hearing·from·you!¶

Figure 5.13 Line spacing controls spacing between lines, while paragraph spacing relates to space between paragraphs.

Paragraph and Line Spacing

Documents can be single spaced, double spaced, or even spaced between single and double (1.5). In fact, the specificity with which you can select line spacing has almost no limit. If you select a line spacing option before typing, all subsequent text will be formatted in that spacing. Otherwise, you can change the spacing of existing text by selecting paragraphs to be affected (or clicking within only one paragraph), and selecting a new line spacing option. As shown in Figure 5.12, the Line and Paragraph Spacing command in the Paragraph group enables you to select a spacing option.

Although the two terms sound similar, *line spacing* and *paragraph spacing* are completely different settings. **Line spacing** is the amount of space between lines of text within a paragraph. **Paragraph spacing** is the amount of space between paragraphs. The document in Figure 5.13 shows single spacing between lines, and 6 pt spacing after each paragraph. A point is actually 1/72 of an inch. Therefore, 6 pt after paragraph spacing means that 6/72" of space is left after each paragraph.

You can select paragraph spacing in the Paragraph dialog box, shown in Figure 5.14. Click the **Paragraph Dialog Box Launcher**, located in the lower-right corner of the Paragraph group, to open the dialog box. Note that you can select spacing before or after a paragraph, although the choice of which spacing to select is not all that critical. Selecting spacing before one paragraph results in the same appearance as if you had selected spacing after the preceding paragraph, so just use your judgment in making a selection. You can also select paragraph spacing in the Paragraph group on the Page Layout tab (Figure 5.15).

Tabs

Tabs are used to position text in columns. A tab is actually a marker that aligns text and helps organize a document. By default, a tab is set at every half inch, but you can change tab settings to make them appropriate for your document. Probably the easiest way to work with tabs is to use the **Ruler**. To display the Ruler, click the **View tab** and then click **Ruler** in the Show group. You can also display the Ruler by clicking **View Ruler** (Figure 5.16). To set a tab, simply click the **Ruler** at the location of the tab. Figure 5.16 shows two left tabs—one at the 0.5" mark and another at the 4" mark.

Quick Tip

Inserting Page Numbers

You can add page numbers to any document when you click the **Insert tab** and then click **Page Number** in the Header & Footer group. Select a position (e.g., top, bottom) and then select a style. You can remove page numbers by following the same steps, but select **Remove Page Numbers** instead of indicating a position.

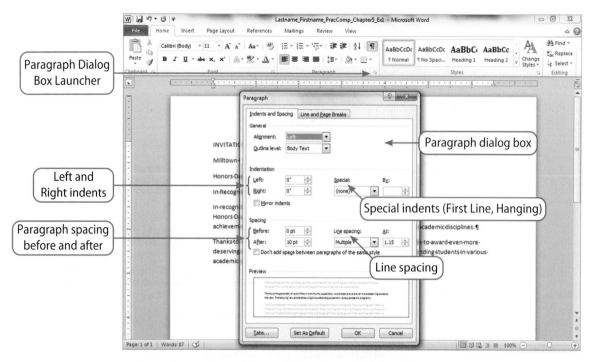

Figure 5.14 Selections in the Paragraph dialog box enable you to set indents and control spacing.

Figure 5.15 The Page Layout tab provides quick access to spacing and indent options.

Before setting a tab, you should consider whether the tab should be a left, right, center, or decimal tab. A left tab aligns text to the left of the tab, while a right tab aligns text to the right. Similarly, a center tab centers tabbed text, and a decimal tab aligns tabbed numeric items at the decimal point. The tab selector, located at the left edge of the Ruler (Figure 5.16), enables you to select a tab type.

A Look Back

Major Word Processors

Although word processor choices are many, several have risen to the top during their era. WordStar, released in 1978, was the first commercially successful word processor that was widely available for personal computers. It actually enabled you to see what you typed on a full screen, make corrections, and print a document. Even so, it included special codes for such character formatting as boldface and italics, making an on-screen document appear disjointed and difficult to read. WordStar dominated the market until the late 1980's with the advent of WordPerfect. With localized spell check features, enhanced editing, and a true WYSIWYG (What You See Is What You Get) interface, WordPerfect produced well-prepared documents with minimal effort. In the end, Microsoft has dominated the market with Microsoft Word, a word processor with comprehensive features and tight integration with the Windows operating system. With Microsoft's marketing muscle behind it, Word is now the dominant word processor and is likely to hold that position for the indefinite future.

Figure 5.16 Use the Ruler to set tabs.

Each time you click the tab selector, the tab selection changes. When you place the pointer over the tab selector, a ScreenTip shows the tab type. Having indicated a tab type, simply click a position on the Ruler to place the tab. When you set tabs, they apply only to any text that you type *after* setting the tab or to text that you select *before* setting the tab. Therefore, different parts of a document can have different tab settings.

You can also set tabs by using the Tabs dialog box (Figure 5.18). To open the Tabs dialog box, you must either double-click **a tab on the Ruler** or click the **Paragraph Dialog Box Launcher** to open the Paragraph dialog box. In the Paragraph dialog box, click **Tabs** in the lower-left corner, as shown in Figure 5.17. After indicating a tab stop position and an alignment, you have the option of including a leader (Figure 5.18). A leader is a row of dots or dashes that precedes a tab stop. You have seen leaders on restaurant menus where the food item is followed by a row of dots leading to the price. Even if you have previously set a tab on the Ruler, you can use the Tabs dialog box to add a leader to the tab stop. If you are modifying a tab stop that has been previously set, you can open the Tabs dialog box by double-clicking the tab on the Ruler.

Indenting

Although the two are sometimes confused, indenting a paragraph is not the same as using tabs. When you **indent** a paragraph, you control the distance of the paragraph from the left or right margin. If you have ever written or reviewed a

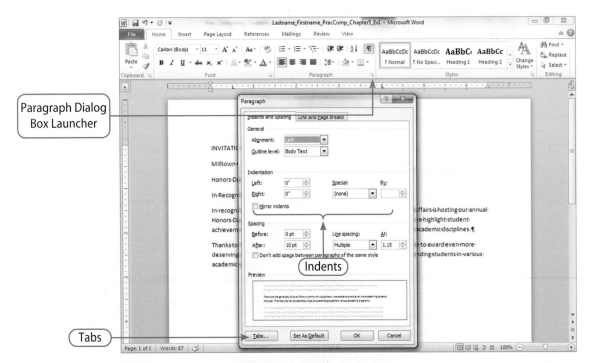

Figure 5.17 One way to set tabs is to click Tabs in the Paragraph dialog box.

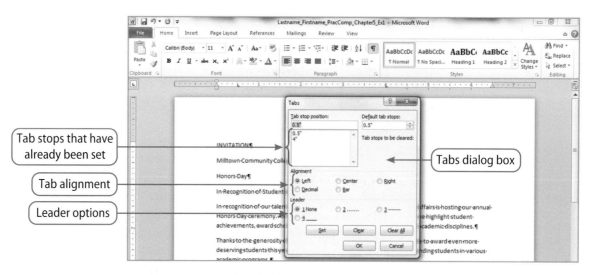

Figure 5.18 The Tabs dialog box enables you to identify precise tab locations and to set leaders.

research paper, you have most likely viewed paragraphs with a **first line indent** of 1/2". The first line of each paragraph was indented 1/2 inch from the left margin. In the same research paper, you might have noticed a lengthy quote that was indented from both the left and right margins, so the quote stood out from the rest of the paper. In that case, a **left indent** and a **right indent** were applied to the paragraph. Finally, the research paper most likely included a bibliography or works cited page, in which each source began at the left margin, with each successive line indented 1/2 inch from the left margin. Such an indent is called a **hanging indent**. Each of those indent types is shown in Figure 5.19. Use the Paragraph Dialog Box (Figure 5.17) to apply indents. A first line indent and a hanging indent are considered Special indents, available when you click the **Special arrow** in the Paragraph dialog box.

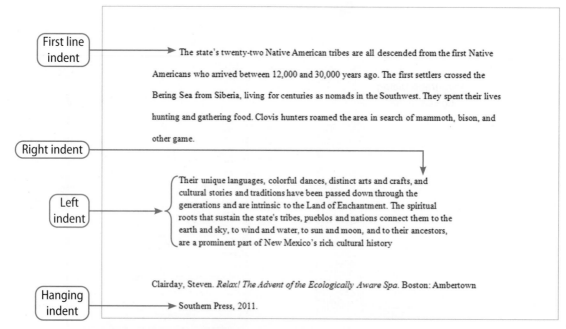

Figure 5.19 Word supports various types of indents.

Figure 5.20 You can specify indents by dragging indicators on the Ruler.

You can also use the Ruler to set indents. As shown in Figure 5.20, the indicator on the left side of the Ruler actually consists of three parts (Left Indent, Hanging Indent, and First Line Indent). Each part can be dragged to indicate an indent. For example, before typing the body of a memorandum, you might determine that each paragraph should be indented by 1/2". Simply drag the First Line Indent marker to the 1/2" mark on the Ruler. The Right Indent marker is located on the right side of the Ruler. Drag the marker to position an indent from the right margin. Of course, you can apply indents to previously typed text by selecting the text to be affected before identifying an indent.

Formatting a Document

Formatting a document involves such activities as setting margins, changing page orientation, inserting headers and footers, bordering pages, changing page color, and working with themes. You can also apply a **watermark**, which is text or a picture that appears behind document text. When you format a document, there is no need to select text, as changes apply to the entire document. For the most part, document settings are located on the Page Layout tab, as shown in Figure 5.21.

Page Orientation

By default, documents are displayed and printed in **portrait** orientation, which means they are taller than they are wide. Most often, that orientation is appropriate. Occasionally, you might find that a document is better situated in **landscape orientation**, where the document is wider than it is tall. You might even identify a single page within a document that should be oriented differently. For example, a document might include a table that would be more attractive in landscape orientation, although the remainder of the document should remain in portrait orientation. Word enables you to change the orientation of part or all of any document by making selections on the Page Layout tab (Figure 5.21).

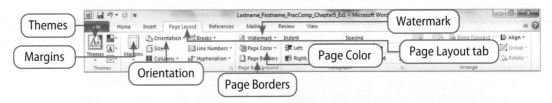

Figure 5.21 Formatting options on the Ribbon can change the appearance of a document.

In Depth

Understanding Sections

You can apply various settings to different parts, or sections, of a document. For example, suppose you are authoring a book and want to number the first few pages (often called the front matter) using Roman numerals, while the rest of the book should be numbered in a 1, 2, 3, . . . format. You can identify the front matter as one section that is formatted with unique page numbers. Perhaps you are preparing a newsletter, and want the title of the newsletter to be centered across the width of the page. However, remaining text should be displayed in two columns. Simply define the title as one section, and the columnar text as another. Then format each appropriately. You can even apply different margins or orientation (landscape or portrait) to different sections.

The key is to insert section breaks within a document so those sections can be uniquely formatted. To insert a section break, position the insertion point where the new section should begin. Click the **Page Layout tab**, and then click **Breaks** in the Page Setup group. Select a break in the Section Breaks area. If the break is to divide text on the same page into sections (as in the case of formatting the newsletter title differently from the remaining text), select **Continuous**. If the break is to divide text on separate pages so that they can be formatted differently (as in the case of formatting the front matter differently from the remainder of the book), select **Next Page**. To display the location of section breaks, make sure nonprinting characters are displayed (click the **Home tab** and select **Show/Hide** in the Paragraph group if nonprinting characters are not already displayed). You can delete a section break just as you delete any other character.

In Depth

Using Themes

As you learned earlier, you can apply individual character attributes (such as boldfacing, underlining, font size, and color) to text selections in a document. Unlike those individual settings, a theme is a collection of coordinated colors, fonts, and effects that will apply to all document content. Using a theme, you can create matching documents, worksheets, and PowerPoint presentations, because other Office 2010 software includes the same themes. Even within the same document, components such as tables, charts, and text will be attractively color coordinated. The Themes gallery is located on the Page Layout tab (Figure 5.21) when you click **Themes** in the Themes group. Live Preview shows the effect of a theme as you place the pointer over a theme selection.

Margins

Every document has a top, bottom, left and right **margin**. By default, those margins are set at 1". By selecting **Margins** (Figure 5.21), you can select from a predesigned set of margins, or click **Custom Margins** to define your own. As shown in Figure 5.22, you can type new margins, and you can either apply them to the whole document or to this point forward. If you intend to use the same margin settings for all documents you create, you can even click **Set As Default**. At that point, all documents you begin will include your custom margins.

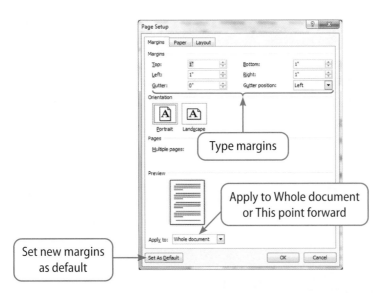

Set new margins as default

Type margins

Apply to Whole document or This point forward

Figure 5.22 Margins can be applied to a document or to a section of a document.

Page Borders and Watermarks

A **page border** is a line or graphic that surrounds a page. Although not often used in business documents, a page border might be appropriate for newsletters or flyers. A watermark appears behind text in a document. You might use a *Draft* watermark to identify a document as a first attempt, not the final copy. Both page border and watermark options are available in the Page Background group on the Page Layout tab (Figure 5.21).

Checking Spelling and Grammar

As you create a document, you might notice a red wavy underline under certain words. Other areas might be underlined in green or blue. Those underlines are Word's alert that you might have misspelled a word or committed a grammatical mistake or word usage error. The underlines will not print, so you can ignore those warnings; however, it is probably wiser to explore the possible mistake and correct it if necessary.

If a word is not recognized, you will see a red wavy line under it. It is important to understand that this does not necessarily mean the word is misspelled, only that it is not included in Word's dictionary. Right-click the underlined word to check spelling options. If the word is actually spelled correctly—perhaps it is a person's last name—you might want to add it to the dictionary by selecting **Add to Dictionary**. However, if the word is misspelled, you should correct it. If the correct spelling is given as a choice on the shortcut menu, click it to correct the spelling. If you do not see the correct spelling listed, click outside the menu to return to your document and then manually correct the word. The red wavy lines are not printed, so if a word is spelled correctly but Word identifies it as misspelled (by underlining it), you can simply continue typing. If you like, you can remove the red underline from the correctly spelled word when you right-click the word and select **Ignore** (or **Ignore All** so that the same word is not flagged later in the document).

Green wavy underlines indicate a possible problem with grammar. Right-click an underlined area to see Word's suggestions. The problem might be a

Activity 5.2 Formatting Characters and Paragraphs

As you continue to work with the Honors Day flyer, you will use character formatting to draw attention to certain areas, and you will adjust alignment, spacing, and indents to make the document attractive and eye catching.

a. Open Word. Click the **File tab** and then click **Recent**. Click **Lastname_Firstname_PracComp_Ch5_Ex1** in the Recent Documents list to open it.

b. Click **Show/Hide** to show nonprinting characters. Position the pointer in the left margin to the left of *Invitation*. Drag down to select the first four lines (paragraphs). Click **Center** in the Paragraph group. Click the **Font Size arrow** and select **20**. Click anywhere to deselect the text.

c. Press **Ctrl+A** to select the document. Click the **Font arrow**, scroll down, and select **Verdana**. Click anywhere to deselect the text. Drag to select **Honors Day ceremony** in the first paragraph underneath the centered lines. Click **Bold** in the Font group.

d. Drag to select the two paragraphs, beginning with *In recognition* and ending with *academic programs*. Do not select the last empty paragraph. Click the **Paragraph Dialog Box Launcher** to open the Paragraph dialog box. Click the **Line spacing arrow** and select **Single**. Click the **Spacing After up arrow** to increase spacing after each selected paragraph to **12 pt**. Click the **Special arrow** and select **First line**. Click **OK**. Do not deselect the paragraphs.

e. Click **Line and Paragraph Spacing** (Figure 5.23) in the Paragraph group and select **1.5**. Click anywhere to deselect the text. Click to place the insertion point after the word *Achievement* in the last centered heading line. Press **Enter** to create some empty space after the heading area.

f. Press **Ctrl+End** to move to the end of the document. Type **$500 Candlewick Industries**

Scholarship – Biotechnology (be sure to leave a space before and after the dash). Press **Enter**. Type **$2,500 (plus books) Valu-Brite Scholarship – Pre-Engineering** (there is no space before or after the hyphen in *Pre-Engineering*). Press **Enter**. Type the following two scholarships, pressing **Enter** after each, and leaving a space before and after the dash.

$1,350 Hanover Clark Memorial Scholarship – Computer Information Systems
$25,000 Perpetual Scholarship (awarding $1,500 per semester) in memory of Elizabeth Chatham – Accounting/Economics

g. Select the scholarship lines, beginning with *$500 Candlewick Industries*, and ending with *Accounting/Economics*. Do not select the last empty paragraph. Click **Bullets** in the Paragraph group. Be sure to click the Bullets button, not the arrow. Click anywhere to deselect the bulleted list.

h. Press **Ctrl+End** to position the insertion point at the end of the document. If the Ruler is not showing at the top of the document, click **View Ruler** (Figure 5.21). The tab selector should show a Left tab, as shown in Figure 5.23. Click at **1"** on the Ruler. Click the **tab selector** twice to select **Right Tab** 🔲. Click at **4.5"** on the Ruler.

TROUBLESHOOTING

If a tab is incorrectly positioned, click **Undo** on the Quick Access Toolbar and click to place the tab on the Ruler. You can also remove a tab by dragging it off the Ruler.

i. Press **Tab**. Type **Date** and then press **Tab**. Type **May 8, 2013** and then press **Enter**. Press **Tab**. Type **Time** and then press **Tab**. Type **10:30 a.m.** and then press **Enter**. Press **Tab**. Type **Place** and then press **Tab**. Type **Clark Gymnasium** and then press **Enter**.

---

sentence fragment or an incorrect subject-verb agreement. The problem could be that you have left too many spaces between words, an error that can be corrected by deleting the extra space. The green wavy underlines will not be printed, so you can simply ignore the concern if it is irrelevant.

Word can also attempt to identify words that are spelled correctly, but used incorrectly. For example, the words *their* and *there* are often confused, as are *too* and *to*. A blue wavy underline indicates a possible usage error.

Instead of addressing each spelling and grammatical error individually (by checking for underlined areas), you might want to let Word check for errors

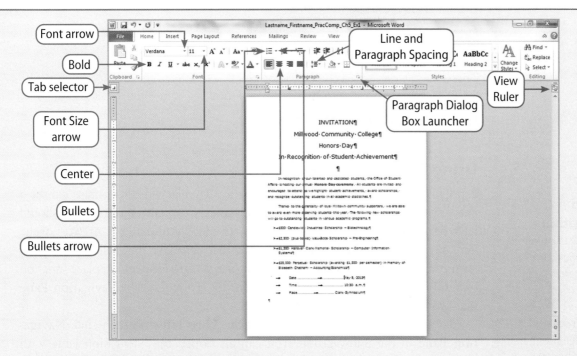

Font arrow

Bold

Tab selector

Font Size arrow

Center

Bullets

Bullets arrow

Line and Paragraph Spacing

Paragraph Dialog Box Launcher

View Ruler

Figure 5.23 The Ribbon includes various character and paragraph formatting options.

j. Select all three tabbed lines. Double-click **a tab on the Ruler** to open the Tabs dialog box.

TROUBLESHOOTING

If the Tabs dialog box does not open, you did not click precisely on a tab. Click the **Paragraph Dialog Box Launcher** and then click **Tabs**.

k. Click **4.5"** in the Tab stop position area. Click **2** in the Leader group to select a dot leader. Click **OK**. Click anywhere to deselect the text.

l. Select all the bulleted lines. Click the **Paragraph Dialog Box Launcher**. Deselect **Don't add space**

between paragraphs of the same style (if the option is already checked). Click the **Spacing After up arrow** twice to increase the spacing after to **18 pt**. Click **OK**.

ON YOUR OWN

With the bulleted scholarship items selected, click the **Bullets arrow** in the Paragraph group on the Home tab and select a different bullet. Deselect the bullets.

m. Click **Save** in the Quick Access Toolbar. Keep the document open for the next exercise.

when you are finished with the document. To do so, click the **Review tab**, and then click **Spelling & Grammar** in the Proofing group. If Word finds any errors, they will display in a Spelling and Grammar dialog box (Figure 5.24). If a suggested correction is appropriate, you can click the suggestion and click **Change** (or **Change All** to change it throughout the document). If, instead, the word is not misspelled (perhaps it is an unusual medical term, or someone's last name), click **Ignore Once** (or **Ignore All** to ignore it throughout the document). You can also click **Add to Dictionary** to add the word to the dictionary so that it will no longer be flagged as misspelled.

Figure 5.24 Word can check your spelling and grammar.

Quick Tip

Spelling and Grammar Options

Use Word Options to indicate whether Word should check for spelling and grammatical errors as you type. Click the **File tab**, and then click **Options**. Click **Proofing**. Indicate your preferences by making selections from the *When correcting spelling and grammar in Word group*.

Using Find and Replace

Especially with a long document, finding a particular word or phrase can be a challenge. Perhaps you are certain you mistakenly capitalized a term that should have been lowercase. Word makes it easy to quickly find all occurrences of the item so you can correct them. If you find that you have misspelled a technical term consistently throughout a document, use Word's Find and Replace function to automatically replace all instances. Word 2010 includes a **Navigation Pane** that provides even more options for finding text.

To open the Navigation Pane, click the **View tab**, and then click **Navigation Pane** in the Show group. You can also open the Navigation Pane with the keyboard shortcut, **Ctrl+F**. The Navigation Pane opens to the left of the document, as shown in Figure 5.25. Using the Navigation Pane tabs, you can browse a document by headings or pages. You can also indicate a search term, with all matches highlighted in the document. Click **Next Search** or **Previous Search** to move to matches within the document so you can make corrections or changes.

A more traditional approach to finding and replacing text is found in the Editing group on the Home tab (Figure 5.26). Click **Replace** to open the Find

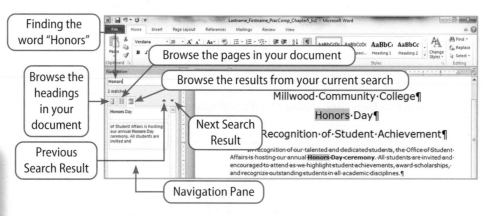

Figure 5.25 The Navigation Pane is a new feature of Word 2010.

Quick Tip

Creating a Cover Page

Although you can certainly design a cover page yourself, centering text vertically on the page, you can let Word do the work for you. Simply click the **Insert tab** and then click **Cover Page** in the Pages group. Select from a gallery of cover pages and then personalize the text for your project.

Figure 5.26 The Editing group on the Home tab enables you to find and replace text.

Figure 5.27 Word makes it easy to find and replace text.

and Replace dialog box, as shown in Figure 5.27. After indicating what text you want to find and what you want to replace it with, you can click **Replace** (to stop at each occurrence, enabling you to choose whether to replace the item) or **Replace All** (to automatically replace all found text with the indicated replacement). For more specificity, click **More**. You can then choose to match case, find whole words only, or even to use a **wildcard**.

A wildcard broadens a search to include one or more characters of any sort. For example, to locate all occurrences of the words *forester* and *forestry*, you could specify *forest** in the Find what: box. The asterisk is a wildcard character, indicating any number of characters. In addition to locating *forester* and *forestry*, then, you might also find *forestation*. The question mark is also a wildcard, but it replaces only one character. Assume you are searching a document for all occurrences of the family name *Conwill*. However, you know that the name is sometimes misspelled as *Conwell*. Using the search term, *Conw?ll*, you would find both instances of the name.

Cutting, Copying, and Pasting

Seldom is a document in final form when you finish typing it. Instead, you are likely to find that some paragraphs would flow better if rearranged. Text from one location could be copied to another to keep from recreating it. All those actions are possible because you can easily **cut**, **copy**, and **paste** text and objects, both within a single document as well as across document types. For example, you could copy a paragraph from a Word document and then paste it in a PowerPoint slide. What makes those actions possible is the **Clipboard**, which is a holding area in RAM. After cutting or copying a selection to the Clipboard, you can paste it to a receiving area. Typically, you will paste an item immediately after cutting or copying it.

To cut or copy a selection, click **Cut** or **Copy** in the Clipboard group on the Home tab (Figure 5.28). Then click where the selection is to be placed and click the upper half of the **Paste button** in the Clipboard group. You can also cut or copy when you right-click a selection and click **Cut** or **Copy** on the shortcut menu. Then right-click the receiving location and click **Paste**.

Unless you open the Clipboard pane, the Clipboard holds only one selection at a time. With the Clipboard pane open, however, you can cut or copy up to 24 items before pasting any. Click the **Clipboard Dialog Box Launcher** to open

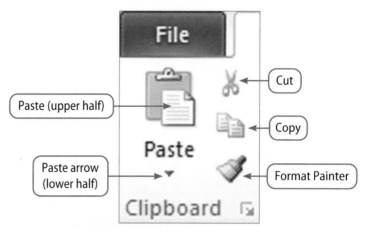

Figure 5.28 The Clipboard temporarily holds items that you cut or copy.

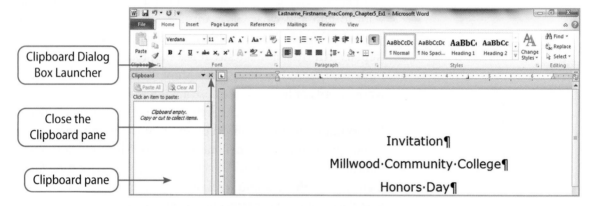

Figure 5.29 The Clipboard pane displays up to 24 cut or copied selections.

the Clipboard pane (Figure 5.29). As you cut or copy a selection, it is shown in the Clipboard pane. Items are listed in the order of activity, with the most recent selection shown first. To paste an item from the Clipboard pane, click where the paste should occur and then point to the item. Click the subsequent arrow and select **Paste** (or **Delete**, if you want to remove the item from the Clipboard

In Depth

Using Format Painter

Having achieved just the right look by adding formatting features to selected text, you might want to duplicate that look elsewhere in the same document. For example, assume you have formatted a heading with a specific font size, color, and text effect. Recreating those settings in subsequent headings would require a great deal of effort, especially if there were multiple headings throughout the document. Instead, you could use Format Painter to copy all formatting from one area to another. Select the area to be copied, and click **Format Painter** in the Clipboard group on the Home tab (Figure 5.28). Then select the area you want to format identically. All formatting attributes are copied. If you want to format several areas identically, select the item whose format you want to copy, and double-click **Format Painter**. Then, one by one, select all receiving areas. Press **Esc**, or click **Format Painter** again, to stop painting the format.

pane). When finished with the Clipboard pane, you can click **Close** (located at the upper right corner of the Clipboard pane) to close it.

Previewing and Printing a Document

When you create a document, you probably will want to print it. Before printing, it is important to have an idea of the way a document will look so you can make adjustments or corrections before using paper and printer ink. Previewing a document is as simple as clicking the **File tab** and then clicking **Print**. From Backstage view, you can not only see a preview, but you can adjust print settings as well. Print settings enable you to specify how many copies of a document to print, which pages to print, and even whether to print on both sides. You can also change margins and page orientation in Backstage view, as shown in Figure 5.30.

Print options in Backstage view include the Print All Pages area, from which you can specify whether you want to print the entire document, only the current page, a selected area, or a custom range of pages. If you choose to print a custom range of pages, specify them by page number, such as 1, 5, 9–12, which would print page 1, page 5, and pages 9 through 12. A comma indicates individual pages, whereas a hyphen specifies a range of pages to print. You can also use the Copies area to indicate the number of copies you want. Other settings enable you to select a printer and specify paper size. Having selected print options, click **Print** to print the document.

Including Headers and Footers

Headers and **footers** display in the top and bottom margins of a document. A page number is a typical footer. If you have prepared a research paper, you know you are required to include your name or student ID as a header. Unless

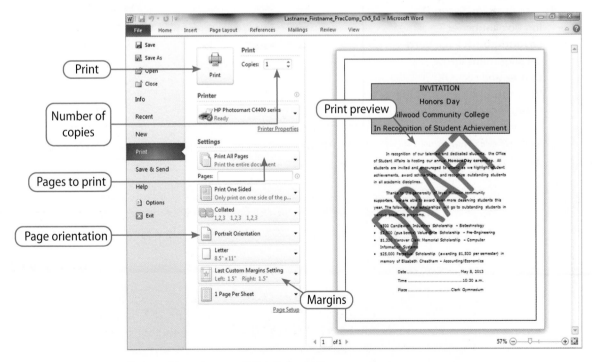

Figure 5.30 Print options are available in Backstage view.

Activity 5.3 Formatting a Document

With a little more effort, the flyer will be ready to go. You will add a page border and a watermark indicating that the document is awaiting approval of the Dean. After checking spelling and repositioning a few selections, the flyer will be almost complete.

a. Click the **View tab** and then click **One Page** in the Zoom group to see how well-positioned the document is on the page. Click **100%** to return to normal size. Drag to select the first four heading lines. Click the **Home tab** and click **Bold**. Click anywhere to deselect the text.

b. Click the **Page Layout tab** and then click **Page Borders** in the Page Background group. Click **Box** and click **OK**.

c. Click **Watermark** in the Page Background group. Scroll down and select **Draft 1**. Click **Watermark** and then click **Custom Watermark**. Click the **Color arrow** and then click **Automatic**. Click **OK**.

d. Click the **Page Setup Dialog Box Launcher**. Click the **Layout tab**. Click the **Vertical alignment arrow**, select **Center**, and click **OK**. Click the **View tab** and then click **One Page**. Figure 5.31 shows the finished document.

e. Save the document and keep it open for the next exercise.

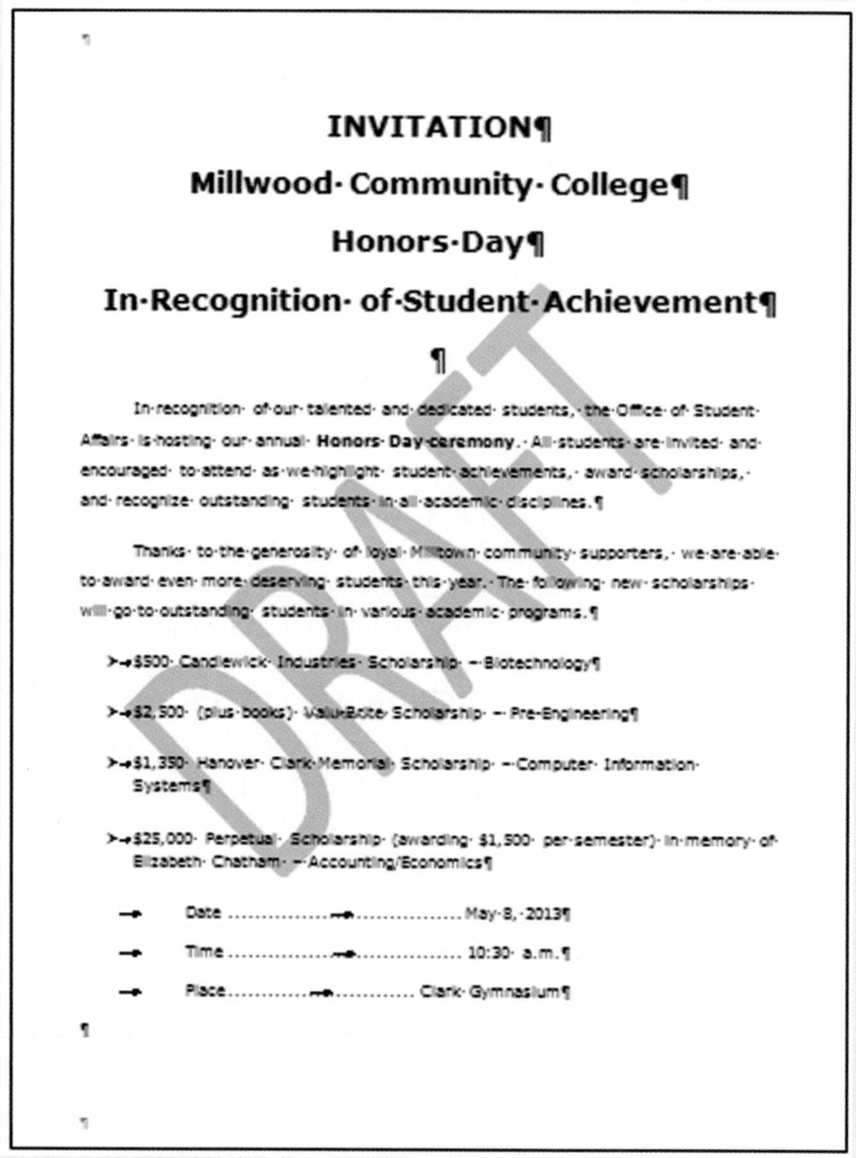

Figure 5.31 Using document formatting, you can put the finishing touches on a document.

you specify otherwise, headers and footers display on every page in a document. However, you can only view them in Print Layout view.

To insert a header or footer, click the **Insert tab** and then click **Header** or **Footer** in the Header & Footer group. Select from a gallery of header and footer styles or click **Edit Header** (or **Edit Footer**) to create a simple header or footer. You can align the header or footer and format it as you would any other text. Click **Close Header and Footer** in the Close group on the Design tab to return to the document (or simply double-click in the document area).

Hands-On

Activity 5.4 Inserting Headers and Footers and Previewing a Document

Before printing the flyer, you will preview it. You will also place identifying information in the header area.

a. Click **100%** in the Zoom group. Click the **Insert tab** and then click **Header**. Click **Edit Header**. Type **Office of Student Affairs** Press **Tab** twice. Type your first name and last name. Click **Close Header and Footer**.

b. Click the **File tab**. Click **Print**. Click the **Copies up arrow** to increase the number of copies to **5**. Click **Print All Pages**. Because the flyer is only one page, there is no need to specify which pages to print, so click **Print All Pages** again to close the print options.

c. Click **Portrait Orientation** and then click **Landscape Orientation**. Because the new orientation is not attractive, click **Landscape Orientation** and then click **Portrait Orientation** to return to the original orientation.

d. Click **Normal Margins** and then click **Custom Margins**. Click the **Left box**, remove existing text, and type **1.5** Click the **Right box**, remove existing text, and type **1.5** Click **OK**.

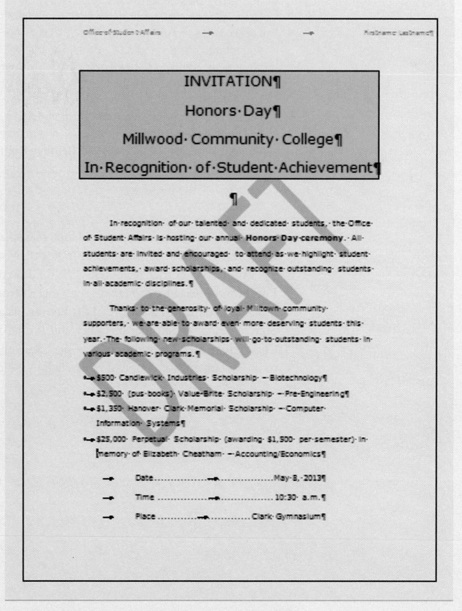

Figure 5.32 Finalize the document by modifying print options and adding a header.

ON YOUR OWN

Change the top and bottom margins to .5". Add a footer, showing the current date. You will simply type the date. Click **Close Header and Footer**.

e. Click the **View tab**. Click **One Page**. The document should display as shown in Figure 5.32. Although you have explored print options, you will not actually print this project. Click **Save**. Click the **File tab** and click **Exit**.

Chapter Summary

- Word processing is one of the most commonly used computer applications, enabling you to create, edit, format, and print documents. *182*

- The Word interface includes a Ribbon, Tabs, the Quick Access toolbar, and document area. *187*

- You can save a document to a flash drive, hard drive, or SkyDrive. *190*

- You can format characters by applying attributes such as boldfacing, underlining, and italicizing. *193*

- Paragraph formats include alignment, bullets, numbering, line spacing, and paragraph spacing. *197*

- Headers and footers display in the top and bottom margins. *209*

- Backstage View enables you to see a document preview. *209*

- Using Find and Replace, you can find all occurrences of specified text, replacing it with another. *206*

- Word's Navigation Pane makes it easy to browse headings and pages in a document, finding specified text. *206*

Key Terms

Backstage view *184*
Clipboard *207*
Copy *207*
Cut *207*
Draft view *188*
First Line Indent *200*
Font *187*
Footer *209*
Full Screen Reading view *188*
Hanging Indent *200*
Hard return *185*
Header *209*
Indent *199*
Insertion point *182*
Landscape *201*
Left Indent *200*
Line spacing *197*

Margin *202*
Microsoft Office 2010 *182*
Microsoft Word 2010 *181*
Microsoft Works *182*
Mini toolbar *195*
Navigation Pane *206*
Outline view *188*
Page border *203*
Paragraph spacing *197*
Paste *207*
Portrait *201*
Print Layout view *188*
Quick Access Toolbar *187*
Ribbon *187*
Right Indent *200*
Ruler *197*
ScreenTip *188*

Soft return *186*
Status bar *187*
Tabs *197*
Title bar *187*
Typeface *193*
Watermark *201*
Web Layout view *188*
Wildcard *207*
Word processing *181*
Word wrap *185*
WordPerfect Office *182*
Zoom Slider *187*

view
word star
Quick access toolbar
template
Know the difference b/t
Red Blue + Green way y
line

Multiple Choice

1. When Word automatically returns the insertion point to the next line, that action is called
   a. a hard return.
   b. a tab.
   c. word wrap.
   d. a forced Enter.

2. The Word feature that groups several of the most common formatting options in a location near selected text is
   a. the Mini toolbar.
   b. Live Preview.
   c. Backstage view.
   d. the Quick Access Toolbar.

3. You might want to display nonprinting characters so you can
   a. troubleshoot a document.
   b. remove soft returns.
   c. identify and correct spelling errors.
   d. format a document.

4. Which of the following is *not* a tab position?
   a. Justify
   b. Right
   c. Left
   d. Decimal

5. A line or graphic that surrounds a page is a
   a. box border.
   b. outline border.
   c. page border.
   d. grid.

6. The blinking vertical bar that indicates where text will be typed is the
   a. pointer.
   b. type point.
   c. blinker.
   d. insertion point.

7. The major purpose of Backstage view is to
   a. provide a location for actions and settings related to an open document.
   b. provide free online storage space.
   c. enable you to see how a proposed change would affect the appearance of a selection or object.
   d. group common formatting commands in an easily accessible area.

8. Before applying changes, such as boldfacing or italicizing, to existing text, you must
   a. click the Page Layout tab.
   b. press Ctrl+A.
   c. select the text.
   d. display the Ruler.

9. The Navigation Pane
   a. provides options for finding text.
   b. enables you to use a formatting mark to find matches.
   c. is located in the Editing group on the Home tab.
   d. displays selections you have cut or copied.

10. To identify a document as not in final form, you could use a
    a. different page orientation.
    b. draft watermark.
    c. page stamp.
    d. formatting mark.

11. A template is a
    a. set of formatting characteristics that you can apply to selected text.
    b. predesigned document that you can personalize.
    c. graphic or symbol that denotes an item of interest.
    d. temporary holding area in RAM.

12. A bibliography in a research paper typically uses this type of indent:
    a. Hanging.
    b. Dropping.
    c. First Line.
    d. Right.

13. The difference between line spacing and paragraph spacing is that line spacing is
    a. limited to single and double spacing whereas paragraph spacing provides many more spacing choices.
    b. an option on the Page Layout tab whereas paragraph spacing is accessed only on the Home tab.
    c. the number of lines between paragraphs whereas paragraph spacing is the number of points between paragraphs.
    d. the amount of space between lines of text within a paragraph whereas paragraph spacing is the amount of space between paragraphs.

14. The Word view that does not display the Ribbon is
    a. Draft view.
    b. Print Layout view.
    c. Outline view.
    d. Full Screen Reading view.

15. Text that is placed in the top margin is called a(n)
    a. heading.
    b. gutter.
    c. object.
    d. header.

True/False

Circle **T** if the statement is true or **F** if the statement is false.

T F 1. An indent is the same as a tab.

T F 2. You can define custom margin settings as the default.

T F 3. The Clipboard is a holding area in RAM.

T F 4. To copy the format of one selection to another, click Copy in the Clipboard group.

T F 5. A Word document is in overtype mode by default.

T F 6. Using Backstage view, you can preview a document before printing it.

T F 7. The Outline view enables you to see the hierarchical organization of a document.

T F 8. Cut, copy, and paste are features that are unique to Word 2010.

T F 9. Unless you open the Clipboard pane, the Clipboard holds only one item at a time.

T F 10. You can use the Ruler, as well as the Tabs dialog box, to set tabs.

End of Chapter Exercises

Guided Exercises

1. You will prepare achievement certificates for presentation at Honors Day at Millwood Community College. After preparing one, you can use it as a pattern for others. The first will be a certificate for Computer Information Systems.

   a. Open Word. Click the **File tab** and click **Save As**. Navigate to the location where you save projects. Click the **File name box** and type **Lastname_Firstname_PracComp_Ch5_Certificate**. Type your last name instead of Lastname and your first name instead of Firstname. Click **Save**. If necessary, click **Show/Hide** to display nonprinting characters.

   b. Click the **Page Layout tab**, click **Orientation**, and select **Landscape**.

   c. Click **Margins** and then click **Custom Margins**. Click in the **Top box** and type **2** (removing existing numbers). Click in the **Bottom box** and type **2** (removing existing numbers). Similarly, change left and right margins to **2**. Click **OK**.

   d. Click the **Home tab** and click **Center** in the Paragraph group.

   e. Click the **Font arrow** and select **Arial**. Click the **Font Size arrow** and select **28**.

   f. Type **COMPUTER INFORMATION SYSTEMS**. Because the current font size results in text that extends over two lines, you will adjust the font size. Select **COMPUTER INFORMATION SYSTEMS**. Click the **Font Size arrow** and place the pointer over any font size. Continue "trying out" font sizes, using Live Preview to determine the best fit. Click **24**.

   g. Click anywhere to deselect the text. Press **Ctrl+End** to move to the end of the document (which is the end of the first typed line) and press **Enter**. Click the **Font Size arrow** and select **20**. Type **Award of Excellence** Press **Enter**.

   h. Click the **Font arrow** and select **Lucida Handwriting**. Type **is hereby granted to** and press **Enter**. Because the first letter of the new line is automatically capitalized, you will change it to lowercase. Click immediately after the letter, press **Backspace**, and type a lowercase **i**.

   i. Select **is hereby granted to** and change the font size to **16**.

   j. Click anywhere in the line containing the text **Award of Excellence**. Click the **Paragraph Dialog Box Launcher** and click the **Spacing after up arrow** twice to increase the paragraph spacing to **18**. Click **OK**.

   k. Press **Ctrl+End** to move to the end of the document. Change the font size to **36**. Type **Melinda Ann Allen** and press **Enter**. Select the name you just typed. Click **Underline** in the Font group. Click after the words granted to and press **Enter** twice.

   l. Press **Ctrl+End** and change the font size to **16**. Press **Enter**. Type **For outstanding performance and highest academic achievement**

   m. Because the document now extends over two pages, you will change the top and bottom margins to 1". Click the **File tab**. Click **Print**. Click **Previous Page arrow** (at the bottom center of Backstage view) to return the view to the first page. Click **Last Custom Margins Setting**. Click **Custom Margins**. Change the top and bottom margins to 1. Click **OK**. Does the document now display on one page? Note that you can also change margins by clicking the **Page Layout tab**, **Margins**, and **Custom Margins**.

   n. Click the **Home tab**. Press **Enter**. Click **Align Text Right** in the Paragraph group. Type **Millwood Community College** and press **Enter**. Type **May 8, 2013** (Do not press Enter.) Select the last two typed lines and click **Line and Paragraph Spacing** in the Paragraph group. Click **1.0**. Click the **Page Layout tab** and click the **Spacing after down arrow** twice to change paragraph spacing after to **0**. With the last two lines still selected, click the **Home tab** and change the font to **Arial**.

   o. Select all text except for the last two right-aligned lines. Click the **Font Color arrow** and select **Dark Blue, Text 2, Darker 50%** (row 6, column 4). Click the **View tab** and then click **One Page**. Because the text of the last two lines is not attractive in a different color, select the last two lines. Click the **Home tab**. Click **Font Color** (the button, not the arrow) to apply the most recently selected color. With the last two lines still selected, click **Bold**. Similarly, bold the recipient's name (Melinda Ann Allen). Deselect any selected text.

p. Click the **Page Layout tab**. Click **Page Borders**. Click **Shadow**. Click the **Color arrow** and select **Dark Blue, Text 2, Darker 50%**. Click the **Width arrow** and select **1 1/2 pt**. Click **OK**.

q. Click **Margins**. Click **Custom Margins**. Click **Layout**. Click the **Vertical alignment arrow** and select **Center**. Click **OK**.

r. Click the **Home tab**. Click **Show/Hide** in the Paragraph group to remove the display of non-printing characters. Click the **Review tab**. Click **Spelling & Grammar** to check spelling. Ignore or accept any errors, as appropriate. Click **OK** when complete.

s. Click the **Page Layout tab**. Click **Page Color**. Click **Dark Blue, Text 2, Lighter 60%** (row 3, column 4). Click **Page Color**. Click **Fill Effects**. Click **Vertical** (under Shading styles). Click the selection in the first row, second column of Variants. Click **OK**.

t. Click the **Home tab**. Select **Award of Excellence** and change the font size to **28**. Bold the title **Computer Information Systems**.

u. Save the document and exit Word.

2. You are preparing an employment letter to use in your upcoming job search. You will consider a template, but will ultimately develop a letter with details specific to your job search.

a. Open Word. Click the **File tab**, and then click **New**. Under the Office.com Templates category, click **Letters**. Click the **Employment and resignation letters** folder. Click the **Applicant letters** folder. Double-click the **Letter announcing your job search (Blue Line design)** file.

b. Because the letter is not appropriate for your particular situation, and would require a great deal of revision, you decide to create your own. Click the **File tab** and then click **Close**. If asked whether you want to save the document, click **Don't Save**.

c. Click the **File tab** and then click **New**. Double-click **Blank document**. Click the **File tab** and click **Save As**. Navigate to the location where you save projects. Click the **File name box** and type **Lastname_Firstname_PracComp_Ch5_Letter** Type your last name

instead of Lastname and your first name instead of Firstname. Click **Save**.

d. If nonprinting characters do not display, click **Show/Hide**. Click **No Spacing** in the Styles group. Type your first name and last name. Press **Enter**. Type your street address (or make up a fictional address) and press Enter. Type your city, state, and zip. Be sure to place a comma after the city, and a space between the two-letter state abbreviation and the zip code. Press **Enter** twice.

e. Type the current date and press **Enter** twice. Type the following address, pressing **Enter** after each line:

Mr. Lawrence Campbell, President
Campbell Industries
3019 Glasgow Drive
Burlington, VT 05401

f. Press **Enter**. Type **Dear Mr. Campbell:** Press **Enter** twice. Click the **Paragraph Dialog Box Launcher**. Click the **Special arrow** and select **First line**. Click **OK**.

g. Type the following paragraph, allowing Word to automatically wrap each line. Press **Enter** at the end of the paragraph.

Please accept my application for the system analyst position advertised in the Times Courier. As requested, I am enclosing a job application, a resume, and three references.

h. Type the following paragraph, but do not press Enter at the end of the paragraph.

The position is very interesting to me because I believe that my strong technical experience and education are well suited to its requirements. Having completed a degree in Systems Analysis from the University of Rockport, I believe that I am an excellent candidate for the position. The key strengths that I possess include:

i. Select both paragraphs that you just typed and click the **Page Layout tab**. Click the **Spacing After up arrow** twice to increase spacing to **12 pt**. Click anywhere to deselect the text. Press **Ctrl+End** and press **Enter**.

j. Drag the **First Line Indent marker** ▽, located at the left side of the Ruler, back to the left margin. Click the **Home tab**. Click **Bullets** in the Paragraph group. Type the following items, pressing **Enter** after each.

Successful design, development, and support of systems

Excellent team-building skills

Demonstrated written and oral communication skills

k. Click **Bullets** in the Paragraph group to remove the final bullet. Select the first two bulleted items, click the **Paragraph Dialog Box Launcher** and click the **Spacing After down arrow** twice to reduce the spacing to **0 pt**. Click **OK**.

l. Press **Ctrl+End** to move to the end of the document. Type **Please refer to my resume for additional information and references**. Press **Enter**. Type **I can be reached at rsh3002@ httnet.net or at 504-555-8971**. Press **Enter**. Right-click the e-mail hyperlink (colored area) and select **Remove Hyperlink**. Click to place the insertion point after the period (before the paragraph mark) following the word *references*. Press **Delete** so the final two paragraphs are shown as one. Press **Spacebar** to insert a space between the two sentences.

m. Click the **Paragraph Dialog Box Launcher**. Click the **Special arrow** and select **First line**. Click **OK**. Press **Ctrl+End**. Type **Sincerely,** and press **Enter** twice. Type your first name and last name.

n. Select the words **Times Courier** in the first paragraph of the letter. Click **Italic** in the Font group. Press **Ctrl+A** to select the entire

document. Click the **Font arrow** and select **Times New Roman**. Click the **Font Size arrow** and select **12**. Click anywhere to deselect the text.

o. Click the **Review tab** and click **Spelling & Grammar** to check spelling. Correct or ignore any errors.

p. Click the **View tab** and then click **One Page**. Click the **Page Layout tab** and then click **Margins**. Click **Custom Margins**. With the value in the Top box selected (or having removed existing text), type **2** Click **OK**.

q. Click the **View tab** and click **100%**. Click the **Home tab** and click **Replace** in the Editing group. You will replace the name *Campbell* with *Crowell* throughout the document. With any text in the **Find what: box** selected, type **Campbell** Click in the **Replace with: box** and type **Crowell** Click **Replace All**. Click **OK**. Click **Close**.

r. Double-click the word **oral** in the third bullet. Click **Cut** in the Clipboard group. Click to place the insertion point before the word **written** in the same bullet. Click **Paste** in the Clipboard group. Type **and** and press **Spacebar**. Double-click **and** after the word **written** and press **Delete**. Adjust any awkward spacing between words.

s. Save the document and exit Word.

Unguided Project

Your company is putting together a training manual for new users of Word 2010. Clerical staff have already typed much of the document, so you will simply edit and modify the document to get it ready to distribute. Complete the steps below to perform that task.

a. Open **PracComp_Ch5_Manual** from the location of your data files. Save the document as *Lastname_Firstname_PracComp_Ch5_Manual*. If necessary, show nonprinting characters.

b. Select and center the first four lines. Bold all four lines. Select only the first two lines and change the font size to 18.

c. Triple-click the multi-line paragraph beginning with *Baker Enterprises* to select it. Change line

spacing to **1.15**. Align the selected paragraph at Justify.

d. Select the line containing the text *Table of Contents*. Center the selected line and change the font size to **16**. Bold the selection. Select the following six lines, beginning with *Beginning a New Word Document* and ending with *Formatting a Document*. Click the tab selector twice to select a right indent. If the Ruler is not shown, click **View Ruler**. Click at 6" on the Ruler to set a right tab.

e. Double-click the **right tab stop** on the Ruler to open the Tabs dialog box. Click **2** in the Leader group. Click **OK**. Click to place the insertion point after the word *Document* (in the *Beginning a New Word Document* line). Press **Tab**. Type **2** Similarly, enter page numbers as shown here for the remaining items in the Table of Contents.

f. With the insertion point after the number *10*, hold **Ctrl** and press **Enter** to begin a new page. Press **Delete** to remove the empty paragraph ¶ at the top of the second page.

g. Select all text on the second page and change the line spacing to **2.0**. Add a First line indent and change the paragraph spacing after to **12 pt**.

h. Press **Ctrl+Home**. Preview the document in Backstage view. Click **Previous Page** and **Next Page** to view all pages, one by one. Press **Esc**.

i. Check spelling, correcting any errors identified (if they are actually errors). The word *Backstage* should be capitalized, so it is not an error.

j. You are not certain whether you capitalized Word wherever it occurred in the context of the software name, so you will use the Navigation Pane to locate all occurrences. Click the **Home tab** and click **Find** in the Editing group. Click in the **white box** at the top of the Navigation Pane and type **Word** (removing any existing text). Scroll through the document, checking each highlighted occurrence for correct capitalization. Close the Navigation Pane.

k. Triple-click the second paragraph on page 2 (beginning with *Using Microsoft Word*). Cut the paragraph and paste it before the first paragraph on the same page.

l. Click the **Insert tab** and click **Page Number**. Point to **Bottom of Page** and select **Plain Number 2** to center the page number. Check **Different First Page** in the Options group to suppress the display of a page number on the first page. Double-click the center of the page to close the Footer.

m. Scroll up and click anywhere on page 1. Click the **Page Layout tab** and click **Page Borders**. Apply a Box border, with a Color of Automatic and a Width of 1/2 pt. Apply the border to **This section – First page only** and click **OK**.

n. Bold the words *insertion point* the first time they occur in the second paragraph on page 2. Bold the word *Ribbon* the first time it appears in the last paragraph on page 3.

o. Preview the document in Backstage view. Save the document and exit Word.

Photos by Monkey Business Images/Shutterstock;
Sergej Khakimullin/Shutterstock

CHAPTER **SIX**

Working with Excel

THE EASIEST WAY TO VISUALIZE A SPREADSHEET IS to think about a grid of columns and rows. Without even giving much thought to the concept of a computerized spreadsheet, you can identify many practical applications of a simple grid on paper. For example, how would you organize your monthly budget? Most likely, you would list income and expense categories in one column, with dollar values in the next. With formulas to calculate total expenses and net income, your budget spreadsheet might be similar to the sample budget shown in Table 6.1. Whether you choose to summarize the budget spreadsheet in a computer spreadsheet program, such as **Microsoft Excel 2010**, or whether you prefer to maintain it on paper, the concept of organizing data in a grid of columns and rows is a common feature of both computerized and manual spreadsheets.

OBJECTIVES

When you complete this chapter, you will:

▶ Become familiar with Excel basics.

▶ Understand how to modify a worksheet.

▶ Create formulas.

▶ Work with absolute and relative referencing

▶ Work with functions.

▶ Conduct what-if analysis.

Table 6.1 A spreadsheet enables you to organize data.

Monthly Income	$3,250
Expenses	
Rent	585
Car	525
Miscellaneous	1,200
Total Expenses	2,310
Net Income	940

The primary purpose of organizing data in spreadsheet form is to express relationships between sets of numeric data. One advantage of using a computer spreadsheet over a paper spreadsheet is the ability to "try out" various scenarios and to copy formulas from one location to another so you can quickly summarize a large amount of data. Your instructor probably uses spreadsheet software to organize class grades, similar to the spreadsheet shown in Table 6.2. Instead of calculating each student's final average with a handheld calculator, she can enter a formula to calculate the final average for the first student, and then copy the formula down the column for every other student. Although each student's test scores are different, the general formula is the same, adding all exam scores and then dividing by the number of exams. Experimenting with scores for the final exam, your instructor can then help you understand what score is necessary for a particular letter grade. Trying out various exam scores and experimenting with different scenarios is an example of the "what-if" capability of a computer spreadsheet. The versatility of a computer spreadsheet with respect to modeling different scenarios can provide information that leads to better decision making. Therefore, spreadsheet software is often considered **decision-support software**.

Table 6.2 A computer spreadsheet is made up of a grid of columns and rows.

	A	B	C	D	E	F
1	Last Name	First Name	Exam 1	Exam 2	Exam 3	Final Average
2	Archer	Marilyn	95	83	98	92
3	Cale	Michael	72	65	85	74
4	Matthews	Sarah	90	90	75	85

The spreadsheet shown in Table 6.2 summarizes data in columns and rows. As you begin to work with Microsoft Excel, you will learn that Excel refers to **spreadsheets** as **worksheets**. Each column is identified with a letter (A, B, C, . . .), while each row is numbered. The intersection of every column and row is called a **cell**. Each cell is identified by a unique address, composed of the column letter and the row number. For example, cell A1 (identified by the column letter and the row number) contains the words *Last Name*, while cell B1 contains the words *First Name*. The final average values shown in column F (cells F2, F3, and F4) were actually calculated. For example, the formula to calculate Marilyn Archer's final average is (C2+D2+E2)/3. Similarly, Michael Cale's final average formula is (C3+D3+E3)/3. Relatively speaking, the formulas are the same, so after entering the formula once in cell F2, you could simply copy the formula down the column. Regardless of whether the class enrollment was 3 students or 300, the formula could be quickly copied down the column, saving an inordinate amount of time calculating final averages.

Using a spreadsheet, you can get answers to such questions as "What will the payment be on a new car if I borrow $20,000 over four years at 7.25% interest rate?" or "How much clear income will I have if my rent goes up by $100 per month?" As a businessperson, you might wonder how sales will be affected if the state raises the tax rate by 1%. By modeling such scenarios with spreadsheet software, you will have well-organized data on which to base decisions. Spreadsheet software is considered a "what-if" tool with which you can tie formulas to data so that if the data changes, the result of the formula reflects that change. For example, to determine net income after a $100 increase in rent, simply increase the rent figure on the computer spreadsheet by $100 and you will immediately see the resulting change in net income. Of course, to be used in that manner, the spreadsheet must be set up correctly, which you will learn to do later in this chapter.

A Look Back

VisiCalc

Introduced in 1979, VisiCalc was the first computer spreadsheet program. It was immensely successful. Companies that invested time and money in recording financial information on manually calculated spreadsheets jumped at the chance to automate that information. One of the developers of VisiCalc, Dan Bricklin, estimated that VisiCalc took work that had required 20 hours per week and turned it into only 15 minutes of effort. Dan Bricklin and Bob Frankston teamed up to develop VisiCalc. Shortly thereafter, they started their own company, Software Arts, to develop and market the product. Initially produced for the Apple II, versions were quickly developed for the Tandy TRS-80, the Commodore PET, and the Atari 800. By October, 1979, VisiCalc was a top seller at $100. Lotus Development Corporation purchased VisiCalc in 1983 and developed it into the Lotus 1-2-3 program.

Understanding Excel

Microsoft Excel 2010 is spreadsheet software included as a component of Microsoft Office 2010. As such, it is recognized worldwide as a powerful, yet easy to learn and use, software package. From the most basic applications to the most complex, Excel enables you to create worksheets (computer spreadsheets) that effectively summarize data so it is easy to understand and from which you can draw well-based conclusions. Excel is widely used in business and educational settings, so if you learn to use only one spreadsheet software package, it is a good choice.

If Excel is installed on your system, you will find it by clicking **Start**, **All Programs**, **Microsoft Office**, **Microsoft Excel 2010**. The Excel window will open, as shown in Figure 6.1. The worksheet area comprises columns and rows, set off by gridlines. You can type words, numbers or formulas in each cell, which you have learned is the intersection of a column and row. Each cell is identified by a **cell address**, which is the column letter and row number, such as A1 or B28.

Just as a book is made up of a series of pages, a **workbook** is made up of one or more worksheets. Each worksheet is an electronic grid of columns and rows in which you can enter data. When you save an Excel file, you are actually saving a workbook. A worksheet is one "page" within the workbook. For example, if your workbook is actually a summary of sales information of various branches of your company, you can place each branch's information on a separate worksheet, label it accordingly, and move among worksheets, comparing sales data. The workbook you save will include several worksheets, each summarizing a branch's performance.

A worksheet is simply a grid of columns and rows, identified by letters and numbers. The lines separating cells are called **gridlines**. What you see on-screen is actually only a small portion of the entire worksheet area. You are not limited to the portion of a worksheet that is shown on-screen at one time. In fact, you have access to 1,048,576 rows and 18,278 columns in each worksheet. Use the

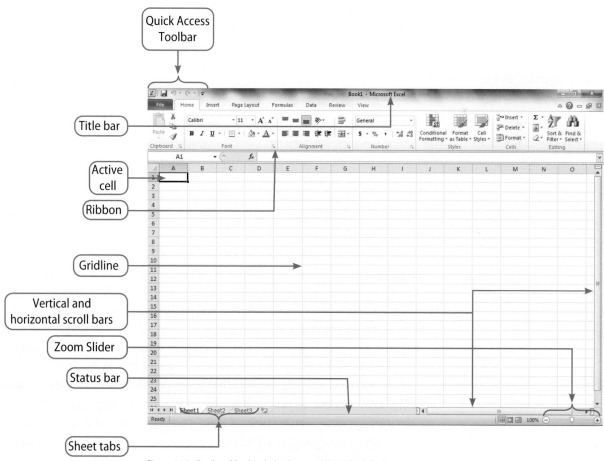

Figure 6.1 An Excel workbook includes three worksheets by default.

Understanding Excel   **223**

Quick Tip

Using the Zoom Slider

Drag the tab on the Zoom Slider (Figure 6.1) to the left to reduce the size of text in a worksheet, or to the right to increase it. Remember that reducing the view size does not actually change the font size or modify the way the worksheet will print. It simply enables you to zoom in or out to view the worksheet differently. Click the percentage indicated on the left side of the Zoom Slider to open a dialog box, enabling you to select a specific percentage or to indicate a custom setting.

Quick Tip

Using Shortcut Keys

To quickly move the active cell to the upper-left corner of a worksheet (cell A1), press **Ctrl+Home**. Use **Page Up** and **Page Dn** to move up or down an entire screen. Use **Alt+Page Up** to move one full screen to the left and **Alt+Page Dn** to move one full screen to the right.

vertical or horizontal scroll bars (Figure 6.1) to view areas that are off-screen. Columns are labeled from A to Z, and then AA, AB, and so forth, ending at column XFD. Rows are numbered sequentially.

The **Ribbon** (Figure 6.1), located at the top of the Excel window, contains groups of commands that are similar to those found in other Office applications, such as Word and PowerPoint. A few groups that are unique to Excel relate to such tasks as generating formulas and organizing data. The **title bar** lists the filename and includes the **Quick Access Toolbar**, which is the location of commonly accessed commands such as Save, Undo, and Redo. Just as in other Office applications, the **status bar** provides information related to the open file or process, as well as View buttons and a Zoom Slider.

After you have created a worksheet, you can customize its appearance by adding formatting features, much like those available with a word processor. You can center items and make them boldface, change the appearance of numbers by adding dollar signs or commas, and include borders and shading. In addition, you can print a worksheet (or a selected area within a worksheet) with or without gridlines.

Beginning and Opening an Excel Workbook

When you open Excel, a blank worksheet displays. The **active cell** is A1, as identified by a black border that surrounds the cell (Figure 6.1). Any data you type or any formatting or edits you apply will affect the active cell. To select a new active cell in which to enter data, simply click the cell. As you move the pointer over a worksheet, the pointer will resemble a large white plus sign. You might think of that sign as a selection indicator. A cell or group of cells that you click or drag (when the pointer is a large white plus sign) will be the location for entering data. When working with Excel, carefully note the pointer shape, as the shape is actually an indication of what will occur if you click or drag. As you will learn later in this chapter, the pointer shape is an indication of whether you will select, copy, or even adjust column width or row height, when you click and drag a worksheet area.

A new workbook includes three worksheets, with each worksheet available on a sheet tab as shown in Figure 6.1. You can rename sheet tabs to better represent worksheet contents. You can also delete, insert, and move sheets to other locations within the workbook. Excel does not impose a limit on the number of worksheets you can add; the only limitation is your computer memory. However, most workbooks can be organized with only a few relevant worksheets. It is much more common to create separate workbooks for varied tasks rather than to include a large number of worksheets within one workbook.

As shown in Figure 6.3, the **Name Box** displays the address of the active cell. You can also use the Name Box to move to another cell. Simply click in the **Name Box** and type the cell to which you want to move. Press **Enter** to reposition the active cell in the new location. The **Formula Bar** displays the contents of the active cell or the formula that produced the result shown in the active cell. The Formula Bar is very helpful when you are attempting to determine why a formula produced an incorrect result. You can even make corrections on the Formula Bar if necessary, to avoid retyping the entire formula if you find the formula

Renaming, Inserting, Moving, and Deleting Worksheets

A worksheet is a page within a workbook. Because each worksheet is likely to represent a component or activity related to the workbook as a whole, you might want to identify each worksheet appropriately. By default, worksheets are identified as Sheet1, Sheet2, and so on, but such identification is not very descriptive. You can rename a worksheet by right-clicking a sheet and selecting **Rename** from the menu that displays (called a shortcut menu). Then type a new name and press Enter. Similarly, you can delete a worksheet, or even change the tab color, when you right-click a sheet and select accordingly from the shortcut menu (Figure 6.2). To move a sheet, simply drag the sheet tab to a new location before or after other sheet tabs. Finally, you can insert a new worksheet when you click **Insert Worksheet** (Figure 6.2).

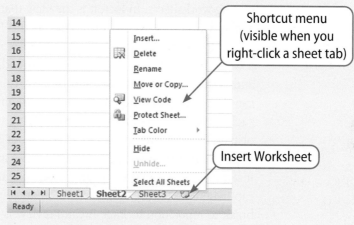

Shortcut menu (visible when you right-click a sheet tab)

Insert Worksheet

Figure 6.2 Each worksheet displays on a separate tab.

to be in error. You can also edit the content of cells containing text or numbers by selecting the cell and then making changes on the Formula Bar.

Entering data is as easy as selecting (clicking) a cell, typing the data, and pressing Enter. You can enter three types of data—text, values, and formulas (including **functions**, which are shortcut formulas). Characters that you type in

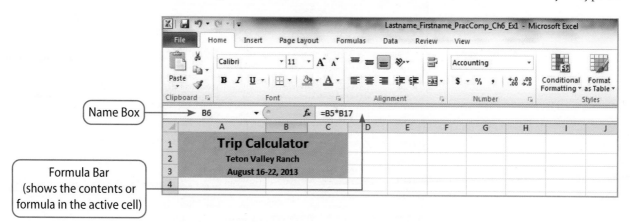

Name Box

Formula Bar (shows the contents or formula in the active cell)

Figure 6.3 The Formula Bar makes it easy to see formulas and other cell contents.

Quick Tip
Navigating a Worksheet
To move to another cell, simply click the cell. If the cell to which you want to move is not on-screen, you can type the cell address in the Name Box and press **Enter**, or drag the vertical or horizontal scroll bar to reposition the view and then click the cell.

a cell determine the data type. If the first character is a letter, the entry is considered to be text. If all characters in a cell are numeric, the entry is identified as a value, and if the first character is an equal sign, the data is assumed to be a formula.

To open a previously saved workbook, click the **File tab** and then click **Open**, navigate through your folder structure to locate the Excel workbook, and double-click the file to open it. When you click the File tab, **Backstage view** opens, which is a collection of common actions and settings related to the current workbook.

Identifying Excel Views

Excel 2010 enables you to view a worksheet in several different ways, as shown in Figure 6.4. You can change views when you click the **View tab** and then select a view from the Workbook Views group. **Normal view** is useful for building and editing worksheets. In fact, it is the view that displays by default when you begin a new workbook. With full access to the Ribbon, Normal view is the setting you will use most often as you develop worksheets. **Page Layout view** shows a worksheet as it will appear when printed. Page Layout view adds horizontal and vertical rulers, with left and right margins shown. In Page Layout view, you can drag a margin on the ruler to increase or decrease it. Any headers or footers, such as page numbers or other identifying information, as well as the locations of page breaks, are shown in Page Layout view. Similar to Page Layout view, **Page Break Preview** displays page breaks as blue lines. A page break you have inserted, called a manual page break, appears as a solid line. Dashed lines indicate where Excel breaks pages automatically. You can drag either type of page break to reposition it. Page Break Preview is useful when you want to make sure that printed worksheet pages are attractive, with the desired amount of information shown on each printed page.

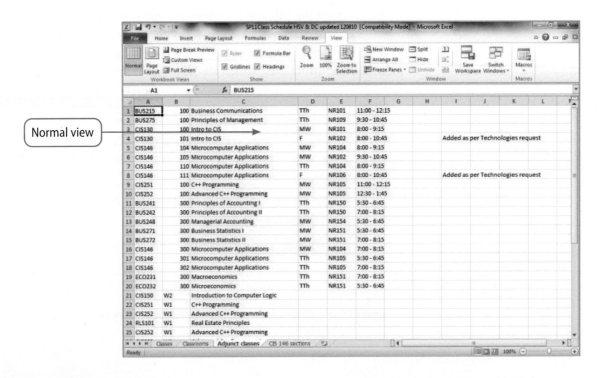

Normal view

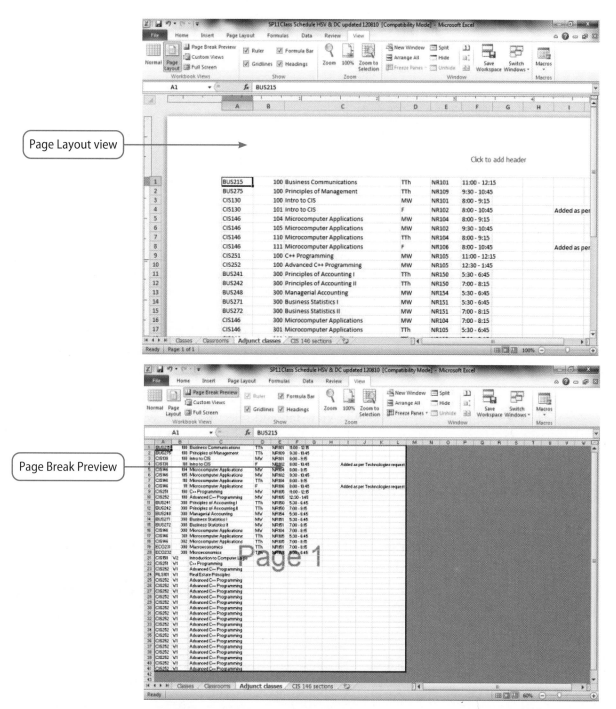

Page Layout view

Page Break Preview

Figure 6.4 Each Excel view shows a worksheet in a different way.

In Depth

Inserting, Moving, and Deleting Page Breaks

After previewing a worksheet, you might determine that a page break is necessary in a location where Excel has not placed one. When you insert a page break, it is called a manual page break. With a worksheet shown in Page Break Preview, select the row below where you want to insert a horizontal page break or select a column to the right of where you want to insert a vertical page break. Click the **Page Layout tab** and then click **Breaks** in the Page Setup group. Click **Insert Page Break**. To quickly remove all manually inserted page breaks, click **Breaks** in the Page Setup group and select **Reset All Page Breaks**. To move a page break, drag the page break to a new location.

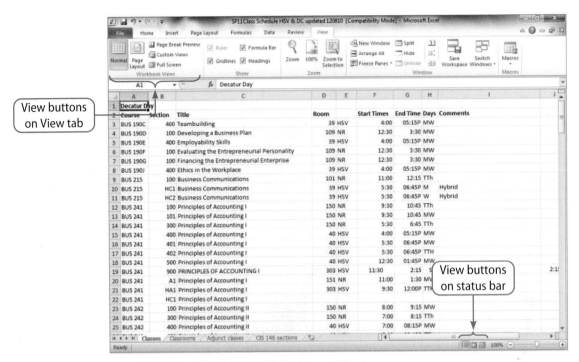

Figure 6.5 Change views with selections on the View tab or in the status bar.

To select an Excel view, click a **View button** on the status bar (Figure 6.5), or click the **View tab** and select from the Workbook Views group. In addition to Normal, Print Layout, and Page Break Preview views, the Workbook Views group includes a Full Screen view selection. **Full Screen view** hides the Ribbon, Formula Bar, and Name Box features, as well as the status bar. Figure 6.6 shows a worksheet in Full Screen view. You might use Full Screen view when you want to see more of a worksheet without the distraction of other on-screen elements. To return to Normal view, press **Esc** (or right-click anywhere and then click **Close Full Screen**). When you select **Custom Views**, you can design your own view settings.

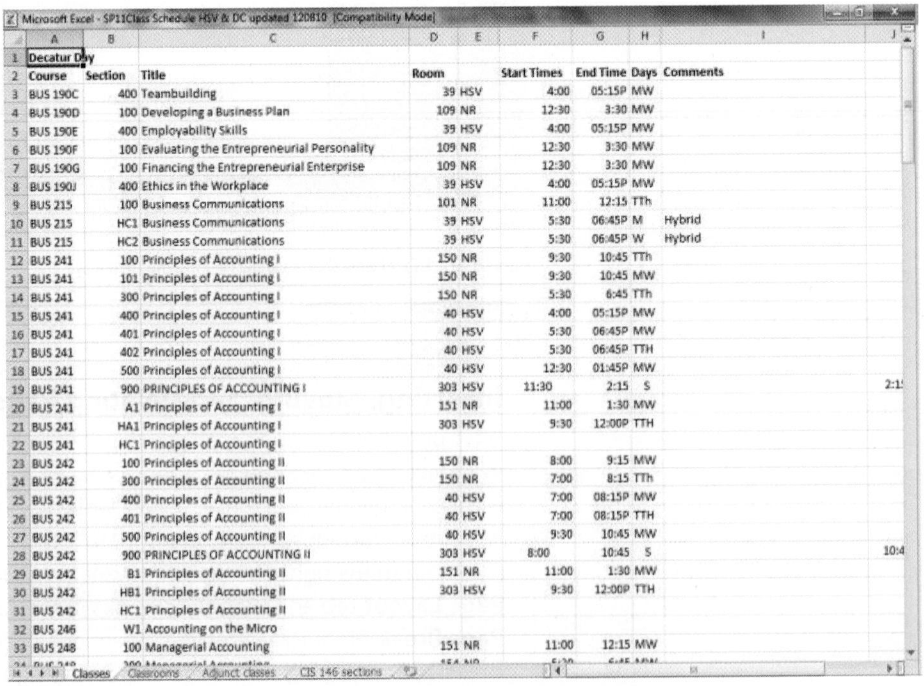

Figure 6.6 Full Screen view provides the most space possible for an open workbook.

In Depth

Using AutoComplete

As you type a cell entry, you might find that Excel attempts to automatically complete the entry for you. That happens if the first few characters you type are identical to a cell you previously typed in the same column. AutoComplete can be helpful if you are repeating information, but it can also be distracting if the entry is actually different. To turn AutoComplete off (or on), click the **File tab**, and then click **Options**. Click **Advanced**. Click **Enable AutoComplete for cell values** in the Editing options choices and click **OK**. To reverse the setting, repeat the steps, but click to deselect **Enable AutoComplete for cell values**.

Saving a Workbook

An Excel workbook, including all its worksheets, is essentially a file. Therefore, when you save a workbook, all worksheets included in that workbook are saved under one filename. Excel 2010 files are saved with an extension of *xlsx*, which is a file format based on Office Open XML. Therefore, a workbook you might save with the filename *Travel Costs* will actually be saved on your disk as *Travel Costs.xlsx*. The Office Open XML file format is a Microsoft standard related to file and document management. Because both Office 2007 and Office 2010 are based on the XML standard, Excel 2007 users can open files that are saved in Excel 2010 with very few compatibility issues.

To save an Excel workbook, click the **File tab**, and then click **Save** or **Save As**. A dialog box similar to that shown in Figure 6.7 enables you to indicate the

Technology Insight

New Features in Excel 2010

For those who currently use Excel 2007, the move to Excel 2010 is not very dramatic. In fact, many Excel users will take comfort in the fact that most of the activities and features they enjoy in Excel 2007 are also found in Excel 2010. With the same basic file format, Excel 2010 files can be opened in Excel 2007. That fact alone makes the transition from Excel 2007 to Excel 2010 much less intimidating for a typical Office user. Even though Excel 2007 and Excel 2010 are very similar on the surface, Excel 2010 incorporates some new features and improvements "under the hood" that make it a very real improvement over previous versions of Excel. First, the Office button is replaced with the File tab. When you click the File tab, Backstage view opens, where you manage files and obtain information about them. Using Excel Options, available in Backstage view, you can even customize the Ribbon so the commands you use most often are only a click away. Excel 2010 introduces sparklines, which are small charts that fit inside a single cell. Using a sparkline, you can include a bit of detail and explanation right next to the data that is charted, providing a quick snapshot of an item of interest. For those who rely more heavily on the computing power of smartphones than on personal computers, Excel Mobile 2010 brings the worksheet to your phone. Power users of Excel 2010—those who delve into the deeper realm of processing power and security—will notice much more improvement in Excel 2010 than will those who are less tech-savvy. The bottom line is that if you are familiar with Excel 2007, you will appreciate the familiarity of a similar interface, while still enjoying some of the new features of Excel 2010 as you begin to work with the newer version.

Hands-On

You are considering traveling to Wyoming for a vacation at a lodge near Yellowstone. The lodge is designed as a ranch with cabins, horseback riding, and daily activities. Because the lodge is a considerable distance from your home in Kentucky, you are thinking about whether to fly or drive. You will use Excel to assist in making that decision, taking into consideration airfare, rental car, and lodging expenses.

a. Click **Start**, **All Programs**, **Microsoft Office**, and **Microsoft Excel 2010**. Click the **File tab** and click **Open**. Navigate to the location of your student data files and double-click **PracComp_Ch6_Ex1**.

b. Click the **File tab** and then click **Save As**. Navigate to the location where you save your student files and save the file as *Lastname_Firstname_ PracComp_Ch6_Ex1*.

c. Click **cell A6** and type **Airfare**. Press **Enter**. In **cell A7**, type **Car rental** Press **Enter**. Pressing Enter between each entry, complete column A as shown below.

   Gas for rental car
   Ranch accommodations
   Jackson Lake Lodge
   Hotel on return
   Miscellaneous

TROUBLESHOOTING

If you make a mistake as you type, you can either press **Backspace** and correct it (before you press **Enter**), or click in the cell and retype the entry (after you press **Enter**).

d. Click **cell B5**. Type *2* and then press →. Type *4* in cell C5. Press **Enter**. You have two young nieces who might make the trip with you, so you will determine the price for two travelers (you and a friend) as well

as four (including your nieces). Click **cell B10**. Type *275* and then press **Enter**. Type *150* and then press **Enter**. Type *500* and then press **Enter**. The entries you place in column B will shorten the display in column A, but you will widen the column later, so leave the entries as they are.

TROUBLESHOOTING

If you place the entries from Step d in column C instead of column B, select the incorrect entries and then press **Delete**. Then enter them correctly in column B.

e. Click **cell A16**. Type *Per Person Cost* and then press **Enter**. Complete cells A17 through B20 as shown below. When you type the entries in column B, the items in column A will be truncated (cut off). You will correct that problem later.

	A	B
17	Airfare (round trip)	280.80
18	Ranch	998
19	Rental Car Cost/Day	29.99
20	Rental Car Days	7

TROUBLESHOOTING

As you type *280.80* for the airfare, Excel is likely to show only *280.8*. Unless you format the number differently, Excel will not display trailing zeroes in a position to the right of the decimal point. You will learn to format values later in this chapter, so leave the entry as it is typed.

f. Click the **View tab** and then click **Page Layout** in the Workbook Views group. Click **Zoom** in the Zoom group and select **75%**. Click **OK**.

g. Your worksheet should appear as shown in Figure 6.9. Click the **File tab** and then click **Print**. The preview on the right shows that the worksheet will print on one page without gridlines. Click **Portrait Orientation** in the middle area of Backstage view and click **Landscape Orientation** to orient the page so it is wider than it is tall. Although you will not print the worksheet at this point, you have practiced selecting print settings, so you could simply click Print to print the worksheet as you have prepared it.

h. Click the **View tab** and click **100%** in the Zoom group. Click **Normal** ⊞ on the status bar. Right-click

Sheet1 and then click **Rename** on the shortcut menu. Type **Air and Car** and then press **Enter**.

ON YOUR OWN
Rename Sheet2 to *Rental Car*. Click to select the **Air and Car worksheet**.

---

i. Click **Save** on the Quick Access Toolbar. Keep the workbook open for the next exercise.

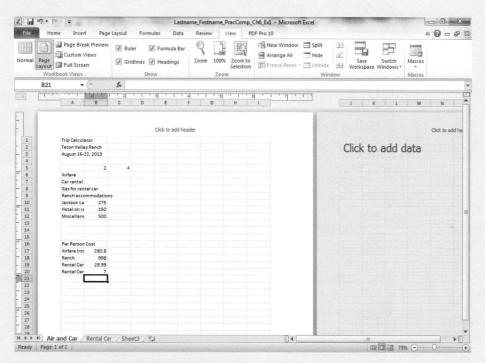

Figure 6.9 Calculating trip expense is a breeze for Excel.

Figure 6.7 Indicate a filename and a location when you save a workbook.

In Depth

Using Excel Web App

As an online companion to Excel 2010, Excel 2010 Web App enables you to work with Excel workbooks from any computer. The computer does not even have to have Excel installed because Excel Web App is actually an online version of Excel, with a few limitations. With your free SkyDrive account, you can access Office Web Apps, which includes an online version of Word 2010, PowerPoint 2010, Excel 2010, and OneNote (a digital notebook designed for making notes, gathering information from other applications, and sharing notes with others). Because Excel Web App (shown in Figure 6.8) facilitates simultaneous editing of a workbook, you can easily collaborate on a single project without dealing with various iterations of the same workbook. To begin to work with Office Web Apps (including Excel), simply create a SkyDrive account (http://skydrive.live.com) and upload any Office files. Then sign in to SkyDrive and open a file to begin to work in Web Apps.

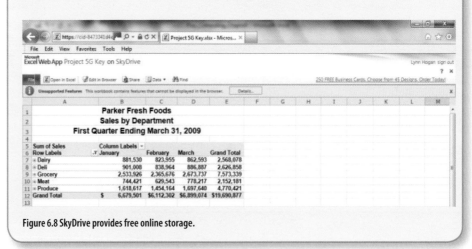

Figure 6.8 SkyDrive provides free online storage.

location where the file is to be saved, as well as the filename. As you develop an Excel workbook, you will want to save it often to avoid losing your work.

You can even save the workbook to **SkyDrive** if you have an account. SkyDrive is free online storage made available by Microsoft. Visit http://skydrive.live.com to create an account. To save a workbook to SkyDrive, click the **File tab** and click **Save & Send**. Click **Save to Web**. Follow the prompts to enter your SkyDrive login information and select an online folder. You might consider saving files to SkyDrive for a couple of reasons. First, having a workbook available online means you can open the file from any computer. Suppose that a workbook is necessary for a class, but you left the flash drive on which the workbook was saved at home. If you had also saved the workbook to SkyDrive, you could open it from there, regardless of the availability of your flash drive. On a similar note, saving a workbook to SkyDrive insures that you have a backup copy. If the original workbook file is lost or damaged so that it is unreadable, the SkyDrive copy enables you to continue to work with the file.

Modifying a Worksheet

Although Excel is not a word processor, it does include many of the formatting features often associated with a word processor. A worksheet can be both functional and attractive when you adjust text alignment and modify font size and color. You can include borders and highlighting, adjust column width and row height, and center headings across the width of a worksheet. By showing or hiding gridlines (the lines separating columns and rows), you can produce a finished product that clearly delineates categories of information or displays more like a document than a columned worksheet. Regardless of whether you have shown or hidden them, gridlines do not print unless you indicate that preference (by using a selection on the Page Layout tab).

Excel's strength lies in statistical operations. Not only can you develop simple formulas to summarize worksheet data, but you can include complex statistical, financial, and even trigonometric functions. Underlying its user-friendly exterior, Excel is capable of supporting complicated numbers-driven business and accounting applications, providing well-organized numeric data on which to base business decisions. As powerful as it is, Excel does not require you to be well versed in math terminology or to have an extensive math background. A basic understanding of business math will set you well on your way to developing effective worksheets. In this section, you will learn to modify worksheets by formatting numbers, aligning text, and adjusting column width and row height. In addition, you will begin to develop basic formulas that can be easily copied to other areas within a worksheet. Finally, you will practice copying and moving data from one area to another.

Selecting a Range

A **range** is a selection of one or more cells. With the pointer showing as a large white plus sign, you can drag any number of cells to select a range. You might select a range to format the cells in a certain way, or perhaps you want to delete, copy, or move the contents of a selected range. You can even give a range a name, if you like, for later reference in formulas or other actions.

Selecting the Entire Worksheet

To quickly select the entire worksheet, including all cells in every column and row (even those that you cannot see on-screen), click the **Select All button**, which is the small square located at the top-left corner of a worksheet (in the worksheet frame immediately above row 1 and to the left of column A). You can also select the entire worksheet when you click in any cell and then press **Ctrl+A**.

Although the simplest way to select a range that includes only a few cells is to drag the cells, you can also select a range by typing the range address in the Name Box. Especially when selecting a large range including cells that extend beyond the visible worksheet area, typing the range in the Name Box is very effective. A range is identified by its top-left and bottom-right corner. For example, the range shown in Figure 6.10 is identified as A6:B12. The colon in the range address is referred to as "through," as in "A6 through B12." That means all cells from A6 through B12, in a rectangular shape, are included in the range. You can select the range by dragging from A6 through B12, or by typing *A6:B12* in the Name Box and pressing **Enter**. Note that the entry of cell addresses is not case sensitive. Therefore, you could just as easily type *a6:b12* when indicating the range. All of the selected range will be shaded, except for the top-left cell (which is the active cell). Even though the active cell is not shaded, it is still included in the range.

By giving a name to a range, you can make formulas in your worksheet much easier to understand. For example, the formula *=SUM(Qtr1_Sales)* is much easier to understand as summing all Quarter 1's sales amounts than would be *=SUM(A15:A52)*, assuming cells A15 through A52 contained sales amounts for Quarter 1. You will learn much more about the =SUM function later in this chapter; it merely serves here as a reference point for the value of using range names.

To name a range, you must first select the cell or range that you want to name. Then click in the **Name Box** and type a name for the range (up to 255 characters). The first character must be a letter, an underscore, or a backslash.

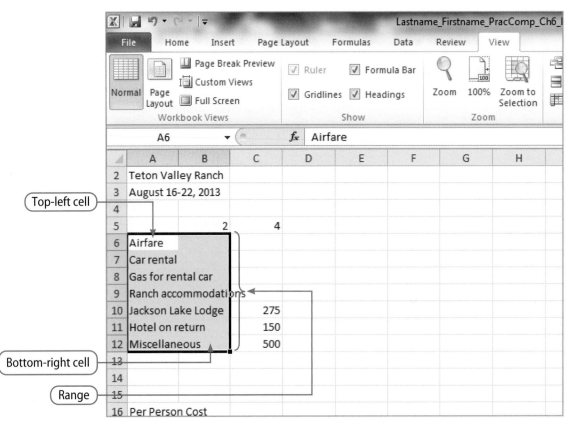

Figure 6.10 A range is one or more cells.

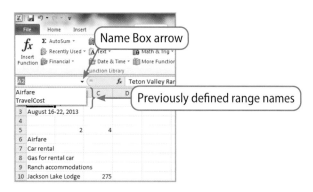

Figure 6.11 Use the Name Box to quickly locate named ranges.

Quick Tip

Selecting a Nonadjacent Range

Although most often the cells to be included in a range are located beside or beneath each other, occasionally the cells to be included are separated. For example, you might want to select separate areas of a worksheet to be included in a chart. For that to happen, all cells must be selected as one range. Drag over the first series of cells, press and hold **Ctrl**, and select other areas while continuing to hold **Ctrl**. When you release the mouse button and **Ctrl**, nonadjacent cells are selected for inclusion in a range.

No spaces are allowed in a range name, and the range name cannot be the same as a cell address. For example, you cannot name a range *D25* because that is actually a cell address. To go to a range name that you have defined, click the **Name Box arrow** and select the range name (Figure 6.11). You can also use the range name in a formula.

Editing Cell Contents

As you have learned, entering data in a worksheet is as simple as selecting a cell and typing. Inevitably, however, you will make mistakes as you enter text and numbers. If you make a data entry mistake and have not yet pressed Enter, you can press **Backspace** to clear the mistake and continue typing. More often, however, you find mistakes *after* you have pressed Enter. You can correct mistakes in the following ways.

- Click to select the cell and retype the entire entry. Press **Enter**.
- Click to select the cell, click the **Formula Bar**, make changes, and then press **Enter**.
- Click to select the cell, press **F2**, make the corrections, and then press **Enter**.
- Double-click the cell, make the corrections, and then press **Enter**.

Occasionally, you will want to clear cell contents. You can do so in any of the following ways.

- Click to select the cell or drag to select a range and then press **Delete**.
- Right-click the cell or selected range and then click **Clear Contents**.
- Select a cell or range, click the **Clear arrow** in the Editing group on the Home tab (Figure 6.12), and then click **Clear Contents**.

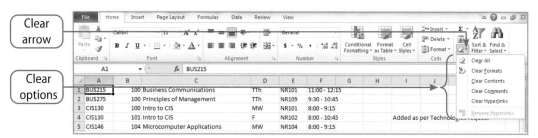

Figure 6.12 Use the Clear command in the Editing group to remove cell contents.

Table 6.3	
Symbol	**Action**
+	Add
-	Subtract
*	Multiply
/	Divide
^	Exponentiation

Including Formulas

Excel makes it easy to include formulas in worksheets. Totaling columns of numbers, calculating averages, and determining monthly payments are just a few of the things that Excel does in a snap. To perform calculations like these, you need to know how to build formulas. A **formula** is a group of instructions that tells Excel how to perform a calculation. You can either build formulas from scratch or use one of the many functions that are built into Excel.

You must first tell Excel that you are beginning a formula. The way to do that is to type =in a cell. Then continue with the formula, pressing **Enter** at the end. When typing a formula in a cell, you will work with a predefined group of arithmetic operators, as shown in Table 6.3.

Although a formula can include a constant (a number, such as 10 or 25), it is much more common to develop a formula primarily using cell addresses where appropriate. That way, if the contents of cell addresses change, the results of the formula will adjust, but you will not have to modify the formula. For example, the worksheet shown in Figure 6.13 illustrates a sales scenario. The sales amount for each item is determined by multiplying the price by quantity. Therefore, the formula in cell D5 will be entered as *=B5*C5*, which is the price of that item multiplied by the quantity sold. A similar formula will be placed in cells D6 and D7. For example, the formula in cell D6 will be *=B6*C6* while the formula in cell D7 will read *=B7*C7*. If the price of any of those items changes, or if the quantity is adjusted, the formulas will not have to be modified because the formulas only refer to the cell addresses, not the specific content. Therefore, cell contents can change without the need to also change associated formulas.

Although you can enter formulas by typing cell addresses, you can also simply point to cells you want to include in a formula. The less you type, the less likely you are to make mistakes, so you might prefer to point to cells. For example, to enter the formula *=D28*E14* in cell E28, click cell E28 and type = (an equal sign). Then click **cell D28** to select it. Next, type * (an asterisk). Finally, click **cell E14** and press **Enter**.

Quick Tip
Clearing Formatting

To remove formatting from a cell, click the **Clear arrow** in the Editing group on the Home tab and then click **Clear Formats** (or click **Clear All** to remove both formatting and cell contents).

Quick Tip
Typing Formulas

Capitalization is not relevant when typing formulas. The formula =B1+D1 is the same as =b1+d1. Whether or not you capitalize cell addresses is a matter of preference.

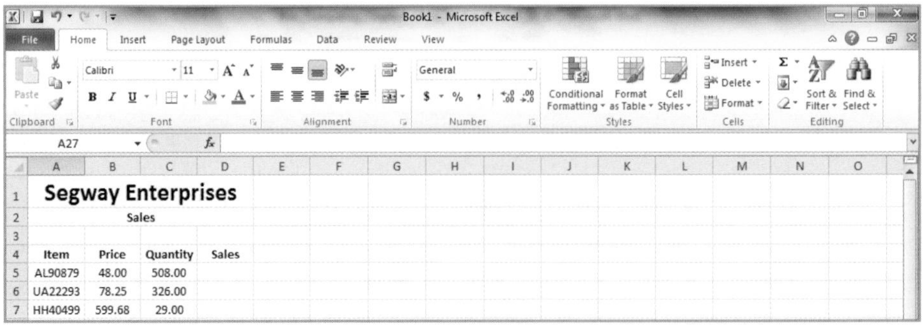

Figure 6.13 Excel's strength is enabling you to create formulas.

Understanding the Order of Precedence

Often, a formula will include more than one arithmetic operator. For example, the formula A8+B8+C8/3 makes use of two operators, + and /. Will Excel divide by 3 first, or will it add A8, B8, and C8 before dividing? It all depends on the order of precedence, sometimes called the order of operations, which is a set of rules that determines the order in which mathematical operations are to be calculated. The standard order of precedence is:

1. Any operation in parentheses is calculated first.
2. Any exponentiation operation (raising numbers to a power) is done next.
3. Next comes any multiplication and division. If both operators are present, the order is determined from left to right.
4. Finally, any addition and subtraction operations are calculated—from left to right if more than one operator is present.

In the previous example, C8 will be divided by 3 first, and then A8 and B8 will be added to the result. If the formula's purpose is to determine the average of three grades, located in cells A8, B8, and C8, the result will be in error. Instead, you could rephrase the formula as *(A8+B8+C8)/3* to force the 3 cells to be added first, with the result divided by 3 to produce an average. Calculations included within parentheses are completed first, so using parentheses is an excellent way to force the addition of A8, B8, and C8 to occur before the division. You can even use nested parentheses, so a calculation in the innermost set of parentheses will be completed before any in the outer set. Preceding the formula with an equal sign, as in *=(A8+B8+C8)/3* would be the proper Excel format for the formula.

Adjusting Alignment

If you are familiar with word processing, you understand the concept of alignment. A left-aligned paragraph begins evenly on the left, while a right-aligned paragraph is just the opposite. Excel worksheets also include alignment options, although they are slightly different. Instead of aligning an entire paragraph between margins, Excel alignment is only relevant to individual cells. Data that is left-aligned in a cell begins evenly on the left edge of a cell, while right-alignment aligns cell data on the right. You can also center data within a cell. All those alignment options are actually considered horizontal alignment, as they align text horizontally within a cell.

Excel also enables you to align data vertically within a cell, an alignment that is especially relevant in a cell that has a great deal of vertical space. Figure 6.14 shows horizontal and vertical alignment options in the Alignment

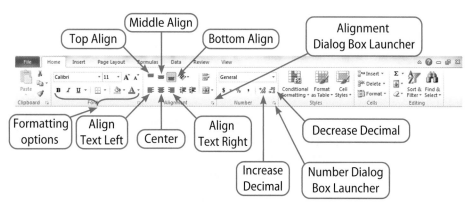

Figure 6.14 Through selections in the Home tab, you can easily align cell contents and format numbers.

group on the Home tab. Vertical alignment options enable you to align at the top, middle, or bottom of a cell, while horizontal alignment is oriented to the left, center, or right.

Often, you will want to center a selection across a series of cells, such as when a major heading is centered across all of the columns that make up the worksheet area. The Merge & Center option in the Alignment group on the Home tab joins selected cells together to form one cell, and then centers text within the newly created cell. Although you can only merge and center one row at a time, it is an effective way to improve a worksheet's appearance. Simply drag the number of cells in a row to merge, including the text to be centered, and then click **Merge & Center** in the Alignment group.

Formatting Data

You can format data in one or more cells in a variety of ways. In fact, having selected a range of cells, you can apply boldfacing, italicizing, or underlining, much as you would in a word processing document. As shown in Figure 6.14, formatting options are found in the Font group on the Home tab. You can also change the font and font size and apply shading and borders to selected cells.

Hands-On

Activity 6.2 Creating Formulas, Formatting Data, and Adjusting Alignment

As you continue to analyze costs associated with the Wyoming trip, you see that several items are dependent on the number of people traveling. The airfare is determined on a per-person basis, as is the ranch accommodation charge. Alignment will also improve the appearance of the worksheet, making it easier to read.

a. Click **cell B6**. The airfare formula is determined by multiplying the number of people traveling by the per-person airfare shown in cell B17. Type =B5*B17 and press **Enter**. The car rental formula will multiply the number of days rented by the cost per day. Type = and then click **cell B20**. Type * and then click **cell B19**. Press **Enter**. Click **cell B9**. Ranch accommodations are equal to the number of people traveling multiplied by the ranch cost per day. Use either of the methods just described to multiply B5 by B18, placing the result in cell B9.

TROUBLESHOOTING

If you forget to begin a formula with = Excel will interpret the formula as a label, showing the formula instead of the result. Click the cell and retype the formula, beginning with =.

b. Drag to select **cells A1 through A3**. Click the **Home tab**, if necessary, and then click **Bold** in the Font group. Click to select **cell A1**. Click the **Font Size**

arrow and then select **18**. Drag to select **cells A1 through C1** and then click **Merge & Center** in the Alignment group.

TROUBLESHOOTING

If you click the Merge & Center arrow instead of the Merge & Center button, you must then click **Merge & Center**.

ON YOUR OWN

One at a time, merge and center cells A2 through C2 and cells A3 through C3.

---

c. Select **cells A1 through A3**. Click the **Fill Color arrow** and select **Dark Blue, Text 2, Lighter 60%** (row 3, column 4). Click anywhere to deselect the cells.

TROUBLESHOOTING

If the font color changes instead of the fill color, you selected the *Font Color* arrow instead of the *Fill Color* arrow. Click **Undo** on the Quick Access Toolbar and repeat Step c.

TROUBLESHOOTING

If the cell fill color is not blue, you clicked the Fill Color *button* instead of the Fill Color *arrow*. Click **Undo** on the Quick Access Toolbar and repeat Step c.

Most Excel worksheets contain numbers that can be formatted in a variety of ways. Depending on the context of the numbers shown, you can format them as currency, percentage, or with a comma separating them where appropriate. As shown in Figure 6.14, you can also increase or decrease the decimal positions displayed. For even more detail, click the **Number Dialog Box Launcher** to display a dialog box with the Number tab selected where you can indicate such settings as how negative numbers should display, or what format a date should assume.

Inserting and Deleting Columns and Rows

Seldom does the first attempt at a worksheet meet your approval. Even with your best effort, you are likely to forget a heading or to determine that a column of data is unnecessary. You have learned how to delete cell and range contents, but that is sometimes not enough. Occasionally, an entire column or row should be deleted.

Although Excel provides several ways to insert and delete those items, the easiest way might be to use a shortcut menu. Simply place the pointer on a row or column heading in the worksheet frame, so the pointer appears as a downward or right-pointing arrow (Figure 6.16), and click. The entire column or row is shaded, indicating that it is selected. Right-click in the shaded column or row and select **Insert** (to insert a column or row) or **Delete** (to delete the selected

Quick Tip
Using the Ribbon to Insert and Delete

With one or more rows or columns selected (click a column or row heading in the worksheet frame, or drag several), click the **Home tab** and then click the **Insert arrow** or the **Delete arrow** in the Cells group to select from several options to insert or delete cells, rows, columns, or even worksheets.

d. Select **cells B5 through C5**. Click **Center** in the Alignment group.

e. Select **cells B6 through B12**. Click **Comma Style** in the Number group.

ON YOUR OWN

Apply the Comma Style format to cells B17 through B19, and center the entry in cell B20. Shade cells A16 through B20 with the same Fill Color as that used in Step c. (Hint: Because the shade you seek is the most recently used color, you can simply click the **Fill Color button** instead of the **Fill Color arrow**.)

f. Right-click the **Air and Car sheet tab** and point to **Tab Color**. Click **Red** (second from left in Standard Colors). You will see only slight change in the color until you select another tab. Right-click the **Rental Car sheet tab** and change the tab color to **Yellow** (fourth from left in Standard Colors).

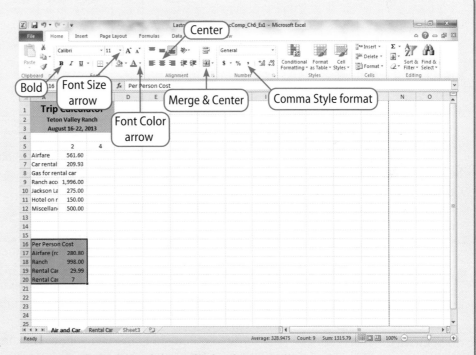

Figure 6.15 You will make the trip calculator workbook much more attractive.

Click the **Air and Car sheet tab**. The Air and Car worksheet should display as shown in Figure 6.15.

g. Save the workbook. Keep it open for the next exercise.

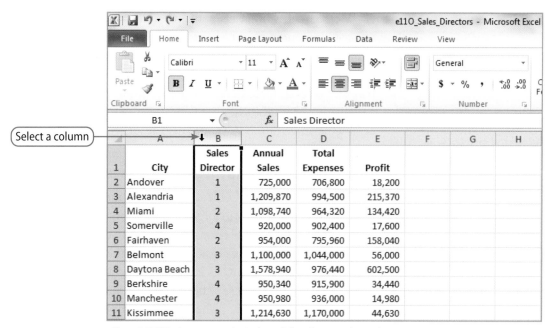

Figure 6.16 Click a letter or a number in the worksheet frame to select a column or row.

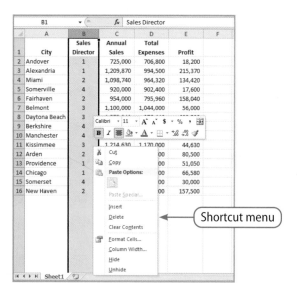

Figure 6.17 Use a shortcut menu to insert or delete a selected column or row.

Select a column

Shortcut menu

Quick Tip

Selecting Nonadjacent Columns and Rows

To select multiple rows or columns that are not adjoining, select the first column or row and then press **Ctrl**. Holding down **Ctrl**, select any other rows or columns, no matter how far removed from the original selection. When you release **Ctrl** and the pointer, all indicated rows or columns will be selected. You might want to select multiple rows and columns to delete, format identically, or provide data for charts.

column or row) from the shortcut menu shown in Figure 6.17. An inserted row is placed immediately above a selected row, while an inserted column is placed to the left of a selected column.

You are not limited to inserting or deleting one column or row at a time. You can select multiple columns and rows and then use the shortcut menu to insert or delete items. With the pointer on a row number or column letter in the worksheet frame, simply drag to select multiple rows or columns. Then right-click the selected area and select **Insert** or **Delete** from the shortcut menu. The number of rows or columns you have selected will be the number inserted or deleted.

Changing Column Width and Row Height

Columns and rows are uniformly sized when you begin a new workbook, according to the theme selected. Because it is unlikely that the size will be suitable for

Quick Tip

Manually Resizing a Row or Column

To manually resize a row or column, point to the right border of the column or to the bottom border of the row to be resized, so the pointer appears as a two-headed arrow. As you drag to resize the row or column, a ScreenTip will show the column width or row height in points and pixels. Release the pointer to select a height or width.

Quick Tip

Using a Shortcut Menu

At times you will be at a loss for how to accomplish a task in Excel. Although it is not a foolproof solution, your best bet is often to select the item in question (perhaps a cell or a column) and then right-click the selection. From the shortcut menu that displays, you will often find an option that might be just what you are looking for.

all columns and rows in a worksheet, you need to understand how to change column width and row height. Often, a column is too narrow for text you enter, and occasionally a column might even be too narrow to display formula results. You might find that you want to narrow a column for a better display of data, or that a row height could be expanded to better accommodate multi-line headings. Excel makes it easy to modify column widths and row heights.

It is not necessarily a problem when you type text that extends beyond a column's border. As long as there is nothing in the column to the right, such an occurrence might require no attention at all. The problem occurs when the column to the right of a lengthy entry is occupied. At that point, text that is too wide for the column is truncated, or cut off from display. Characters are not actually removed; they are simply not shown. You can always click a cell and check the Formula Bar to reassure yourself that the text remains. To expand a column's width so all text in the column is shown, position the pointer in the worksheet frame at the top of the worksheet, on the right border of the column that is too short. The pointer will appear as a two-headed arrow. Simply double-click to **AutoFit** the column for the widest entry. Using AutoFit, you allow Excel to determine the appropriate column width. Note that AutoFit has no effect unless a column contains data. If a column containing numeric entries is too narrow to display all of the numbers, pound signs (####) will display in the column. At that point, you can use AutoFit to expand column width as necessary. If, instead, you want to manually adjust column width, drag the column border (when the pointer is a two-headed arrow) to the right to expand the column or to the left to narrow it.

For more precise column width and row height adjustment, select one or more columns or rows. Click **Format** in the Cells group on the Home tab. You can then select an AutoFit option or indicate that you want to manually adjust column width or row height, as shown in Figure 6.18. Column width is measured by the number of characters of the default font that will fit in a column. As shown in Figure 6.19, the default column width is 8.43 for the particular theme in effect, which means that slightly more than 8 characters of the default font will fit in the column. However, various themes prescribe unique default column widths, so the default column width depends on the applied theme. Regardless, you can adjust the column width setting if you like, by making a selection from the menu shown in Figure 6.18. Row height is measured in points, with each

In Depth

Hiding a Column and Worksheet

Occasionally, you might want to hide a column before you print a worksheet or show the worksheet to someone else. Perhaps information in the column is confidential or maybe the column is not necessary to show as part of a printout. Select a column to hide and then right-click the selected column. Click **Hide**. The column will no longer display as part of the worksheet. However, a break in column lettering lets you know that a column is hidden. For example, having hidden column C, columns will then be labeled A, B, D, E, . . . with an obvious gap at column C. To "unhide" the column, select the columns before and after the hidden column. In this example, you would select columns B and D. Right-click within the highlight and click **Unhide**. You can also hide an entire worksheet. Right-click a worksheet tab to hide and select **Hide** from the shortcut menu.

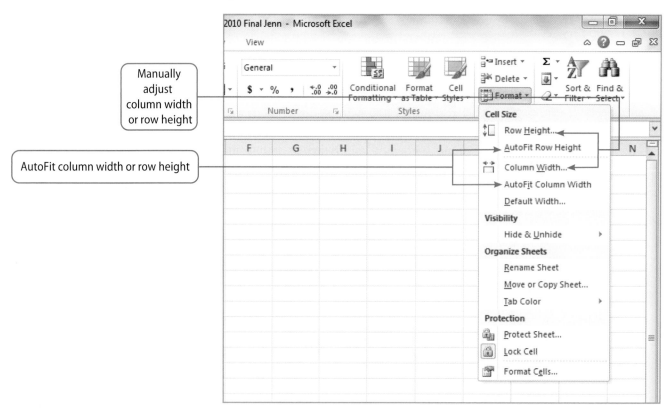

Manually adjust column width or row height

AutoFit column width or row height

Figure 6.18 You can manually resize a column or row or allow Excel to automatically determine the appropriate size.

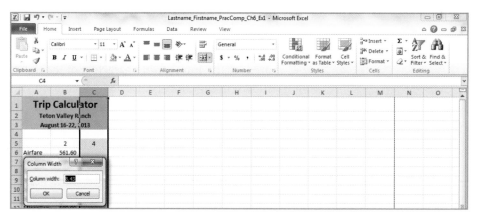

Figure 6.19 Specify an exact column width in this dialog box.

Quick Tip

Changing Several Column Widths

You can simultaneously change the width of several adjacent columns so they are a uniform size. Select the columns to be adjusted, and then drag a border between any two of the selected columns to the desired size. All selected columns will be adjusted identically. Similarly, you can adjust row heights by selecting several rows and adjusting them all.

point representing 1/72 inch. Just as you can adjust column width, you can adjust row height by selecting one or more rows, clicking **Format** in the Cells group on the Home tab, and selecting **Row Height**.

To add pizazz to a row of headings, or to make better use of limited space, you can angle text within cells. In doing so, you also require less horizontal space. Select the cells to be affected and click the **Alignment Dialog Box Launcher** (or for less specificity, click **Orientation** in the Alignment group on the Home tab, as shown in Figure 6.21, and select an angle). Drag the red diamond in the Orientation area in the Alignment dialog box, or type a specific degree of rotation in the Degrees text box. Click **OK** to complete the alignment.

In Depth

Wrapping and Orienting Text

To fit more text within a specified column width, or simply to make a worksheet more attractive, you can wrap text within a cell. Row height automatically adjusts to accommodate the wrapped text. Select one or more cells (or select an entire row or column) and click **Wrap Text** in the Alignment group on the Home tab (Figure 6.20). You can also create another line within a cell when you hold **Alt** and press **Enter**.

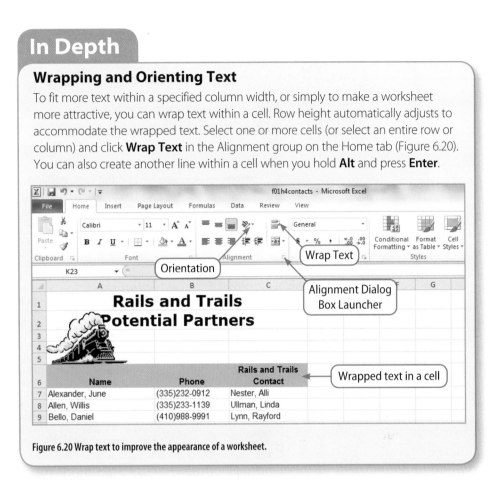

Figure 6.20 Wrap text to improve the appearance of a worksheet.

Copying and Moving Cell Contents

You can easily copy and move data from one area of a worksheet to another, or even between worksheets. Moving data is called cutting and pasting. Duplicating data from one location to another is called copying and pasting. When you **cut** or **copy** a selection, it is temporarily placed on the **Clipboard**, where it is held until you **paste** the selection or until it is replaced with another cut or copy. If you plan to cut or copy multiple items, you should open the Clipboard pane by clicking the **Clipboard Dialog Box Launcher** (Figure 6.20). The Clipboard pane holds up to 24 items that have been cut or copied. You can view the contents of the Clipboard in the Clipboard pane, selecting an item to paste, or removing items at will.

To cut or copy one or more items:

1. Select the cell or range to cut or copy. You can also select an object, such as clip art, a picture, or even SmartArt. If you plan to cut or copy multiple items, click the **Clipboard Dialog Box Launcher** to open the Clipboard pane.
2. Click the **Home tab** and click **Copy** (or **Cut**) in the Clipboard group. If cutting or copying multiple items, and the Clipboard pane is open, continue the process of cutting or copying.

To paste one or more items:

1. Select the cell or range to which the selection should be pasted.

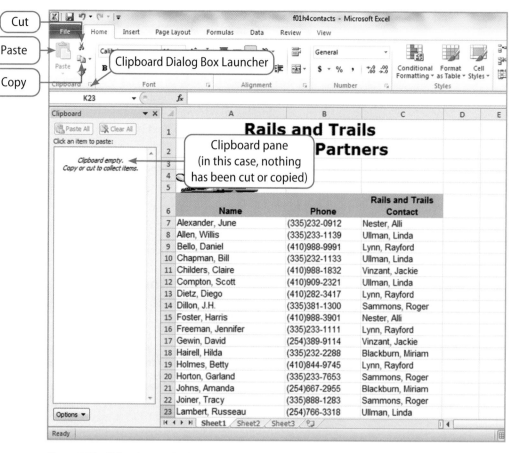

Figure 6.21 The Clipboard pane can hold multiple items that have been cut or copied.

Quick Tip

Copying a Series

Use the fill handle to copy items such as months and days, as well as a recognized series. Having entered *March* in one cell, drag the fill handle to adjacent cells to display succeeding months (e.g., *April, May.*). You can do the same for days of the week, and for any pattern that Excel can recognize. Having entered the number *100* in one cell and *200* in the next, select both cells. Then drag the fill handle at the bottom right of the selected range to other cells to continue the pattern through *300, 400,* and so on.

2. If the Clipboard pane is not open and you are pasting the most recently cut or copied item, click **Paste**. If you are selecting an item from the Clipboard pane, click the item in the Clipboard pane (or click the arrow to the right of the item and click **Paste**).

If you are copying contents or a formula from one cell to adjacent cells, the quickest way is to drag the **fill handle**, which is the small black square located at the bottom-right corner of the active cell or range (Figure 6.22). When you point to the fill handle, the pointer appears as a small black plus sign. If you are copying a formula, the formula will adjust relative to its new location. For

In Depth

Understanding the Pointer Shape

As you learned earlier, the shape of the pointer often indicates a selection or process. Learning to identify the following pointer shapes and the processes the shapes represent will help you develop effective worksheets and avoid common mistakes.

⊞	Select one or more cells
↓	Select one or more columns
→	Select one or more rows
↘	Resize a column or row
▣	Drag fill handle to copy cell contents or a formula
↖	Move cell contents (or copy, if you also hold **Ctrl**)

Quick Tip

Moving and Copying by Dragging

You can drag to move and copy cell contents to another location, even if the location is not adjacent. Select one or more cells you want to move or copy and point to the border of the selection. The pointer will appear as a four-headed arrow. Drag to a new location to move the selection, or press and hold **Ctrl** while you drag to a new location to copy the selection.

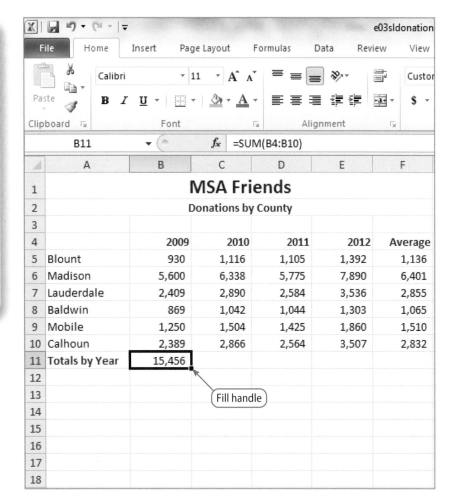

Figure 6.22 To copy a formula or cell content from one cell to one or more additional cells, drag the fill handle.

example, copying the formula =A10+B10 to the next row will result in =A11+B11. If you are copying anything other than a formula, the cell contents will be duplicated in the new location. The only exception to that rule is if the range you are copying is a series, such as 1, 2, and 3. In that case, Excel will continue the pattern as it fills subsequent cells, so they appear as 4, 5, and so on.

Absolute and Relative Referencing

When a formula is copied, its cell references normally adjust according to the copy location. For example, if you copy the formula =B5+C5 down one row, the formula will be adjusted to =B6+C6. Most often you want the formula to be adjusted, but occasionally one or more of the cell references should remain unadjusted, or absolute.

Consider the example given in Figure 6.24. Each salesperson earns a commission on the amount sold. The commission rate is shown in one cell while each sales amount is listed beside the corresponding salesperson. The Commission formula for each salesperson is Sales multiplied by Commission Rate. The formula to calculate Joseph Morton's commission (in cell C8) is =B8*B5 (multiplying Joseph Morton's sales by the commission rate).

It seems logical to copy the formula from Joseph Morton's commission down the column to every other salesperson, because relatively speaking, the commission for each salesperson is calculated in exactly the same way. With so many

Quick Tip

Correcting a Formula

When you become aware that the results of a formula are incorrect, double-click the cell containing the erroneous formula. Correct the formula in the cell and press **Enter**. You can also select the cell and take a look at the Formula Bar, which shows the formula that created the results. You can simply correct the error on the Formula Bar and press **Enter**.

Hands-On

Activity 6.3 Formatting a Worksheet and Using Absolute Referencing

You have determined several of the costs associated with traveling as a pair. But how do the costs change if there are four in the party? Because the formulas you used for two people are basically the same formulas as those that would be used for four, you will copy the formulas from one column to the next. You will also adjust column widths, include an additional heading, rearrange some text, and use absolute references where appropriate.

a. Select **cells B6 through B12**. Because all the formulas in column B are basically the same as those required in column C, you will copy them all at one time. Point to the **fill handle** located at the bottom-right corner of the selected area. When you point to the fill handle, the pointer becomes a small black plus sign. Drag the **fill handle** to the right to include **cells C6 through C12**. Release the mouse button. Several of the travel costs copied correctly, but several did not.

TROUBLESHOOTING

If the formulas were moved instead of copied, or there was no effect, you did not drag the fill handle, Click **Undo** and repeat Step a.

b. Click **cell C6**. The cell displays a dash, which is an indication of a null value (0). Take a look at the Formula Bar. The formula is =C5*C17. Can you tell what is wrong with the formula? The first reference in the formula (C5) refers to the cell containing the number of travelers. The second reference, however, refers to cell C17, which is empty. Therefore, the result of the formula is 0. What should have happened is that the number of travelers was multiplied by the per-person airfare cost (located in cell B17). When you copied the formula (along with the others in column B) to column C, the original formula was adjusted to the right, resulting in the erroneous formula for airfare.

c. Click **cell B6**. Click **to the left of B17** on the Formula Bar. Type $ and then click **to the left of the number 17**. Type $ and then press **Enter**. You will see no change, because you have not yet copied the formula to column c.

d. Click **to the left of B20** on the Formula Bar. Type $ and then click **to the left of the number 20**. Type $ Because the car rental charge is based only on the number of days rented and the cost per day, and will not vary based on the number of travelers, the formula should not be adjusted at all as it is copied to the right. Therefore, you will make each entry in the car rental formula absolute.

e. Click **to the left of B19** on the Formula Bar. Type $ and then click **to the left of the number 19**. Type $ and then press **Enter**. Select **cells B6 through B7**. Drag the **fill handle** to the right to include **cells C6 through C7**. Because you adjusted the original formulas to include absolute references to those elements that should not be adjusted, the formulas copied correctly. Do not be alarmed with the ##### that display. The column is too narrow to display the result, but you will correct that in Step f.

TROUBLESHOOTING

If you make any mistakes when entering a formula (or any other text), select the cell in which the error occurred and correct the mistake on the Formula Bar or simply retype the entire formula. Then press **Enter**.

f. Click **cell C6**. The cell displays #####, indicating that the column is too narrow to display the result. Point to **the border between columns C and D** (in the worksheet frame) so the pointer becomes a two-headed arrow. **Double-click** to AutoFit the column. Click cell B9. Click the Formula Bar and change cell B18 to an absolute reference (B18). Press Enter. Click cell B9. Drag the fill handle to copy the formula from cell B9 to C9.

ON YOUR OWN

Column A appears to be too narrow to display all contents. AutoFit column A.

g. Select **cells A1 through A3**. You will copy those cells to the Rental Car worksheet. Click **Copy** (the *button*, not the *arrow*) in the Clipboard group on the Home tab (Figure 6.23). Click the **Rental Car sheet tab**. Click **cell A1**. Click the **Paste button** (not the Paste arrow).

When pasting several entries, you only need to click the top-left corner of the range to paste to. All copied cells will fill in from there.

h. AutoFit column A to fit all cell entries in that column. Select **cells B5 through C5**. Click **Center** in the Alignment group on the Home tab. Click **cell B6**. Type =B17*B18 and then click **Enter** (✓) beside the Formula Bar. You indicate absolute references in the formula because the two cells used to determine rental car cost (B17 and B18) should not be adjusted as the formula is copied to the next column (when you determine the cost for traveling with 4 people).

TROUBLESHOOTING

If the active cell moves to the next row, you *pressed* Enter instead of *clicking* Enter (✓) beside the Formula Bar. Click **cell B6**.

i. Drag the **fill handle** to copy the formula to cell C6. Click **cell B7**. Because the ranch accommodation charge is based on the number of travelers, you will enter a formula with an absolute reference when referring to the per-person charge. That way, when you copy the formula to the right, it will adjust appropriately. Type =B5*B16 and click **Enter** (✓) beside the Formula Bar. Drag the fill handle to copy the formula to cell C7. Click anywhere to deselect the range.

j. Point to the border between Columns C and D in the worksheet frame. Double-click to AutoFit the column, showing all entries.

k. Complete entries in column B as follows:

Two-night hotel on drive up	300
Jackson Lake Lodge	275
Gas for rental car	
Two-night hotel on return	300
Miscellaneous	500

l. Select **cells B8 through B12**. Drag the **fill handle** to the right to include **cells C8 through C12**. Format the selected cells in **Comma Style** (click **Comma Style** in the Number group on the Home tab).

TROUBLESHOOTING

If the selected cells were moved instead of copied, you did not drag the fill handle (when the pointer is a small black plus sign). Click **Undo** on the Quick Access Toolbar and repeat Step l.

ON YOUR OWN

Center cells A16 through A18. Shade cells A16 through B18 with Dark Blue, Text 2, Lighter 60% (row 3, column 4).

m. Click the **number 12** in the worksheet frame (when the pointer appears as a right-pointing arrow) to select the row. You will insert a row above the

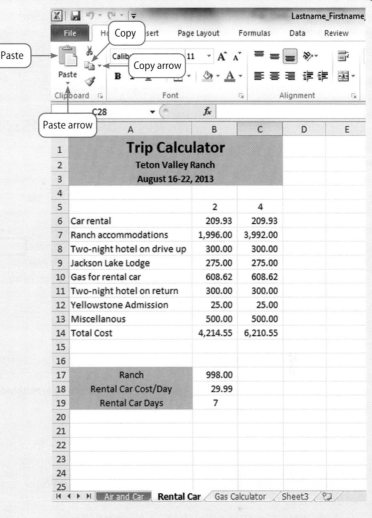

Figure 6.23 The Clipboard group includes options to cut, copy, and paste selections.

selected row. Right-click the **selected row** and click **Insert** on the shortcut menu. Click **cell A12**. Type **Yellowstone Admission** and then press →. Type *25* and then click **Enter** (✓) beside the Formula Bar. Drag the **fill handle** to copy the contents of cell B12 to C12. Because Yellowstone charges admission by the car, you will not need to determine a per-person cost.

ON YOUR OWN

Insert a row above row 12 in the Air and Car sheet. Copy the contents of cells A12 through C12 on the Rental Car sheet to cells A12 through C12 on the Air and Car sheet.

n. Click the **Rental Car sheet tab** and press **Esc** to remove the dashed border from the cells that were just copied.

o. Save the workbook. Keep it open for the next exercise.

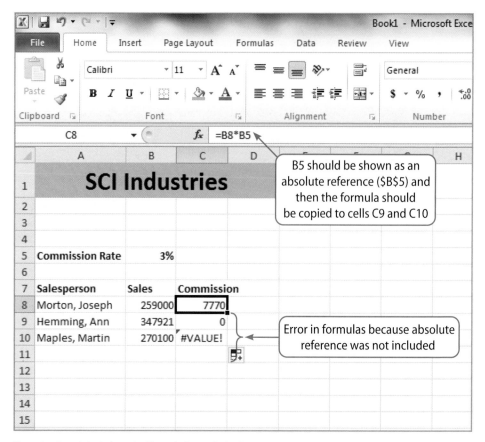

Figure 6.24 Commission is determined by multiplying sales by the commission rate.

Quick Tip

Shortcut for Absolute Reference

If you have access to function keys on a keyboard, you can create an absolute reference by pressing F4 either before or after typing a cell address in a formula. You can also click in the cell reference on the Formula Bar (if you have previously typed the formula) and press F4.

salespeople, retyping the formula for each employee is not feasible, so you could simply drag the fill handle down the column to copy the formula. The results of the copy, however, would not be what you expect. Remember that a formula is adjusted relative to its new position when it is copied. Therefore, the original formula (=B8*B5) becomes =B9*B6 when it is copied, with each cell reference adjusting in a relative manner. Although it is true that the next salesperson's sales are in cell B9, so that particular adjustment is appropriate, what is in cell B6? Because nothing is in cell B6, the formula actually multiplies Ann Hemming's sales by 0, which means that she receives no commission. As the formula is copied to the next salesperson, it gets even worse. The formula is adjusted to =B10*B7, and although the B10 cell reference is correct, cell B7 actually contains text. Because text cannot be used in a formula, the commission for Martin Maples is completely erroneous. The bottom line is that the first reference in the formula, the sales amount, should be copied relatively. However, the second reference, the commission rate, should not be adjusted because it appears in only one cell in the worksheet. It should remain an **absolute reference**.

To indicate that a cell reference in a formula should be considered absolute, place a dollar sign before each affected reference. For example, in the situation described above, the formula =B8*B5 multiplies sales by commission rate. Because the reference to the commission rate, which is only found in one cell, should not be adjusted as it is copied, the formula should be stated as =B8*B5. When the formula is subsequently copied down the column, it adjusts to =B9*B5 and then =B10*B5. The reference to the sales figure correctly adjusts with each move down the column to a different salesperson.

However, the reference to the commission rate does not adjust, as it is an absolute reference that refers to the one cell in which the commission rate resides. In rare cases, you might need to make either the cell or row reference absolute, while leaving the other component of an address relative. For example, when including cell C10 in a formula, you might want to hold row 10 as an absolute, while leaving column C relative. In that case, you could specify the cell reference C$10 in a formula. Such a reference is called a **Mixed reference**.

Keep in mind that you should only use an absolute reference when you are going to copy a formula. If you plan to retype the formula for each successive entry, you can simply type the formula correctly without the need to indicate absolute referencing. However, because it is much more timesaving to copy a formula, especially if the copy is to extend to numerous rows or columns, understanding absolute referencing is an invaluable skill.

Working with Multiple Worksheets

By default, Excel 2010 provides three worksheets for every new workbook. Each worksheet contains approximately 16 billion cells, so it would seem that three worksheets would be more than enough space for any application. The fact is, however, that worksheets are used as much for organization as for available space. For example, suppose you are an instructor responsible for three classes. It would make sense to include grade records for each class on a separate worksheet, titled appropriately. Then, when called upon to check grades for a particular student in one of those classes, you could simply click the class sheet tab and retrieve the information. It might even be possible to design the class records so they include the same formulas in the same cells on each worksheet. So if the final averages for each class are calculated in the same manner and are included in the same column on each worksheet, you could enter the formula once, and then *fill* it across the other class worksheets. Perhaps you include a Summary worksheet where you want to summarize final averages for all classes. By linking formulas from all the class worksheets, you can easily accomplish that task. In this section, you will learn to move, copy, insert, and delete worksheets. You will also create linking formulas, so you can consolidate data from several worksheets in one formula.

Copying, Moving, Inserting, and Deleting Worksheets

Although you can copy and move worksheets in several ways, the simplest method is to drag a sheet tab to another location. The workbook shown in Figure 6.25 includes three worksheets, each of which is named. You will recall that you can rename a worksheet when you right-click the sheet tab, click **Rename**, type a name, and press **Enter**. Suppose you want to rearrange the sheet tabs so that American History is placed before English Lit. Simply drag the sheet tab to reposition it. Release the sheet tab when a small black triangle indicates that the sheet will be positioned appropriately. If you want to copy a worksheet instead of moving it, press and hold **Ctrl** while you drag the worksheet to a new position. A copy of the worksheet will be placed in the new location, titled with the worksheet name followed by (2).

To insert a worksheet so it appears as the last worksheet in the workbook, click **Insert Worksheet** (Figure 6.25). If you want to place a new worksheet elsewhere within the worksheets, right-click the sheet tab before which you want the new worksheet to appear. Click **Insert**, click **Worksheet** and then click **OK**

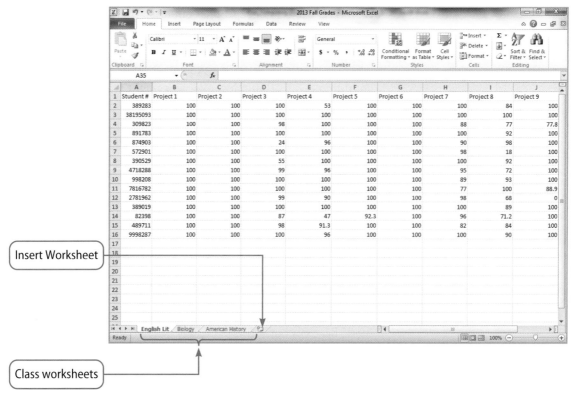

Figure 6.25 Placing related data in named worksheets is a great way to organize data.

(or simply double-click **Worksheet**). To delete a worksheet, right-click the sheet tab and then click **Delete**. If the worksheet contains data, you will have to agree to remove the worksheet, including all data.

Grouping Worksheets

Especially if worksheets are organized similarly, you might enjoy the time-saving feature of grouping worksheets so that edits made to one worksheet are applied to all. Think back to the example of listing class grades for each class on separate worksheets. Suppose that each class worksheet included the same column for final averages. Although the data for each class is different, the column in which the final average appears contains identical formulas. As you format the final average column to display only one place to the right of the decimal point, you want the same format to apply to all other class worksheets. First, group the worksheets by clicking the first sheet tab and then pressing **Shift** as you click the last worksheet in the group. If worksheets that you want to group are not adjacent, hold **Ctrl** while you click all sheet tabs to be included. Several class worksheets are selected, as indicated by the word *Group* on the title bar (Figure 6.26). Adjust the format for the currently displayed worksheet, and the same format applies to all of the selected worksheets. As you type text in one worksheet, the same text is placed in the same location of all selected sheets. In fact, any edit or format that you apply to the current worksheet is automatically applied to all selected worksheets. Remember to ungroup worksheets after you have completed all edits.

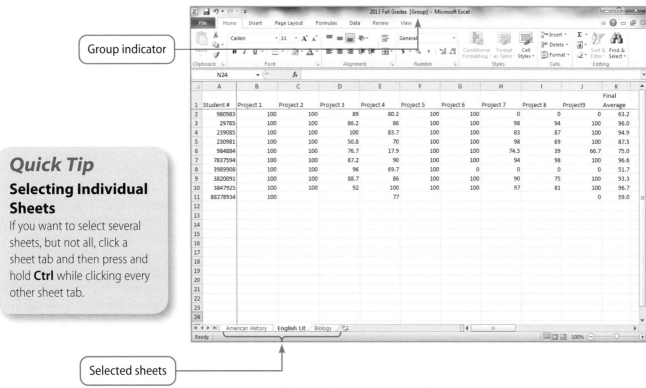

Figure 6.26 Grouping worksheets enables you to edit several worksheets simultaneously.

To ungroup, simply click one of the worksheet tabs or right-click a worksheet tab and click **Ungroup Sheets**.

Referencing Other Worksheets

A formula can include cells both within the same worksheet as well as from other worksheets. For example, to determine the total sales of all company branches (assuming each branch is shown on a separate worksheet within the same workbook), you can create a formula on a Summary sheet that links to sales data in each of the branch worksheets. As shown in Figure 6.28, each branch includes total sales in cell B15. The Summary worksheet includes a grand total in cell B5, which is a collection of all branch totals. All the worksheets are included within one workbook. To begin the grand total formula, click **cell B5** of the Summary worksheet. Type = and then click the first branch sheet tab. Click **cell B15**. Type + and click the next branch sheet tab. Click **cell B15**. Continue in that manner, adding all branch sales to the grand total. Press **Enter** after clicking the last sales amount. The grand total on the Summary sheet will reflect the total of all branch sales. The grand total formula precedes each branch total with the worksheet name, as in ='Caldwell Branch'!+'Blake River'!B15. Although you could certainly type a formula that includes references to other worksheets, it is much easier to click those cells to be included, as in the previous example. You are also much less likely to make mistakes that way.Quick Tip

Hands-On

Activity 6.4 Working with Multiple Worksheets

A determining factor in your choice of transportation to Wyoming is the cost of gasoline. You will either rent a car to drive from your home in Kentucky, or you will fly to Salt Lake City and then rent a car for the five-hour trip from Salt Lake City to Jackson, Wyoming. Either way, you will incur gasoline expense. To determine the cost, you will add a worksheet. Then you will create formulas in the other two worksheets to incorporate the gasoline cost.

a. Right-click the **Air and Car sheet tab** and then click **Insert**. Click **Worksheet** and then click **OK**. A new worksheet is inserted before the Air and Car worksheet. Right-click the **Sheet1 tab** and click **Rename**. Type **Gas Calculator** and press **Enter**.

b. Click **cell A2**. Type **Rental Car** and then press **Enter**. Type **Miles Traveled** and then press →. Type **Mileage** and then press →. Type **Cost/Gallon** and then press →. Type **Total Cost** and then press **Enter**. Click **cell A6** and then type **Air and Car Press Enter**.

c. Select **cells A3 through D3**. Right-click **the selection** and then click **Copy** on the shortcut menu. Right-click **cell A7** and click the **Paste** selection under Paste Options on the shortcut menu. The Paste selection is the first option on the left. Press **Esc** to remove the dashed border around the first selection. Click anywhere to deselect the pasted range.

d. Point to the **border between columns A and B** in the worksheet frame and double-click (when the pointer is a two-headed arrow). You have used AutoFit to adjust column A to show the longest entry in the column. Similarly, AutoFit Column C.

e. Select **cell A4**. Type **1926** and then press →. Type **25** and then press →. Type **3.95** and then press **Enter**. Select **cell A8**, type **275** and press **Enter**.

ON YOUR OWN

Copy cells B4 through C4 to cells B8 through C8.

---

f. Select **cell D4**. Enter a formula that divides Miles traveled by the Mileage and then multiplies the result by the Cost/Gallon. The formula is =A4/B4*C4

g. Select **cell D4**. You will copy the formula to cell D8. The formula will adjust relative to its location so that it calculates the gasoline cost for the Air and Car option. Click the **Home tab**, if necessary. Click **Copy** (the button, not the arrow) in the Clipboard group. Select **cell D8**. Click **Paste** (the button, not the arrow) in the Clipboard group. The formula should be copied to cell D8. Press **Esc** to remove the dashed line from the original formula.

h. Click the **Air and Car sheet tab**. Select **cell B8**. Type **=** Click the **Gas Calculator sheet tab** and select **cell D8**. Click **Enter** (✓) beside the Formula Bar. The Formula Bar displays the linking formula that shows the gasoline cost from the Gas Calculator worksheet.

i. Click on the Formula Bar to the left of **D8**. Type **$** and then press →. Type **$** and then press **Enter**. Because the gasoline cost will be the same regardless of whether two or four travelers make the trip, you will copy the Gas for Rental Car formula to the next column. You make the cell reference absolute, so it will not adjust incorrectly for the new location.

j. Select cell **B8**. Drag the fill handle to the right to include cell C8. The formula is copied to cell C8, showing the same gasoline cost.

k. Click the **Rental Car sheet tab**. Select **cell B10**. Type **=** Click the **Gas Calculator sheet tab** and select **cell D4**. Click **Enter** beside the Formula Bar. Repeat Step I, changing cell D4 in the formula to an absolute reference. Use the **fill handle** to copy the formula from cell B10 to cell C10.

l. Click the **Gas Calculator sheet tab**. You realize that the number of miles traveled is for a one-way trip, when it should be for a round trip. Change the miles traveled for the Rental Car to *3852* and the miles traveled for Air and Car to *550*. Select the **Air and Car worksheet**. Note that the Gasoline cost is adjusted to reflect the round trip miles. Similarly, select the **Rental Car worksheet** and see that the Gasoline cost has been adjusted there as well.

m. Point to the **Gas Calculator sheet tab** and drag to place it after the Rental Car worksheet (Figure 6.27). A small black triangle will indicate the placement of the tab before you release the sheet tab.

n. Save the worksheet. Keep it open for the next exercise.

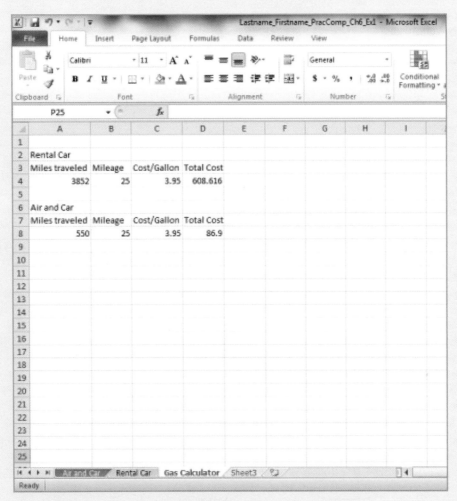

Figure 6.27 The Gas Calculator worksheet summarizes the cost of gasoline for the trip to Wyoming.

Grand Total Formula
(referencing other worksheets)

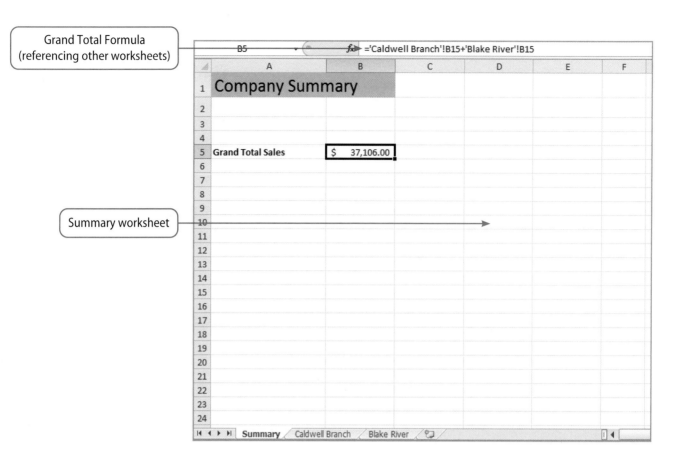

Summary worksheet

| | B5 | | f_x | ='Caldwell Branch'!B15+'Blake River'!B15 |

Company Summary

Grand Total Sales | $ 37,106.00

Summary | Caldwell Branch | Blake River

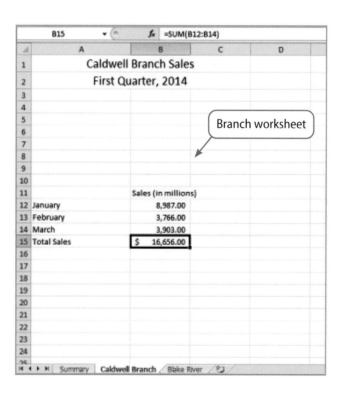

| | B15 | | f_x | =SUM(B12:B14) |

Caldwell Branch Sales
First Quarter, 2014

Branch worksheet

	Sales (in millions)
January	8,987.00
February	3,766.00
March	3,903.00
Total Sales	$ 16,656.00

Summary | Caldwell Branch | Blake River

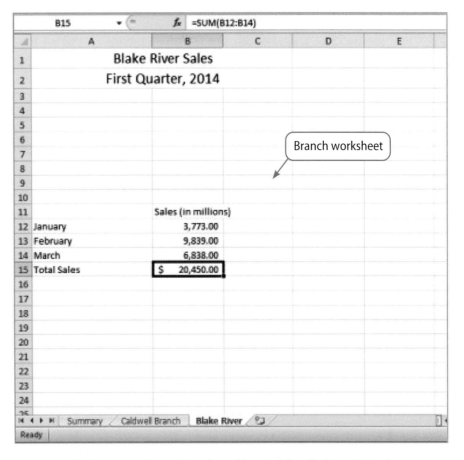

Figure 6.28 Excel makes it easy to reference cells on other worksheets, including cell references in formulas.

Working with Functions

Some formulas are quite complex. Especially if math is not your strong suit, you might find yourself avoiding even the suggestion of a lengthy calculation. Although Excel is perfectly capable of working with any formula you devise, it is also well stocked with **functions**, which are shortcut formulas. Functions simplify even the most complex formulas so you can select a function, supply the necessary data, and let Excel do the work. You can select functions from several categories, including financial, statistical, trigonometric, and logical.

Suppose you are considering purchasing a new car and must procure a bank loan to make the purchase. Armed with the purchase price, the interest rate charged, and the number of years in which you plan to repay the loan, you can select a PMT function, supply the loan variables, and instantly see the monthly payment that would be required. If the payment is more than you can afford, use Excel's "what-if" capability to identify the price you can afford if the interest rate and the repayment time remains the same. Such analysis is possible through Excel's Goal Seek feature.

Technically, all functions include at least one parenthetical argument that includes variable information. For example, the PMT function described in the preceding paragraph could be =PMT(28000,60,.07/12) where the loan amount is $28,000, the number of months for loan payback is 60, and the interest rate is 7% (divided by 12 to determine a monthly rate). The loan variables are called **arguments**. Most often, the arguments are cell addresses instead of constants, so a more realistic PMT function would be =PMT(B5,C5,D5/12). In very few functions

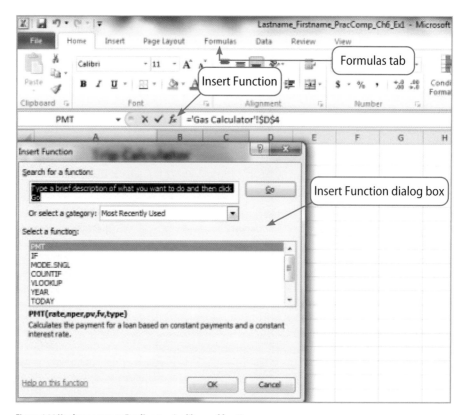

Figure 6.29 You have access to Excel's extensive library of functions.

the argument is actually null, or empty, but the parentheses are still included. For example the =NOW() function returns the current date and time, without a specific argument within the parentheses. Even so, parentheses are included.

Because it is nearly impossible to remember the format of all functions, you can find functions in a couple of places. Click **Insert Function** (Figure 6.29) to open the Insert Function dialog box. From there, you can select a function. You can also click the **Formulas tab** and select a function category in the Function Library group. Select a function and enter any required variables.

You will use a few functions so often that you will memorize them. The most common function is =SUM. It is used to total a series of numbers. Its format is

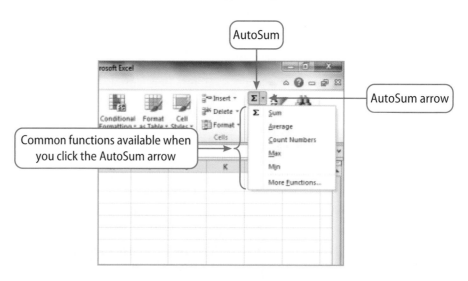

Figure 6.30 Some of the most common statistical functions are included in the Editing group.

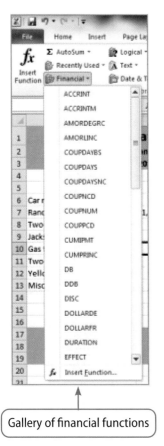

Gallery of financial functions

Figure 6.31 Selecting from a gallery of functions means that you do not have to memorize the format of each function.

=SUM(cell1:cell2), where the argument is a range of cells to sum. Also called AutoSum, you will find the =SUM function very helpful in quickly summing ranges. Similarly, the =AVERAGE function averages a range of numbers. Both AutoSum and Average are available in the Editing group on the Home tab as shown in Figure 6.30. In this section, you will be introduced to statistical, financial, and logical functions. In addition, you will explore Excel's "what-if" capability.

Using Statistical and Financial Functions

From basic activities such as sum, average, median, and mode to more complex statistical distribution and probability tests, Excel provides a full slate of statistical functions. Using those functions, you can analyze spreadsheet data in various ways. The most common statistical functions, and those you will most likely remember, are SUM, AVERAGE, MAX, MIN, and MEDIAN. In all those cases, the format of the function is the function name followed by the range of cells to be summarized. For example, the function =AVERAGE(C20:C25) returns the average of the values in cells C20 through C25. Similarly, =MAX(C20:C25) returns the largest value in that range. =MIN identifies the smallest value, and =MEDIAN finds the median (middle value).

Financial functions, such as those shown in Figure 6.31, enable you to analyze financial data. Although the choices are many, you will most likely use only a few, unless you become involved with business finances. When you select a function from a gallery such as that shown in Figure 6.31, you are able to place function arguments in a dialog box. When you click OK, the function is built automatically for you, sparing you the necessity of memorizing a specific function's format. Figure 6.32 illustrates the process of preparing a PMT function.

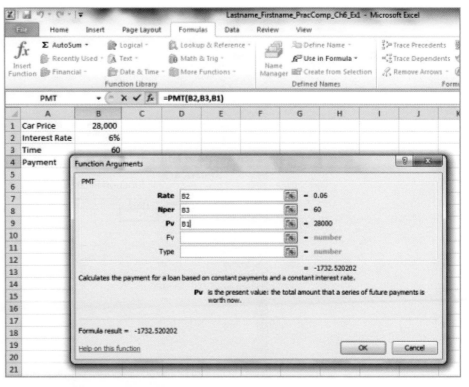

Figure 6.32 Use a dialog box to create a function quickly.

Using a Logical Function

A logical function is a versatile decision-making tool. With seven logical functions, all of which are available on the Formulas tab, you can instruct Excel to make a determination of cell content after comparing values in other cells. The most commonly used logical function is IF. The IF function includes three components—a comparison, an action to take if the comparison tests true, and an action to take if the comparison tests false. As with other functions, you do not have to remember the exact **syntax** (rules regarding the wording of the function) because Excel enables you to use a dialog box to identify function components.

Consider the worksheet shown in Figure 6.33. A physical education program at a local high school awards two different levels of achievement to its student athletes. If a student completes 50 hours or more of training, he is designated a Gold athlete. Anything less than 50 hours results in a Silver designation. So you do not have to make that determination yourself, you can build an IF function to automatically place the correct designation in cell C5—either *Gold* or *Silver*. That determination comes after comparing the contents of cell B5 with 50. If the value is greater than 50, then the word *Gold* is placed in cell C5. Otherwise, the word *Silver* is placed in cell C5. When worded in that manner, it becomes simple to identify the three parts of the IF function. The *comparison* is B5>50. The condition if the comparison tests *true* is "Gold," and the condition if the comparison tests *false* is "Silver." The correct IF function to place in cell C5 is =IF(B5>50,"Gold","Silver"). Each component, or argument, within the parentheses is separated by a comma.

Of course, the more you type, the more likely you are to make mistakes. In addition, you will not want to remember the exact syntax of many functions. Therefore, you can use the Formulas tab to simplify the development of functions. In the case of the IF statement described in the preceding paragraph, you

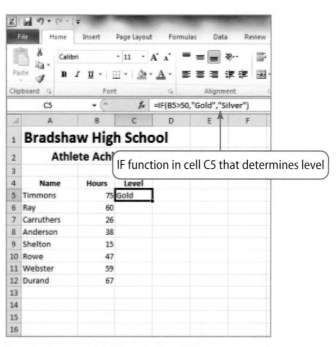

Figure 6.33 The result determined by a logical function is based on a comparison.

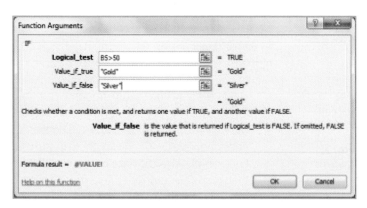

Figure 6.34 If an athlete has more than 50 hours, he is considered "Gold;" otherwise, he is a "Silver" athlete.

Figure 6.35 After the 5IF function is copied down the column, all athletes are categorized as Gold or Silver.

would click in cell C5. Then click the **Formulas tab** and click **Logical** in the Function Library group. Select **IF**. Complete the Function Arguments dialog box as shown in Figure 6.34. Note the placement of the three components discussed earlier. After copying the function to other cells in column D, the resulting worksheet is shown in Figure 6.35.

Using What-If Analysis

Excel can summarize data so you are able to make better decisions. You can use Excel's **what-if analysis** to assist in the process. What-if Analysis is located in the Data Tools group on the Data tab. One of those tools, **Goal Seek**, enables you to set a goal and see how variables must be modified to achieve that goal. Suppose you have identified a house to purchase. You will need to borrow money for the house, and you want to pay it back within 15 years. The interest rate is fixed at a certain percentage. After using a PMT function to determine the monthly payment, you realize that you cannot afford to make the payment. You are only prepared to pay a certain amount each month. With that figure in mind (your goal), you can use Excel's Goal Seek feature to modify the only variable that you can, or are willing to, change—the purchase price. At that point, you have a clear understanding of the amount you can borrow, so you begin to shop for a house that costs no more than what you can afford. Goal Seek is an excellent example of Excel's ability to help you make better decisions.

Hands-On

Activity 6.5 Working with Functions and What-If Analysis

In finalizing the Wyoming travel worksheet, you will include functions to summarize total costs. In addition, you will use a PMT function and data analysis to make a purchase decision regarding a new home.

a. Click the **Air and Car sheet tab**. Press **Ctrl** and click the **Rental Car sheet tab**. Both sheets are selected, as indicated by the word *Group* in the title bar. Click **cell A14**. Type **Total Cost** and then press →.

b. Click the Home tab, if necessary, Click **AutoSum** Σ in the Editing group. (Be sure to click the AutoSum button, not the arrow.) The suggested function shown is *=SUM(B5:B13)*. Note that the function is incorrect because it includes cell B5, which designates the number of travelers, but is not actually a trip cost. Click on the **Formula Bar to the right of B5**. Press **Backspace**. Type *6* and then press **Enter**.

c. Click **cell B14**. Drag the **fill handle** to copy the formula to **cell C14**. Click the **Rental Car sheet tab** and note that the =SUM function was also placed on that sheet (because the two sheets were grouped). Right-click the **Rental Car sheet tab** and select **Ungroup Sheets**. Having completed the travel analysis, which mode of travel is the best choice with respect to total traveling with two? How about four?

d. Save the workbook. Click the **File tab** and then click **Close**. Click the **File tab** and then click **New**. Double-click **Blank workbook**. Complete the worksheet as shown in Figure 6.36.

ON YOUR OWN

Expand column A as necessary to show all cell entries. Format cell B3 as Accounting Number Format ($ in the Number group on the Home tab).

---

e. Save the workbook as *Lastname_Firstname_PracComp_Ch6_Ex2*. Click **cell B4**. Click **Decrease Decimal** in the Number group on the Home tab to display only one place to the right of the decimal.

ON YOUR OWN

Decrease the decimal places of the purchase price in cell B3, so no places are displayed to the right of the decimal point.

---

f. Click **cell B6**. Click the **Formulas tab** and click **Financial** in the Function Library group. Scroll through the functions and click **PMT**. Complete the dialog box as shown in Figure 6.37. Instead of typing the cell references, however, you can click them in the worksheet. For example, click the **Rate box**, click **cell B4**, and then type */12*. Complete the remaining areas of the dialog box as shown in Figure 6.37 and click OK.

	A	B	C
1	Home Purchase		
2			
3	Loan Amount	175000	
4	Interest	6.50%	
5	Years	15	
6	Payment		
7			
8			
9			

Figure 6.36 Variables include purchase price, interest rate, and payment periods.

The Rate in cell B4 is divided by 12 so that the annual interest rate is shown at a monthly rate. Nper, which is the number of payments, is multiplied by 12 because you will be paying by the month. Finally, Pv (Present Value) is the amount of the loan, shown in cell B3.

g. The payment amount is shown as a negative value, because it is technically an outflow. To reverse the sign to positive, click **cell B6**. Click on the **Formula Bar before the PMT function** (but after the =). Type - (a negative sign) and then press **Enter**.

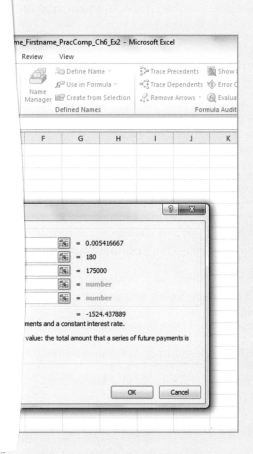

name_Firstname_PracComp_Ch6_Ex2 - Microsoft Excel

Review   View

Name Manager | Define Name | Use in Formula | Create from Selection

Defined Names

Trace Precedents | Show
Trace Dependents | Error C
Remove Arrows | Evalua

Formula Audit

	= 0.005416667
	= 180
	= 175000
	= *number*
	= *number*
	= -1524.437889

ments and a constant interest rate.

value: the total amount that a series of future payments is

OK   Cancel

ON YOUR OWN

Rename Sheet1 as *Payment Calculator*. Delete the remaining sheets (right-click a sheet tab and click **Delete**).

---

h. Click **cell B6**. Because you can only afford a $1,000 monthly payment, you will use Goal Seek to determine the purchase price that will meet your payment goal. Click the **Data tab**. Click **What-If Analysis** in the Data Tools group and select **Goal Seek**. Cell B6 is shown in the *Set cell* box because it is the current cell (and the one that you are setting a goal for). Click the **To value box** and type **1000** (because you can only afford a payment of $1,000). *Do not type the dollar sign or comma*. Click the **By changing cell box** and click (or type) **B3**. The variable you are willing to adjust to meet your payment goal is the purchase price, which is located in cell B3. Click **OK**. Click **OK** again. What is the highest possible purchase price you can borrow money for and stay within your payment goal?

i. Save the workbook and exit Excel.

Chapter Summary

- Spreadsheet software simplifies the task of organizing numeric data on an electronic grid of columns and rows. *221*

- A workbook includes one or more worksheets. *224*

- You can type data in a worksheet as text, numbers, or formulas. 225

- Before making any changes to worksheet data, you must first select the cells to be changed. *233*

- A range is a group of one or more cells. *233*

- You can select ranges, columns, and rows. *240*

- A formula is a set of instructions that tells Excel how to perform a calculation. *236*

- Functions are predefined formulas that simplify complex operations. *255*

- Absolute cell references in a formula do not change as the formula is copied to another location, whereas relative cell references change, relative to the position from which they are copied. *248*

- When you make changes to a worksheet, such as aligning data, formatting numbers, or changing the appearance of worksheet data, you are formatting it. *233*

- The Goal Seek feature enables you to set a goal and see how variables must be modified to achieve that goal. *259*

- You can manage multiple worksheets, adding, deleting, and renaming them. *249*

- You can include cells from multiple worksheets in a formula. *251*

Key Terms

Multiple Choice

1. How many worksheets can be included in a workbook?
   a. The number is limited only by the computer's memory.
   b. 255.
   c. 3.
   d. 10.

2. A range is identified by
   a. a worksheet name.
   b. the cell addresses at all four corners of the range.
   c. the cell address of the top-left and bottom-right cell within the range.
   d. the bottom-left and top-right cell within the range.

3. An example of a "what-if analysis" tool is
   a. Scenario Guide.
   b. Data Estimator.
   c. Goal Seek.
   d. AutoSum.

4. When developing a formula in which at least one component refers to a cell address that should not be adjusted if the formula is copied, you would use a(n)
   a. relative reference.
   b. absolute reference.
   c. fixed reference.
   d. static reference.

5. To display a shortcut menu,
   a. right-click an area or selection.
   b. click the Data tab and then click Shortcut.
   c. select Shortcut in Backstage view.
   d. select an area or item and then click Shortcut on the Mini toolbar.

6. An advantage of grouping worksheets is that
   a. all worksheets in a workbook can be given the same name.
   b. all worksheets are saved as one workbook.
   c. formatting changes and formulas can be applied to all the grouped worksheets.
   d. all the worksheets can be referred to with one worksheet name.

7. The feature that enables Excel to adjust the column width for the widest entry is
   a. Merge & Center.
   b. AutoFit.
   c. FreeFit.
   d. Goal Seek.

8. The formula =SUM(Units_Sold) is an example of the use of a(n)
   a. order of precedence.
   b. predefined formula.
   c. worksheet name.
   d. range name.

9. The small black square, located at the bottom-right corner of an active cell or range, that enables you to copy cell contents is the
   a. fill handle.
   b. data fill handle.
   c. sizing handle.
   d. copy handle.

10. The value of the Formula Bar is that it
    a. provides formula templates from which you can select when developing a formula.
    b. provides quick access to functions, which are shortcut formulas.
    c. displays the formula or contents of the active cell, so you can make corrections, if necessary.
    d. informs you of syntax errors if you enter a formula incorrectly.

11. Arguments of a function are located
    a. within quotation marks after the function name.
    b. in the selected cell after the function is executed.
    c. within parentheses after the function name.
    d. immediately preceding the function name.

12. Which of the following is an example of vertical alignment?
    a. Middle Align.
    b. Center.
    c. Left.
    d. Justify.

13. The Excel view that hides the Ribbon, providing the most space possible for an Excel worksheet is
    a. Normal view.
    b. Page Layout view.
    c. Page Break Preview.
    d. Full Screen view.

14. Free online storage, made available by Microsoft, is called
    a. Excel Live.
    b. SkyDrive.
    c. Backstage.
    d. Excel 2010 Web App.

15. When you copy a formula from one cell to an adjacent cell,
    a. the results of the formula are copied, but not the formula itself.
    b. you are asked to confirm the copy.
    c. cell addresses in the formula are adjusted relative to the new location.
    d. the formula is copied, but the resulting value is the same because cell addresses in the formula are not adjusted.

True/False

Circle **T** if the statement is true or **F** if the statement is false.

T F 1. One way to manually expand column width is to point to the border on the right side of the column (in the worksheet frame) and drag to the right.

T F 2. You can position a worksheet between two existing worksheets.

T F 3. You must begin a formula with an equal sign.

T F 4. The Excel view that shows margins and special features, such as headers, is Normal view.

T F 5. The IF function is considered a logical function.

T F 6. By default, Excel provides five worksheets for every new workbook.

T F 7. A formula can include cell references from the same worksheet as well as from other worksheets.

T F 8. With the Clipboard pane open, you can copy or cut up to 24 items before pasting any.

T F 9. You can only insert or delete one row or column at a time.

T F 10. To indicate that a cell reference is absolute, place a dollar sign before each element of the cell reference that is to remain fixed; for example "H5".

End of Chapter Exercises

Guided Projects

1. You will spend the summer as a counselor for a weight loss camp for children. The camp combines fun with weight loss, offering a variety of sports and fitness programs along with guided nutrition. With an emphasis on fun, Camp Rainbow Trails has a proven success record. Affiliated with Scottwood Camps, Inc., Rainbow Trails is one of only two Scottwood weight loss camps in the nation. The other, Camp Wasilla, offers identical programs. In this exercise, you will prepare a worksheet for each camp, listing camp income. You will also develop a summary worksheet showing combined camp income.

   a. Start Excel and open **PracComp_ Ch6_Camps** from your student data files. Save the file as *Lastname_ Firstname_PracComp_Ch6_Camps*.

   b. Click **cell A4** in Sheet1, type **Session** and then press →. Type **Duration** and then press →. Type **Dates** and then press →. Type **Cost** and then press **Enter**.

   c. Place the pointer on the number **4** in the worksheet frame and drag to **highlight rows 4 and 5**. Right-click **the shaded rows** and click **Insert**. Two rows are inserted.

   d. Click **cell E6**, type **Total** and then press →. Type **% of Total** and then press →. Type **Location** and then press **Enter**. Place the pointer on the border between columns A and B (in the worksheet frame) so a two-headed arrow appears. Drag to the right, watching the ScreenTip, to expand the column to **12.14** (or **90 pixels**). Double-click **the border between columns B and C** to AutoFit column B.

   e. Select **columns D, E, and F**. (Drag columns D through F in the worksheet frame.) Click the **Home tab**. Click **Center** in the Alignment group. Drag to select **cells A6 through C6**. Click **Center**. Select **row 6** (click the number 6 in the worksheet frame). Click **Bold** in the Font group on the Home tab. Click **Italic** in the Font group.

   f. Right-click **Sheet1** and select **Rename** from the shortcut menu. Type **Camp Rainbow Trails** and then press **Enter**. Likewise, rename Sheet2 to **Camp Wasilla**. Click the **Camp Rainbow Trails sheet tab**.

   g. Select **column E** (click the letter E in the worksheet frame). Right-click in the shaded column and click **Insert**. Click **cell E6**, type **Campers** and then press **Enter**. Complete cells E7 through E15 as follows:
   38
   24
   30
   36
   42
   31
   27
   45
   52

   h. Click **Select All** (the box immediately to the left of the letter A in the top worksheet frame and above the number 1 in the left worksheet frame). Click **Copy** in the Clipboard group on the Home tab. Click the **Camp Wasilla sheet tab**. With the active cell in A1, click **Paste**. (If you click the Paste arrow instead of the Paste button, click **Paste**, which is the first option under Paste.) The contents of the Camp Rainbow worksheet should be copied to Camp Wasilla.

   i. Click **cell A1**. Edit the entry in the Formula Bar to read *Camp Wasilla* and press **Enter**. Type **Bluewater, New York** and then press **Enter**. Click **cell E7**, type **31** and then press **Enter**. Continue changing the number of campers in cells E8 through E15 as follows:
   40
   43
   28
   60
   53
   27
   56
   49

j. Click the **Camp Rainbow Trails sheet tab** and click cell **A1** to deselect the previous selection. Press **Ctrl** and click the **Camp Wasilla sheet tab**. Both worksheets are selected, as indicated by the word *Group* on the title bar. Select **cells A1 through G1**. Click **Merge & Center** in the Alignment group on the Home tab. Similarly, merge and center **cells A2 through G2** and **cells A3 through G3**.

k. Click **cell A1**. Click **Bold** in the Font group. Click the **Font Size arrow** and select **20**. Select **cells A1 through A3**. Click the **Fill Color arrow** and click **Light Green** (fifth from the left in Standard Colors).

l. Click cell **F7**. Type = and then click **cell D7**. Type * and then click **cell E7**. Press **Enter**. Click **cell F7**. Drag the **fill handle** to copy the formula through cell F15. With cells F7 through F15 selected, click **Comma Style** in the Number group on the Home tab. Click **Decrease Decimal** twice.

m. Click cell **F16**. Click **AutoSum** (the button, not the arrow) in the Editing group on the Home tab. Press **Enter**. Click cell **F16**. Click the **Border arrow** in the Font group and click **Top and Double Bottom Border**.

n. Click cell **G7**. Type = and then click **cell F7**. Type / and then click **cell F16**. Press **Enter**. Click cell **G7**, On the Formula Bar, edit **F16** to be F16 and then press Enter. Click cell **G7**. Drag the fill handle to copy the formula to **cells G8 through G15**. With cells G7 through G15 selected, click **Percent Style** in the Number group on the Home tab. Click **Increase Decimal** once.

o. Click the **Camp Wasilla sheet tab** to verify that all the formatting and formulas copied correctly to that worksheet. Double-click the **Sheet3 tab**, type Summary and then press **Enter**. In cell A1, type **Camp Summary** and then press **Enter**. Click **cell A1**, change the font size to **20**, and then click **Bold**.

p. Click cell **A5**, type **Session** and then press →. Type **Total** and then press **Enter**. Click the **Camp Wasilla sheet tab**, select **cells A7 through A15**, and right-click within the selected area. Click **Copy** on the shortcut menu. Click the **Summary sheet tab**, right-click **cell A6** and click **Paste** (the first selection under Paste). Expand column A to **12.14** (or **90 pixels**).

q. Click cell **B6**. Type = and then click the **Camp Rainbow Trails sheet tab**. Click **cell F7**. Type + and then click the **Camp Wasilla sheet tab**. Click **cell F7** and then press **Enter**. Click **cell B6** in the Summary worksheet and see the formula on the Formula Bar that references other worksheets. Double-click the **fill handle** to copy the formula to **cells B7 through B14**. Format cells B6 through B14 as **Comma Style** with no decimals.

r. Click cell **A15**, type **Total** and then press →. Click **AutoSum** in the Editing group, and then press **Enter**. Bold cells A15 and B15, and apply a top and double bottom border to both cells.

s. Click the **Camp Rainbow Trails sheet tab**. Click **cell H7**. Depending on the number of campers, sessions will be held either at Siesta Lodge or Sonora Cabins. If the number of campers is greater than 35, sessions are at Siesta Lodge. Otherwise, they are at Sonora Cabins. Click the **Formulas tab**. Click **Logical** in the Functions Library group. Click **IF**. Click **cell E7**. (If the dialog box obscures cell E7, drag the title bar to reposition the dialog box and then click cell E7.) Type >35 and then click the **Value_if_true box**. Type **Siesta Lodge** and then click the **Value_if_false box**. Type **Sonora Cabins** and then click **OK**. Because the number of campers in the PreCamp session is greater than 35, the location is Siesta Lodge. Drag the **fill handle** to copy the function to **cells H8 through H15**.

t. Click the **Camp Wasilla sheet tab**. Click **cell H7** and enter an IF function similar to that completed in Step s. If the number of campers is greater than 35, sessions are at Poco Campground. Otherwise, they are at Falls Lodge. Copy the function to cells H8 through H15.

u. Save the workbook and exit Excel.

2. You have identified a house you want to purchase. The house costs $128,900. You have been approved to borrow that amount of money at 5.25%. You are now considering whether to borrow the money for 15 years or for 30 years, and will use Excel to calculate the payment. If the payment is not within your means, you will use Goal Seek to help determine the amount that you can borrow.

a. Open Excel. Save the blank workbook as *Last-name_Firstname_PracComp_Ch6_House*.

b. Click **cell A1**. Type **Home Purchase** and then press **Enter**. Click **cell A3**, type **Price** and then press **Enter**. Type **Rate** and then press **Enter**. Type **Years** and then press **Enter**. Type **Payment** and then press **Enter**.

c. Click **cell B3**. Type **128900** and press **Enter**. Type **5.25%** and press **Enter**. Type **15** and press **Enter**.

d. Click **cell B3**. Click **Accounting Number Format** in the Number group on the Home tab. Click **Decrease Decimal** twice.

e. Click **cell B6**. Click the **Formulas tab** and click **Financial** in the Function Library group. Scroll down and click **PMT**. Click **cell B4** and type **/12** (dividing the rate by 12 to obtain a monthly rate). Click the **Nper box** and click **cell B5**. Type ***12** (multiplying the number of years by 12 to obtain the number of monthly payments). Click the **Pv box** and click **cell B3**. Click **OK**.

f. Double-click the **Sheet1 sheet tab**, type **15 Years** and then press **Enter**. Double-click the **Sheet2 sheet tab**, type **30 Years** and then press **Enter**. Click the **15 Years sheet tab**. Click the **Formula bar** between = and PMT. Type **–** and then press **Enter**. The Payment is now positive. You have reversed the case of the Payment value from negative (representing an outflow) to positive, which is more understandable. Click **cell A1**, click the **Home tab**, and click **Bold** in the Font group of the Home tab. Click the **Font Size arrow** and select **18**.

g. Select **cells A3 through B6**. Click the **Fill Color arrow** and click **Aqua, Accent 5** (row 1, column 9). Select **cells A1 through B6**. Click **Copy** in the Clipboard group on the Home tab. Click the **30 Years sheet tab**. With the active cell in A1, click **Paste** in the Clipboard group.

h. AutoFit Column B (double-click the right border in the worksheet frame). Click **cell B5**, type **30** and then press **Enter**. Note the reduced monthly payment over **30** years. Click the **15 Years sheet tab** and click **cell D3**. Type **Total Payment** and then press **Enter**. Type **=B6*B5*12** and then press **Enter**. You have multiplied the monthly payment by the number of years, and then multiplied the result by 12 (the number of payments each year) to obtain the total that you will pay for the house over 15 years.

i. Select **cells D3 through D4**. Right-click the selected area and select **Copy** from the shortcut menu. Click the **30 Years sheet tab** and click **cell D3**. Click **Paste** in the Clipboard group on the Home tab. Double-click the **border between columns D and E** to AutoFit column D. Click the **15 Years sheet tab** and press **Esc** to deselect the selection. Note the total payment and then compare it with the total payment in the 30 Years worksheet. How much more would you pay over 30 years?

j. Click the **15 Years sheet tab**. Because you want to pay off the house in 15 years, but the monthly payment is slightly high, you will use Goal Seek to determine how much you can borrow so that the monthly payment is no higher than $1,000.

k. Click **cell B6**. Click the **Data tab** and click **What-If Analysis** in the Data Tools group. Click **Goal Seek**. Click the **To value box**. Type *1000* and then click the **By changing cell box**. Click **cell B3**, click **OK**, and then click **OK** again. What is the most you can borrow for the house to keep the payment at $1,000?

l. Right-click the **15 Years sheet tab**, point to **Tab Color**, and click **Red** (second from left in Standard Colors). Change the **30 Years sheet tab** to **Blue** (third from right in Standard Colors).

m. Save the workbook and exit Excel.

Unguided Project

1. You have developed a set of plans for building an Adirondack chair and an Adirondack swing. The building supplies company for which you work is preparing a promotional flyer with a materials list for each project, along with an invitation to attend a free Adirondack workshop. In this project, you will edit a workbook with plans for both projects.

a. Start Excel and open **PracComp_Ch6_Plans** from your student data files. Save the file as *Lastname_Firstname_PracComp_Ch6_Plans*.

b. Group Sheet1 and Sheet2. Select **columns A through D**. Place the pointer on the border between any two of the selected columns and double-click to AutoFit all of the columns. Select **row 4** and wrap the text (click Wrap Text in the Alignment group on the Home tab). Change the width of column C to **9.57** (or **72 pixels**).

c. Delete column D. Select **row 4** and click **Middle Align** in the Alignment group on the Home tab. Center columns B and C.

d. Type **Discount** in cell E4. One at a time, merge and center cells A1 through E1 and cells A2 through E2. Apply a fill color of **Tan, Background 2, Darker 10%** to cells A1 through A2.

e. Ungroup the worksheets. Rename Sheet1 as *Adirondack Chair* and rename Sheet2 as *Adirondack Swing*.

f. Select **cell D5** in the Adirondack Chair worksheet. Type * and then click the **Price List sheet tab**. Click **cell B3**. Type * and click the **Adirondack Chair sheet tab**. Click **cell C5** and press **Enter**. You multiplied the price per inch for a 1x6 (from the Price List worksheet) by the number of inches required (in the Adirondack Chair worksheet). So that you can copy the formula to other chair parts that require 1 × 6 lumber, without adjusting the per inch cost, you will make the reference to cell B3 absolute. Click **cell D5**. Click the **Formula Bar** and change the reference to cell B3 to *B3*. Press **Enter**.

g. Select **cell D5**. Click **Copy**. Select **cell D7** and click **Paste**. Click **Copy**. Select **cell D9** and click **Paste**. Click **Copy**. Select **cell D11** and click **Paste**. Press **Esc**.

h. Select **cell D6**. Enter a formula that multiplies the price per inch for a 1 × 4 (on the Price List worksheet) with the number of inches in cell C6 on the Adirondack Chair worksheet. Make the reference to the price per inch absolute, and copy the formula to other items requiring 1x4 lumber. Press **Esc**.

i. Complete the Total Cost column in the Adirondack Swing worksheet as you did in Steps f–h for the Adirondack Chair worksheet. Be sure to make the reference to the price per inch for each item absolute and copy the formula to the appropriate cells.

j. Group the Adirondack Chair and Adirondack Swing worksheets. Type **Total** in **cell A12** and press Enter. Select **cell D12**. Include an Auto-Sum function to sum the entries in column D.

k. Select **cell E5**. Include an IF function to enter the word "Yes" if Total Cost is greater than $10, and "No" if it is not. (Hint: Do not include $ in the logical test when comparing Total Cost to $10). Copy the IF function to cells E6 through E11. Ungroup the worksheets.

l. Save the file and exit Excel.

Photos by sheelamohanachandran2010/Shutterstock; almagami/Shutterstock

CHAPTER SEVEN

Understanding Networking and Computer Security

WHETHER YOU REALIZE IT OR NOT, COMPUTER networking has become an essential part of our everyday lives. Most businesses today cannot function without a network that enables a business to coordinate internal communication, share files and devices, connect to the Internet, and send and receive e-mail. A computer network facilitates communication and the exchange of information by linking one or more computers and peripheral devices. A network can be wired and/or wireless, with devices connected by cables or communicating wirelessly. In this section, you will learn about **networking** basics and how you can easily create your own home network.

Understanding Networking Basics

Regardless of whether a network is designed to connect computers globally or simply within one home, the common element is hardware. At its most basic level, a computer network connects computers so that they can communicate and share devices and files. On a large scale, the Internet connects computers around the world, facilitating such activities as research, shopping, banking, and file sharing. In your home, you might want to share an Internet connection with multiple computers, or perhaps you intend to connect several computers wirelessly

OBJECTIVES

When you complete this chapter, you will:

▶ Understand basics of networking.

▶ Be able to identify hardware and software needed to network devices.

▶ Understand and explain the two main types of network architectures.

▶ Be aware of security and privacy risks as they pertain to networking.

▶ Explain how to set up and protect a home network.

▶ Understand network threats such as viruses, spyware, and malware and know how to protect against them.

▶ Become familiar with Windows 7 privacy and security features.

Quick Tip

Test Your Connection Speed

If you have an Internet connection at home, you can test its speed. Visit http://www.whatismyip.com/tools/internet-speed-test.asp, scroll down slightly, and click the city nearest your location. Then watch as your download and upload speed is tested and shown.

Quick Tip

What is a Gateway?

A gateway joins several networks, such as a home network and the Internet. A gateway is usually associated with a router, although a computer can act as a gateway, as well.

to one printer so they can share the device. You can even share documents and other files between computers in your home if you have access to a home network.

To create a home network, you will need more than one computer, a device such as a router and/or modem, software (such as an operating system or other application) to coordinate communication, and a path for the information to travel from one computer to another. The path can be wired or wireless, although the most common configuration is a wireless home network.

In most cases, a home network is designed to enable several computers to share a single Internet connection. Suppose you connect to the Internet through a broadband connection, such as cable. Your cable provider will set up a cable modem in your home so you can access the Internet. If you use a desktop computer (as opposed to a laptop), the computer might not be configured for wireless access, so you can connect to the modem with a **CAT 5 Ethernet cable**. Cable modems are typically designed to provide wireless access as well, so you could also connect to the Internet with a laptop if the laptop includes a **network interface card (NIC)** or if you plug a **wireless network adapter** into the laptop's USB port. Other modems, such as DSL or satellite, might require that you purchase and connect a **wireless router** to the modem so several computers can simultaneously access the Internet. A **router** is a device that transmits data along a network; the device can be wired (connected by cable to computers and other devices) or wireless (receiving wireless signals from computers). Figure 7.1 illustrates several of those hardware devices and cable.

Let's look at these hardware devices using an example. Connie lives in Detroit and wants to send an e-mail to her sister, Claudia, in Orlando. She types an e-mail on her laptop, which is connected to the Internet. Her computer is configured with a NIC, which facilitates communication on a network. Especially if the computer is a laptop, it is very likely that a NIC is included. Some desktops, but not all, include a NIC, as well.

Connie's e-mail (or data) is sent as a group of **data packets** to its destination. Data messages—Connie's e-mail, in this example—are broken into smaller

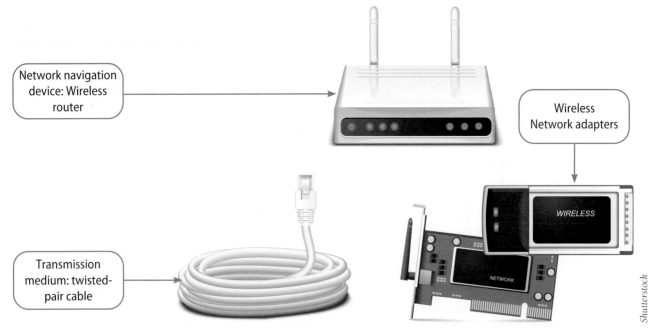

Network navigation device: Wireless router

Wireless Network adapters

Transmission medium: twisted-pair cable

Shutterstock

Figure 7.1 In addition to software, networks require hardware devices to transmit data across a network.

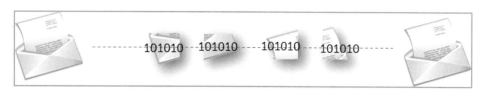

Figure 7.2 Data messages and files are broken into smaller components and sent across the network as data packets.

components, called data packets (Figure 7.2), so they can be sent more easily along the network. They will be reassembled once they reach their destination. Connie will not see or have to deal with data packets. She simply types the e-mail and sends it.

But how does an e-mail sent from Detroit get to Orlando without getting lost somewhere in Ohio? Similar to the way that an item mailed through the U.S. Postal Service makes its way through several stops, carried by several mail vehicles and sorted by various devices, data packets are directed through a computer network by various computer servers and routing devices. You might compare a data packet to an addressed envelope, which contains routing information that assists in transferring contents appropriately. Not only do data packets include routing information but they also contain the actual pieces of data being sent, as well as information about how to reassemble the pieces.

Routers and switches are instrumental in getting data packets where they need to go. Used most often in a wired setting, a **switch** sorts and distributes data packets between devices on a **local area network (LAN)**. On the other hand, a router is capable of directing wireless and wired traffic, while at the same time determining the most efficient way to route the transmission. A router not only directs data packets in an effective manner but also serves as a **gateway**, connecting any combination of LANs, **wide area networks (WANs)**, and the Internet. Connie's message may be sent through several of these routing devices before it reaches its final destination in Orlando.

Network Architecture

Network architecture is the way a communications network is designed. A network's design includes the hardware, software, data formats, and the functional organization that ties the network components together. A **peer-to-peer network (P2P)** links two or more computers without going through a central server computer. The linked computers can then share resources and devices. In a **client-server network**, a central computer handles all the network's security and file-sharing requests. A home network is typically organized as a peer-to-peer network, while a client-server network is more often found in a business setting, where centralization of resources and network security are priorities.

Peer-to-Peer (P2P) Networks

Suppose you want to share music, pictures, or files between two computers in your home. Using a peer-to-peer network, you can do just that. In a peer-to-peer network (Figure 7.3), each computer on a network can communicate with others on the same network, sharing files and other resources. A peer-to-peer network, which can be wired, wireless, or some combination of the two, has no central computer that acts as a storehouse for files, software, and devices. Instead, each computer on the network is able to share resources with others, provided the administrator of a computer has *shared* those resources. For example, User A can access a printer that is connected to User B's computer only if User B has made that device available

Figure 7.3 Peer-to-peer networks permit the sharing of resources between computers and devices. Peer-to-peer networks are often found in home networks.

to others. Similarly, User B can access a document that is stored on User A's hard drive if User A has shared the hard drive (or a folder on the hard drive). Most operating systems, including Windows 7, enable you to create **workgroups** to share files, printers, and other resources. A workgroup is a collection of computers on a network that shares resources. The term *workgroup* is actually synonymous with a *peer-to-peer network*, as no computer on the network acts as a server.

An Internet-based peer-to-peer (P2P) network allows a group of computer users to share resources from one another's hard drives. Although any file type can typically be shared, the type most often transferred is music. That fact is of great concern to record companies and copyright holders who question what they consider illegal sharing of copyrighted content. In fact, Napster, which today is an online music store, originated as a peer-to-peer file sharing service specializing in sharing audio files (accessed from Napster's music database). Legal difficulties that arose over copyright infringement caused the company to cease operations. Later acquired by Roxio and then by Best Buy, the company has been retooled into a profitable online music seller. Other Internet projects, such as Gnutella, Freenet, and eDonkey, offer decentralized, peer-to-peer file sharing among users. Although all file sharing is susceptible to copyright infringement concerns, the difference between the current generation of Internet P2P file sharing and such projects as Napster is that the shared files are typically housed on the hard drives of those individuals who download file sharing software and connect to an online P2P network—not from a company's database. The responsibility, then, is shifted to individual users. Even so, concern over the protection of copyrights and the liability incurred with copyright infringement causes many colleges and public entities to prohibit access to such sites as Gnutella and Freenet. In its purest form, however, Internet P2P file sharing frees individuals to share information directly with one another, without the supervision or monitoring of third parties.

Client-Server Networks

A client-server architecture is a type of network in which several **client** computers are connected to a **server**. A server is a computer that provides services and resources to client computers that are connected to the server. A server manages disk drives, printers, and network traffic. By definition, a client is a computer that requests and receives information over a network. Desktop computers, laptops, and mobile devices can all function as clients. Unlike a peer-to-peer model, in which computers share resources and communication on equal footing without a central point of direction, a client-server network relies on a powerful centralized computer to provide access to files, software, and even security. As illustrated in Figure 7.4, a typical client-server arrangement connects several clients to a server. As clients request services, the server responds.

Quick Tip

Domains and Workgroups

Networked computers can be part of either a workgroup or a domain. In a workgroup, no computer acts as a server; in a domain, one or more computers are servers. While workgroups are typical of home networks, domains often represent subnetworks within a business network, such as departments.

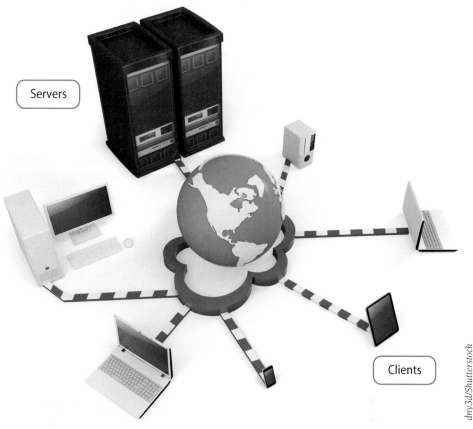

Figure 7.4 In a client-server network, your computer is a client computer. It makes requests of the server, a computer that provides resources to the client-server.

In Depth

Sneakernet

Sneakernet, in computer jargon, is the process by which electronic information is transmitted between computers by physically carrying it on a form of storage media, such as a USB drive or a CD. For example, if you save a document on a USB drive and then give the drive to a colleague so she can save the document on her computer, you have used a sneakernet. The play on words originates from the idea that the person carrying the storage device is using his feet (or *sneakers*) instead of the company's network to transfer data. An odd mix of the newest technology and the oldest form of transportation, the sneakernet model is actually the conceptual basis for today's peer-to-peer networks, in which information is equally shared between computers without the need for a central server.

Sneakernets can also be used in less mundane ways. For example, the compound in which Osama Bin Laden was killed was reported to have no phone or Internet connections. Yet U.S. Intelligence was well aware that much of Al Qaeda's business was conducted through e-mail. How, then, was Bin Laden able to maintain e-mail communication with his followers, if his home had no Internet connection? Most likely, he used a human courier, or sneakernet, to act as the last mile between his computer and the Internet. Speculation is that Bin Laden would type a message on his computer, save it on a USB drive, and then pass the drive to a trusted courier. From a distant Internet connection, the courier would copy Bin Laden's message into an e-mail and send it. At the same time, he would copy any incoming e-mail onto the USB drive which Bin Laden could then read offline.

A Look Back

Origins of the Internet as a Peer-to-Peer Network

In its original inception, the Internet of the 1960s was a peer-to-peer network. ARPANET, the first iteration of the Internet, was designed to share computing resources around the United States. The challenge of integrating independent networks so they all communicated with one another led to the development of a network system in which all users were peers who shared resources. The original Internet lacked security safeguards, as researchers and educators shared all sorts of files with one another without fear of viruses, hacking, or malware. Of course, the use of obscure and specialized protocols (methods of communication) created a system where security breaches were rare and relatively harmless. That all changed with the transition of the Internet in the 1990s from a scholarly research network into a bustling commercial arena in which ordinary people began to send e-mail, view websites, shop, and bank. Not only did the basic communication model shift toward a client-server arrangement, but users also found a need for enhanced security, typically in the form of a firewall.

Beginning in the 1990s, use of the Internet became much more centered on downloading data, causing a switch from a P2P model to that of a client-server. With the advent of the browser, a common scenario became one in which a client (a user at home) connected to a server (providing access to the Internet), downloaded or read information, and then moved on to another application. The straightforward client-server model actually works well for everything from online shopping, streaming video, and playing interactive games, to participating in online college classes or buying stock. The client-server arrangement has been typical of the Internet for at least the past 20 years. Because a computer that accessed the Internet could theoretically be accessed by others on the same network, firewall security became absolutely necessary.

Today, software developers are very attuned to collaboration and joint projects, many of which are only possible with the incorporation of more P2P file sharing online. For that reason, emphasis is currently being placed on enabling secure online communication and file sharing in a peer-to-peer model among individual users. The Internet might actually be considered a *hybrid* model that encourages both client-server and peer-to-peer communication, depending upon the application. The transition of the Internet from a peer-to-peer model of communication to one that emphasizes client-server sharing seems to have evolved into a workable combination of the two.

In many of its activities, the Internet acts as a client-server arrangement as Web servers provide gateways to the Internet for client computers. Web servers also deliver the display of websites to browsers, facilitating such applications as online banking, shopping, and research. For example, you can use the browser on your computer (a client) to access a favorite website (supported by a Web server) to make a purchase.

A peer-to-peer network is typically suitable for a home or small business network, while larger enterprises often prefer a client-server model. A peer-to-peer network is usually cheaper to install, requiring less high-powered equipment; also, microcomputer operating systems often provide tools to easily configure a peer-to-peer network. In addition, without a central server to go through, peer computers can transfer information quickly, without any routing delay. On the downside, each microcomputer in a P2P network must not only manage its individual user requests but also act as a conduit for other network traffic. Large businesses, with a greater need for strong network security, especially appreciate the dedicated processing power and security features of a client-server network. For them, the additional equipment cost and network configuration and management requirements are not really disadvantages when compared with the benefits of a secure and effective network.

Creating a Home Computer Network

A home computer network can simplify sharing resources between computers and can provide a common point of Internet access. However, many people find the very thought of creating a network overwhelming. The truth is that it is not as difficult as it may seem; in fact, almost anyone can easily configure a home computer network, even someone who does not consider himself computer literate.

As you consider a network, you should first determine your needs, budget, and how you plan to use the network. Keep in mind that a home network can be designed to share resources between computers, such as files and peripheral devices, and also to provide Internet access so that several computers in the home can simultaneously access Web pages. Before you begin, ask yourself the following questions. What do I expect from a network? How many computers do I want to connect? Do I have a printer or other peripheral device that I want to share? Do I want to use my laptop in any room in the home? Answering those questions will help you determine the most effective network configuration for your purposes. In this section, you will identify components of a home network and you will explore ways to configure a home network so that it best fits your needs.

Wired and Wireless Home Networks

A home network can be wired, wireless, or some combination of the two. If you plan to physically connect devices, you will most likely use Cat 5 (short for Category 5), a form of twisted pair cable. Also known as Ethernet cable, Cat 5 is an industry standard for network and telephone wiring. Although connecting devices in close proximity with one another is fairly simple, stretching cables between devices that are in different rooms or not near one another can be quite cumbersome, not to mention unsightly. Cable that is run under floors or through walls can be difficult to manage and install. However, the benefits of a wired network, including reliability, performance, and cost are attractive. Some newer homes are prewired with Cat 5 cable, making the task a bit easier.

In addition to cabling, a wired network often requires the use of connecting devices like **hubs**, switches, and routers to connect computers to a local home network so resources can be shared. A hub is an inexpensive device that simply enables computers to transmit data along the network. Unlike a switch or router, a hub has no built-in program that facilitates optimized traffic direction. In a network with heavy simultaneous computer traffic, a hub can be overwhelmed, causing delay in communication and data transfer. Although it costs a bit more than a hub, a switch provides much more efficient transfer on a heavily traveled local network.

A wired network is appropriate if equipment you are connecting is not mobile. If your home network includes primarily desktop computers and stationary devices such as printers, then using cable as a primary conduit is a viable networking solution. Cables, hubs, and switches are inexpensive and easy to maintain. Even if you choose to use a broadband router, the slightly higher cost (when compared to a switch or hub) is offset by the enhanced security and easy installation. An Ethernet (wired) network is extremely reliable, with loose cabling being the most often-cited problem that might occur—and obviously one that is easy to correct. Wired LAN speed is generally acceptable for home file sharing, interactive gaming, and high-speed Internet access. As it is likely that you will use a home network for Internet access, security is a primary concern, regardless of whether the network is wired or wireless. Wired Ethernet hubs and switches do not support internal firewalls; however, you can install firewall software on individual computers (or use the Windows 7 firewall). A broadband router typically includes built-in firewall capability, as well.

With the increasing popularity of laptops and other wireless mobile devices, wireless networks are becoming more prevalent in homes. The central device that supports a wireless home network is a wireless router, as shown in Figure 7.5. As you learned earlier in this chapter, a router transmits information between two networks. For example, using a router, you can connect all the computers and wireless devices in your home (including laptops, wireless printers, e-readers, portable music players, and other mobile equipment) to a modem, which then enables you to connect to the Internet. At that point, you can download music to an iPod, acquire electronic books for an e-reader, stream video, and browse the Internet. In addition to wireless devices, a wireless router includes capacity to connect wired devices, such as desktop computers and printers. You can purchase a wireless router at an office supply or electronics store and set it up yourself by following the directions included with the device. Most often, you can simply insert a CD that accompanies the wireless router, and follow the on-screen directions to install the router.

A router serves as a **Wireless Access Point (WAP)**, routing devices to the Internet and/or to each other. Technically, a WAP is a bridge between a wireless and a wired network. For example, a wireless access point can connect a wireless LAN to a preexisting Ethernet network. A wireless router not only serves as a WAP, but it also supports Internet connection and provides firewall protection.

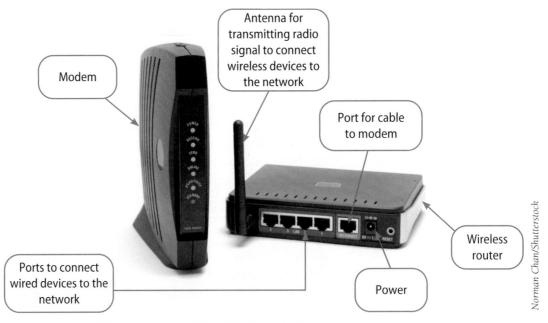

Modem

Antenna for transmitting radio signal to connect wireless devices to the network

Port for cable to modem

Ports to connect wired devices to the network

Power

Wireless router

Norman Chan/Shutterstock

Figure 7.5 Wireless routers are central to a wireless home network.

Quick Tip

Connecting a Wired Computer

Even if you work with a computer that does not include a wireless adapter, you can still use a wireless router to connect the wired computer as well as wireless devices in your home to the Internet. A wireless router includes a port into which you can connect a Cat 5 cable between the computer and the router. At that point, the wired computer is connected through the router to the Internet modem. Wireless devices in your home can also access the Internet through the same wireless router, although they will not be physically connected.

Not all wireless routers are alike. Although all wireless routers use the **IEEE 802.11 standard**, also called **Wi-Fi (wireless fidelity)**, various subsets of the standard further define a router. Each Wi-Fi standard subset supports a maximum bandwidth across which data can be transferred. Subsets of the 802.11 standard include *802.11a*, *802.11b*, *802.11g*, and *802.11n*. At this point, 802.11n is the newest and fastest of those subsets, supporting data transmission of over 100 mbps (megabits per second). The 802.11n standard also provides a wide range of coverage, approximately 230 feet indoors.

It is important to be aware of the wireless standard a device supports so you can make sure that all equipment in a wireless network is compatible. Linksys, Belkin, D-Link, and Netgear are common brands of wireless routers, but, with so many choices available, it is best to consult product reviews before purchasing a wireless router for your home. Websites such as CNET (www.cnet.com) and Consumer Search (www.consumersearch.com) are excellent sources for unbiased product reviews.

In Depth

Internet-Enabled Home Appliances

In the future, your home might include Internet-enabled appliances that actually help you save energy and money, while providing related information. For example, a refrigerator (Figure 7.6) might provide recipes or a digital shopping list. An Internet-enabled appliance, such as a dishwasher or dryer, can monitor utility price information and take action to lower power usage during critical periods of time, all with little or no user input. A freezer might postpone an energy-hogging defrosting cycle until the early hours of the morning when utility cost is cheaper.

Courtesy of Samsung

Figure 7.6 Appliances like Samsung's Wi-Fi enabled refrigerator (above) are the future of networking technology.

Aside from their more glitzy applications, Internet-enabled appliances are attractive because of their energy saving potential. General Electric markets a home energy management system called Nucleus, which is a small device that tracks electricity use, making connected appliances aware of low-cost energy usage hours. Appliances can then automatically adjust their operation so they take advantage of low-cost energy. With a Nucleus smart phone app, you can monitor home energy data and even adjust home temperature remotely. Similarly, Cisco is preparing to market a home energy controller that manages appliance energy use and connects to a wireless thermostat so you can program home heating and cooling. Complete integration and communication between all home devices—appliances, computers, and mobile phones—will likely be a reality for homes in the near future.

As with most wireless devices, the router's placement in the home is very important. Because the signal radiates in all directions from the router, it is best to put the device in a central location where you are more likely to direct the signal to all parts of your home. Cement walls, thick insulation, and even water, such as a fish tank, can interfere with a wireless signal, so use good judgment when locating a wireless router, to ensure an unobstructed signal.

Hands-On

Activity 7.1 Considering a Home Network

You are considering setting up a home network, primarily for shared Internet access, although you also plan to share a printer that is currently connected to a desktop computer in your home office. You own an iPod Touch and have recently acquired an e-reader, which is a device that enables you to download and read books. Both wireless devices are capable of downloading media if they can connect to a wireless network either in your home or elsewhere. In addition, you have a laptop with wireless capability. Your spouse has an older laptop with no wireless network adapter. Your desktop computer is currently connected by a cable to a DSL modem, which provides Internet access to that computer. However, the modem does not have wireless capability built in. Your home is single-story, encompassing approximately 2500 square feet.

Others have told you that creating a home network is relatively simple if you have the right equipment. In this exercise, you will explore networking equipment, identifying components that are appropriate for your needs.

a. Connect to the Internet. Go to www.microsoft.com/athome. Explore the site (Figure 7.7), clicking links of interest. Identify any that relate to home networking (perhaps by clicking a **Setup + Maintenance** link).

b. Click in the **Search Microsoft.com box** and type **creating a wireless home network.** Press **Enter**. In the result list, click **How to set up a wireless network (WLAN) in your home**. If the link is not in the results link, click any other that appears to provide the information you seek.

TROUBLESHOOTING

If you find that the website does not include helpful information related to wireless home networking, click the **Back button** at the top of your browser to return to the search results. In some cases, you might have to close the browser tab, instead (if the results open on a separate tab).

---

c. Make a list of equipment you think you will need to include in your network. Be as specific as possible, providing specific examples of equipment, specifications, and price range. Record your responses on paper.

Microsoft Corporation

Figure 7.7 The Microsoft website can help get you started with your own home network.

Configuring a Network

Configuring a home network can actually be quite simple. Now that you are familiar with basic networking terminology, you will be comfortable setting up a home network so that several computers can connect to the Internet or you can share devices and files. Even a task as simple as sharing a printer is easily accomplished with a simple home network. Figure 7.8 illustrates a typical home network.

If part of your goal is to provide Internet access to devices in your home, you will first need to contract with an Internet Service Provider (ISP). An ISP is typically a cable or telephone company that provides an Internet connection, usually for a monthly service charge. As you learned in Chapter 3, you have a great deal of choice in Internet connectivity, ranging from cable or telephone options to satellite connection. In most cases, you can easily connect a router to the modem supplied by your ISP so you can provide Internet access to devices throughout your home. Newer modems supplied by an ISP often include built-in wireless capability, so you will not need an additional wireless router.

Following the setup guidelines that accompany a router you purchase, you can easily configure the router to fit into your home network. The guidelines are often located on a CD or DVD that is packaged with the router. Called a setup wizard, the step-by-step instructions on the disc enable you to physically connect the router to other equipment and to secure the router against unauthorized access.

Figure 7.8 A home network might include wired and wireless devices connected to a wireless access point.

Quick Tip

Networking Various Operating Systems

All computers in a HomeGroup must have Windows 7 installed. If you are networking computers with various operating systems—perhaps Windows XP or Windows Vista—search online for information on creating a home network so all those computers can share resources.

Windows 7 enables you to configure a peer-to-peer network through its HomeGroup networking feature. Although you do not have to use HomeGroup to configure a network, the feature enables you to create and join a home network quickly and easily. After setting up a home network, you can easily share files and resources with any computer connected to the network. For example, from your laptop in the living room, you can access a file stored on the desktop computer in your home office. Or perhaps you want to send a document from your laptop to print on the printer connected to the office computer. From within a Windows 7 HomeGroup, you can even stream media to an electronic device such as a digital picture frame or a television.

As you set up or join a HomeGroup, you will select the libraries and printers you want to share. You can easily change those later, even excluding certain files or sharing them with some people but not with others. With built-in security,

In Depth

Sharing a Printer

Computers on a home network can share a printer. The cheapest and most common way to share a printer is to connect it to one of the computers through a USB port or with another type of printer cable. Make sure the printer is turned on and functional. Then log in to the computer as an administrator, click **Start** and then **Devices and Printers**. Right-click the **printer icon** and then click **Printer properties**. Click the **Sharing tab** and select **Share this printer** (unless it is already checked). Click **OK**. Now that the printer is shared, each computer on the network should add the printer. To do so, you should log in to the computer to which you are assigning printer access. Click **Start** and then click **Devices and Printers**. Click **Add a printer**. Click **Add a network, wireless or Bluetooth printer**. In a few seconds, the shared printer should display. Click to select the printer, if necessary, and then click **Next**. Click **Next** to acknowledge that the selected printer has been installed. Click **Print a test page** to make sure the connection is active. Click **Finish**. The computer can now print documents on the printer remotely (as long as both the printer and the computer to which it is connected are turned on).

A second approach to sharing a printer is to use a print server, which is a device that takes the place of the computer in the previous solution. A print server has network interfaces (Ethernet and Wi-Fi) and printer connections. The print server is connected to a WAP (perhaps a wireless router), just as are other wireless devices on the home network. It is recognized as a connected device. Each laptop, then, can access the print server (and the printer) through the wireless access point. An advantage of using a print server is that a dedicated computer (always on) is not necessary for other computers to use a networked printer. A print server can also easily manage multiple computers. Not always a separate hardware device, a print server is sometimes integrated with a broadband wireless router.

A third solution is to use a wireless printer, which has built-in wireless capability. Simply connect the wireless printer to a WAP so other computers on the network see it as just another device. Because they can all access the printer through the WAP, shared printing is a breeze. Even easier, a wireless printer can be added to the network directly. Simply follow the setup instructions that accompany the printer, adding the printer to the existing home network. At that point, all networked computers can send print jobs to the printer.

Quick Tip

Sharing Libraries on a HomeGroup

Members of a HomeGroup can select libraries to share. Click **Start**, **Control Panel**, and then **Choose home-group and sharing options** (under Network and Internet). Check those items you want to share (or uncheck those you want to remove from sharing). You can also view or change the Home-Group password as well as leave the HomeGroup.

Quick Tip

Sharing Additional Folders with a HomeGroup

You can share any folder on your system with others in your HomeGroup. Click **Start** and then click your user name (on the right side of the Start menu). Navigate to the folder to share and right-click it. Click **Share with**. Choose to share with your **HomeGroup** in either a *Read* format (which means that HomeGroup members can read files in the shared folder but cannot change them) or in a *Read/Write* format. You can also lock a folder so it is not available to anyone.

the Windows 7 HomeGroup feature enables you to set passwords that protect shared files and devices. All members of a HomeGroup must run Windows 7. If you are using Windows 7 Starter or Windows 7 Home Basic, you can join a HomeGroup, but you cannot create one.

To create a HomeGroup, you must be signed on to a computer as the administrator. Then click **Start**, **Control Panel**, **Network and Internet**, and then **HomeGroup**. Click **Create a homegroup**. Check those items you wish to share (Pictures, Documents, Music, Printers, and/or Videos) and then click **Next**. Window 7 will then generate a password to allow other users to join the HomeGroup. Click **Print password and instructions**. Then click **Finish**. In a matter of a few seconds, you can create a HomeGroup!

If running Windows 7, other computers on your home network can join the HomeGroup you just created. Having logged on to a computer, click **Start** and then click **Control Panel**. Click **Network and Internet** and then click **HomeGroup**. Click **Join Now**. In the Join a HomeGroup window, type the password for the HomeGroup and then click **Next**. The password should have been printed when the HomeGroup was created. Having joined the **Home-Group**, click **Finish**.

After other computers have joined your HomeGroup, all members of the HomeGroup can access any files and resources that were shared. Click **Start** and then click your user name (on the right side of the Start menu). Click **Homegroup**, as shown in Figure 7.9. Double-click a HomeGroup member on the right and navigate the folder structure of shared items to locate documents, music, pictures, or video.

Click Homegroup

Figure 7.9 The Microsoft HomeGroup in Windows 7 makes it easy to network computers to share documents, photos, music and more.

A HomeGroup is a collection of computers that shares resources on your home network. To be included in a HomeGroup, each computer must run Windows 7. Although you are most likely in a computer lab setting, and therefore unable to create a HomeGroup, think about how you would organize computers in your home.

To continue the example from Activity 7.1, you have at least three computers that will share resources. One of the computers has a printer connected. You have already put into place all necessary networking hardware. Now, you will focus on using the operating system to create a HomeGroup. Using Windows Help and Support (and any other resources), complete the items below. Where indicated, record your responses on paper for possible submission to your instructor.

d. Click **Start** and then click **Help and Support**. In the Search Help box, type **creating a homegroup** and press **Enter**. Click **Create a homegroup**.

e. Click **Go to the Windows website to watch the video**. Click the **large arrow in the center of the graphic** to begin the video. After watching the video, close the browser.

f. Click the **Browse Help icon** at the top right side of the Windows Help and Support window. Click **Networking—connecting computers and devices**. Click **Start here to set up a home network in Windows 7**. What are the six steps involved? Record your response on paper.

g. Close Windows Help and Support. Open your browser. Visit www.microsoft.com/athome/. Click in the Search Microsoft.com box, type **wireless networking tips** and then press **Enter**. Identify and visit a page that includes wireless networking tips. Record at least three tips on paper, as well as the URL where you found the tips. The tips can relate to wireless network setup or security.

h. Close the browser.

Securing a Home Computer

Securing a home computer involves taking precautions against common threats such as viruses, spyware, and hackers, as well as ensuring that wireless Internet communication is private. Software is available to identify and remove viruses and spyware, and firewall software keeps computer hackers at bay. In addition, taking steps to protect a home network from unauthorized access can keep personal information safe and out of the hands of would-be criminals. In this section, you will learn to identify safety concerns and protect your home network from unauthorized access and the transfer of potentially destructive software such as viruses and spyware.

Home Computer Network Security

In 2011, a New York man's home was raided by police when he was suspected of downloading thousands of files containing child pornography. Authorities broke down the door to his home and arrested him. They thoroughly searched his home and computers but came up empty. In the end, authorities determined that because the suspected perpetrator had not protected his wireless network with a password and appropriate security, his neighbor had accessed the network and downloaded the offending material. By taking a few simple steps, the unjustly accused person could have protected his network against such unauthorized access, preventing the unfortunate incident.

As you configure a wireless router for a home network, you will want to ensure that the network is as secure as possible. You will do so by uniquely identifying your network with a personal password and security key. In addition,

Piggybacking

Gaining access to a network that is not your own, even one that does not require a password, is called piggybacking. Piggybacking (Figure 7.10) is considered a felony in some states and certainly raises ethical concerns even if it is not illegal in other areas. Some argue that piggybacking is acceptable if a network is not password protected, because the owner of the network obviously does not care enough to secure it. In effect, he is asking for trespassers. Others argue that piggybacking is an ethical violation. They compare piggybacking with leaving the front door of a house unlocked. Just because the door is open does not mean that everyone is welcome. However you feel about the issue, the safest advice is that you should never connect to a network unless you own it or unless it is a public Wi-Fi hotspot.

Konrad Bak/Shutterstock

Figure 7.10 Gaining access to a network that is not your own and is not open to the public is called piggybacking. Piggybacking is considered a felony in some states.

you will need to set data encryption so that data transmission cannot be read by unauthorized people. Wireless networks are especially susceptible to security breaches because the signal does not necessarily stop at the property line. In fact, unless it is properly secured, a wireless signal can be intercepted up to 300 feet away from the source. As you set up a wireless router, you should take all suggested security precautions.

Later in this chapter, you will consider ways to keep a computer secure. Using a firewall, virus scanner software, and other security measures, you can be relatively certain that a computer is adequately protected against the most common security and privacy threats. When using a wireless router, however, a new level of security concerns must be addressed to ensure that your network is not susceptible to piggybacking. Having purchased a router, you will find that it is preconfigured with a default user name and password. The problem is that the standard user name and password is widely known, so it actually does little to secure the network. You should certainly be prepared to change the identifying information. The following In-Depth section provides suggestions for creating a strong password. You will also want to change the **network service set identifier** from "SSID" to something that better describes your network. Keep in mind that the network name, or SSID, will be seen by others even if they do not know the password. Although the network name is visible, it is not likely that anyone can access your Internet connection without the password.

As you configure a wireless router, you will indicate an **encryption** standard. This is a very important step, as encryption encodes the data that is being sent across your network so a hacker cannot read the data without an encryption key. A **hacker** is someone who gains access to a computer system, often without authorization. Encryption methods include **WPA**, **WPA2**, and **WEP**. When possible, use WPA (Wi-Fi Protected Access) or WPA2 instead of WEP (Wired Equivalent Privacy), as those encryption standards are more secure and less likely to be decoded than WEP. Both WPA and WPA2 encrypt network data, insuring that only authorized users can access the network. Although WPA2 is more secure than WPA, it might not work with older wireless network adapters. For more information about the standard employed by your router, visit the router manufacturer's website.

Using Public Wi-Fi Hotspots

A **Wi-Fi hotspot** is a place, such as a library or coffee shop, which offers Internet access over a wireless local area network. Using a laptop that is equipped for wireless access, as most laptops are, you can connect to the Wi-Fi hotspot and browse the Internet, usually free of charge. Most colleges provide wireless access to students and staff, although most are password protected. Even hotels typically provide wireless Internet access to guests.

Figure 7.11 Wi-Fi hotspots like cafes are often a prime target for identity thieves.

Public Wi-Fi hotspots (Figure 7.11) usually do not use encryption and are therefore not as safe as your secure home network. You should always assume that anyone can see what you do on a public Wi-Fi network. Therefore, it is wise to refrain from using any passwords or accessing any financial sites that contain your personal information when connected to a public network. The following tips will help you understand how to safely use a public Wi-Fi network.

1. Verify that Windows Firewall is turned on, or that you have alternate firewall software installed. If you are using the Windows 7 Firewall (discussed later in this chapter), click **Start**, **Control Panel**, and then **System and Security**. Click **Windows Firewall**. Click a link in the left pane to turn on the firewall if it is not already on.
2. Keep your computer's protection current. Click **Start**, **All Programs**, and then **Windows Update** to ensure that you have downloaded all updates suggested by Microsoft. Updates are posted periodically by Microsoft to address security and privacy issues, as well as to keep your computer running optimally. Most likely, your computer is configured to automatically download and install Windows updates, but you can also periodically check them manually.
3. Refrain from banking and shopping at public hotspots. Do not log in to banking, credit card accounts, or other sensitive accounts. Do not use your credit card to shop online from a public hotspot. (Hint: some credit card companies offer virtual card numbers that are only good for 24 hours and do not reveal your real account numbers. You could get a virtual account number using a computer on your home network and then use it online in a pinch at a hotspot.)
4. Do not automatically save and store passwords.
5. Disable Wi-Fi (and Bluetooth if you have it) when you are not using them. Newer computers include a key or button you can press to disable wireless connection. Check your computer documentation to learn how to disable yours.

Securing a Home Computer   **285**

Connecting to a Public Wi-Fi

Using a laptop configured for Internet access (which is true of most laptops), you can connect to a public network that provides access to the Internet (called Wi-Fi hotspots). Starbucks, Panera Bread, local libraries—maybe even your college—often provide free wireless Internet access. Some hotels boast of Wi-Fi capability, as well. Following a few steps, you can connect to a network and begin browsing the Web.

1. Locate the wireless network icon in the Notification area of your computer (on the right side of the taskbar). The icon should resemble a bar graph.
2. Click the icon to see a list of available networks (Figure 7.12). If you cannot identify the icon, click **Start**, **Control Panel**, **Network and Internet** and then click **Connect to a network** (under Network and Sharing Center).
3. Click to select a network and then click **Connect**.
4. If the wireless network is secured, you must enter the network password. The hotel or public location will most likely supply you with the password upon request (if the network is intended for public use).
5. Indicate whether the connection should be considered Home, Work, or Public, as shown in Figure 7.13. Windows 7 will provide security appropriate for the network location.

Having completed all steps, you should be connected to the Internet. Open your browser. You may have to accept terms and conditions to actually get Internet access.

Figure 7.12 A list of available wireless networks is shown.

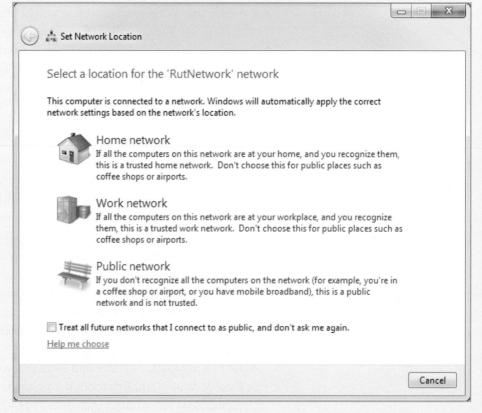

Figure 7.13 Selecting the location for a network (i.e. home, work, public) will apply the correct security settings to the network.

6. Beware of the evil twin. An **evil twin** is a Wi-Fi hotspot that appears to be legitimate but has been created by a hacker. For example, if you see a network name in your network list like "free Wi-Fi" in or near a location that you know does not have free Wi-Fi, it is probably an evil twin. If you are not sure, do not connect.

If you find that you must use Wi-Fi hotspots regularly, you might consider signing up for a paid subscription to a hotspot network provided by cell phone companies such as T-Mobile and Verizon. Also called *mifi* the service enables you to get online from thousands of locations through your own personal mobile router. It acts as a private hotspot with built-in, password-protected security. The portable router looks like a thick credit card with a power button, a status light, and a swappable battery. You can connect up to five Wi-Fi enabled devices (laptops, tablets, music players, gaming consoles, and more) to high-speed Internet through your mobile wireless router. The device costs approximately $50 or more, and you must also pay for a usage plan. Plans vary among providers, so check with your cell phone company for details.

Security Threats

Using a computer for work or pleasure is an activity that most of us engage in every day. Using a computer is not without risk, though. Your computer can acquire viruses from infected e-mail attachments or programs you download. Spyware can track your travel on the Internet and change browser settings. Hackers can access files on your computer, perhaps even stealing your identity. Before you decide that the solution is to refrain from using a computer at all, ask yourself if you would stop driving a car simply because risk is involved. Recognizing that risk, you probably lock the doors, take the keys when you are not in the car, and buckle your safety belt when traveling. Similarly, you can take precautions when using a computer to prevent your computer from being compromised. Using common sense, along with software (antivirus software, spyware removal software, and a firewall), you can be assured that your computer is well protected from the most common privacy and security threats.

Viruses

A computer **virus** is a program that can cause harm to a computer or its contents. Never accidental, a virus is intentionally written to be annoying or destructive. Much like a human virus, a computer virus passes from one computer to another, infecting as many as possible. Often attached to e-mails, viruses are also spread through networks and may travel with a USB drive or other portable media on which infected files have been copied. Some viruses wreak havoc as soon as they are copied, while others lie dormant until triggered by later circumstances. For example, a virus might wait until a hard drive is 80% full before wiping it out.

A virus is actually considered a type of **malware** (short for *malicious software*). Malware includes programs such as viruses, worms, Trojan horses, and spyware that are designed to cause damage to a computer or electronic

Quick Tip
Computer Security Site
Visit www.microsoft.com/athome/security for a wealth of information, videos, and software related to securing your home computer.

device. Specific types of malware are discussed later in this chapter. Although some viruses are merely annoying, others can crash computers and cause billions of dollars in damage. A virus is not easy to identify, as it is often disguised as a legitimate program or file. Fortunately, you can install software that will assist in identifying and removing viruses from your computer system.

In Depth

Viruses on Mobile Devices

Viruses are not unique to laptops and desktops. They are also prevalent on mobile devices such as smartphones and tablets. Of particular concern for smartphone users who frequently log in to various financial accounts or transmit sensitive data, a virus could be stealing login information, selling e-mail contacts to marketers and spammers, and replicating itself to other devices. It might delete all your contact information and calendar entries, lock up certain applications, or even crash your device completely. Some suggest that future viruses could bug phones, recording numbers you call and listening in on conversations. A mobile device virus spreads through Internet downloads, applications from add-on sites (such as ringtones or games), and Bluetooth transmissions.

The best way to protect yourself is never to open anything suspicious, and be sure to install security software. An Internet search for *mobile device antivirus software* will return multiple sources for security software. You might also visit http://www.symantec.com/business/mobile-device-security for information on a wide range of protection.

Because they can cause a great deal of damage, computer viruses should be taken very seriously. It is important for your computer to have **antivirus software** (Figure 7.14) installed and to maintain current software at all times so it can identify and remove even the newest virus threats. Most often, a new computer will have a trial version of antivirus software installed. You will be alerted when the trial

© Jeff Morgan 16/Alamy

Figure 7.14 Programs can alert you to viruses.

subscription is about to expire. At that time, you can make a decision to renew the subscription or to purchase another type of virus protection. You might even choose to download a free version, such as AVG Antivirus (http://free.avg.com/us-en/ homepage), although you should keep in mind that free software often has fewer features than programs that you purchase. Norton Antivirus, McAfee, Microsoft Security Essentials, and ZoneAlarm are also popular antivirus programs. You might check online for trial versions of any of those programs if you want to try before you buy. Also, your Internet Service Provider might provide free antivirus protection.

Antivirus software scans your computer periodically for viruses, removing any that are identified (or alerting you of problems with removal). Most often, antivirus software will be configured to automatically download virus updates (new virus definitions) so it can continue to identify even the newest virus threats. Depending on the antivirus software in use, you can schedule virus scans so your computer is checked often for viruses. You can even check your computer between scheduled scans if you have reason to suspect a virus or simply want to ensure that a downloaded program is virus free.

In Depth

Malware Symptoms

How do you know if your computer is infected with a virus or malware? You might suspect a problem if you experience some of the following symptoms.

- **Pop-up advertising** Pop-up ads display that are unrelated to a website you are viewing. Never click a link in a pop-up ad, even if it appears to be alerting you to a serious problem with your computer.
- **Additional browser components** Toolbars you do not want or need are added to your browser. Even when you remove the toolbars, they reappear when you restart your computer.
- **Computer is slow to respond** Your computer might take longer than usual to complete routine tasks or might stop responding at all.
- **Slow boot-up** Your computer might take a long time to boot up and display the desktop. You might see a message that you are missing certain files.
- **Computer restarts** Your computer might restart on its own, even if you are actively working with a project.
- **Unusual display or sound** Windows and on-screen items might appear distorted. Unusual colors or sounds can be symptoms as well.
- **Software fails** Software begins to act erratically, fails to open, or locks up while you are using it.
- **Browser home page changes** The page you usually see when you open your browser is different. You may not be able to reset it.
- **Antivirus program is disabled** Your antivirus program no longer functions.
- **New icons or programs appear** You do not recognize some desktop icons, and new programs are installed.
- **Hard disk thrashing** You notice that the hard disk seems to be constantly working, as if it is continually accessing disk space. As a result of the constant activity, system performance is reduced.

If you suspect that your computer has been infected, you should install the latest Windows Updates from Microsoft (click **Start**, **All Programs**, and **Windows Update**) and scan your computer with your antivirus software. Also scan your computer with spyware removal software, and if necessary, seek help from a computer professional. Antivirus software and spyware removal software are addressed later in this chapter.

Hackers

A hacker is a person who gains access to a computer or computer network without permission. Hackers have many motivations for accessing computers; some simply want to prove that they can, others are motivated by greed or revenge. Whatever the motivation, accessing a network or computer without permission is illegal. In fact, unauthorized access, especially if it results in damage or theft of information, is a federal crime—punishable by up to 20 years in prison. In this section you will explore safeguards against hacking.

A **firewall** (Figure 7.15) is software that prevents unauthorized access to your computer by monitoring incoming and outgoing traffic. For example, an attempt to access files or other resources on your computer by an external program or computer will be blocked by a firewall unless you specifically indicate that the request should be allowed. Occasionally, software on your computer will attempt to access files on the Web, such as when your antivirus software initiates an update. A firewall will block that communication, as well, unless you specify that the software should always be allowed to access the Internet. You might think of a firewall as a shield between your computer and the Internet—a layer of protection that makes your computer invisible to others. If a firewall becomes too restrictive, as it might in certain cases, you can disable it temporarily or indicate that certain traffic should be allowed. Although you can purchase firewall software, or download a free version, Windows 7 includes a bidirectional firewall, (named Windows Firewall) that monitors both incoming and outgoing traffic. Think of a firewall as the front door to your home. When the door is locked, intruders cannot come in. However, if visitors are invited, you can unlock the door and let them in. Hackers and unauthorized programs are prohibited by a firewall as uninvited incoming traffic. Occasionally, programs on your computer attempt to access the Internet. Although such outgoing activity is usually necessary, as is the case when your antivirus software updates its virus definitions, your firewall will prohibit spyware that is housed on your hard drive from communicating information on your Internet travel. The Windows 7 firewall is turned on by default when Windows 7 is installed, but you can turn it off temporarily or adjust its settings through the Control Panel.

Shutterstock

Figure 7.15 A firewall protects a computer by monitoring incoming and outgoing traffic.

To check firewall settings, click **Start**, **Control Panel**, **System and Security**, and then **Windows Firewall**. As shown in Figure 7.16, you can turn the firewall on or off and you can change the way traffic is blocked.

Although the Windows 7 firewall is effective, you can choose to install another. You should only run one firewall, however, so if you install another, you should ensure that the Windows 7 firewall is turned off. Most often, the newly installed software disables the Windows 7 firewall, but you should always check.

Spyware and Other Forms of Malware

Spyware is a form of malware that collects personal information about you and your surfing habits without your knowledge. Some forms of spyware collect

Quick Tip

Hackers and Crackers

Although the term *hacker* is most often used to describe someone who gains unauthorized access to a computer system, its original definition is actually someone who likes to tinker with things to see how they work. On the other hand, a *cracker* is someone whose purpose is to circumvent or break security measures. Regardless of technical correctness, it is likely that we will continue to recognize a hacker as someone who breaks into a system, usually with ill intent.

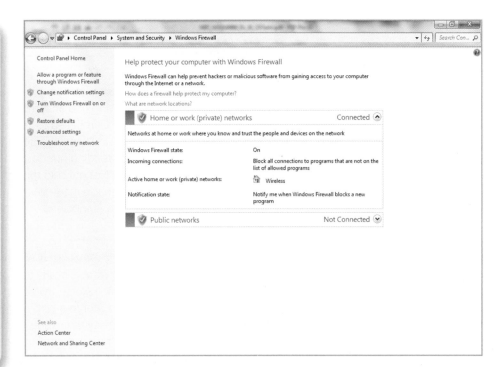

Figure 7.16 The Windows firewall screen is where you can turn on or off your firewall.

passwords and other personally identifiable information that can then be used in criminal activity such as identity theft. Spyware often causes unwanted pop-up ads to appear and might even change your browser settings. Both a security and privacy risk, spyware is becoming a huge problem for computer users.

Spyware typically accompanies downloaded software. However, that does not mean that every program you download carries spyware along with it. Whether or not you realize it, you might even agree to accept spyware when you agree to the terms of use of software that you download and install. Such agreement is usually found in the small print of an end user license agreement, often worded as agreement to accept third-party software (which might, in fact, be spyware).

Antispyware software identifies and removes spyware from your system. Often included as part of an Internet security software package, antispyware software is also available as a stand-alone product. Although it is not free, Webroot Spy Sweeper (http://www.webroot.com/En_US/consumer-products-spysweeper.html) is a leader in antispyware software, providing continuous monitoring and detection. You can also download very effective free antispyware software (Ad-Aware and Spybot Search and Destroy) from http://free.lavasoft.com/products2.aspx and http://www.safer-networking.org/en/download/.

A **Trojan horse** is a form of malware that masquerades as a useful program when it is instead destructive. A Trojan horse cannot replicate itself on its own, but it can still do a lot of damage. Hackers often use Trojan horses to gain entry into a computer system, from which they can steal information or wreak havoc. Antivirus programs can typically detect and remove Trojan horse software, but you should take steps to avoid acquiring a Trojan horse. For example, only download programs from reputable websites and do not open unexpected e-mail attachments.

Considered a form of malware, a **worm** sends copies of itself to other computers without your awareness or involvement. Unlike a virus, a worm does not need to be attached to a program or code. Also, its target is less often a receiving computer; instead it focuses on causing harm to a network, often by simply consuming massive amounts of bandwidth. Often, a worm exploits vulnerabilities in operating systems, so it is very important to make sure your computer is downloading and installing Windows updates regularly. Antispyware and antivirus software often identify and remove worms, as well.

Windows Defender is software that identifies and removes malware from your computer. It is included in Windows 7 and is also available as a free download at http://www.microsoft.com/windows/products/winfamily/defender/default.mspx. Windows Defender addresses spyware and other malware threats, blocking the download of potentially dangerous programs and removing spyware. At your direction, Windows Defender will periodically scan your computer for malware. It offers real-time protection, which means that it is constantly on guard, preventing problems before they occur.

To adjust Windows Defender settings or to initiate a scan, click **Start**. In the Search box, type **Windows Defender**. Click the resulting link. As shown in Figure 7.17, you can scan your computer, check for updates, or change the way scheduled scans occur.

Cookies

Did you know that your computer has **cookies**? Unfortunately, they are not of the chocolate chip variety. Rather, they are small text files placed on your computer by websites you visit. Most cookies are designed to be helpful, as they "remember" your shopping preferences or perhaps assist you in logging back in to a class website. A cookie might save your shopping cart information or indicate your user preferences so it can direct you accordingly the next time you

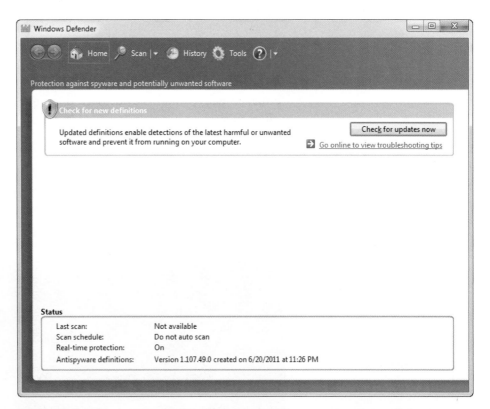

Figure 7.17 Windows Defender software is built into Windows 7 and protects your computer against security threats like spyware.

Quick Tip

Phishing Tip

The best way to prevent a phishing attack is to learn how to recognize one. Often, phishing e-mail contains spelling errors and uses poor grammar. It might even appear to be from someone you know (called *spear phishing*).

If you are unsure of whether an e-mail is a phishing attempt, you can place the mouse pointer over any hyperlink that is included in the e-mail. You will then see the actual URL for the link, which often does not match the one included in the e-mail. Never click a link included in what appears to be a phishing attempt. Instead, call the financial institution at the phone number listed on your account or open a browser and type the URL for the financial institution.

visit a particular website. Suppose you visit a weather site and enter your zip code so you can keep up with the weather each day. The next time you open the weather site, it appears to have remembered your zip code, displaying the local weather without your having to ask for it. Most likely, a cookie was placed on your computer the first time you visited the weather site, recording your preference for weather for your zip code. That is an example of how a cookie can be useful. Concern arises, though, when advertisers begin tracking the habits of their visitors. A tracking cookie might be placed on your computer, which traces your Internet browsing as you visit other websites. The owner of the website that placed the tracking cookie can then make determinations about who its customers are with regard to their shopping habits and interests. Alarmingly, cookies can also be put to malicious use by hackers intent on gaining access to an account or on collecting personal information for illegal purposes. Indeed, the line between spyware and tracking cookies is blurred, as both can be used to track your movements online.

Phishing

Phishing is a very real concern for those who use the Internet often. Phishing is an e-mail scam in which a sender attempts to dupe you into providing personal information such as your Social Security number, account passwords, or other sensitive information that could be used to steal your identity. Phishing can also be perpetrated through social media, online chats, text messages, and other sources.

A typical phishing attempt might involve an e-mail from a sender posing as an official from a financial institution. A phishing e-mail typically includes a link to an "official" site, which is actually a link to another website where the criminal can capture sensitive and personally identifiable information. The e-mail usually contains a message that creates a sense of urgency and alarm, often suggesting a quick response to forestall some impending credit card or bank account fraud.

In Depth

Prevention of Identity Theft

Identity theft (Figure 7.18) is prevalent and has become easier to perpetrate with the heightened availability of online and mobile technologies. According to the Federal Trade Commission, approximately 9 million Americans have their identities stolen each year. Thieves often use personal information to steal bank account records, Social Security, and credit card account numbers.

If you find what appears to be a mistake on a credit card statement, call the credit card company and report the concern immediately. Most credit card companies do

Figure 7.18 The Internet has become an appealing place for identity thieves.

Shutterstock

not hold you liable for fraudulent charges and will reverse the charges, but you must report possible fraud as quickly as possible. If you suspect identity theft, you should report the event to the financial institution involved, immediately file a police report, and notify the credit reporting agencies as soon as possible.

The following tips can help you prevent identity theft.

- Shred documents containing Social Security numbers, account numbers, and other personally identifying information.
- Do not carry your Social Security card with you. Instead, keep it in a safe place in your home.
- Never log in to your bank or credit card account on a public wireless Internet connection.
- Be aware of phishing techniques. Do not click on a link in an e-mail that asks for account numbers or other sensitive information. Instead, type the URL of the financial institution in a browser to go directly to the correct website. Do not provide account information in an e-mail or on the phone unless you are certain that you are speaking with an official of the organization with which you do business.
- Keep your antivirus software up to date and ensure that scans occur regularly.
- Use strong passwords that contain letters and numbers, avoiding the use of obvious information like a child's or pet's name or even your birthdate.
- Opt out of pre-approved credit card notices, which can be easily stolen out of your mailbox and used to set up an account. To opt out, you can call 1-888-5OPTOUT (1-888-567-8688).
- Ask for a free credit report. By law, each of the three major credit reporting companies (Equifax, Experian, and Transunion) must provide you with a free copy of your credit report once each year at your request. Visit www.annualcreditreport.com, or call 1-877-322-8228, to request a credit report.

Hands-On

Activity 7.3 Exploring Security Risks

Having set up your home computer network, secured the wireless connection, and explored ways to safely connect wirelessly in other locations, you will turn to protecting each computer on your home network. You are aware of security threats such as viruses, malware, phishing, and hackers. You are also familiar with software and behavioral solutions that minimize those risks. In this exercise, you will prepare a plan to protect the computers on your home network. Where indicated, record your responses on paper for possible submission to your instructor.

a. Open your browser. Visit www.microsoft.com/athome/security/. Click **Protect my computer** on the left side of the browser window. Explore additional links to learn more about spyware. Provide a written set of steps you can follow to prevent spyware.

b. Explore links on the current page, or identify others that provide tips on creating a strong password. Following those tips, create a password for use with an e-mail account you want to create. Record your password.

c. Visit www.howsecureismypassword.net. Type the password you created in Step B. How long would it take a computer to crack your password?

Record your answer. Visit https://www.microsoft.com/security/pc-security/password-checker.aspx and type your password in the space provided. How strong is your password? Record your answer.

d. Visit www.symantec.com. Friends have encouraged you to install Internet security software on your computer. Identify Internet security software provided by Symantec. How much does it cost and what components are included? Will it protect you against more than viruses? Provide a written summary of the software. Is it available for trial before you buy?

e. Locate information on Microsoft Safety Scanner. What is it, how do you acquire it, and how could it help keep your computer more secure? Although you should not download or run the software in a computer lab, you might want to try the product on your home computer. Provide a summary of the product.

f. As a Facebook user, you enjoy online social interaction with friends. What you may not know is that social networking can be a vehicle for identity theft. Conduct online research to determine how that is possible and record your findings. How can a social networking site be used by identity thieves? How can you protect yourself?

Chapter Summary

- A computer network facilitates communication and the exchange of information by linking one or more computers and peripheral devices. *269*

- A network can be wired and/or wireless, with devices connected by cables or communicating wirelessly. *275*

- A computer network requires specific hardware components in order to function. At a minimum, you need a computer, a device (such as a router and/or modem), software (such as an operating system or other application) to coordinate communication, and a path for the information to travel from one computer to another. *270*

- Network architecture is the way that a communications network is designed. There are two main types. A peer-to-peer network (P2P) links two or more computers without going through a central server computer. The linked computers can then share resources and devices. In a client-server network, a central computer handles all of the network's security and file-sharing requests. *271*

- A home network is typically organized as a peer-to-peer network, while a client-server network is more often found in a business setting, where centralization of resources and network security are priorities. *274*

- It is important to know and understand the real threats to a network and how to protect against them. Threats such as viruses, spyware, and malware can be harmful to a computer's data and threaten personal privacy. *287*

Key Terms

Antivirus software *288*
CAT 5 Ethernet cable *270*
Client *272*
Client-server network *271*
Cookies *292*
Data packet *270*
Encryption *284*
Evil twin *287*
Firewall *290*
Gateway *271*
Hacker *284*
Hub *275*
IEEE 802.11 standard *277*
Local Area Network (LAN) *271*

Malware *287*
Networking *269*
Network architecture *271*
Network interface card (NIC) *270*
Network service set identifier (SSID) *283*
Peer-to-peer network (P2P) *271*
Phishing *293*
Router *270*
Server *272*
Spyware *290*
Switch *271*
Trojan horse *291*
Virus *287*

WEP *284*
Wide Area Network (WAN) *271*
Wi-Fi (wireless fidelity) *277*
Wi-Fi hotspot *284*
Windows Defender *292*
Wireless Access Point (WAP) *276*
Wireless network adapter *270*
Wireless router *270*
Workgroups *272*
Worm *291*
WPA *284*
WPA2 *284*

Multiple Choice

1. Connecting one or more devices to share resources such as peripherals or files is considered
   a. phishing.
   b. networking.
   c. Wi-Fi.
   d. sharing.

2. The term workgroup is synonymous with
   a. wide area network.
   b. client-server network.
   c. peer-to-peer network.
   d. local area network.

3. Data is sent through a transmission medium such as CAT 5 Ethernet in the form of
   a. SSID.
   b. HTML.
   c. switches.
   d. data packets.

4. Which of the following is a method you would use to protect your computer against privacy and security concerns?
   a. Turn your firewall off.
   b. Ensure that your antivirus software is kept up to date.
   c. Leave your computer network open.
   d. Download spyware.

5. A form of malware that collects personal information about you and your surfing habits without your knowledge is called
   a. a virus.
   b. an evil twin.
   c. spyware.
   d. a Trojan horse.

6. Which of the following would be considered a strong password?
   a. A single five letter word that can be found in the dictionary.
   b. Numbers, uppercase, and lowercase letters, at least 8 characters.
   c. Only uppercase and lowercase letters.
   d. 12 characters that contain an anniversary and a birthdate.

7. Which network navigation device serves as a gateway and routes data between networks?
   a. Hub.
   b. Switch.
   c. Router.
   d. NIC.

8. The software that assists in connecting your computer to a wireless network is the
   a. user account control.
   b. operating system.
   c. Windows firewall.
   d. wireless access point (WAP).

9. A _____ is device that enables computers to transmit data along the network; it has no built-in program to optimize network traffic.
   a. hub
   b. switch
   c. router
   d. modem

10. _____ is a term for the act of using open wireless networks that are not public.
    a. Phishing
    b. Encryption
    c. Spoofing
    d. Piggybacking

11. A _____ is a layer of protection that makes your computer invisible to others.
    a. firewall
    b. switch
    c. hacker
    d. hub

12. In a client-server network
    a. each computer on the network is equal.
    b. each computer can communicate directly with any other.
    c. a central computer handles all of the network's requests.
    d. the network must be wired.

13. A _____ is a computer that provides services and resources to _____ computers that request and receive the information.
    a. server, client
    b. client, server
    c. peer, client
    d. client, peer

14. A network's _____ can often be seen by other computers and is the network name.
    a. WEP
    b. WPA
    c. identifier
    d. SSID

15. To secure a home computer network you should do all of the following EXCEPT
    a. use the standard username and password for access your router.
    b. password protect access to your network.
    c. encrypt your network.
    d. use a firewall.

True/False

Circle **T** if the statement is true or **F** if the statement is false.

T F 1. The Internet is a network.

T F 2. Wired networks are the only type of network.

T F 3. A router and a switch are both considered network adapters.

T F 4. The network service identifier is the name of the network as it is broadcast wirelessly.

T F 5. Trojan horses are a type of Internet cookie.

T F 6. Downloading and installing antivirus software is enough to keep your computer safe.

T F 7. Wired networks are faster and more secure than wireless networks.

T F 8. WEP is a more commonly used wireless protocol and is also safer to use than WPA or WPA2.

T F 9. A network using an 802.11g signal will be faster than one using an 802.11n signal.

T F 10. Cookies can infect your computer with viruses.

T F 11. Emails and other files that are sent across a network are sent as a single data packet.

T F 12. Routers can direct only wireless traffic.

T F 13. A gateway joins several networks.

T F 14. The Internet is a large, client-server network.

T F 15. A server is necessary in a peer-to-peer network.

End of Chapter Exercises

Safer Networking

In this project, you will create a flyer (using Microsoft Word) for your workplace about the importance of taking precautions when travelling and using Wi-Fi hotspots. Your flyer should include at least 10 tips that every business traveller should know. Use the Internet or explore Windows Help and Support for further information.
Save your file as LastName_FirstName_PracComp_Ch7_Networking.

Antivirus Software

Your friend recently purchased a new computer. She is having problems with it, but she does not know what is wrong. Based on her description, you suspect that her computer may be infected with a virus. In your document, discuss some of the signs and symptoms that suggest that a computer might be infected. Open a Word document and summarize the information on viruses that you would provide to your friend.
Save your file as LastName_FirstName_PracComp_Ch7_Security.

Internet Search Activity: Antivirus Software Programs

Now that you have learned how to protect yourself from various forms of malware, use the Internet to search for information on three antivirus software programs. Using Microsoft Word, create a table similar to the one shown below. In the Word document, compose at least one paragraph that provides your rationale for selecting a particular antivirus program from the list of three that you provided in the table.

Product name	Product website	Primary features (list 3)	Cost	Subscription length

Save your file as LastName_FirstName_PracComp_Ch7_AntivirusSoftware.

CHAPTER **EIGHT**

Exploring Online Communication and Cloud Computing

ONE OF THE MOST-CITED REASONS FOR USING THE Internet is to communicate with others online. The most common way to communicate online is through electronic mail (e-mail). Other methods of communicating include social networking, instant messaging, blogging, and using the Internet to place video and voice calls through Voice over Internet Protocol (VoIP).

Your connection to the Internet through an Internet Service Provider (ISP) or company network makes it possible for you to send and receive e-mail messages, as well as use other forms of online communication, which have become an indispensable tool for both business and home users. They enable people of all ages to keep in touch with coworkers, friends, and relatives.

E-mail

Electronic mail, or **e-mail** (Figure 8.1), is a letter or message sent over the Internet or other network (for example, a business network). You no longer have to wait for the mail carrier to deliver a letter; instead, you can send a message through e-mail so it is delivered almost instantaneously. E-mail has become the standard for sending messages, newsletters, and

OBJECTIVES

When you complete this chapter, you will:

▶ Understand the concept of electronic mail.

▶ Be aware of e-mail privacy and security risks.

▶ Be familiar with the basic rules of e-mail etiquette.

▶ Be able to send and receive an e-mail message.

▶ Know how to create an e-mail account using a Web-based e-mail service.

▶ Understand how to send and receive e-mail attachments.

▶ Be familiar with the basics of instant messaging.

▶ Understand the concepts of blogging, social networking, wikis, and RSS.

▶ Be familiar with the concept of cloud computing and its application.

Figure 8.1 According the Pew Research Center, 94% of adult Internet users in the U.S. send and read e-mail.

other communications. An e-mail message is usually short and informal, except in some business situations where a greater degree of formality is often required.

In addition to speed of delivery, another advantage of sending an e-mail is that you can attach files, such as photographs and documents. An **attachment** is a saved file that is located on your computer system. The recipient of an e-mail can open and save your attachment if appropriate software is available on his computer. For example, if an attached file is an Excel workbook, the recipient can only open the attachment if he has access to Microsoft Excel.

File sizes can vary greatly, depending on file content and type. A file composed primarily of text, such as a typical word processing document, requires much less storage space than a graphic file, such as a photograph. You should be aware that most e-mail systems place an upper limit on the size of an attached file, so plan accordingly before attaching very large files. Also, corporate e-mail systems might ban certain file types, such as program files, usually in an effort to minimize the risk of viruses and malware, or to conserve hard drive space.

Given the amount of time you are likely to spend working with e-mail, it is a good idea to learn to manage it well. In this section, you will learn to send and receive messages, work with attachments, and control the type and amount of e-mail you receive.

In Depth

E-Mail Security and Privacy

Be careful when opening an e-mail sent with an attachment. Viruses are often sent by e-mail, so if you do not know the sender of the e-mail, do not open it. You should also make sure your antivirus program automatically scans incoming e-mail for viruses. Additionally, do not send account numbers or other sensitive information through e-mail. Such communication is not necessarily private. In fact, you should assume that anything you send in an e-mail can be read by others. Most workplaces have e-mail policies related to what can and cannot be sent through company e-mail. Keep in mind that many people have been fired after sending e-mail that was not considered appropriate or that violated company policy. Always keep security and privacy in mind when working with e-mail.

E-mail Software

The ISP with which you contract typically provides e-mail software that enables you to send and receive e-mail. As such, your e-mail address is associated with the ISP; for example, if you contract with America Online, your e-mail address is *username@aol.com*, where the user name is what you use to log in to America Online. E-mail software can be *client-based*, meaning the program is downloaded and runs from your computer, or *Web-based*, meaning the program operates through your browser, thereby making it unnecessary to download software to your computer.

Client-based e-mail is accessible when you are logged in to the computer that is configured with the e-mail software you use to read and send e-mail. Technically, client-based e-mail limits you to reading and sending e-mail only on the computer on which the client software is stored; however, businesses and colleges usually provide a Web-based equivalent so you can actually access your e-mail from any Internet-connected computer as well as your office desktop. For example, your company might install client e-mail software on your computer at work. Using the client software on your work computer, you have access not only to your e-mail but to features that enable you to organize and sort e-mail, as well as maintain a calendar and appointment scheduler. From your home computer, you can also access your work e-mail, although you will access a website and enter login information to do so. The Web-based equivalent to your work e-mail client typically only provides access to e-mail—not to any special features. Programs such as Microsoft Outlook, Windows Live Mail, and Mozilla Thunderbird are examples of client-based e-mail; they all include features that go beyond basic e-mail to include more in-depth personal information management features.

If you choose to work with a program such as Microsoft Outlook, you must first obtain an e-mail address from an ISP, your workplace, or another source. You can then use Microsoft Outlook or another client-based e-mail program to manage your e-mail. In addition to client e-mail software, most ISPs also enable you to access your mail by logging in to a website. In that way, you can read and respond to e-mail from any Internet-connected computer, although the Web-based version is likely not as full featured as its client-based equivalent.

If you prefer the flexibility of accessing e-mail from any Internet-connected computer, you might consider Google Gmail or Yahoo! Mail, both of which are examples of Web-based e-mail programs. You can easily register for a free account online, selecting your own e-mail address, as long as it has not already been taken. Once registered, you can access the Web-based account from any computer, as long as you are connected to the Internet. Most Web-based e-mail accounts include the capability to create an address book, maintain a calendar, organize e-mail, and filter out junk e-mail (spam).

Regardless of how your primary e-mail account is configured, you might find it helpful to create an additional Web-based e-mail account that you can use when you are required to provide an e-mail address; for example, when shopping online or taking part in an online survey in which you are asked for an e-mail address. In that way, you can segment your e-mail by purpose, hopefully diverting e-mail that is not personal into another account that you might check less often.

Address Books

As you gain proficiency with sending and receiving e-mail, you will find that it can be time consuming to type an e-mail address, especially if you do not remember the recipient's e-mail address and must look it up. In that case, you will probably enjoy using an electronic address book, in which you can record the names and e-mail addresses of people to whom you send e-mail. Those e-mail addresses are called Contacts. By recording your Contacts in an electronic address book, you can simply list a recipient's name in an e-mail message, with the e-mail address retrieved automatically. Most e-mail programs include an easy-to-use Address Book or Contact List feature.

Spam

Earlier in this chapter, the delivery of e-mail was compared to the postal system. To continue that analogy, consider the amount of postal junk mail you receive each week. Now triple that number and you have some idea of how much electronic junk mail will land in your e-mail inbox every day. **Spam** is

unsolicited, and usually unwanted, e-mail. To make matters worse, spam can potentially be offensive, sometimes including pornographic material. The reason you receive spam is the same reason you receive junk mail. Advertisers hope to convince you to purchase a product. Because most spam goes unanswered, advertisers must send it out in great volume, hoping to attract a few buyers. The result can be an inbox that contains a few personal messages but is monopolized by unwanted e-mail. Figure 8.2 shows an e-mail inbox, filled with unsolicited e-mail.

What can you do about spam? You can do exactly what you do with some junk mail—you can delete it without reading it. Although it does take time and might be annoying to have to select and delete multiple messages, it is one sure way to remove them from your e-mail account. However, similar mail will just reappear the next day. If the same spam comes regularly, you can set filters to delete it or block it automatically from your Inbox. Check with your ISP for directions on filtering. In many cases, an ISP filters what appears to be junk e-mail before it even makes it to your inbox. Software products that attempt to control spam are available, but some might require

ene/Shutterstock

Figure 8.2 Spam, unwanted bulk e-mail, is a negative aspect of e-mail.

E-mail **303**

Activity 8.1 Creating a Web-based E-Mail Account and Sending an E-Mail

In this scenario, you are the manager of a restaurant that serves stone oven pizzas. You have prepared a flyer, publicizing the pizza selections, for distribution in the community. Before finalizing the flyer, you will e-mail it as an attachment to a colleague for review. For the purpose of this hands-on activity, think of an e-mail address to which you can send a message. You might ask a classmate for an address, or you can send the message to your home e-mail address, if you have one. The address should be in the form user_name@mail_server .xxx. Before you send the e-mail, you will create an e-mail account with a free Web-based e-mail service. You can use a fictitious name, if you like, and you can delete the account when you have completed this chapter.

a. Use the following steps to create a free Web-based e-mail account using Google's Gmail service.

1. Open your browser and type **www.gmail.com** in the Address bar. Press **Enter**.
2. Click **Create an account**.
3. Type **your first and last names** (or create a fictitious name) in the first two boxes. Create a unique login name—one that is unlikely to have been already claimed by someone else. You might consider including both letters and numbers, but be sure the login name is something that you can remember. Click **check availability!**. If the login name is available, continue to complete the on-screen form. If the login name is unavailable, create another one and check its availability.

As you complete the form, you will be asked to type a series of characters that appear in a box. The set of characters is called a *captcha*. It is a challenge response test to make sure that a human, not a computer, is completing the form. You will often see captchas when you are completing online forms and transactions. For example, when purchasing online concert tickets, you will most likely have to fill in a captcha before the transaction is completed. That way, automated software cannot overwhelm the system with requests— a ploy often attempted by people intent on harming a system or creating a nuisance.

4. Read the Terms of Service agreement, and then click **I accept. Create my account** (Figure 8.3).

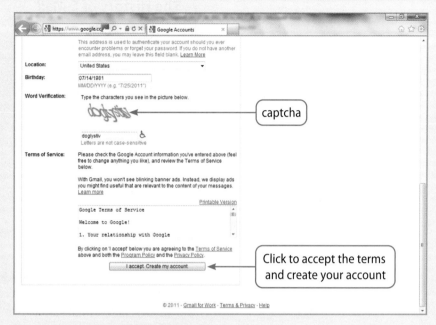

Figure 8.3 Create a free, Gmail account by completing the registration form.

TROUBLESHOOTING

In some cases, Gmail must provide a verification code before your account is finalized. If prompted, follow the directions on-screen to receive and enter your verification code.

5. Click **Show me my account**. You will be directed to your Gmail Inbox, which includes a few messages from the Gmail Team related to your new account (Figure 8.4).

b. Having created an e-mail account, you find that your Inbox has a few messages in it. Use the following steps to read an e-mail.

1. Close any boxes containing e-mail tips.
2. Point to any of the bold words in the first e-mail message in your Inbox and click. Read the message.

Figure 8.4 A new Gmail account already has a few e-mails from the Gmail Team.

3. Click **Inbox** on the left side of the browser window, as shown in Figure 8.5.

c. Use the following steps to compose a message to your colleague, asking him to review the flyer before it is finalized.

  1. Click **Compose mail** on the left side of the browser window. An empty e-mail message area appears, as shown in Figure 8.6. Maximize the window, if necessary.

  2. Click in **the box beside To:** and type a friend's e-mail address (or perhaps your home e-mail address). Click in **the box beside Subject:** and type **Attached Flyer**.

  3. Click in **the large white message area** and type **Hi Sam,** and then press **Enter**. Type **I've attached the Spring Stone Oven Pizzeria flyer for your review. Please let me know what you think about it.** Do not press Enter as you type, but allow lines to automatically wrap.

  4. Press **Enter**. Type **Thanks,** and then press **Enter**. Type **your first and last names.**

d. Use the following steps to attach the flyer to the e-mail. The flyer is located with the student data files that accompany this text.

  1. Click **Attach a file** in the area above the e-mail message.

  2. Click **Computer** in the left pane of the window. In the right pane, double-click the disk drive containing your student data files, and then

navigate through the folder structure to locate **PracComp_Ch8_Flyer.docx**. Click the file and then click **Open**.

  3. Click **Send**.

e. Click **your e-mail address** in the top-right corner, as shown in Figure 8.6. To see that the e-mail was sent, click the **Sent Mail** folder on the left. Note that the e-mail is shown. If you like, you can double-click the e-mail to read it again. Click **Sign out**. It is especially important to sign out if you are working at a public computer so your account is not available to anyone who might work at the computer after you leave.

f. Close the browser.

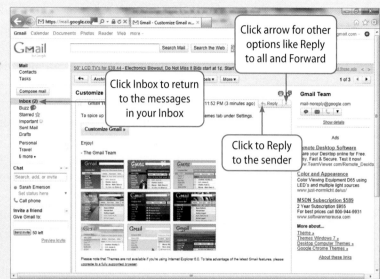

Figure 8.5 This is an e-mail message in Gmail.

Click arrow for other options like Reply to all and Forward

Click Inbox to return to the messages in your Inbox

Click to Reply to the sender

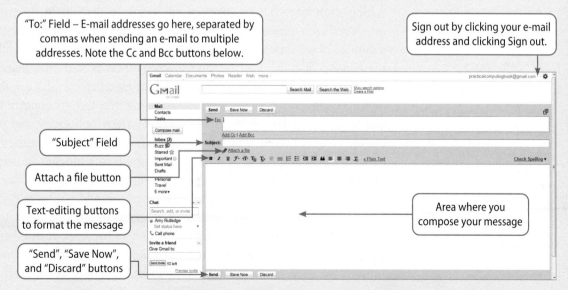

"To:" Field – E-mail addresses go here, separated by commas when sending an e-mail to multiple addresses. Note the Cc and Bcc buttons below.

Sign out by clicking your e-mail address and clicking Sign out.

"Subject" Field

Attach a file button

Text-editing buttons to format the message

"Send", "Save Now", and "Discard" buttons

Area where you compose your message

Figure 8.6 The compose mail window shows an e-mail ready to be typed.

more management than you may want to deal with. Also, anti-spam software is often included in Internet security packages, including Norton Internet Security and McAfee Internet Security. You should never respond to unwanted e-mail, or send a note asking to be removed from the mailing list. That just confirms that your e-mail address is valid, possibly adding you to even more spam mailing lists.

Although it is virtually impossible to stop spam once it has started, consider the following ideas in an attempt to minimize spam:

- If subscribing to anything on the Web, always indicate, if asked, that you do not want your e-mail address or personal information shared with anyone else.
- Never reply to any junk e-mail or visit any website suggested in the e-mail.
- Never reply to a request from a mailer asking if you want to be removed from the mailing list.
- Be familiar with your ISP's suggestions for dealing with unwanted e-mail. Some ISPs ask that you forward unwanted e-mail to a special account so they can help filter future e-mails from the sender. Other ISPs like Yahoo! Mail and Google Mail contain built-in filtering that you can turn on and use to manage spam.
- Create a separate e-mail account, and use that address for those situations when you must provide a valid e-mail address but do not want the e-mail sent to your personal account.
- Install an Internet security software package or anti-spam software.

> ### Quick Tip
> **Filtering Junk Mail**
> If you do not see an e-mail message you are expecting, check the junk mail folder (or a folder similarly named). Your e-mail provider might have redirected what appeared to be spam into a junk mail folder.

Online Communication

As the Internet continues to evolve, new forms of online communication are introduced. In addition to e-mail, you can also use blogs, social networking, and instant messaging to keep connected. Other communication tools with which you may already be familiar include Twitter, Skype, and VoIP. All these methods of communication are discussed in this section.

Blogs

A **blog**, short for web log, is an electronic journal posted on the Internet. Most blogs are shared with others and allow visitors to leave comments. People keep blogs for a number of reasons. Some write blogs as a personal online diary, while others may use blogs to discuss a specific topic or keep others posted on activities. For example, a new mother might keep a blog so family members can share in the excitement of a new baby. Or perhaps a person traveling in a foreign country keeps friends and family up to date on his adventure. Celebrities, politicians, and political activists use blogs to keep interested followers informed. As with just about any form of online communication, privacy is never assured, so a **blogger** (a person writing a blog) must always assume that what is written on the blog can be seen by anyone. Therefore, sensitive information or photographs should not be posted in a blog.

Creating a blog is easy; anyone with access to a computer with an Internet connection can be posting a blog in a matter of minutes. A number of free blog websites exist, such as www.blogger.com and www.wordpress.com. These sites simplify the process of creating and maintaining a blog. A blog can include text, pictures, videos, and links to other Web pages. Figure 8.7 shows an example of a Travel blog from TravelPod (www.travelpod.com).

Figure 8.7 Travel blogs allow people to share their adventures with others.

In Depth

E-Mail Etiquette

Although e-mail is often an informal method of communication, you should still be aware of standard rules of etiquette related to composing an e-mail message. Use the same care with writing an e-mail that you would when writing a business letter or memo. Plan your wording carefully and always check for grammatical and spelling errors before sending.

1. Include a subject line that relates to the e-mail. Not only is it courteous to include a subject so your reader knows what to expect, but it also suggests that the e-mail is not actually a virus. Viruses that replicate themselves through e-mail often contain no subject.

2. The first line should contain a proper greeting. If the e-mail is informal, you might simply include the recipient's first name; otherwise, use a greeting similar to one you would use in a more formal business letter, such as *Dear Dr. Jones.*

3. Always include a signature line, with your name and any other relevant identifying information, such as your position or phone number. To save time, you can create a signature line and have it automatically attached to all e-mail that you send.

4. Be concise. An e-mail is no place for wordiness, as most people expect to read through e-mail messages fairly quickly.

5. Only address the e-mail to the person(s) to whom it is intended. If you are replying to an e-mail, avoid replying to everyone who was addressed in the original message (the Reply All option) unless you are certain the response should be sent to all. Most e-mail software includes a Reply and a Reply All option. Make sure you select the option that is correct for your purpose.

6. Do not use all caps in an e-mail message—IT APPEARS THAT YOU ARE YELLING.

7. In most cases, a simple black font is appropriate. Unless the e-mail is very informal, avoid unusual fonts and bright color.

8. Use proper spelling and grammar. Most e-mail software provides a spelling checker you can use to check an e-mail before sending it. You can also copy the message and paste it into a Microsoft Word document, checking the spelling and grammar there.

9. Always proofread an e-mail, for both spelling and grammatical errors as well as general readability, before sending it.

10. If you are angry, wait a bit before sending an e-mail in which you air your frustration. It is likely that such an interval will give you time to rethink the repercussions of sending an e-mail you might regret later.

11. Use humor and sarcasm sparingly, if at all, in an e-mail message. Remember that body language is difficult to convey in written form, so your reader might misinterpret your tone.

12. Avoid the urge to forward chain e-mails. They are annoying to many people who see them as a waste of time and computer resources. Chain e-mails are messages that instruct receivers to redistribute the message to a larger group of people. Most workplaces discourage or prohibit chain letter activity.

Writing very short blog posts has become a popular option for communicating online. Known as a **microblog**, a short blog usually contains a post about what is happening in the blogger's life at that moment. Twitter and Tumblr are popular microblog sites.

Some bloggers enjoy video blogging. A **vlog** (short for video blog), displays a video instead of text. You can find vlogs on websites such as www.youtube.com.

Social Networking

Social networking has become an extremely popular form of online communication among people of all ages. A **social network** is an online community of people with common interests, who connect with each other to share information and experiences. Most social networking sites, such as Facebook (www.facebook .com), are free to join. Through such a social network, you can connect with old and new friends, posting comments and photographs related to your life. Social networking is not only popular with individuals but also with businesses who use the service to market themselves.

With over 800 million active users, the most notable social networking site is **Facebook**. **LinkedIn** (www.linkedin.com) is another popular site, aimed at building professional networks for career-related purposes. LinkedIn users can post an online resumé and connect with recruiters. Figure 8.8 shows an example of a typical LinkedIn page.

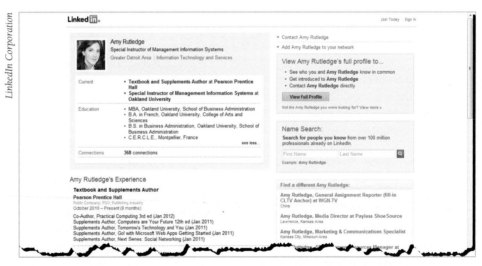

Figure 8.8 LinkedIn is a professional social networking site. Member profile pages resemble a resume.

Social networking sites tend to include common elements. Each user has her own page containing information that she chooses to make available to others. In addition to text, you can include photos or videos, making them public or private (available only to those you have confirmed as "friends").

When you first create an account on a social networking site, you will create a **profile**, in which you can choose to provide information such as your hometown, profession, school attended, and birthdate. A profile often includes a photo, which you can change often. Profile information is typically available to everyone, even those who are not yet your friends, so avoid providing too much detail (your home address or phone number, for example). A typical social networking site includes an area where a user can post an update, similar

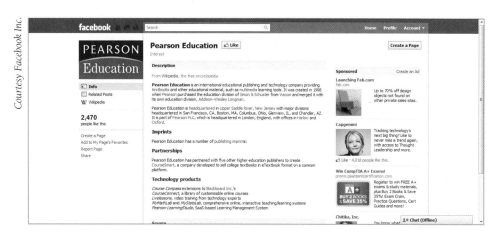

Figure 8.9 With over 800 million users, Facebook is the most popular social networking site. A Facebook profile page is shown.

to a blog or microblog. In Facebook, this area is known as the *wall*. You can upload photos, videos, links to sites of interest, and multimedia content to your social networking account. As shown in Figure 8.9, companies such as Pearson Education often maintain a Facebook wall.

People you choose to communicate with through a site such as Facebook are called your contacts, or **friends**. Depending on your privacy settings, contacts are usually the only people who can see (and respond to) the content posted on your social network page.

Social media has its advantages but should be used with caution. Consider setting privacy settings at the highest level and refrain from posting personally identifying information such as a phone number. Also, do not be generous with details about your travel plans or work schedule. Too much information might invite unscrupulous people to burglarize your home or otherwise take advantage of your property while you are away. You should also be aware

In Depth

Staying Safe Online

Communicating online can be enjoyable, but be sure to take all precautions to protect yourself and your identity. When using social media for networking with friends, posting to blogs, or communicating in other ways, it is important to manage your online reputation as well as your privacy. Privacy is always a concern when you use a social networking website. Always be aware of the privacy settings on your social networking site, and adjust those settings, if necessary, to provide the greatest protection against online predators. Many social networking sites offer a way to view your page as the general public sees it; if such is the case on the site that you use, check to see how your account appears to others. Additionally, keep in mind that when using social networking sites, others may be able to see your posts, even if those people are not your friends. For example, friends of your friends on Facebook can often see your posts, even though you have appropriately managed your privacy settings. It is best to think of a post as an advertisement on a billboard. If you would not want your post to be seen on a billboard, then do not post it on Facebook. Be very cautious about the information you share on social networking sites. Your pet's name, mother's maiden name, birthdate, address, and phone number can all be used for identity theft. Finally, you should never confirm as a friend someone that you do not know very well.

Online Communication **309**

that prospective employers often check the social networking sites of potential employees; many people have been denied jobs based on questionable content posted by the job seeker.

Twitter

Twitter is a microblogging and social networking site used by private individuals, celebrities, and even businesses. As you recall, a microblog is a very short post, typically related to your immediate activity, or a brief thought. Using Twitter (www.twitter.com), you can create an account and then post, or **tweet**, status updates or other comments. General Twitter messages can be seen by anyone, but you can also send private tweets. With each Twitter post limited to 140 characters, status updates are relatively brief. A **follower**—a person who reads the tweets of others—can access tweets through the Internet, by text message, or by using a smartphone application, commonly called an *app*. You do not have to tweet to take advantage of Twitter. You can simply register for an account and follow other Twitter users' tweets. Twitter is not used simply for entertainment. Businesses also make use of Twitter as an advertising tool and to stay connected to clients. Figure 8.10 shows an example of a Twitter page. People often place hash tags, the # symbol, into a tweet to mark keywords or topics. A user could click on a hashtagged word in a tweet to show all of the other tweets containing that same word.

Figure 8.10 A Twitter page features tweets, or messages, that are limited to 140 characters.

Voice over IP

Voice over Internet Protocol, known as **VoIP** (referred to as Voice over IP), enables you to make phone calls through a broadband Internet connection. VoIP customers can use a landline phone to make calls; however, the calls are transmitted over the Internet instead of along telephone lines. To make a call from your home phone, you need a traditional phone, a phone adapter (usually provided by the VoIP service), and an Internet connection. You can also make VoIP calls using a computer with a speaker and microphone. When using a computer, a phone adapter is not necessary; however, you must install VoIP software before you can make any calls.

Video Conferencing

Businesses have found video conferencing to be a way to save money and time, and gain efficiency. Video conferencing allows people to conduct online sales presentations, meetings, and training through the use of video and audio transmissions. Using video cameras, the Internet, and video output devices (such as video monitors, television screens, or projectors) you can conduct a meeting as if the person (or people) you were meeting with were actually in the room with you. Video conferencing can be accomplished in one of two ways, through the use of a dedicated system or a desktop program. A dedicated system is usually found in a corporate conference room or auditorium. To function, a camera (or cameras) are mounted in the room along with microphones to capture images and sound. Incoming sounds and images from the other party are played through speakers and projectors or screens, respectively. Desktop systems use webcams, microphones, and video conferencing software.

VoIP has several advantages over a traditional phone line. It is usually less expensive than a landline, which is why so many people have switched to it. It includes typical features of a traditional phone, such as call waiting, caller ID, and call forwarding. VoIP numbers are also portable. For example, you can take your number with you when travelling so others can reach you wherever you are. All you need is a high-speed Internet connection (not dial-up) and your phone adapter, which will serve as your VoIP connection. Because it uses the Internet to transmit your signal, it does not matter where you are; you can keep your phone number.

VoIP is not without disadvantages. Some customers report dissatisfaction with the sound quality of calls, although sound quality is becoming less of an issue with the greater availability of high bandwidth Internet access. Also, because VoIP requires electricity, a power outage can temporarily disable the service. In response, some VoIP providers include battery backups for phone adapters, so calls can be made during a power failure (although the time is usually limited to a couple of hours).

Two popular VoIP companies are Vonage (www.vonage.com), and Skype, (www.skype.com). Vonage can convert a home line to VoIP and also enables you to make calls on a computer through the Internet, whereas Skype is primarily used for making calls with a computer using the Internet.

Instant Messaging

Instant messaging (IM), also known as online chat, is a form of online **real-time** communication. Real-time communication occurs synchronously, like a face-to-face conversation, as opposed to an e-mail which occurs asynchronously. How does it work? First, you must set up an account with an instant messaging service. Yahoo! Messenger (http://messenger.yahoo.com), Windows Live Messenger 2011 (http://explore.live.com/windows-live-messenger), AOL Instant Messenger (www.aim.com), and ICQ (www.icq.com) are a few of the most popular instant messaging services. You can identify friends who use the same instant messaging service and then communicate with a buddy when you are both online. Social

Using Skype

Skype (www.skype.com) is an application that facilitates instant messaging, as well as VoIP voice and video calls over the Internet. With voice calls, Skype users can call other computer users or can connect to landline and mobile phones. Video calls require a computer equipped with a webcam and a microphone. Using Skype is an excellent way to keep up with family over great distances (Figure 8.11).

Calls to other Skype members, regardless of the distance involved, are free. When using Skype to call a landline or mobile phone, you will incur a small fee (a few cents per minute, depending on location). To use Skype, you must download and install the Skype application. You will also create a Skype account.

If you plan to use Skype on a mobile phone, you will need to download a Skype app. Because so many mobile phone users are interested in video chat (such as Skype), wireless phone companies have begun to include an additional camera in certain phone models to facilitate the video. You will use your mobile phone's Wi-Fi connection to work with Skype.

Some newer television models have built-in capability to make Skype calls. Even so, you might prefer not to be seen on a 52" flat screen!

Courtesy Skype Technologies S.A.

Figure 8.11 Skype has online video chat. There is no fee to chat with other Skype members.

networking sites, such as Facebook, usually include a form of instant messaging so you can "talk" with your friends who are also logged in to the site.

Instant messaging is becoming more popular in the workplace as well. Internal business messaging programs enable colleagues to chat with each other about work-related topics (Figure 8.12). Of course, the employer can monitor instant messages on the company network, so you should insure that a message is business related before sending it. Companies in particular industries, such as banking, are even legally required to archive instant messages for a number of years.

Chat rooms provide another means of instant messaging. Unlike the forms of instant messaging described previously, a chat room can include unknown users discussing a particular subject. Your instructor might offer to host a chat room for students interested in further study, or perhaps your ISP schedules a chat room where you and others can share thoughts on a topic of interest.

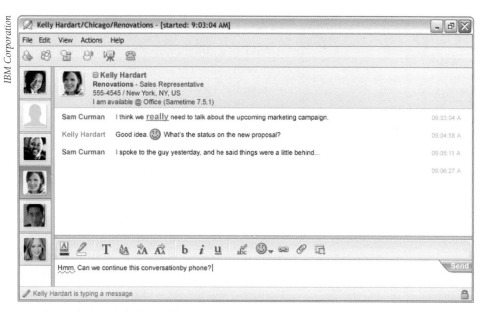

Figure 8.12 In recent years, instant messaging has gained popularity as a business productivity tool. Many companies utilize internal chat programs such as IBM's Lotus Sametime Chat.

In Depth

Chat Lingo

When using instant messaging programs, users often shorten phrases into acronyms rather than spelling each word. A component of *chat lingo*, those shortcuts are extremely popular and are becoming increasingly recognizable by almost everyone who uses any form of online communication. The following list shows commonly used shortcuts.

AFAIK	As Far As I Know		NP	No Problem
BRB	Be Right Back		OMG	Oh My Gosh
BTW	By The Way		ROFL	Rolling On Floor, Laughing
F2F	Face To Face		THX	Thanks!
FAQ	Frequently Asked Question		TTFN	Ta-Ta For Now
FYI	For Your Information		TTYL	Talk To You Later
L8R	Later (usually used for good bye)		YW	You're Welcome
LOL	Laughing Out Loud			

In addition to shortcuts, *emoticons* are used to convey emotions or facial expressions. An emoticon is created by combining keys on the keyboard. For example, the emoticon for a happy face is actually a colon, followed by a right parenthesis. Common emoticons are shown in the following table. You can find a more comprehensive list by conducting an Internet search for emoticons. Because they are considered very informal, emoticons and shortcuts are not appropriate for communications in a business or educational setting.

:)	Smile (happy)
:(	Frown (sad)
;)	Wink

Wikis

A **wiki** is a collaborative website that enables you to share ideas and information with other contributors. Wikis such as wikiHow (www.wikihow.com) and Wikipedia (www.wikipedia.org) encourages content contribution from the public so that topic coverage remains current and relevant. Obviously, the downside to such open access contribution is that information is not necessarily verified for accuracy. At the same time, such open access encourages more experts to contribute, possibly yielding even more complete coverage than would have been possible with only one author.

Among other things, wikis can be used for collaborative learning, online manuals, project management, a company knowledge base, and more. PBworks (www.pbworks.com) and Wikispaces (www.wikispaces.com) are popular with some businesses and organizations that encourage online collaboration for business purposes. Most wikis provide some level of free access, with additional features available for a one-time cost or monthly fee.

At a site such as www.wikispaces.com, you can create an account and invite others to contribute to your wiki. A typical wiki includes privacy features, ensuring that only people to whom you have granted access can view or edit content. Your wiki page will be assigned its own Web address (URL), which invited contributors can easily access. Wikis are easy to edit; most use a simple text editor, which means you do not need to be familiar with a Web programming language. Inserting links to other wiki pages or adding additional content like photos and videos is easy. Figure 8.13 shows a wiki page used in higher education. The page allows the students of an online course to declare the company they have chosen to research for their project.

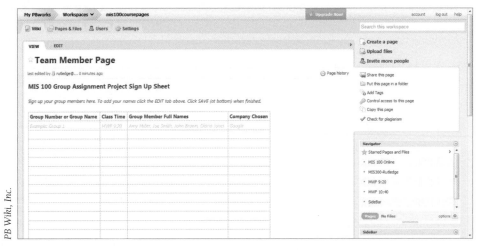

PB Wiki, Inc.

Figure 8.13 Wikis can be used in education to facilitate learning or simply to aid the instructor with tasks such as group project assignment sheets.

RSS Feeds

RSS, short for really simple syndication, is a Web technology in which news and other content is pushed out to a subscriber of a site. Rather than have readers go to a website to check for updated content, an RSS feed provides a short summary to subscribers of the feed as soon as an update is available. For example, suppose you are interested in travel to Oregon. Having accessed an Oregon travel site, such as www.traveloregon.com, you might locate an RSS link (usually at the bottom of

In Depth

Wikipedia

Wikipedia (www.wikipedia.org) is an online, wiki encyclopedia. Using Wikipedia, you can search for information on just about any topic. Simply type the topic in the search box, as shown in Figure 8.14. According to a Pew Research poll, 53 percent of adult Internet users use Wikipedia to search for information.

Unlike a traditional encyclopedia, which is edited by scholars and is confirmed to be accurate, Wikipedia is open access. This means that information contained in Wikipedia is contributed by anonymous users. Because content can be added by anyone, regardless of whether it is actually true, educators and professionals typically disregard Wikipedia as a legitimate source for research. Although several studies have shown that the content is most often accurate, you should never base a research study on Wikipedia or assume that what you read is necessarily correct.

In a traditional encyclopedia, you often find references to related topics. For example, when reading about George Washington, you might see the words *see also Continental Army*. Similarly, Wikipedia provides links to related topics, although those links are actually on-screen text that you can click for more information. Having looked up *George Washington* in Wikipedia, you might find that the words *Continental Army* are shown in a different color. When you point to the words, the mouse appears as a pointing hand, which is an indication that clicking the *link* will display an article related to the Continental Army. As shown in Figure 8.14, the Wikipedia article on George Washington includes several hyperlinks to other topic pages.

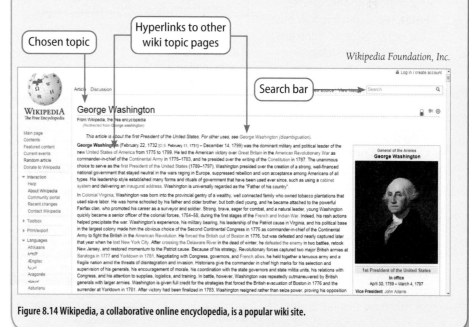

Figure 8.14 Wikipedia, a collaborative online encyclopedia, is a popular wiki site.

a page). Click the link and respond to additional prompts to subscribe to the RSS feed. By subscribing, you will receive periodic updates on travel to that state. An RSS feed is a common feature of many news, travel, and commercial sites.

Some e-mail clients, such as Mozilla Thunderbird and Outlook 2010, enable you to subscribe to an RSS feed. Otherwise, you can download an **aggregator** or **reader** to which the updated content, or **feed**, will be sent. NewsGator (www.newsgator.com/rss-readers.aspx) and Google's Reader (www.google.com/reader) are two examples of RSS aggregators, both of which you can sign up for online. Then you can subscribe to RSS feeds you find on your favorite Web pages. Simply

Hands-On

Activity 8.2 Setting up Feeds in Google Reader

Have you ever felt as if you were out of the loop when others were discussing the latest news? Do you find yourself often checking your favorite sites for the newest information? You can keep yourself better informed with very little effort by using an RSS reader such as Google Reader. In this activity, you will create a Google Reader account and subscribe to several RSS feeds. To complete this activity, you must have a Gmail account, like the one that was created in Hands-On Activity 8.1.

a. Connect to the Internet. Type **www.google.com /reader** in the Address bar and then press **Enter**.

b. Sign in using your Gmail user name and password (from the account you created in Hands-On Activity 8.1).

c. Click **Add a subscription** on the left side of the window, as shown in Figure 8.15.

d. Type **TechCrunch** in the search box and then press **Enter**. TechCrunch is a website that provides information and news feeds on developments in technology. Results from your search appear on the right, with a TechCrunch link shown at the top of the list (Figure 8.16).

e. Click **TechCrunch**. Scroll through the articles, reading a few that interest you. Next, you will subscribe to the feed.

f. Scroll to the top of the page and then click **Subscribe**.

A message lets you know that you have subscribed to Tech-Crunch. You will also see TechCrunch on the left under the Subscriptions heading. If you wish to unsubscribe later, point to the subscription and click the blue arrow that appears on the right. Then click **Unsubscribe**.

ON YOUR OWN

Search for at least two other websites or publications for which you would like to receive news feeds. If you have nothing specific in mind, try searching for Time or Better Homes and Gardens. Both of these sites provide feeds.

---

g. Click **All items** at the top of the left pane. The view expands to show short summaries of all feeds. Click **List** in the upper-right corner. The view now resembles an e-mail Inbox (Figure 8.17).

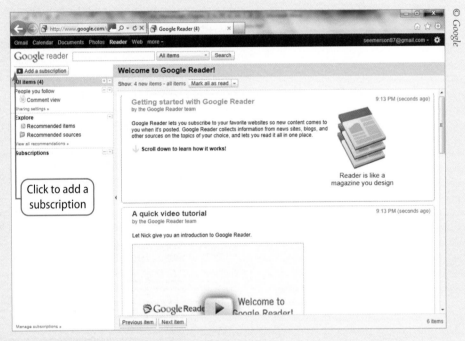

Figure 8.15 The Google Reader subscription page.

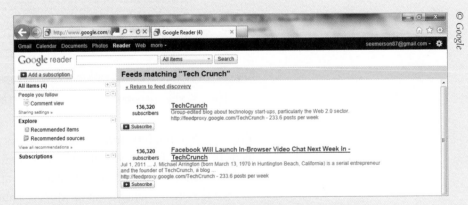

Figure 8.16 This is the Google Reader subscription page. Note the TechCrunch link that is listed first.

h. Click **Expanded** in the upper-right corner. Click **the title of a news item** in the list on the right. Scan the article, if you like, and then close the article's tab.

You can add a newsfeed directly from your favorite sites. Check to see if the site has an RSS symbol on the home page (shown in Figure 8.19), or another indication of an RSS feed, and click on it.

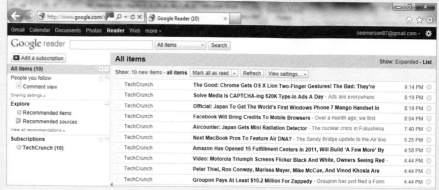

Figure 8.17 In this view, only the title of each article is listed.

i. Go to http://online.wsj.com and look for the RSS symbol. You may need to scroll to the bottom of the page to find it.

j. Click the **RSS Feeds link**. You will be taken to the Wall Street Journal RSS page.

k. Click **U.S. News** (beside the words *Get Feed*).

l. A list will appear with various RSS aggregators. Click **Google Reader**.

m. You will be taken to your Google Reader page where you can add the Subscription to your feeds. Click **Subscribe**.

n. Click **your user name** in the top right corner and then click **Sign Out**.

o. Close the browser.

TROUBLESHOOTING

If you are taken to a page where you must choose whether to add to your Google homepage or add to Google Reader, click **Add to Google Reader**. Log in with your Gmail user name and password. Repeat Step m if you do not see a list of Wall Street Journal articles. Otherwise, continue to Step n.

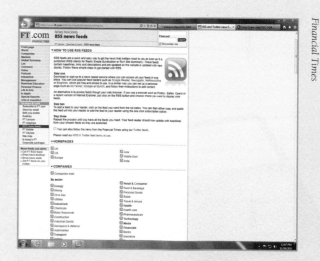

Figure 8.18 This is the Financial Times RSS News Feeds page.

Figure 8.19 This image represents the symbol for RSS (really simple syndication).

identify and click an RSS link (Figure 8.19), often located at the top or bottom of a Web page. Follow all subsequent directions to prepare for the feed. You might consider an RSS feed as a personalized newspaper. As a feed is sent to the aggregator, it is shown as a link or short summary. A link often directs you back to a location on the host website, where you will find more information on the topic.

Social Bookmarking

You have just learned about the benefit and enjoyment of accessing RSS news feeds that are related to your interests. But what if you want to share a news feed with a friend or be made aware of a news story that is of interest to others? **Social bookmarking** sites enable users to share (or bookmark) online content they find interesting. At sites such as www.digg.com, you will find links for the news stories that Digg members have an interest in. The top stories are those that many users have bookmarked. News stories are also arranged by topic, so you can see what users identify as the most interesting stories for a particular topic. As a user of a social bookmarking site, you can bookmark stories you enjoy. Some of the most widely used social bookmarking sites are digg.com, delicious.com, reddit.com, and StumbleUpon.com.

Podcasts and Webcasts

Do you occasionally miss your favorite television or radio show? You might be able to find it online in the form of a webcast or podcast. Many television networks and radio stations offer content online. Have you ever wanted to learn a new language or fix your kitchen sink yourself? With podcasts and webcasts the possibilities are endless.

Webcasts are audio and video files broadcast over the Internet. Audio and video files are streamed to the computer (much like television and radio content). For example, if a live graduation ceremony or sports event were being recorded and broadcast over the Internet, you could watch it online. Or, if you wanted to learn French you could sign up for a **webinar**, a Web-based seminar or online lesson. You would need media player software to watch a webcast on your computer. A number of free media players are available, such as iTunes and Windows Media Player.

Figure 8.20 Podcasts allow you to download and play content offline on an iPod or portable media player.

Podcasts (Figure 8.20) are similar to webcasts in that they are audio or video files that can be downloaded from the Internet to play on a computer, **iPod**, or **portable media player** (devices that play digital audio and/or video files). The term podcast is derived from the word iPod and broadcast. Despite what the term suggests, you do not need an iPod to listen to or watch a podcast.

Cloud Computing

Cloud computing refers to using the Internet as a host for certain services, such as file storage or remote applications. Enabling you to enjoy computing anytime and anywhere, cloud computing is designed to release you from the confines of your desktop or laptop computer. The "cloud" is actually the Internet—a reference to its availability from any location (Figure 8.21). With a computer and access to the Internet, you can use certain software applications, even though they may not

Quick Tip

Podcasts

Just like news feeds, you can subscribe to a podcast through an RSS aggregator.

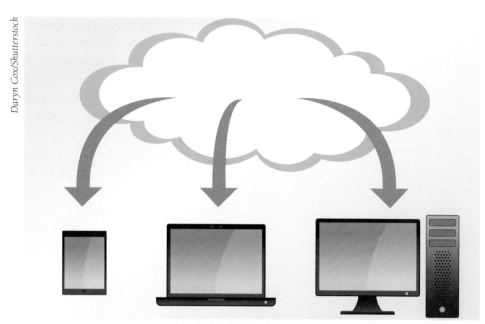

Figure 8.21 Cloud computing involves using the Internet to accomplish various tasks.

be installed on your computer. You can also save files, such as documents and photographs, in the "cloud" so they are available to you from any location. Such file storage also enables you to make backups of files you do not want to lose.

The newest version of Microsoft Office, Office 2010, incorporates cloud computing capability in its Web Apps companion to the traditional desktop Office version. **Microsoft Web Apps** is an online version of Office components—Word, Excel, PowerPoint, and OneNote—which means that you can use the software even if you do not own a license for it. Although Web Apps versions are limited in functionality, you are still able to create and work with Office documents, even sharing them with others online. Other companies, such as IBM, offer cloud versions of software so that businesses can access and pay for software only as they need it. Although those cloud versions may not be free, the cost of using the software is significantly less than it would be if a company had to buy and install the complete version on company computers.

In this section, you will learn how you can use the cloud to increase productivity and to collaborate with others. You will also explore options for saving files online so you can access them from any Internet-connected computer.

Quick Tip

Creating a Presentation in the Cloud

Do you have to make a presentation but you do not have Microsoft PowerPoint? You can use the Web Apps version of PowerPoint to create and save the presentation.

Document Saving and Sharing

Cloud computing makes it simple to share files with others. In fact, document saving and sharing will probably be one of the first applications of cloud computing that you explore. Having recently returned from a vacation to an exciting venue, you might share your photographs online with others. Or perhaps you want to collaborate with coworkers on a proposal that is due very soon. Sharing the proposal online insures that everyone has the opportunity to review and modify the document. In both examples, the common element is the fact that you were able to make your files available online, or in the "cloud."

When you store or share files online, those files are uploaded to a Web server from which others can access them. Most online storage sites offer a certain amount of space for free, with additional space available for a fee. For example, Dropbox .com (www.dropbox.com) provides space where you can share documents, photos, and videos. Even if your goal is simply to save files so you can access them later or be assured of a backup (although you should never rely completely on online storage for backup of critical files), online storage sites can be your answer. Most online storage sites are similar in nature to another disk drive to which you can save and from which you can retrieve files. Having created an account with an online service, you can simply upload files from your computer to an online location. In most cases, you can even create a series of folders to organize the files that you upload.

In addition to Dropbox.com, you might want to explore Google Docs (http://docs.google.com), which not only enables you to save and share files, but also to create documents, spreadsheets, and presentations online. Similarly, Microsoft SkyDrive (http://skydrive.live.com) provides 25 GB of free online storage space, as well as access to Web Apps. You can easily share files and collaborate on projects with others using any of these services. You will find directions on how to save and share files when you visit those sites.

Online Applications and Services

True to its name, cloud computing is difficult to categorize in a neat bundle. Its nebulous nature, as much concept as reality, creates overlap in various areas. Applications of cloud computing relate not only to online file storage and sharing but also to software that supports the development of documents that you can then share online. In fact, some online services, such as Microsoft's **Windows Live**, bundle cloud applications, file sharing, and online storage with entertainment and communication facilities, making a concise definition or categorization even more difficult. What is clear is that applications that at one time were available only locally (on one computer at a time) are now becoming commonplace, and often free, entities that can be accessed remotely.

More than simply a service, Windows Live is actually a free collection of services and programs that coordinate to provide a complete package of entertainment and productivity software, communication, and file management. Microsoft makes Windows Live available at http://home.live.com, where you can create a Windows Live ID and begin enjoying the many Windows Live features. If you already have a Hotmail, SkyDrive, or Windows Messenger account, your sign-in is your Windows Live ID. Windows Live includes access to Windows Live Essentials, a collection of entertainment, multimedia, and communication software that even enables you to synchronize files between your SkyDrive account and other computers. Including mail, instant messaging, file and calendar sharing, and even Web page hosting, Windows Live seamlessly integrates your PC with the larger world of cloud computing. You can learn more about Windows Live at http://explore.live.com.

Accessible with a Windows Live ID, Microsoft Web Apps are Microsoft productivity software programs that are available free as a link from your SkyDrive account. As shown in Figure 8.22, you can create a new Word, Excel, PowerPoint, or OneNote document from SkyDrive. Also, having uploaded an Office document to your SkyDrive account, you can simply double-click the document to open it automatically in the Web Apps version of the program that created the file. While missing some of the capabilities of a full-featured Office program that might be installed on your desktop or laptop, Web Apps versions of the same programs are sufficient for most projects, and the price is right—free! Using Web Apps, you can collaborate with others without juggling a single document back and forth. Multiple edits can occur on the same document simultaneously, with no need to coordinate versions. Anytime, anywhere computing is definitely a reality with Microsoft Web Apps.

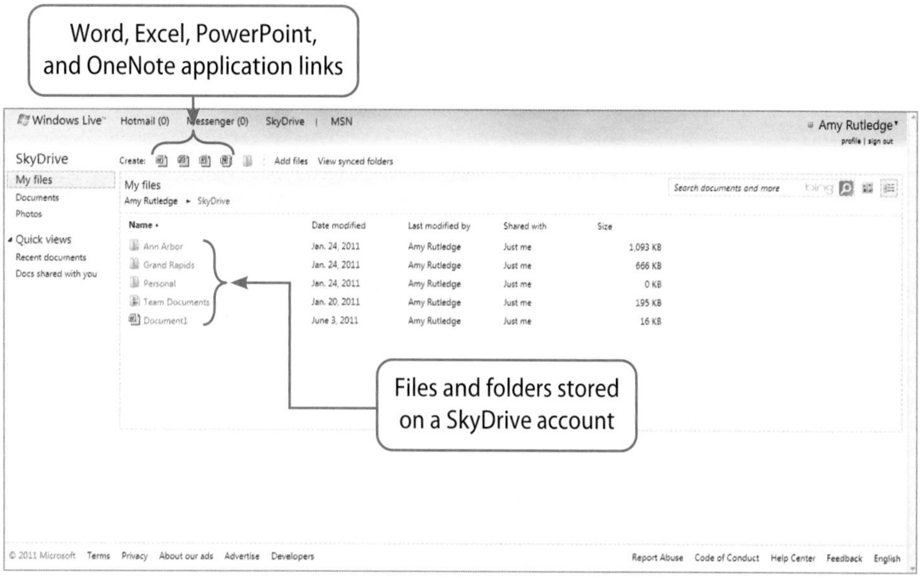

Files and folders stored on a SkyDrive account

Figure 8.22 Microsoft Web Apps are free, online versions of Microsoft Word, Excel, PowerPoint, and OneNote.

Technology Insight

Cloud Players: Play Your Music from Anywhere

Did you ever wish you could listen to your favorite songs from anywhere at any time? With Amazon's online music application, that is entirely possible. Amazon's Cloud player (Figure 8.23) uses the cloud to store music and video content so it can be accessed from a computer or Android phone. When you sign up for the Cloud Drive (of which the Cloud Player is a part), Amazon gives you 5 GB of free storage space where you can upload your own personal music and video files already stored on your computer. Amazon sells music and video downloads, and any purchases can be saved to the cloud player as well. Those files do not count against the 5 GB of free space. You can make your own playlists and access music from home, work, or literally any computer with an Internet connection. Similar to the way a webcast works, the player will stream music to your computer. Amazon also has an app for Android phones that can play music right from the mobile phone.

© NetPhotos/Alamy

Figure 8.23 Amazon's Cloud Player enables you to access music or video content from a computer or Android phone.

Apple has also introduced its own cloud player, named iCloud. The player works with the iTunes software program to allow users to store their music on remote servers similar to the way Amazon does.

Hands-On

Activity 8.3 Exploring Google Docs: Creating and Sharing Documents

In this activity, you will take a tour of Google Docs and create and share a document. You will use the Gmail account you created in Activity 8.1. Before beginning this exercise, think of an e-mail address you can use when sharing the document you work with in this exercise. You might ask a classmate for an address, or you might share your document with your home e-mail address, if you have one. Assume that you work for a marketing company that is planning a summer employee picnic. You need to collaborate with your colleagues to determine a list of supplies for the event. Not everyone works in the same office location, so you decide that Google Docs would be the best way to collaborate.

a. Open your browser and go to www.gmail.com. If necessary, sign in to your Gmail account, using the user name and password you created in Hands-On Activity 8.1.

b. Click **Documents** in the bar at the top of the window. The Documents page opens in a new tab as shown in Figure 8.24. Close any tips window that might open.

c. Click **Create new** and then click **Document** from the list of file types.

As shown in Figure 8.25, the document window has features that are common to other word processing programs, such as Microsoft Word.

Figure 8.24 Google Docs is a free productivity software suite from Google.

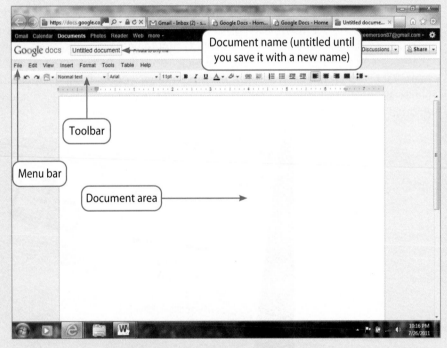

Figure 8.25 Google's text editor enables you to create documents.

d. Type **Supply List for the 4th Annual Company Picnic** and then press **Enter** two times. Type the following items, pressing **Enter** after each.
Silverware
Napkins
Plates
Condiments
Tablecloths

e. Click **Untitled document** at the top of the window so you can give the document a name. Type **Prac_Comp_PicnicList** and then click **OK**.

f. Click the **Share button**. Click in the **Add People box** (Figure 8.26) and type the e-mail address you collected before beginning this exercise. If you were sharing the document with several individuals, you would separate e-mail addresses with a comma.

g. Click the box beneath the addresses you just typed, type **For your review** and then press **Enter**. Type **Please add supplies as necessary,** and then press **Enter**. Type **Sincerely,** and then press **Enter**. **Type your first and last names.**

h. Click **Share & save** and then click **Close**.

i. Close the Prac_Comp_PicnicList tab. The document now appears in the Google Docs list (Figure 8.27). You have access to the most up-to-date version of the document. If your colleagues edit the document, you

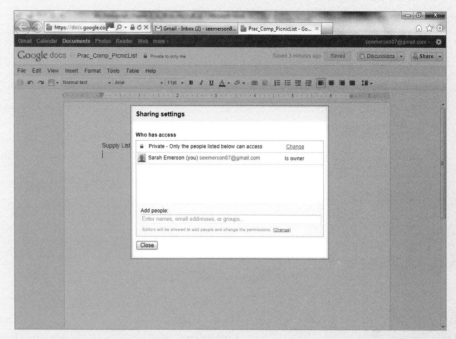

Figure 8.26 Share your document.

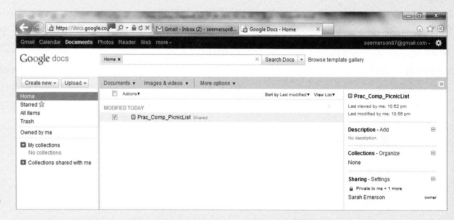

Figure 8.27 Your document is stored here and can be accessed from any computer.

will be able to see the changes the instant they happen. You can access the document when you sign in to your Gmail account and go to Google Docs.

j. Close the browser.

Chapter Summary

- The most common way to communicate online is through electronic mail (e-mail). It is important to understand how to send and receive e-mail as well as attach documents and photos to e-mails. *300*

- In addition to e-mail, other methods of communicating include social networking, instant messaging, blogging, and using the Internet to place video and voice calls through Voice over Internet Protocol (VoIP). *306*

- A social network is an online community of people with common interests, who connect with each other to share information and experiences. Most social networking sites, such as www.facebook.com, are free to join. *308*

- Instant messaging (IM), also known as online chat, is a form of online real-time communication. Real-time communication occurs synchronously, like a face-to-face conversation, as opposed to an e-mail which occurs asynchronously. *311*

- A blog, short for web log, is an electronic journal posted on the Internet. *306*

Key Terms

Aggregator *315*	**iPod** *318*	**Spam** *303*
Attachment *301*	**LinkedIn** *308*	**Tweet** *310*
Blog *306*	**Microblog** *308*	**Twitter** *310*
Blogger *306*	**Microsoft Web Apps** *319*	**Vlog** *308*
Chat room *312*	**Podcast** *318*	**Voice over Internet**
Cloud computing *318*	**Portable media player** *318*	**Protocol (VoIP)** *310*
E-mail *300*	**Profile** *308*	**Webcast** *318*
Facebook *308*	**Reader** *315*	**Webinar** *318*
Feed *315*	**Real-time** *311*	**Wiki** *314*
Follower *310*	**RSS** *314*	**Windows Live** *320*
Friend *309*	**Social bookmarking** *318*	
Instant messaging (IM) *311*	**Social network** *308*	

Multiple Choice

1. Messages that are sent over the Internet and are usually short and informal are called
   a. wikis.
   b. VoIP.
   c. e-mail.
   d. spam.

2. Unsolicited e-mails sent to your e-mail address are called
   a. postal mail.
   b. spam.
   c. computer mail.
   d. virus mail.

3. A _____ is an online community of people with common interests who connect with each other to share information and experiences.
   a. blog
   b. VoIP
   c. cloud
   d. social network

4. _____ are collaborative websites that allow the sharing of thoughts or ideas by multiple authors.
   a. Wikis
   b. Blogs
   c. E-mail
   d. Social networks

5. A means of making phone calls via a broadband Internet connection is called
   a. VoIP.
   b. blogging.
   c. webcasting.
   d. podcasting.

6. A device that plays digital audio and/or video files is called
   a. a Skype.
   b. a chat room.
   c. a portable media player.
   d. a flash drive.

7. Which of the following is a program that can be used to create online documents?
   a. Twitter.
   b. Microsoft Web Apps.
   c. Skype.
   d. LinkedIn.

8. All of the following are a disadvantage of VoIP except
   a. issues with call quality.
   b. power outages that cause VoIP to be offline.
   c. calls that can be hacked like e-mail.
   d. higher cost than traditional phone service.

9. A written conversation that takes place between people on different computers at the same time is called
   a. e-mail.
   b. VoIP.
   c. blogging.
   d. instant messaging.

10. If you want to send an e-mail to someone as a "carbon copy," in which field would you would put the address?
    a. Subject
    b. Cc:
    c. To:
    d. Bcc:

11. Delicious and Digg are examples of
    a. social networking sites.
    b. social bookmarking sites.
    c. RSS.
    d. blogging sites.

12. The method of online communication in which online conversations can occur between people who might be unknown to one another is
    a. VoIP.
    b. Social networking.
    c. a chat room.
    d. electronic messaging.

13. _____ refers to using the Internet as a means to accomplish various tasks.
    a. Client computing
    b. Online search
    c. Cloud computing
    d. Blogging

14. What online feature(s) allow you to save and share your favorite sites with others?
    a. Blogging sites
    b. RSS
    c. Social networking sites
    d. Social bookmarking sites

15. Microsoft Web Apps includes all of the following except
    a. Word.
    b. Excel.
    c. Outlook.
    d. PowerPoint.

True/False

Circle **T** if the statement is true or **F** if the statement is false.

T F 1. Client-based e-mail programs can be accessed from any computer.

T F 2. You should never open an e-mail attachment from someone you do not know.

T F 3. It is fine to type an e-mail in all capital letters.

T F 4. The word blog is short for Web log.

T F 5. A Twitter status update that consists of 140 characters or fewer is called a chirp.

T F 6. When using Facebook, the area where a user can update his or her status, upload photos, and other content is called the wall.

T F 7. Cloud computing requires an Internet connection.

T F 8. A social bookmarking site enables you to share content that you find interesting with others.

T F 9. Facebook and LinkedIn are two social bookmarking sites.

T F 10. Google Docs is downloadable software that runs from your computer as client software.

End of Chapter Exercises

Create a Travel Blog

In this project, you will create your own blog. Imagine that you have just won $50,000 in the lottery. You plan to take the trip of your dreams. Using a travel blogging website like www.travelpod.com, create a blog about your upcoming trip. In your blog, be sure to include your destination(s), method of travel, where you will stay, and what you will see and do while you are there. (If you do not know anything about the destination you have chosen, that is OK. Plenty of sites offer trip information. Use a search engine to help you.)

When you are finished with the assignment, open a Word document, copy the URL for your blog page and paste it into the Word document. Save your files as LastName_FirstName_PracComp_Ch8_TravelBlog.doc. (Note: Make sure that your blog settings are set so your instructor can view your page.)

Podcasts

The company you work for has reassigned you to the Paris office. You will be moving in two months and you need to learn French quickly. You have an MP3 player that you can listen to in your car while driving to and from work. Search for free French lessons you can download to your iPod.

Put your answers in a Word document. Find two websites where you can find these podcasts. Copy and paste the URLs. Do you need to download any sort of software to your computer to download the files? If so, what kind of software? Save your file as LastName_FirstName_PracComp_Ch8_Podcast.doc.

Group Collaboration Project: Microsoft Web Apps

In groups of two or three, create a paper about the advantages and disadvantages of cloud computing. Each group member will take one of the following sections, and the activity will be completed through online collaboration using a single document. Your group is part of the IT department at a local university. The president of the university is considering moving to cloud computing to save costs. As a group, you will research cloud computing and give a recommendation for its application at the school.

Use the following instructions.

1. One member of the group should create a Word document using Web Apps and share it with the other members of the group. Your instructor should assign you a group number. Save your document as *YourGroupNumber*_PracComp_Ch8_WebApps_.doc.
2. Each member of the group will research the following topics. (Be sure to cite your sources if required by your instructor.)
   a. Definition of cloud computing and its application in business.
   b. Advantages of cloud computing.
   c. Disadvantages of cloud computing.
   d. Group recommendations.
3. Use Web Apps to collaborate with your group and add your research to the document.
4. Save your document.
5. Share your document with your Instructor.

Google Docs: Presentations

Using Google Docs Presentations program, create a presentation about one of the technologies presented in this chapter, other than e-mail. Discuss the following topics in your presentation. Each bullet below should correspond to a single slide:

- Overview of the technology
- Application for home use
- Application for business use
- Examples of programs or companies that provide the technology

Add a title slide with your name and course. Add a photo or clip art to your presentation.

Save your file as Lastname_Firstname_PracComp_Ch8_GooglePres. Share the presentation with your instructor.

Photos by Robert Kneschke/Shutterstock; Leigh Prather/Shutterstock

CHAPTER **NINE**

Exploring Digital Entertainment and Multimedia Applications

IT SEEMS THAT THE WORLD HAS GONE DIGITAL. Photo processing locations, record stores, and even video rental stores have all but disappeared as more and more people use digital cameras, MP3 players, and YouTube or Netflix. Gone are the days when you had to worry about wasting a roll of film. Digital cameras can hold hundreds (if not thousands) of pictures without the need for a film change. Music with incredible sound quality can be stored on a compact player the size of a silver dollar. Home movies are easier than ever to create with digital video cameras that are compact, easy to use, and extremely affordable. The advance in technology in these areas has changed how we enjoy pictures and multimedia today. Some of the most enjoyable things you can do with a computer are to listen to music and work with photos and videos.

A Definition of Digital

In the past, music, photos and videos were stored in analog form rather than digital. However, because computers are electronic devices that work with **digital** data (recorded as a series of ones and zeros), text, music, video, and even pictures can be placed on a computer storage device in digital form.

OBJECTIVES

When you complete this chapter, you will:

▶ Understand the concept of digital data.

▶ Be aware of how to use a digital camera and transfer pictures to a computer.

▶ Identify common digital camera specifications.

▶ Be introduced to various types of image editing software.

▶ Be aware of various graphic file types.

▶ Understand how to use a digital camcorder, transfer video files to a computer, and upload them to the Internet.

▶ Be introduced to various types of video-editing software.

▶ Understand digital music formats and players.

▶ Learn how to search for and play digital music.

Technically, digital storage means that a series of numbers (using the binary system of zeros and ones) is generated to represent an image or sound. For example, **analog** music is stored as one continuous wave of sound on a medium such as a VHS or magnetic tape. As humans, everything we hear and see is a continuous transmission of variable data, or *analog*. When recording in digital format, the continuous transmission is converted into a sequence of numbers—digital—that can be read by a computer or device and then played back. In binary, or digital, form, music, video, and pictures can be electronically manipulated, preserved, and replayed perfectly at high speed. As you will see throughout this chapter, digital format offers many advantages over its analog predecessor.

Digital Photography

Many people are discovering an exciting way to take pictures without using film or paying film-processing costs. They often take several pictures of the same subject, viewing pictures immediately, and deleting any they do not like. They might use image editing software to enhance photographs—brightening, cropping, adding borders—for creative projects.These people have discovered the world of digital photography.

Although some will suggest that the printed quality of a film-based image surpasses that of digital, it is usually difficult to tell the difference between the two. If you print digital pictures on photo paper, and keep the printer cartridges or toners fresh (not low on ink), you will enjoy clearly detailed pictures that you can manage with an image editor and then print to your specifications. In addition, you can transfer your digital photos from a camera or computer to a photo processing service, receiving high-quality printed copies in short order. In this section, you will explore digital camera specifications, and you will learn to share and edit digital photos.

Understanding Digital Camera Specifications

A **digital camera** (Figure 9.1), captures images without the aid of photographic film. It records images digitally, so you can download photos to a computer and use a graphics program to manipulate and print the pictures, if you like. You can also send the digital photos to a photo processing center for printing. Most digital cameras enable you to view pictures immediately after you take them. If you do

Technology Insight

Convergence

As you learn about digital photography, video, and music, you will identify a common theme—most (if not all) of these multimedia activities have been integrated into smartphones. It is no longer necessary to carry around a separate camera, music player, or video camera; all these devices have been combined into the smartphone. In fact, one of the best-selling video camcorders (the Flip) has been discontinued because of this convergence of technologies. As related to technologies, *convergence* occurs when separate systems evolve toward performing the same functions on a single device. What additional functions would you like to see in a smartphone?

Figure 9.1 Digital cameras are divided into two main categories: consumer (point-and-shoot) and professional (DSLR).

not like a picture, simply delete it. With relative ease, you can upload photographs to your computer. In addition, you can copy them to a photo website so you can share them with others or have them printed. Regardless of artistic ability, you can use software to edit and fine-tune photos, generating high-quality pictures and photo projects. Digital cameras have become extremely affordable in recent years, with some costing as little as $25. With a wide variety of digital camera capabilities, it is important that you understand a bit about digital camera specifications so you can select the right camera for your needs.

Digital cameras come in all sizes and have a range of features. Some digital cameras can fit in your pocket, whereas others are a bit larger. As you select a camera, be sure to check on how simple the control buttons are to find and use, and how easy the camera will be for you to carry. Also consider your skill level and purposes. As a novice, you might prefer a camera in which most of the settings are automatic, so you simply push a button to take a picture. On the other hand, as a camera enthusiast, you would likely enjoy using a camera that enables you to manually adjust settings, such as shutter speed and aperture.

If you are interested in digital photography, your first question is probably "What type of camera should I buy?" That question has no simple answer; it depends on your budget, as well as the way you plan to take pictures. Digital camera users come in two

In Depth

Why Are Digital Cameras So Popular?

You can purchase a digital camera or simply use the one that is included on just about every mobile phone purchased. Why are they so popular?

- You can immediately view the pictures you have taken. Most cameras include an LCD screen (Figure 9.2), which is a small boxed element in which the currently selected photo can be viewed. You can scroll through photos, deleting any you do not want to keep.

Figure 9.2 Most digital cameras include an LCD viewing screen.

(continued)

- You can print pictures on a color printer (Figure 9.3). You can also use a dedicated photo printer, which enables you to print various photo sizes, or you can upload photos to a professional printing service. If you want to manipulate a picture, perhaps brightening or cropping it, you can copy the photo from the camera to your computer and use image editing software.

Khomulo Anna/Shutterstock

Figure 9.3 Digital photos can be printed at home using an ink jet printer.

- Digital cameras are excellent devices for "spur of the moment" photos. With nothing more than the camera on your mobile phone, you can capture that unexpected rainbow!
- For some professions, such as insurance adjusters and newspaper reporters, digital cameras provide quick photos that can be viewed and printed (or transferred to electronic storage) in a timely fashion.
- You can improve or alter digital photographs with an image editing software package, such as Adobe Photoshop Elements.
- You can post photographs on a website, perhaps to share with friends online, and you can e-mail photographs to friends and family members.
- You can save pictures on a disk or CD for safekeeping and printing later.
- You might become a better photographer because you will not be concerned about wasting film as you experiment with taking pictures.

basic categories—professionals and consumers. Digital cameras are available in various levels of complexity, with a model for just about any budget and skill level. Consumer digital cameras, often called **point-and-shoot cameras**, are appropriate for most of us who take pictures at home and on vacation. They are perfect for anyone who wants a simple-to-use, lightweight camera to capture images. On the other hand, photographers who must manually adjust photo settings and who are more creative with backgrounds and light settings—perhaps even professional photographers—prefer to use the more complex professional digital cameras. **Digital single-lens reflex (DSLR) cameras** offer such features and have interchangeable lenses. These cameras are sometimes much larger and

Digital Camera Considerations

Owning a digital camera can be a lot of fun. On that family outing, when you are able to view a picture immediately after you take it, you will be pleased that you purchased a digital camera. Even so, digital cameras are not without a few disadvantages.

- *Battery life can be disappointing*, especially if you often use the LCD (viewing screen where you can check the photos you have taken). As you view those photos, the camera uses battery power. Some cameras include a rechargeable battery, which is a handy alternative to replacing smaller batteries, but even so, you must remember to recharge the battery.
- *A digital camera tends to become obsolete more quickly* than its film-based counterpart. With advances in technology, a camera that you paid full price for two years ago might be able to do only a fraction of what a new model can do (especially with respect to the number of megapixels and special features included).
- *Learning to use a digital camera requires a steeper learning curve* than learning to use a film-based camera. Although a digital camera might be simple enough to learn to operate, you will most likely want to learn to use image editing software as well so you can enhance photos and create photo projects or multiple prints. You will also need to know how to interpret camera specifications before you purchase a camera, which requires a higher level of awareness than for purchasing a film-based camera.

Even considering the preceding "disadvantages," you are likely to conclude that they are miniscule when compared to the advantages of creating digital photos. The instant gratification of seeing a picture immediately after shooting it, the ability to modify photos and print them at will, and the sheer fun of sharing photos by e-mail or other electronic avenues is enough to interest even the most devoted film-based camera user.

heavier than a point-and-shoot digital camera, offer more megapixels (described later in this chapter), and come with a higher price tag.

Digital cameras might look like film-based cameras, but they have unique requirements and methods of operation. As you read the camera specifications on the packaging, you will find terms such as *megapixels* and *total zoom*. Before you get the idea that you are not cut out to use such a complicated device, you should know that while the specifications may appear unintelligible, they are easy to interpret and understand.

Digital camera specifications do not have to be mystifying. Figure 9.4 lists a few technical terms and measurements that you are likely to see in advertisements and on packaging. Being aware of those terms, and understanding what the specifications indicate, will certainly help as you evaluate camera choices.

A camera's **optical resolution** is measured in **megapixels**, which indicates how many million pixels the camera is capable of working with when it displays images. A **pixel** (short for *picture element*) is an individual square in the color grid that composes a digital image. The higher the camera resolution, or the more pixels in the grid, the more a picture can be enlarged while retaining picture quality. As you can see in Figure 9.5, a portion of a picture that is significantly enlarged shows individual pixels. Although you will most likely never enlarge

Specification	Description
Viewfinder	The area through which you look when taking a picture. Newer digital cameras do not have a viewfinder and only have an LCD display.
LCD display	A liquid crystal display that shows what you are currently recording or a previously captured photo. The LCD enables the user to instantly see the image and reshoot it if necessary. A disadvantage is that the screen can be difficult to see in bright sunlight. Most digital cameras come with an LCD display.
Flash	A brief, intense, burst of light when lighting on the scene is inadequate. Recommended: AutoFlash.
Flash modes	Auto: Automatic flash activation in low-light situations. Red-eye reduction: Flashes several times before taking the picture. Recommended: A camera that includes flash when it is needed, including red-eye reduction.
Self-timer	A built-in self-timer delays the shutter and enables you to include yourself in a picture. Recommended: Depends on user preference.
Interface	The type of physical connection used to transfer digital images to the computer. The standard connection is a USB port. Some cameras are built to connect wirelessly via Wi-Fi network. Recommended: USB AutoConnect and/or Wi-Fi.
Power supply	The number and type of batteries required to support the camera. Optional AC adapters are sometimes included. Recommended: Rechargeable batteries with a battery charger. To lessen the drain on batteries, it is also preferable to have an AC adapter.
Optical and digital zoom	Optical zoom: Uses the camera's optics to bring the image closer while still maintaining photo quality. (Similar to binoculars.) Digital zoom: Digital zoom enlarges the image mathematically. Quality may be sacrificed. Recommended: Optical zoom of at least 3x. If you want to capture high-resolution images from a distance, you should pay more attention to the optical zoom rather than the digital zoom.
Megapixels	The more pixels, the larger the prints can be. One megapixel is adequate for 4 × 6 prints; an 8 × 10 requires at least 2 megapixels. With 4 megapixels, you can make 11 × 14 prints. Recommended: min of 6 megapixels, although most cameras sold today average about 10 megapixels.

Figure 9.4 You should carefully consider various specifications when choosing a digital camera.

a photo to the magnitude of Figure 9.5, the illustration shows that a picture is actually comprised of pixels. It makes sense that the more pixels the grid has, the clearer the image will be as it is enlarged.

With a higher megapixel rating, you can produce larger prints of photos while maintaining an acceptable level of detail. To print good quality photos at a 5 × 7 size, you will need at least a 2- to 3-megapixel camera. If you plan to print photos as large as 8 × 10, you will need a 3- to 4-megapixel camera. Currently, popular consumer model digital cameras include 10 or more megapixels. Keep in mind that most people really only need about 6 megapixels to take great photographs. In fact, professional photographers suggest that it is more important to use good lenses and good techniques than to pay for increasingly more megapixels.

Another camera specification to keep in mind is the amount and type of memory. Just as film-based cameras save images on film, digital cameras save images on a memory device. Most cameras are equipped with removable memory in the form of a card or stick, which lets you save pictures and transfer them later to a computer or printer. When purchasing a camera, it is crucial to know how much memory comes with the camera. Make sure you factor that into

Figure 9.5 Digital photos are composed of tiny pixels that look like squares. As you enlarge a digital photo the pixels become more apparent.

your comparison; otherwise, you might end up spending money for additional memory when you find that the memory card that came with the camera is limited to fewer pictures than you want to store at one time.

A camera's resolution is adjustable. The camera resolution setting is related to the capacity of the camera's memory device. The higher the resolution setting, the more space each picture will use. Typical memory cards will hold anywhere from 100 to 500 pictures. You can also buy additional memory, which enables you to take more pictures by simply swapping out the memory card.

Most cameras use a form of flash memory (Figure 9.6) to store images. **Flash memory** is small, inexpensive, and rugged. It actually uses solid-state chips to store images. Although flash memory is similar to RAM, it has one very important difference. Flash memory requires no batteries and does not lose contents when power is lost. Photographs are retained indefinitely on flash memory.

Although most cameras on the market today use Secure Digital® (SD) or Secure Digital High Capacity (SDHC) format cards, there is no standard flash card format. Each camera manufacturer may use a particular type of flash card. These cards are not usually interchangeable among cameras. That means that any investment you make in flash cards for your camera could be lost when you move to another camera type. Figure 9.6 shows a typical digital SD memory card.

Digital cameras include not just one zoom setting, but two. The **optical zoom** uses the optics (curvature) of the lens to magnify the image, giving a true reproduction, while the **digital zoom** crops the photo and then enlarges the image mathematically using interpolation. In other words, it guesses what the pixels should be. Interpolation may affect the image quality in a negative way because it is not a true reproduction of the image being taken.

SanDisk Corporation

Figure 9.6 Most cameras on the market today use Secure Digital® (SD) or Secure Digital High Capacity (SDHC) format cards to record photos.

Digital Photography

The optical zoom setting does not change the image size or resolution; therefore, if you want to capture high-resolution images from a distance, you should pay more attention to the optical zoom rather than the digital zoom. Do not be impressed with total zoom (optical + digital) rates. Evaluate each specification separately to ensure that you get the most optical zoom you can afford.

If you plan to take action shots, such as at sports events, consider only those cameras that are configured for fast action. In models not designed for fast action, a picture is not captured immediately after you press the shutter button. Rather, it takes one or two seconds to adjust the settings before taking the picture. Between shots, you might have to wait a few seconds while the camera is busy processing, compressing, and storing the image. Although newer digital cameras tend to include a fast-action setting, that is not necessarily true for all.

Some cameras also include a burst mode, which allows the camera to take several pictures in a row by holding down the shutter button. In that way, as many as one to three shots can be captured per second. Especially when taking fast-action pictures, burst mode can be very helpful.

Digital cameras are notorious for running through batteries. The more you use the LCD screen and flash, the sooner you will need more batteries or must recharge a battery. If your camera has an AC adapter, you can plug in your camera to save battery life when viewing pictures or downloading images to your computer.

Transferring Pictures to a Computer

As you take digital pictures, the photos remain in the camera's memory indefinitely. Even after you download them to a computer, or place the memory card in a photo printer for printing, the pictures remain on the card (unless you move them from the card to a storage device instead of simply copying them). Once the pictures are copied or printed, you may want to erase them from the camera memory card so more pictures can be stored. One of the most aggravating occurrences is to see a *full memory card* message as you are taking photos of an event. Prevent that from occurring by regularly removing pictures that have already been copied or printed from the memory card.

To download photos, you will either **tether** the camera, which is the process of connecting the camera to a computer through a cable, usually through the

USB port, or place the camera memory card in a memory card reader, which Windows recognizes as another disk drive. Often, a computer includes memory card slots so you do not have to use an external memory card reader. The computer is able to read memory cards that are inserted into those slots. A major advantage of copying pictures directly from a memory card (not tethering) is that the process does not drain camera batteries or make the camera unavailable during a download. External card readers are available for popular memory card types, and universal card readers are also available, which are configured to work with several of the most common memory cards. With either approach, Windows 7 has built-in features that make downloading images a breeze. With the assistance of **Windows Live Photo Gallery 2011**, as well as other image editing software selections, you have everything you need to download, edit, and print your digital photos.

To download photos by tethering, connect the camera to your computer using the USB cable that came with the camera, and turn on the camera. Wait a few seconds. In the dialog box that appears (Figure 9.7), click **Import pictures and videos**. The next dialog box gives you a chance to tag the photos. For

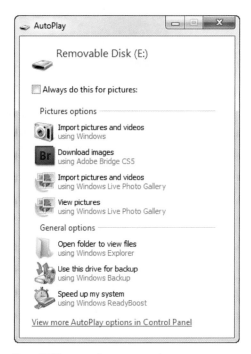

Figure 9.7 When you tether a camera to the computer, you can choose from several options.

example, if all photos on the camera are from a recent beach trip, you might type the tag *Summer 2013 beach* to uniquely identify them. If you want to include several tags, separate them with semicolons. Click **Import**. The imported photos will display. Turn off your camera and disconnect it from the computer. The photos you imported are saved in a subfolder of Pictures, titled with the current date and tag (if you added one earlier).

If the dialog box shown in Figure 9.7 does not appear when you connect your camera, AutoPlay might be turned off. If Windows Live Photo Gallery 2011 is installed on your computer, you can use that software to import your pictures instead. Open Windows Live Photo Gallery 2011. Click **File** and then click **Import from Camera or Scanner**. In the Import Pictures and Videos dialog box, choose your camera and click **Import**.

To download photos by using a memory card reader, remove the memory card from your camera and insert it in the memory card reader slot (or insert it into the computer's built-in card reader slot[s]). If using an external card reader, connect the card reader to the computer's USB port. Respond to the dialog box shown in Figure 9.7 as described in the preceding paragraph.

Unless you specify otherwise, the pictures you download are copied, not moved. That means they still remain in your camera's memory. You can remove them in several ways. The easiest way is to read your camera's instruction manual to determine how to delete them. You can also use Windows 7 to delete them. If you want to use the operating system to manually erase pictures after you import them, leave your camera connected to your computer (and turned on). Click **Start** and then click **Computer**. In the list of disk drives, double-click the removable disk that represents your digital camera or flash memory card. Navigate through the folder structure to locate the digital pictures. Press **Ctrl+A** to select all the pictures (or select a picture and then hold down **Ctrl** as you select any

Graphic File Formats

Image editors and image-capturing devices, such as digital cameras and scanners, assign graphic file types, or formats. Some formats are better suited for e-mail attachments, whereas others are more appropriate for items that are to be printed or saved. The following file types are all bitmap graphic types. Bitmap graphics, created and managed by image editing software, are images composed of a pattern of dots. Devices, such as cameras, will assign an appropriate file type to images you capture, unless you specify that you prefer another file type.

- RAW: A RAW file is essentially a copy of data captured by the digital camera. It is unprocessed data, which means that the file has not been altered, compressed, or manipulated by the camera or computer. When the file is opened with an image editing program, it can be modified and saved in another format.

- BMP: The Windows bitmap format (BMP) is a color-rich, detailed display that is often used for Windows backgrounds or wallpaper. However, bitmap files are very large—any image stored as a BMP is about as large as it can ever be—so BMP files are not often found on Web pages (due to the storage space required and the amount of time it takes to download or view a BMP graphic). Because of their size, BMP files are also not suited as e-mail attachments.

- JPEG: The acronym—pronounced "jay-peg"—stands for Joint Photographic Experts Group. JPEG is one of the most popular methods for displaying images on the Web. It also works well with photographs, supporting up to16 million colors. Because of its compressed size, it is well suited for sending photos as e-mail attachments, or for saving photos on limited disk space. JPEG—also known as JPG—is quickly becoming the standard for transferring images on the Web. You would not want to use a JPEG file for drawing or lettering because it is not well suited for displaying sharp, distinct lines. Because it is a "lossy" format, a JPEG file has actually lost some of its original detail to minimize storage space. However, such loss is usually not detectable by the human eye.

- GIF: Graphics Interchange Format (GIF) is a compressed image format capable of displaying high-resolution color graphics on a variety of hardware devices. GIF graphic files are commonly found on the Web, in such things as color-block banners, logos, line art, and drawings. The strength of the GIF format is seen in images with only a few distinct colors, such as line drawings, although it is sometimes used to represent photographs. Unlike JPEG, GIF format supports transparency, so a color in an image can be made transparent.

- TIFF: Tagged Image File Format (TIFF) is commonly used in desktop publishing, faxing, and 3-D applications. It is often used for transferring images to professional printing companies. Internally, TIFF file headers consist of tagged items, which identify file components to the application software—hence the word "tagged" in the file type name. The TIFF format—also called TIF—was created in 1986 by Aldus Corporation, now Adobe, although Microsoft and Hewlett-Packard also contributed to the effort. TIFF can be used across platforms, including Macintosh, Windows, and UNIX. Because the TIFF format is complex and "lossless," TIFF files are generally larger than GIF or JPEG files.

- PNG: Portable Network Graphics format was originally designed as a replacement for the GIF format. A PNG file can be 5 to 25% more compressed than a GIF file of the same image. It also offers greater color support, better transparency management, and a better method for displaying progressive images. It is used for single images only, not animation.

other pictures to delete). Press **Delete** on the keyboard. Respond affirmatively if asked whether you intend to remove all files. Note that removing pictures from the camera memory card is permanent, so only delete those you are certain you do not want.

Sharing Digital Pictures

Taking photos is fun, but usually the main reason you take photos is to share them. Sharing digital photos with others is easy. Photos can be shared in a number of ways, but most people prefer using e-mail or sharing the photos online. Sending photos by e-mail is convenient when sharing only a few photos. However, attaching more than a few photos to e-mail can be a problem. Most e-mail providers limit the size of attachments, so it may not be possible to attach several photos, regardless of the file type. A JPEG file is compressed so it is typically smaller than a BMP or RAW image. Even so, graphics tend to be large, so e-mail is not the best way to share more than a few pictures. To send an e-mail with photos, simply attach the photos to an e-mail message as described in Chapter 8. You might also use compression software, such as WinZip, to minimize the file size before attaching photos. Often, an ISP, or e-mail provider, automatically compresses graphic files when they are attached.

Photo sharing sites make it easy to share photos with friends and family. As you upload photos to a photo sharing site, you can create digital photo albums, sharing the entire album with friends and family. Many of these sites allow you to upload and share your photos for free, hoping that you, or those you share the photos with, will purchase prints or other photo products. A number of websites like www.flikr.com and www.shutterfly.com (Figure 9.8) enable you to upload photos, share them with others, and create prints, photo books and other memorabilia, such as calendars and mouse pads.

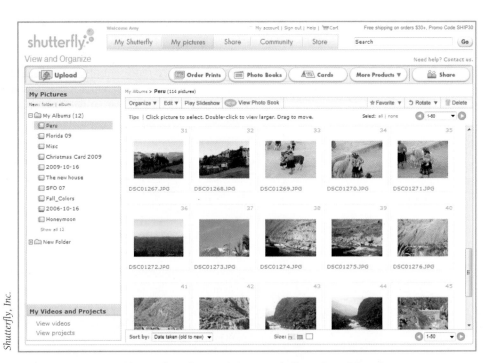

Shutterfly, Inc.

Figure 9.8 Photo sharing sites like www.shutterfly.com make it easy to upload, organize, and share photos.

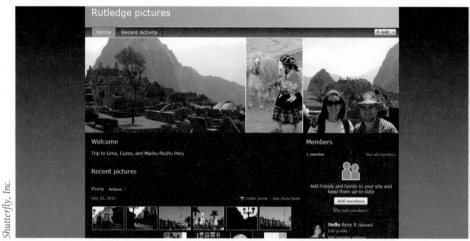

Figure 9.9 Photo-sharing sites enable you to create photo books and even your own website.

How do you upload photos to a photo sharing site? Simply visit a photo sharing site and follow the directions provided. It is usually a very easy process to upload (copy) photos from your computer to the site. Once pictures are uploaded, you can then make minor edits to your photos, such as cropping, adjusting color saturation, and reducing red eye. Photo sharing sites also offer tools to help you organize photos into folders, or albums. Most sites enable you to upload multiple pictures at once so you can quickly move on to the fun task of ordering prints or creating photo projects (Figure 9.9).

Editing Digital Pictures

Using **image editing software**, you can modify pictures, cropping, brightening, or otherwise enhancing photos. Some image editing software is free, such as Windows Live Photo Gallery 2011 (http://explore.live.com/windows-live-photo-gallery), and **Picasa** (http://google.picasa.com), while more full-featured software, such as **Photoshop** and **Photoshop Elements** (www.photoshop.com), costs about $700 and $100 respectively. However, the latter are both available as a free trial for a limited time. Because it is a basic image editing program, Windows Live Photo Gallery 2011 is somewhat limited, but if your goal is to quickly correct color, improve exposure, change composition, or remove red eye, it might be all you need. As your photographic skills improve, you will probably want to explore software that provides more possibilities, such as Adobe Photoshop Elements, but free image editing software is a great way to get started. For the purposes of this chapter, you will learn to edit pictures using Windows Live Photo Gallery 2011.

Using Windows Live Photo Gallery 2011

Windows Live Photo Gallery 2011 is a basic image editor available as a free download. Coordinating with the Pictures folder, the image editing software makes it easy to view, organize, edit, print, and enjoy digital pictures. You can import pictures directly from a digital camera or scanner and save them to folders on a storage device—perhaps a USB, CD, or hard drive. Basic editing includes color correction, adjusting brightness and contrast, cropping, and removing red-eye problems. You can print any number of copies of a picture in any size. In short, although it is not a full-featured image editor, Windows Live Photo Gallery 2011 interfaces well with Windows, enabling you to quickly download, find, edit, and print your pictures. Photos in the gallery are arranged by the date they were taken (Figure 9.10). Using the software, you can easily share photos (and videos) by e-mail or by uploading them to popular sites such as Facebook, Flickr, and YouTube (for video).

Tags make it easy to organize your photos and locate them later. Similar to captions, tags are typically short (usually only one or two words), and they enable the photo to be easily located. For example, you might tag a photo with the name of a location like *San Francisco* or the name of a person like *Daniel*. Then, using the tag, you can quickly locate all of the *San Francisco* or *Daniel* photos for group printing, copying, or editing. Image editing software, such as

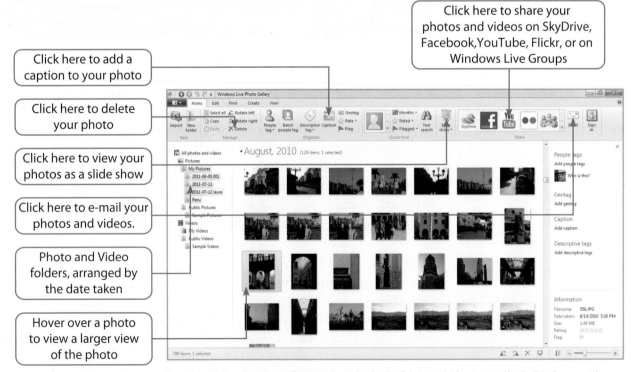

Figure 9.10 Windows Live Photo Gallery 2011 shows thumbnails of photos and videos arranged by the date they were taken.

Image Editing Software: Photoshop Elements and Photoshop Express Editor

Adobe Photoshop has long been recognized as excellent image editing software. However, to take advantage of all its features, you would need hours of training. Preferred by graphic design professionals, it might be overkill for the typical photo enthusiast. For those people, Adobe offers another program—*Photoshop Elements*. Featuring basic editing and photo management features, Photoshop Elements is easy to learn. And its price makes it even more appealing (typically less than $100 for students). Although it is not free, Photoshop Elements includes unique applications like layering, color replacement, and scratch removal. Those features, and many others, might make it well worth its price. Adobe also offers an online program, Photoshop Express Editor, http://www.photoshop.com/tools/expresseditor. The program is free and offers basic photo editing features, including cropping, exposure options, and special effects.

Windows Live Photo Gallery 2011 and Adobe Photoshop Elements, gives you the option of adding a tag to any picture.

Before making changes to a picture, you should save the original. That way you can always return to the original and begin again if you like. Double-click a photo in a gallery to open it. To make a copy using Windows Live Photo Gallery 2011, click the **Edit tab**, and then click **Make a Copy**. Name the photo, indicate a location to save to, and then click **Save**. With the picture open, as shown in Figure 9.11, you can edit or correct the photo.

Click to make a copy of the photo

Click to view the previous picture

Click to view the next picture

Click to auto adjust exposure, color, and to straighten the photo

Drag the sliders to adjust settings

Click to rotate the photo 90 degrees left or right

Drag the slider to zoom in or out

Click to return to the thumbnail view for all photos

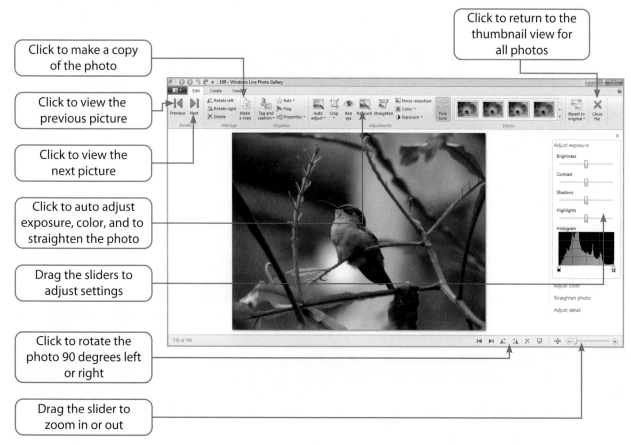

Figure 9.11 Windows Live Photo Gallery 2011 provides editing tools in an easy-to-use interface.

Hands-On

Activity 9.1 Using Windows Live Photo Gallery

You are a travel agent. Having taken some photos during a recent trip to Peru, you want to use those photos to promote your business. In this exercise, you will use Windows Live Photo Gallery 2011 to edit several pictures.

a. Create a folder named *PracComp_Chapter9_Peru* on your flash drive. Copy Peru1.jpg and Peru2.jpg (located on the student data disk) to the PracComp_Chapter9_Peru folder that you just created.

b. Click **Start** and then click **All Programs**. Scroll down, if necessary, and click **Windows Live Photo Gallery**. Windows Live Photo Gallery 2011 opens and displays photos arranged by date. If necessary, sign in to Windows Live.

TROUBLESHOOTING

If Windows Live Photo Gallery 2011 is not installed on your computer, you can download and install the program from http://explore.live.com/windows-live-photo-gallery.

TROUBLESHOOTING

If asked whether to designate Windows Live Photo Gallery 2011 as the program to open various types of graphic files, click **No**.

c. Navigate to the folder you created in Step A. Click on the folder to view the pictures. Double-click **Peru1** (the picture of the Peruvian girl). The picture displays in large view.

TROUBLESHOOTING

If you do not see the folder (or drive) that includes Peru1 and Peru2, click **File** (Figure 9.12) and then click **Include folder**. Click **Add**. Navigate to the folder or drive and click to select it. Click **Include folder**. Click **OK**. Complete Step C.

d. Click **Make a copy**. Save the file as *Prac_Comp_Peru1_yourlastname*.

e. Click **Rotate left** (Figure 9.12). The picture rotates so it is correctly displayed.

f. Click the **upper half of the Crop button**. Place the pointer on a sizing handle (small white box) on the border of the picture so the pointer appears as a double-headed arrow. Drag to crop the picture as shown in Figure 9.13.

TROUBLESHOOTING

If a menu displays when you click Crop, you clicked the lower half of the Crop button instead of the upper half. Click the upper half of the Crop button.

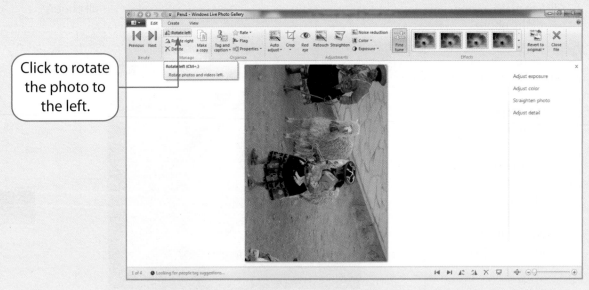

Click to rotate the photo to the left.

Figure 9.12 Rotate the photo.

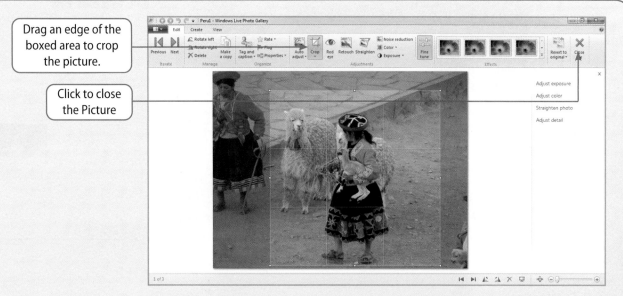

Drag an edge of the boxed area to crop the picture.

Click to close the Picture

Figure 9.13 Crop the photo.

g. Click **Close file**. Double-click **Peru2** (the mountain picture). Click **Make a copy**. Save the picture as *Prac_Comp_Peru2_yourlastname*.

h. Click **Fine Tune**. Click **Adjust color** in the right pane. Drag the **Saturation slider** to experiment with adjusting color (Figure 9.14).

i. Click **Close file**. Click **OK**. Close Windows Live Photo Gallery 2011.

Click to display the pane on the right

Drag the slider to adjust saturation

Figure 9.14 Adjust color saturation.

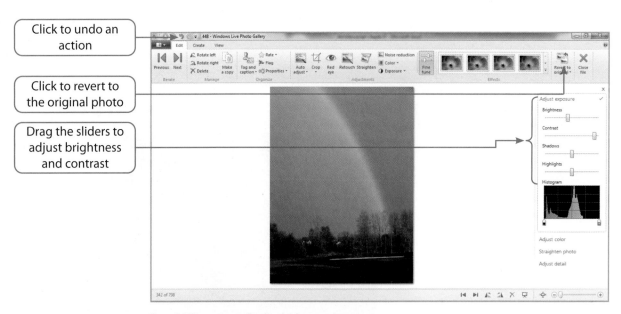

Click to undo an action

Click to revert to the original photo

Drag the sliders to adjust brightness and contrast

Figure 9.15 You can manually adjust brightness and contrast.

Quick Tip

Restoring a Picture to a Previous State

Windows Live Photo Gallery 2011 includes an Undo button that enables you to undo the most recent action. If you are not happy with the results of an operation, simply click **Undo**, as shown in Figure 9.12. If you want to return the picture to its original state, as it was when you first opened the photo, click **Revert to Original**.

To adjust brightness and contrast, you have a couple of choices. You can manually make corrections by clicking **Fine Tune** and then **Adjust Exposure**. Next, move the **Brightness and Contrast** sliders as shown in Figure 9.15. If, instead, you want Windows Live Photo Gallery 2011 to automatically adjust brightness and contrast settings, you can simply click **Auto Adjust** in the Adjustments group. Auto Adjust optimizes brightness, contrast, color temperature, and picture tint in one operation. After using Auto Adjust, you can still manually adjust those settings if you are not entirely pleased with the result.

Undoubtedly, you will want to experiment with color saturation, in which you can actually change the original colors of a photo. To change color, click **Fine Tune** (Figure 9.16) and then click **Adjust Color** in the Fine Tune pane. Drag a slider to increase or decrease color temperature, tint, or saturation. You can create pictures that have little or no color, or highly intense color. You can also adjust the color by selecting a predefined effect (Figure 9.16).

Click Fine Tune to display the panel shown on the right

Select an effect

Drag to adjust color saturation

Figure 9.16 You can manually adjust color saturation.

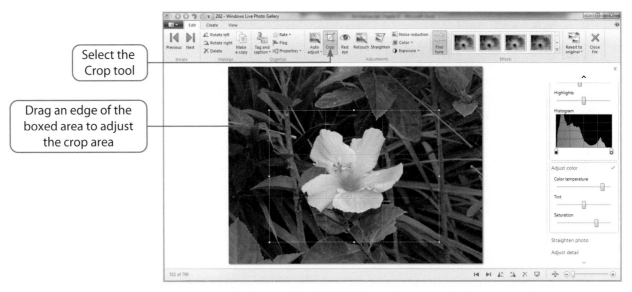

Select the Crop tool

Drag an edge of the boxed area to adjust the crop area

Figure 9.17 Crop a photo by dragging an edge of the boxed area.

When you crop a picture, you indicate an area of a picture that is to remain, discarding everything outside the identified area. You can crop any picture by using the Crop tool, shown in Figure 9.17. When you select the Crop tool, a portion of the current picture is boxed. Drag a box border to increase or decrease the boxed area. The enclosed area is the cropped picture. Click **Apply** (or press **Enter**) to accept changes.

Digital Video

Recording and sharing video is now easier than ever, thanks to digital technology. You can record digital video using various devices. For example, most digital (still) cameras and smartphones have the ability to record short videos. In addition, **digital camcorders**, also called digital video cameras, are designed to record motion images and can record lengthy videos (Figure 9.18). If you plan to record events like recitals or weddings, or if you simply want high-quality video, then a camcorder is your best option. In recent years, camcorders have become extremely affordable (as little as $50), compact, and easy to use. In this section you will learn to record digital video, transfer it to your computer, and share it with others.

Working with Video

A digital camcorder works in much the same way as a digital camera, except that it actually takes multiple still pictures in rapid succession. These still photos are called **frames**, and, when shown one after another, they create the appearance of motion. The number of frames per second is called the **frame rate**.

Figure 9.18 Digital camcorders are designed to record motion images.

Figure 9.19 Digital camcorders come in a number of shapes and sizes. Smaller, compact cameras may include a USB drive for easy transfer of files.

Camcorders and digital cameras share many of the same specifications, such as zoom, megapixels, and memory. They are also available in a number of physical sizes. Small, compact camcorders are the size of a point-and-shoot camera or cell phone. Such camcorders are simple to use, with only a few buttons and a small screen. Often, these small cameras are able to transfer files to a computer or storage device through a USB connection (Figure 9.19). More full-featured (and typically larger) camcorders boast a wide LCD screen (usually about three inches across) as well as more lenses and video features than smaller camcorders.

Video files require a great deal of storage space, so it is important to consider various storage options offered with camcorders. Some camcorders have a built-in hard drive that can typically store up to seven hours of video. When the hard drive is full, however, video files must be deleted or transferred to a computer. Another option is mini DVD (Figure 9.20), in which discs can be removed and viewed on a DVD player. Flash memory is yet another option. Just as with digital cameras, a flash memory card can be swapped out with another when full. This may be one of the best options, since flash memory cards have significantly decreased in price, making them affordable for video storage. Finally, pocket-sized camcorders include a built-in USB drive that can be used to transfer pictures to a computer through a USB port.

Transferring Video to a Computer

After you have recorded a video, you might want to transfer it to your computer so you can edit and share it with others. Transferring videos from a camcorder is similar to transferring pictures from a digital camera. If you are using a camcorder with a hard drive, you can tether the camcorder to the computer. If you are using a camcorder with flash memory, you can use either a card reader or a tether. Some computers have a built-in card reader, so you may not need a stand-alone card reader. If you are using mini DVDs, you can simply put the DVD into your computer's DVD drive. Mini DVDs can be read by a regular DVD drive or a DVD player. You can then transfer the video to your computer, using the software that came with the camcorder, so it can be edited if necessary. If you have a pocket-size camcorder with a built-in USB drive, simply plug the device directly into the computer's USB port and transfer the files.

Editing Video

You can edit a video file, including music, narration, or captions—even trimming (removing) part of the video and adding features such as fades and color change. **Windows Live Movie Maker 2011** is free software that includes basic editing functions. Apple's **iMovie '11** (part of the iLife suite, costing $49), **Adobe Premiere Elements** ($89), and **Adobe Premiere Pro** ($799) are also popular, but they are not free. Most types of video editing software are fairly simple to learn, with many offering templates and other features that enable you to quickly modify a movie.

Figure 9.20 Some camcorders record to a mini DVD.

Uploading Video to YouTube

YouTube, a popular video sharing site owned by Google, is one of the five most frequently visited websites on the planet. Amateur videographers, as well as professional movie makers and major corporations, post videos to the site. Videos posted on YouTube are frequently shared with others. When a video becomes extremely popular it is said to have gone "viral."

You can upload a video you have recorded to YouTube. With various privacy settings, YouTube enables you to control the availability of your video. You must create a YouTube account in order to post, or upload, a video. To create an account, go to www.youtube.com. Click **Create Account**. Complete the registration form, making sure to read the YouTube Terms of Use, Google Terms of Service, and the Privacy Policy. Click **I accept**. In some cases, YouTube will provide a verification code to finalize the account setup. It is especially important to note the sections regarding copyright infringement. Uploading videos containing third-party content such as recorded television shows or songs is considered copyright infringement.

With a YouTube account, you can upload videos. At www.youtube.com, click **Upload**. Sign in and follow directions to upload a video. Remember that video files are large, so transferring video can take a few minutes.

In Depth

Windows Live Movie Maker

Windows Live Movie Maker 2011 (Figure 9.21) is included in Windows Live Essentials, a bundle of free photo, movie, instant messaging, and social networking software. Windows Live Movie Maker 2011 is a simple, easy-to-use movie editing program. You can trim a video, add captions or credits, and include basic visual effects. The software also makes it easy to upload video to a number of popular sites, such as YouTube and Facebook.

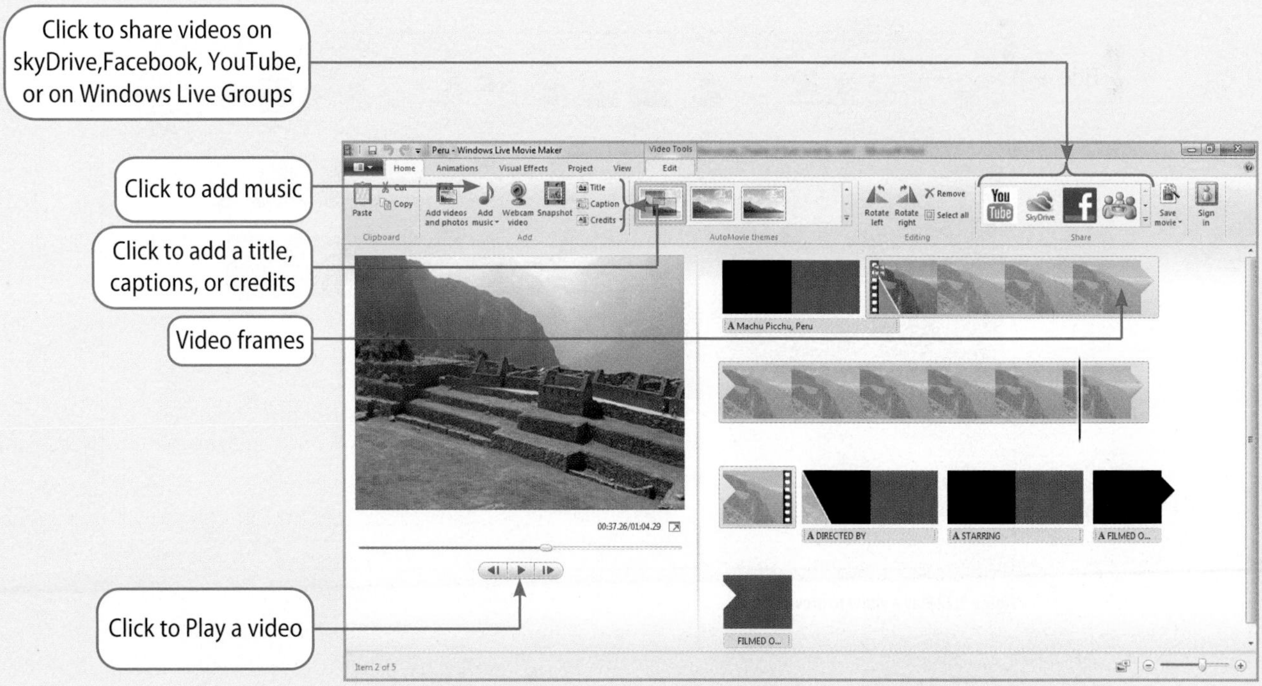

Click to share videos on skyDrive, Facebook, YouTube, or on Windows Live Groups

Click to add music

Click to add a title, captions, or credits

Video frames

Click to Play a video

Figure 9.21 Windows Live Movie Maker 2011 is a free, video-editing software program.

Hands-On

Activity 9.2 Using Windows Live MovieMaker 2011

Typical home videos are often shaky and have unwanted background noise. Using Windows Live Movie Maker 2011, you can correct a video so that it has a more professional feel. On a trip to Peru you took a short video of Machu Picchu, a 15th century Inca village high atop the Andes mountain range. You want to edit your video so you can share it with your friends.

a. Create a folder named *PracComp_Chapter9_Video* on your flash drive.

b. Copy the *Peru_Video* file from the student data disk to the folder that you created in Step A.

c. Click **Start** and then click **All Programs**. Scroll down, if necessary, and click **Windows Live Movie Maker**.

TROUBLESHOOTING

If Windows Live Movie Maker is not installed on your computer, you can download and install the program from http://explore.live.com/windows-live-movie-maker.

d. Click **Add videos and photos** (Figure 9.22). Navigate to the *PracComp_Chapter9_Video* folder and double-click *Peru_Video*.

e. Click the **Play button** below the video screen to play the video (Figure 9.22).

f. Click the **Edit** tab. Click **Video volume**. Drag the slider to the left to mute all sounds.

g. Click **Trim tool**. Click the **Start point box** and type **15.00s**. Leave the End point as is. See Figure 9.23.

h. Click **Save trim**. Play the video.

i. Click the **Speed box** on the Edit tab. Change the speed to *0.5x*.

j. Click the **Home tab**. Click **Title** (Figure 9.22). Change the title to *Machu Picchu, Peru*.

k. With the **Format** tab open, choose an effect (of your choosing) from the Effects group at the top right (Figure 9.24). You can preview effects by hovering over each effect. Click an effect to apply it to the video. Click the **Home tab**.

l. Click **Credits**. Type your name. Click the **Scroll effect** (Figure 9.25).

m. Click **the first frame** in the right pane, titled *Machu Picchu*. Click **Preview full screen** (Figure 9.25). At the end of the video, after the credits, press **Esc** to return to editing the video.

n. Click the upper half of the **Save movie button**. Save the video in the *PracComp_Chapter9_Video* folder as *Prac_Comp_Video_yourlastname*. Click **Close**. Close Windows Live Movie Maker 2011.

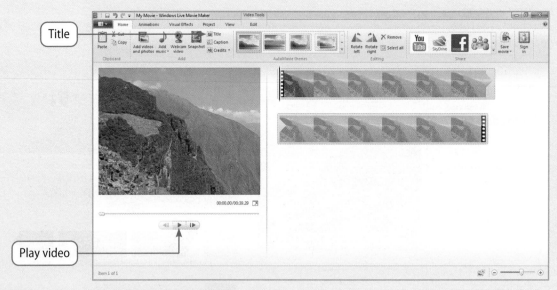

Figure 9.22 Play a video to preview it.

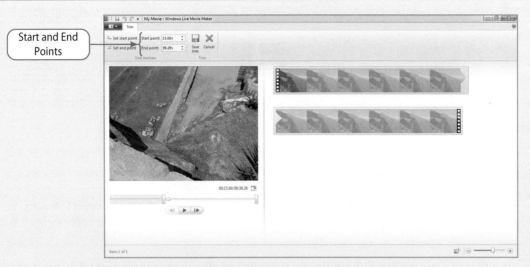

Start and End Points

Figure 9.23 To trim the first few seconds of the video, click the Edit tab and select Trim.

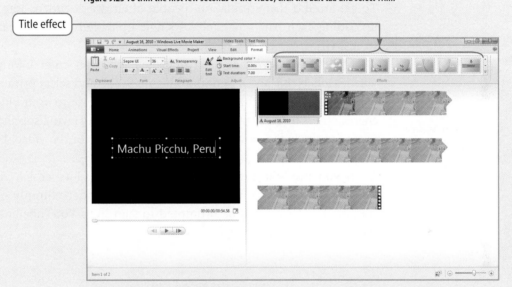

Title effect

Machu Picchu, Peru

Figure 9.24 Add a title to the video and edit the effect.

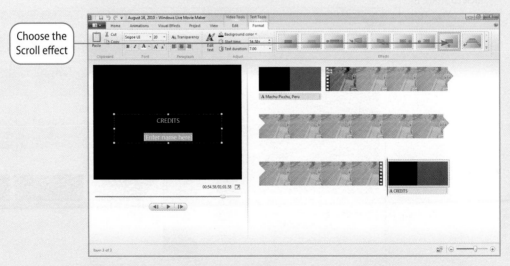

Choose the Scroll effect

CREDITS
Enter name here

Figure 9.25 Add credits to the video and edit the effect.

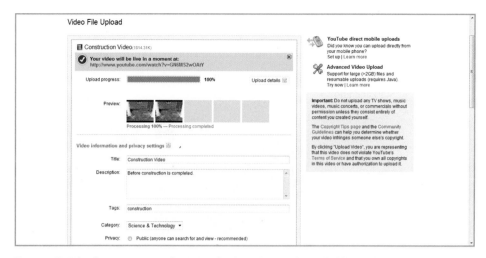

Figure 9.26 YouTube allows you to create a description of a video so that it can be searched for by others.

YouTube only allows you to upload videos that are 15 minutes long or less. To get around that stipulation, people often divide videos into several parts, uploading each part separately. A single uploaded video file can be no larger than 2 GB.

Once your video has been uploaded, you can enter information for the video, such as title and description (Figure 9.26), and select privacy settings. You will also choose whether to grant YouTube a license to your video content, or enable others to freely use and distribute the video. Having specified information related to the video, you will receive a direct URL for the video. Using the URL, others can view the video.

If you use Windows Live Movie Maker 2011 to edit a video, you can also use the software to upload and share a video. Simply click YouTube (Figure 9.27). You will be prompted to sign in to YouTube and then upload the video.

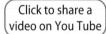

Click to share a video on You Tube

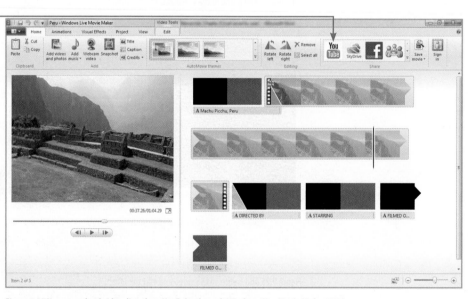

Figure 9.27 You can upload video directly to YouTube through Windows Live Movie Maker 2011.

Music

It seems that no area has been affected more by the digital revolution than music. Today, you can listen to virtually anything, when you want, and where you want. Do you want to listen to Beethoven's 5th as performed by the London Symphony Orchestra or by Brian Setzer (with a jazz flare)? You can simply visit www.iTunes.com or www.Amazon.com, and purchase and download your favorites in a matter of minutes. In this section, you will learn about digital audio files, and how to download and play music on a portable media player.

Figure 9.28 The iPod shuffle is about the size of a U.S. silver dollar. It can hold hundreds of songs and costs about $49.

Working with Digital Audio

In the past, music was stored in analog form on a vinyl record or cassette tape. Music played as a continuous wave of sound—through physical grooves on the vinyl record or through a fluctuation in magnetic recording on a cassette tape. A digital recording is generated when an analog wave is converted into a sequence of numbers that can be read by a computer or other device. The sound is then saved as an audio file. The quality of digital sound is excellent and can be reproduced exponentially without loss of quality (unlike, for example, a photocopy of a photocopy). Also, with advances in storage technology, hundreds (if not thousands) of music files can be easily stored on a device the size of a silver dollar (Figure 9.28).

A music file can be stored in one of several different file types. MP3, AAC, and WMA are common.

- MP3 files – MPEG-1 or Moving Picture Experts Group Layer-3 – the standard format for most digital audio players.
- AAC – Advanced Audio Coding – the standard format for iPod, iPhone, iTunes and some mobile phones. Can be converted to MP3 format so it can be played on other devices.
- WMA – Windows Media Audio – created by Microsoft. Plays on Windows Media Player as well as the Zune player and other digital audio players.

In Depth

The Digital Library

Did you know that some local libraries offer digital content for free? Some offer free downloads of audio books, music, video, and e-books for e-readers like the Kindle. All you need is a library membership, your computer, and your portable music player, Kindle, or smartphone (if you choose to download the files there). If your library has the service, you can go to the library website, and download files without ever having to visit the library! You will first have to download software such as OverDrive (www.overdrive.com) to manage digital books that are under the protection of digital rights management (DRM). What you are permitted to do with the digital content may vary. For example, some audio books may permit you to burn the book to CD, listen to it on your computer, or download it to MP3, while others might not allow all those actions. Just like a printed book, your digital book will have a due date, at which time the files automatically expire.

Using Portable Media Players (PMPs)

As you learned in Chapter 8, you can store and play music and video files using a **portable media player (PMP)**, like an Apple iPod or Microsoft Zune. These players range in features, storage capacity, size, and cost. The iPod Shuffle, for example, does not have a screen, and therefore, you can't see the name of the song that is playing. It does make up for the lack of a screen with its small size, which is attractive to many. Some media players play only audio files, while others play audio and video; some can even store digital photos.

Most players enable you to create your own playlists. Playlists make it easy to arrange music into categories. Most PMPs store music on flash memory or on a hard drive. A player using a hard drive, such as the Apple iPod, provides approximately 160 GB of storage space—enough to save about 40,000 songs. A player with flash memory includes between 1 GB and 32 GB of space for music. Some players allow you to swap out flash cards so you can share music between devices. The number of songs a player can hold actually depends on the **sampling rate**, or the quality of conversion from analog to digital. The higher the sampling rate, the better the quality, but the larger the file size. All PMPs have software that facilitates the transfer of files from a computer to a music player. Most players use a USB connection to connect to the computer in order to transfer files.

Ripping Music

You have a dilemma. You purchased an MP3 player or an iPod and you have a number of music CDs. How do you get the music from a CD to your player? You can use specialized software to **rip**, or copy, the songs into an MP3 or other format. iTunes and Windows Media Player software both include the capability to rip songs from a CD. To rip a song from a CD using Windows Media Player, place the CD into the computer's CD/DVD drive. The steps to follow to rip a CD vary, depending upon the version of Windows Media Player installed. If Windows Media Player is not already open, it will open in the Now Playing mode. Point to the upper-right corner of the Windows Media Player window and click **Switch to Library**. By default, songs on a CD will be ripped in WMA (Windows Media Audio) format; however, you can select a different format (perhaps MP3 or WAV) when you click **Rip Settings** and then **More options**. Change the format and click **OK**. If you do not want to rip all songs on the CD, clear the check box beside any song you do not want to include. Click **Rip CD**. The ripped songs will be saved in the Music Library on your hard drive, accessible when you click **Start** and then **Music**. You can then use the player's software to transfer the songs to an MP3 player.

Downloading Music

One of the biggest advantages of digital music is that you do not have to go to the store to buy music; you can download it right from the Internet. A number of sites sell music downloads, including www.iTunes.com, www.Amazon.com, and www.Rhapsody.com. With sites like iTunes (Figure 9.29) and Amazon, you no longer have to purchase an entire album of songs; most songs are available for individual purchase for about 99 cents each. Some sites, like Rhapsody, offer music on a subscription basis. For about $10 per month, you can stream all the music you want. At a higher subscription level, you can download and transfer music to a portable player. These files cannot be shared, and once you stop paying the monthly fee you no longer have the ability to play the files.

Eldad Carin/istockphoto

Figure 9.29 iTunes is a software program that lets you manage music files. With the iTunes store and iCloud all of your music can be accessed from an iPhone. (Shown above.)

Chapter Summary

- Today, music, photos and videos are stored in digital form. In this context, digital means that a series of numbers (using the binary system of zeros and ones) is generated to represent an image or sound. *329*

- A digital camera captures images without the aid of photographic film. It records images digitally so that you can download them to a computer and use a graphics program to manipulate and print the pictures, if you like. *330*

- There are several specifications that you should be aware of with respect to digital cameras: optical resolution, storage (memory), and optical and digital zoom. *333*

- A camera's optical resolution is measured in megapixels, which indicates how many million pixels the camera is capable of working with when it displays images. *333*

- Most digital (still) cameras and smartphones have the ability to record short videos. *347*

- Digital camcorders, also called digital video cameras, are designed to record motion images and can record lengthy videos. *347*

- Like digital cameras, optical resolution, storage and zoom are also specifications that should be taken into consideration for digital camcorders. *348*

- Music can also be stored in digital form using portable media players (PMPs) like the iPod or Zune which can store thousands of songs on flash memory or on a hard drive. *354*

Key Terms

Adobe Premiere Elements *348*	**Frame rate** *347*	**Point-and-shoot camera** *332*
Adobe Premiere Pro *348*	**Image editing software** *341*	**Portable media player (PMP)** *354*
Analog *330*	**iMovie '11** *348*	**Rip** *354*
Digital *329*	**Megapixel** *333*	**Sampling rate** *354*
Digital camcorder *347*	**Optical resolution** *333*	**Tag** *342*
Digital camera *330*	**Optical zoom** *335*	**Tether** *336*
Digital single-lens reflex (DSLR) camera *332*	**Photo sharing site** *340*	**Windows Live Movie Maker 2011** *348*
Digital zoom *335*	**Photoshop** *341*	**Windows Live Photo Gallery 2011** *337*
Flash memory *335*	**Photoshop Elements** *341*	**YouTube** *349*
Frame *347*	**Picasa** *341*	
	Pixel *333*	

Multiple Choice

1. A device that records images digitally so you can download them to a computer and use a graphics program to manipulate and print them is called _____.
   a. a camcorder.
   b. PMP.
   c. a digital camera.
   d. SLR.

2. A _____ is an image composed of millions of tiny pixels that look like small squares.
   a. DSLR
   b. digital photograph
   c. PMP
   d. tag

3. A graphic file that can easily be sent through e-mail because of its small file size but is not well suited for displaying sharp, distinct lines is a _____ file.
   a. WAV
   b. RAW
   c. BMP
   d. JPEG

4. Similar to a caption, a _____ makes photos searchable.
   a. megapixel
   b. frame
   c. tag
   d. tether

5. Digital cameras most commonly save photos to a _____.
   a. mm film reader
   b. mini DVD
   c. flash memory device
   d. hard drive

6. A device that plays digital audio and video files is a _____.
   a. digital camera
   b. portable media player
   c. camcorder
   d. flash player

7. Which of the following is not a program that can be used to crop photos and adjust color saturation for photo images?
   a. Microsoft Live Photo Gallery 2011.
   b. YouTube.
   c. Picasa.
   d. Photoshop.

8. All of the following should be considered when choosing a digital camera except:
   a. resolution (megapixels).
   b. optical zoom.
   c. camera size.
   d. digital photo sites.

9. _____ is a popular site to view and upload video files.
   a. Flikr
   b. YouTube
   c. iMovie
   d. Shutterfly

10. Still photos, called _____, are shown one after another to create the appearance of motion in a video.
    a. frames
    b. pixels
    c. tags
    d. moves

11. Shutterfly and Flickr are examples of
    a. social networking sites.
    b. photo-sharing sites.
    c. image-editing software.
    d. video-editing software.

12. A portable media player can play _____, a common music file format.
    a. TIFFs
    b. MP3s
    c. PNGs
    d. MPEGs

13. The iPod is a popular _____ device.
    a. portable media player
    b. digital camcorder
    c. digital camera
    d. tablet

14. Digital camcorders may use any of the following storage media except:
    a. mini DVD.
    b. flash memory.
    c. hard drive.
    d. VHS.

15. The act of copying music from a CD to a computer or PMP is called
    a. ripping.
    b. tagging.
    c. deleting.
    d. moving.

True/False

Circle **T** if the statement is true or **F** if the statement is false.

T   F   1. In analog format, a series of numbers is created to represent an image or sound.

T   F   2. Memory cards cannot be reused.

T   F   3. A point-and-shoot camera has interchangeable lenses.

T   F   4. Digital zoom and optical zoom are the same.

T   F   5. A camera's resolution is measured in megapixels.

T   F   6. It is illegal to rip music you purchased from a CD and put it on a portable media player.

T   F   7. AAC is the most common format for digital audio files.

T   F   8. Some digital camcorders use hard drives to save recorded video.

T   F   9. Smartphones most often have built-in digital cameras.

T   F   10. Some digital cameras can be used to record video.

End of Chapter Exercises

Digital Cameras

Your friend is looking into purchasing a digital camera. Write a short summary, in a Word document, about the various features he or she should look for when purchasing a camera. Explain what features you find most important and why. Be sure to discuss the difference between point-and-shoot cameras and DSLR cameras. Explain how much he or she should expect to spend, and how many megapixels would be appropriate. Your friend already has a smartphone with a built-in camera. Explain why he or she might still want to purchase a camera.

Complete an Internet search and find two cameras you would recommend. Be sure to note the websites in your document.

Save your file as LastName_FirstName_PracComp_Ch9_Camera.

Digital Music

You work for an advertising agency and you have just been assigned to work on an orange juice commercial. The commercial will show a farmer picking oranges, and then a family drinking juice at a breakfast table. Your manager has asked you to come up with a few song samples that could potentially be used in the commercial. Using the Internet, search for three songs that would be appropriate for the commercial.

Put your information in a Word document. It may be easiest to create a table to complete the following: List the songs. Provide the URLs of the website(s) where you located the songs. Is any software required to download the music files to your computer? If so, what kind of software? Were you able to listen to a sample of the songs? How much does each song cost?

Save your file as LastName_FirstName_PracComp_Ch9_Music.

Digital Video

You are the owner of a yoga studio. You recently purchased a digital camcorder. Discuss five ways you could use the camcorder for your business.

Put your answers in a Word document. Save your file as LastName_FirstName_PracComp_Ch9_Video.

Appendix

USING A LEARNING MANAGEMENT SYSTEM

A learning management system (LMS), such as Blackboard or Moodle, is a software application that enables you to access course content online. Your instructor might have chosen to use a learning management system to enhance the delivery of course content and/or to facilitate communication, post assignments and assessments, and maintain grades and attendance records of students. Not exclusive to online classes, learning management systems can also support blended or hybrid courses in which you meet with your instructor in class but submit assignments and assessments online, using an online calendar to stay on track and an e-mail or chat function to communicate with others in the class.

Typically, the license to use an LMS is acquired by an educational institution, with the software housed on a campus server. For example, if your college chooses to use Blackboard for online or blended course management, you will most likely visit the website of a college server to log in to your class site. Often, a college also provides online assistance, in the form of a help page (Figure 1), for issues related to student and instructor use of the adopted learning management system. Ask your instructor if such assistance is provided by your college. In addition, an LMS sponsor (such as Blackboard or Moodle) often provides general assistance with questions related to the overall operation of the product (Figure 2), although such assistance is not specific to the configuration of your college's LMS installation.

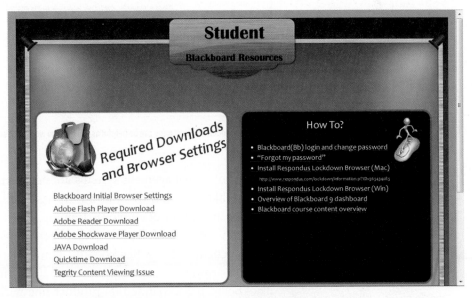

Student
Blackboard Resources

Required Downloads and Browser Settings

Blackboard Initial Browser Settings
Adobe Flash Player Download
Adobe Reader Download
Adobe Shockwave Player Download
JAVA Download
Quicktime Download
Tegrity Content Viewing Issue

How To?

- Blackboard(Bb) login and change password
- "Forgot my password"
- Install Respondus Lockdown Browser (Mac)
  http://www.respondus.com/lockdown/information.pl?ID=363434085
- Install Respondus Lockdown Browser (Win)
- Overview of Blackboard 9 dashboard
- Blackboard course content overview

Figure 1 You can often find help online, related to a learning management system.

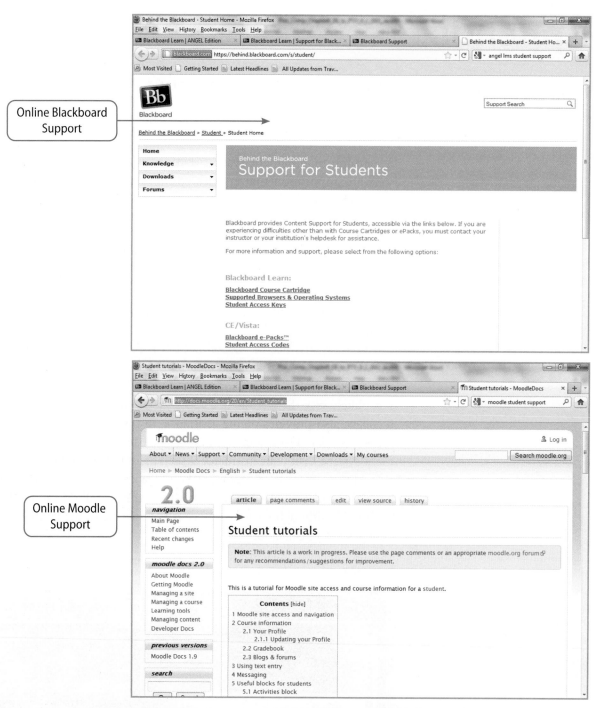

Online Blackboard Support

Online Moodle Support

Figure 2 A student support page can be helpful as you learn to work with an LMS.

Quick Tip

Blackboard Support

Find general support for Blackboard products (including Angel) at https://behind.blackboard.com/s/student/. Moodle provides student support at http://docs.moodle.org/20/en/Student_tutorials.

Learning management systems are not restricted to educational use. In fact, you are likely to find them in businesses of all sizes, as well as in colleges and schools, in support of employee training.

With dozens of learning management systems available, perhaps the most recognizable is Blackboard. Through the acquisition of several electronic learning (e-learning) software solutions, such as WebCT and Angel, Blackboard has expanded its product line within the newest Blackboard LMS release—Blackboard Learn 9.1.

Quickly gaining recognition and market share in the educational community, Moodle is a free LMS. In an open-source system, users can download, change, share, improve, and customize the product. As is true of other LMS platforms, Moodle is used to create online content and encourage user interaction and communication.

If your institution uses an LMS for course delivery and communication, your instructor will most likely include information on the syllabus related to logging in and accessing course material. In the format of frequently asked questions, this appendix provides assistance with general guidelines for using Blackboard, Angel, and Moodle.

Blackboard

Blackboard provides online access to course materials, including assignments, lecture notes and videos, slides, and hyperlinks, as shown in Figure 3. In addition, you can view a class calendar, submit assignments, participate in class discussions, and receive instructor feedback. If your class uses Blackboard, your institution and instructor have customized the interface to include only those items that are relevant to your course. In addition, the version of Blackboard used by your college might vary from the version shown in the figures within this section. For that reason, although your Blackboard interface will be similar to that shown in Figure 3, it will not be identical. In this section, you will explore commonly asked questions regarding Blackboard.

How Can I Log In to My Class?

Your college has provided a user name and password for you to use in logging in to your Blackboard course website. Your instructor will provide the URL as well as login information. When you visit the URL, you will enter your user name and password, as shown in Figure 4. After logging in, click the course in which you are enrolled.

What If I Do Not See My Class Listed?

Your college or instructor must make a class available before you will see it listed. It is possible that the class will not be available until the first class day. Check your syllabus or college's support website for information related to course availability. Your instructor or a member of your college's educational software support staff can let you know when the course will be available or what might be preventing you from accessing the course.

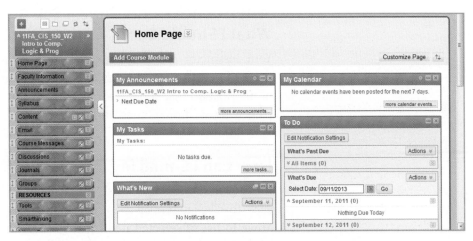

Figure 3 Blackboard is a popular LMS.

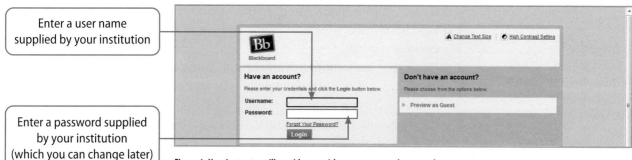

Enter a user name supplied by your institution

Enter a password supplied by your institution (which you can change later)

Figure 4 Your instructor will provide you with a user name and password.

Quick Tip
Blackboard Links
Your instructor or institution might have configured Blackboard to include more or fewer links than those shown in the figures in this section. Buttons on the left might be renamed, rearranged, or categorized differently.

I Am Enrolled in Several Courses That Use Blackboard. However, the Buttons on the Left Are Not the Same From One Course to Another. Why Not?

It is likely that each instructor has customized his or her course to include those buttons that are relevant to the particular course. Blackboard is flexible, so an instructor can easily rename and rearrange buttons, showing some while hiding others. For that reason, it is likely that each Blackboard section in which you are enrolled will have different buttons.

May I Access Blackboard on a Mobile Device?

Blackboard provides a Blackboard Mobile Learn component that your institution might have purchased, making it possible to access a course from a mobile device. Check with your instructor.

Where Can I Find the Course Syllabus?

Typically, the course syllabus is located when you click the Syllabus button on the left. If you do not see a Syllabus button, ask your instructor for the location of the syllabus.

When I Click Home Page, I See Announcements. Is That What I Should See?

Your instructor can customize the Home page to show any course material. Often, the instructor chooses to display announcements so you remain aware of information that should be shared with you. However, the content of a home page will vary from course to course.

How Can I E-mail My Instructor or Another Student?

Click **Course Messages**, as shown in Figure 5. Click **Create Message** and then click **To**. Click to select a recipient (hold **Ctrl** to click multiple recipients). Click the **Move to list of selected items arrow**. Click the **Subject box** and type a subject. Click the **Message box** and type the e-mail message. Click **Submit**.

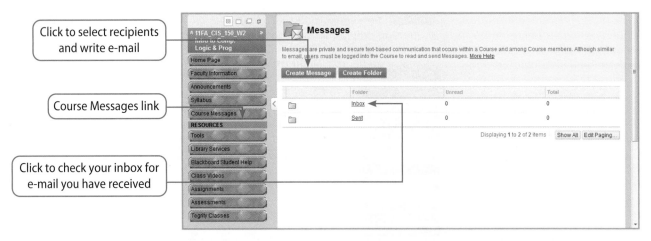

Click to select recipients and write e-mail

Course Messages link

Click to check your inbox for e-mail you have received

Figure 5 Depending upon the settings selected by your instructor, you might have access to class e-mail through Blackboard.

Quick Tip
Check Blackboard Mail
Check for e-mail by clicking **Course Messages**, as shown in Figure 5, and then **Inbox**.

How Can I View Class Announcements?

Click the **Announcements button** on the left. It is also possible that your instructor has configured the Home page to show Announcements. In that case, you will see Announcements when you log in to Blackboard.

How Can I Submit an Assignment?

It really depends upon the configuration of your Blackboard course site and the manner in which your instructor prefers that you submit assignments. Typically, you will click an **Assignments button** on the left. An assignment could be a file that you upload, a video to view, an exam (although exams are more typically included in an Assessments section), or another item. The icon at the left of the assignment indicates the assignment type, as shown in Figure 6. Click the **assignment name**.

If the assignment is a file to upload, read any information supplied by your instructor and then click **Browse My Computer** (or **Browse for Local File**). Locate and double-click the file. Browse for additional files, if necessary. Once all files are attached, click **Submit**.

How Can I Check My Grades?

You can check grades for any assignment or exam submitted, if your instructor has made available the option to check grades. To check your grades, click

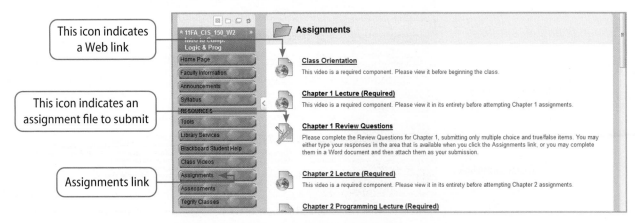

This icon indicates a Web link

This icon indicates an assignment file to submit

Assignments link

Figure 6 Assignments can be files to upload, videos, or quizzes.

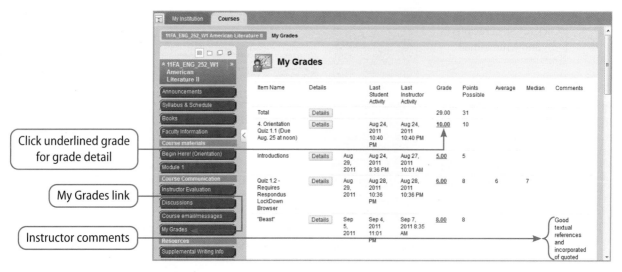

Figure 7 Check your grades in Blackboard.

Click underlined grade for grade detail

My Grades link

Instructor comments

Quick Tip
Blackboard Grades

If your instructor grades an assignment instead of enabling Blackboard to automatically grade it, grades might not be available immediately after submission of assignments. Instead, it may be several days before you can view an assignment grade. An exclamation point will display instead of a score if no grade has been given.

My Grades (or click **Tools** and then **My Grades**). Instructor comments will show in the Comments column, as shown in Figure 7. For additional grade information, click the **exclamation point** or the **underlined score** in the Grade column. If the assignment had multiple attempts, you must click the particular assignment score for additional information.

How Can I Participate in a Class Discussion?

Click **Discussions** (or click **Tools** and then **Discussions**, or **Discussion Board**).

To post to a thread, which is a series of discussions and responses, click the **underlined Forum title**, as shown in Figure 8. Click **Create Thread** and type a subject, which is the title your readers will see. Type your response in the Message box. To attach a file to your discussion post, click **Attach File** and browse for the file. Double-click the file. Click **Submit**.

To read and reply to a discussion post, click the **underlined Forum title** and navigate through any other discussion responses by clicking the underlined titles. Having displayed the item to which you want to reply, click **Reply**, as shown in Figure 9. Type your response, attach a file if desired, and click **Submit**.

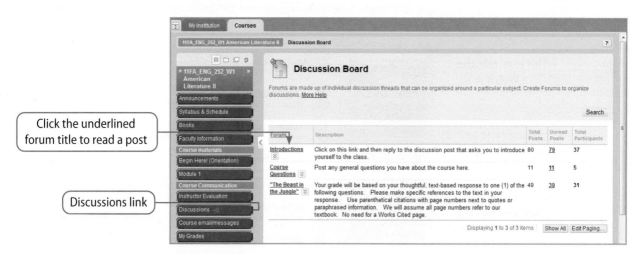

Click the underlined forum title to read a post

Discussions link

Figure 8 Your instructor might ask you to participate in a class discussion.

Click to reply to a post

Figure 9 Reply to a post in the Discussions area.

What If My Instructor Cannot See My Discussion Post?

Most likely, you clicked Save Draft, or Save as Draft, rather than Submit. To locate and resubmit your post, enter the discussion board or forum where your post should be. You might have to point to **Display** and then click **Show All** to see all posts. Look for the word Draft next to your post, and also in the Status column. Click the **underlined post title** and then click **Edit**. Finally, click **Save**.

How Can I Return to a Previously Viewed Page?

Using "breadcrumbs," Blackboard makes it easy to return to a previously viewed area of the current section. Breadcrumbs is a navigation aid found in some user interfaces, such as Blackboard. Typically appearing as a horizontal line across the top of a window, a breadcrumb trail, as shown in Figure 10, enables you to click any segment of the breadcrumb trail to return to that location. The term is borrowed from the trail of breadcrumbs left by Hansel and Gretel in the popular fairy tale. As shown in Figure 10, you can click a parent folder of a current location to trace your steps back (hence, the name *breadcrumbs*). The browser's Back button is another way to return to previously viewed pages within Blackboard.

How Can I Take an Exam?

Click **the button indicated by your instructor** (usually Assignments, Content, Assessments, or Exams, depending upon how your instructor has

Breadcrumbs (click to backtrack to previously viewed pages)

Figure 10 Breadcrumbs are links that enable you to easily return to previously viewed pages.

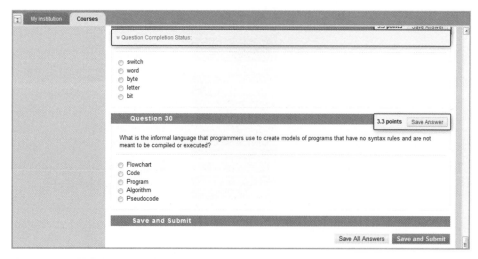

switch
word
byte
letter
bit

Question 30   3.3 points   Save Answer

What is the informal language that programmers use to create models of programs that have no syntax rules and are not meant to be compiled or executed?

Flowchart
Code
Program
Algorithm
Pseudocode

Save and Submit

Save All Answers   Save and Submit

Figure 11   When taking an exam in Blackboard, be sure to save and submit your answers.

set up the class website). Click the **exam title** and then click **Begin**, after reading any instructions provided. Complete the exam and click **Save and Submit** (Figure 11).

In Depth

Exam Tips

Consider the following tips when taking an exam in Blackboard:

- Read all exam instructions carefully. They might tell you exactly how to take the exam and will include any special instructions provided by your instructor.
- Be sure to disable any popup blocker as it could interfere with the display of exam questions. You might also find it necessary to temporarily disable your firewall.
- Only begin an exam when you have plenty of uninterrupted time to devote to it and make sure that no other programs or browser windows are open as you take the exam.
- Be aware of your instructor's policy regarding how technical problems that might occur during an exam will be handled. Such problems might include an inadvertent loss of power or other interruption.
- Read each exam item carefully, and allow the page to load completely before answering a question.
- Do not use the browser's Back and Forward buttons to navigate to previously viewed questions. Instead, use the arrow keys or scroll bars. Note that if the exam displays questions one screen at a time, you may not be able to backtrack.
- Consider saving each question as it is presented (if the exam is configured to provide that option), but do so only if you are certain that you have made the intended response. That way, you are less likely to lose or overlook any responses.
- Be sure to click **Save and Submit** when you have answered all questions. You should see a confirmation page if the submission was successful.

Angel

Angel is an LMS that enables an instructor to manage course materials and to communicate with students online. Formally titled Blackboard Learn Angel Edition, the LMS will be supported by its parent company, Blackboard, through 2014. Using Angel, you can submit assignments and exams, send and receive e-mail, participate in online discussions and chat rooms, and access course material. Schools and companies that use Angel appreciate its capability to be tailored to specific institutional needs. In this section, you will explore Angel. Because it is possible to modify the appearance and tools included in Angel, the Angel interface you work with might vary from that shown in the figures in this section.

How Can I Log In to My Class?

Your college has provided a user name and password for you to use in logging in to your Angel course website. Your instructor will provide the URL as well as login information. When you visit the website, you will enter your user name and password as shown in Figure 12. After logging in, click the course from the list on the left.

What If I Do Not See My Class Listed?

Your college or instructor must make a class available before you are able to see it listed. It is possible that the class will not be available until the first class day. Check your syllabus or college's support website for information related to course availability. Your instructor or a member of your college's educational software support staff can let you know when the course will be available or what might be preventing you from accessing the course.

I See Classes From This Semester as Well as From Other Semesters. How Can I "Unclutter" the Course List?

Point to any class and then click the **subsequent pencil icon**. Deselect any courses that you no longer wish to see, leaving those checked that should remain in your course list. Click **Save**.

May I Access Angel on a Mobile Device Like My iPhone?

Angel's parent company, Blackboard, provides a Blackboard Mobile Learn for Angel component that your institution might have purchased, making it possible to access a course from a mobile device. Check with your instructor.

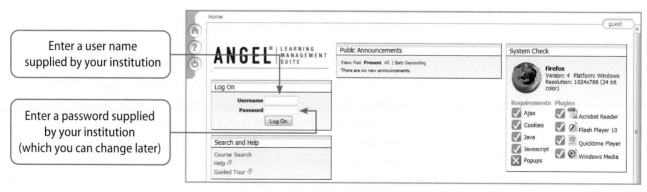

Figure 12 Your instructor will provide you with a user name and password.

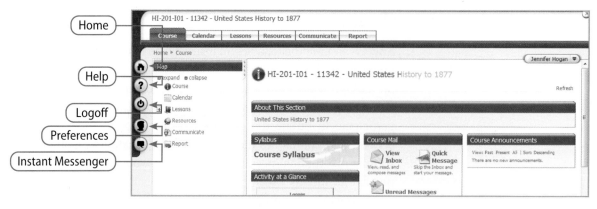

Figure 13 The Angel interface enables you to select from various options.

What Are the Icons on the Left Side of My Angel Course Page?

As shown in Figure 13, the icons enable you to navigate back to the Home page, seek Help, log off, set personal preferences, and engage in instant messaging.

Where Can I Find the Course Syllabus?

After clicking a course from the list on the left of your Home page, the Course tab will be selected, as shown in Figure 14. Most likely, your instructor has made the course syllabus available, so you can simply click the **Course Syllabus** link.

How Can I Return to a Previously Viewed Page?

Click the browser **Back button** (or click an item in the breadcrumb trail to which you want to go) to return to a previously viewed page.

What Are the Links at the Top of My Course Page?

Typically, you will see six links at the top of a course page, as shown in Figure 14.

- Click **Course** to display the Home page for a course. From the Home page, you can access the syllabus, your e-mail inbox, and any other resources your instructor makes available.
- Click **Calendar** to display important dates for the course. The calendar can display in either a grid (similar to a wall calendar) or a list fashion.
- Click **Lessons** to access course material, including videos, assignments, assessments, and drop boxes. Usually organized in folders, the Lessons area is where the bulk of course activity takes place.
- Click **Resources** to access the class syllabus and links to institutional resources. Your institution will most likely have the Resources page customized to include relevant resources and components.
- Click **Communicate** to access class e-mail, course news, discussion forums, and possibly Live Chat.
- Click **Report** to view the Reports Console, which enables you to create reports on your course activity. You can create a report of your grades here, as well.

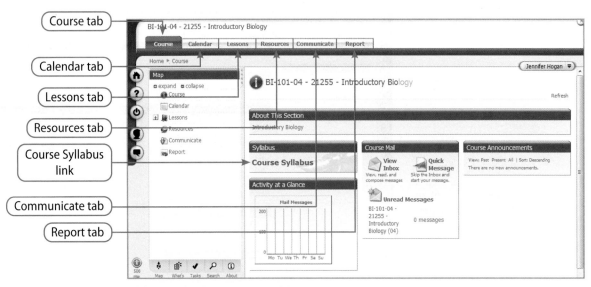

Course tab

Calendar tab

Lessons tab

Resources tab

Course Syllabus link

Communicate tab

Report tab

Figure 14 Click a tab to move to another class area.

How Do I E-mail My Instructor or Another Student?

Click **Communicate**, as shown in Figure 14. Click **Quick Message** and then click **To:**. In the Quick Search box, click **the letter that begins the last name** of the person to whom you want to send an e-mail. Select a recipient and click **To:** (Figure 15). Click **OK**. Click in the **Message area**, type the message, and click **Send**.

How Can I View Class Announcements?

Class Announcements are typically available to two places in Angel, from the Course tab and from the Communicate tab. You can view Past, Present, or All announcements by clicking a link under the Course Announcements tab, as shown in Figure 16.

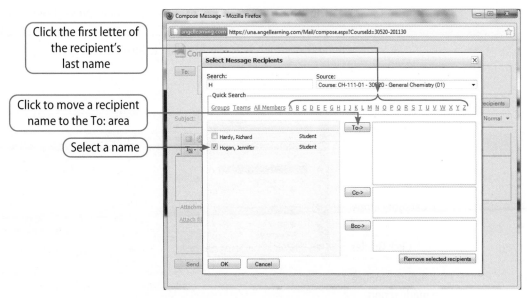

Click the first letter of the recipient's last name

Click to move a recipient name to the To: area

Select a name

Figure 15 You can send e-mail to your instructor or a student in class.

Figure 16 Your instructor will post important class information in announcements.

How Do I Take an Exam?

Depending upon how an exam is configured, it is most often located in the Lessons folder. Click **Lessons** and then click the **exam link**. Read any instructions from your instructor and then click **Begin Now**. Complete the exam and then click **Submit**.

How Can I Check My Grades?

Click **Report**, as shown in Figure 14. Click the **Category arrow** shown in Figure 17 and click **Grades**. Click **Run**.

How Can I Participate in a Class Discussion?

Click **Communicate**, as shown in Figure 18 and then click **a Discussion Forum** that your instructor has posted. Click **New Post** and type a title and your response. If you want to add an attachment, click **add a file**, browse for the file, and double-click the file. Click **Submit**.

Category arrow

Click **Grades**

Click **Run** to produce a grade report

Figure 17 Angel makes it easy to view your grades.

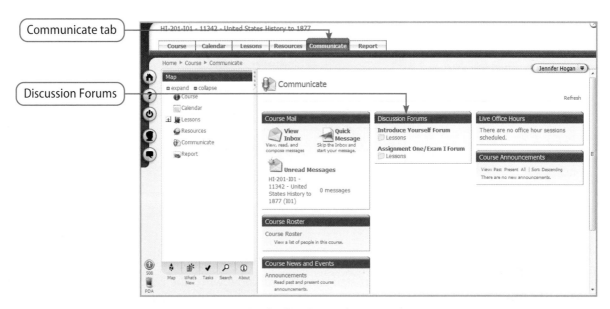

Figure 18 You can participate in a class discussion.

Moodle

Moodle enables students and instructors to access course content online. Instructors can upload course material, collect assignments, post exams, communicate with students, and include links to media and other websites. Students can communicate with instructors and other students, participate in chat sessions and class discussions, take exams, submit assignments, and access course material. In this section, you will be introduced to Moodle components, exploring Moodle's use in a typical class.

How Can I Log In to My Class?

Your college has provided a user name and password for you to use in logging in to your Moodle course website. Your instructor will provide the URL as well as login information. When you visit the website, you will enter your user name and password as shown in Figure 19. After logging in, click the course from the list on the left.

What If I Do Not See My Class Listed?

Your college or instructor must make a class available before you are able to see it listed. It is possible that the class will not be available until the first class day. Check your syllabus or college's support website for information related to course

Figure 19 Log in using a user name and password provided by your instructor or institution.

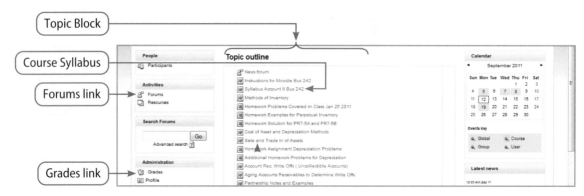

Figure 20 Moodle is organized in Blocks.

availability. Your instructor or a member of your college's educational software support staff can let you know when the course will be available or what might be preventing you from accessing the course.

May I Access Moodle on a Mobile Device Like My iPhone?

Moodle provides a Moodle Mobile service that enables you to log in to a Moodle class from a mobile device. Visit http://docs.moodle.org/20/en/Mobile_Moodle_FAQ for information on Moodle Mobile.

Where Can I Find the Course Syllabus?

The Home page contains a Topic Block, as shown in Figure 20. The Topic Block is often grouped into major categories. Class material, including the course syllabus, is typically placed in the Topic Block. Click a syllabus link, if provided, to view the syllabus.

How Can I Check My Grades?

Click **Grades** in the Administration Block (Figure 20).

How Can I Participate in a Discussion?

Click **Forums** in the Activities Block (Figure 20). Click **News forum** and then click **an underlined post** that you want to read or respond to. If you want to reply to the post, click **Reply**. Type a response in the Message area. If you want to attach a file, click **Browse**, navigate to the file, and double-click it. Click **Post to forum**.

How Can I Post a New Discussion Topic?

Click **Forums** in the Activities Block, as shown in Figure 20. Click **News forum** and then click **Add a new topic**, as shown in Figure 21. Type a Subject, click in the **Message area** and type the post. Click **Post to forum**.

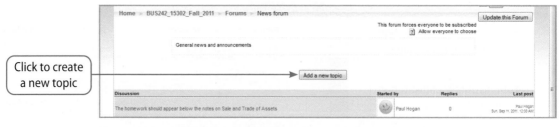

Figure 21 You can post a new discussion in Moodle.

Click to check your inbox

E-mail list Block

Click to compose an e-mail

Figure 22   Using Moodle, you can send and receive e-mail (within the class).

How Can I Send E-mail to My Instructor or Other Students?

If your instructor has made available the E-mail list Block, click **Compose**, as shown in Figure 22. Click **Contacts** and click **To:** beside each recipient's name. Click **Close this window**. Click **Browse** if you want to add an attachment, navigate to the file, and double-click it. Type your message and click **Send**.

How Can I Check My E-mail?

If your instructor has made available the E-mail list Block, click **Inbox**, as shown in Figure 22. Click the **underlined subject** of an e-mail to read. Click **Reply** or **Reply All** to respond to the sender (or to all of those who were also copied on the original message you received). Click in the **Message area**, type a response, and click **Send**.

How Can I Return to a Page I Previously Viewed?

Click a breadcrumb, as shown in Figure 23, to backtrack to a previously viewed page, or click the browser's Back button.

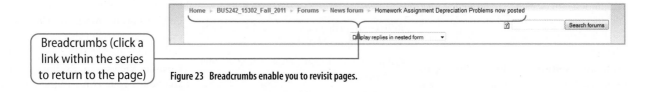

Breadcrumbs (click a link within the series to return to the page)

Figure 23   Breadcrumbs enable you to revisit pages.

Glossary

Absolute reference—a cell address that does not change, even if it is included in a formula that is copied elsewhere.

Active cell—the selected cell in an Excel worksheet.

Active window—the window that displays above all other open windows on the Windows desktop; the window that is selected.

ActiveX Filtering—Internet Explorer feature that allows only approved sites to run ActiveX controls.

Address bar—a bar displayed in a browser window and at the top of every folder shown in Windows Explorer that enables the user to type the address of a website to visit.

Adobe Premiere Elements—image editing software produced by Adobe and marketed to consumer photo enthusiasts.

Adobe Premiere Pro—image editing software produced by Adobe, marketed to professional photographers and graphic design artists.

Aero Flip 3D—Windows 7 feature that displays a continuous cascade of open windows, enabling you to select any one as the active window.

Aero Peek—Windows 7 feature that shows the contents of an open window in a thumbnail when you point to a taskbar icon; it also shows the desktop when you point to the Show desktop button.

Aggregator—software that displays an RSS feed to which you have subscribed.

Alignment—the position of a line or text paragraph related to the left, right, or center of a page, or cell.

Analog—data that is recorded as a continuous wave.

Animation—on-screen movement that includes entrance, exit, and emphasis effects of slide elements such as titles, bullets, and objects.

Antivirus software—software that scans your computer periodically for viruses, removing any that are identified (or alerting you of other options).

Application software—software that enables you to enjoy tasks and activities on a computer, such as word processing and games.

Argument—cell addresses, or contents, that are included in a parenthetical section of a function.

ARPANET—the forerunner of the current Internet, designed to advance communication between government and scientific organizations.

Attachment—a saved file, such as a photograph or document, that is located on your computer system and sent along with an e-mail to a recipient.

Audio—a sound file.

Backbone—a network core composed of high-capacity communication devices.

Background—the base color, or image, displayed on the desktop (behind the icons).

Backstage view—a collection of common actions and settings related to the current presentation, document, or workbook.

Backup—a copy of a file or folder.

Bandwidth—the rate at which signals can travel through a medium, such as cable or DSL.

Blog—an electronic journal posted on the Internet by an individual or group.

Blogger—someone who posts to a blog.

Bookmark—a URL stored for quick retrieval at a later date, sometimes called a Favorite.

Boolean searching—the use of AND, OR, and NOT operators to significantly narrow a Web search.

Broadband—high-speed data transmission, usually in the form of cable or DSL Internet connection.

Broadcast—to make a presentation available on the Internet to audience members in far-flung geographic locations or even those in the same building.

Browser—software that displays the Internet on a computer.

Bullet—a small graphic used to set items apart from other text.

Cable—Internet connection using a cable modem and cable to provide fast access.

CAT 5 Ethernet cable—a form of twisted wire cable that is an industry standard for network and telephone wiring.

CD (compact disc)—a common form of optical disc storage, capable of holding data, graphics, or music.

Cell—the intersection of a column and row in an Excel worksheet.

Cell address—the location of a cell within a worksheet, identified by the column letter and row number (as in cell A5).

Chart—a graphic diagram used to convey numeric information in an understandable way.

Chat room—a form of instant messaging that can include unidentified users discussing a particular subject.

Client—a computer that requests and receives information over a network.

Client-server network—a network in which a central computer (server) handles all of the network's security and file-sharing requests, communicating with connected client computers.

Clip art—an electronic illustration (non-photographic drawing) that is available both online (in Microsoft's clip art gallery) and within a built-in library in a typical PowerPoint, Word, or Excel installation.

Clipboard—a holding area in RAM for items that have been cut or copied and are awaiting pasting in another location.

Close—to remove a window from memory (but not from disk).

Cloud computing—using the Internet as a host for certain services, such as file storage or remote applications.

Computer—an electronic device that inputs data and processes the data into output.

Contextual tab—a tab on the Ribbon that includes one or more groups of commands related to a selected object.

Cookies—text files stored on a user's computer, most often identifying the user and keeping track of his or her online preferences.

Copy—to select text or an object and duplicate it to the Clipboard.

CPU (Central Processing Unit)—the processor, a component that accepts, evaluates, and acts on instructions found in software.

Custom Views—an Excel view in which you design your own settings related to how a worksheet appears on-screen.

Cut—to select text or an object and move it to the Clipboard so it is no longer found at the original location.

Data file—a file that contains various types of information, such as a document, workbook, or photograph; created by a user when working with an application program.

Data packet—a basic unit of information sent over a network.

Datasheet—a table in which data is entered in columns and rows.

Decision-support software—a capability of Excel to model different scenarios, projecting various outcomes based on adjusted variables.

Default—a setting that is assumed unless you specify otherwise.

Defragment—to rewrite a file so it is no longer broken into pieces on a disk.

Desktop—the screen, often containing icons and a taskbar, that is displayed when a computer is turned on.

Desktop computer—a personal computer in which all components, including the keyboard, mouse, monitor, and system unit, are not easily portable; instead the computer remains stationary on a desktop.

Details pane—an area displayed at the bottom of a Windows Explorer window when a file or folder is selected, providing such details as a file name, file size, and author.

Device Stage—a Windows 7 feature that simplifies the management of peripherals.

Dial-up—a seldom-used Internet connection that enables a computer to transmit Internet data over a standard telephone line.

Digital—data that is stored in the form of ones and zeroes (binary digits).

Digital camcorder—a digital video camera designed to record motion images.

Digital camera—a camera that captures images and saves them to flash memory so you can download photos to a computer and manage them with a graphics program.

Digital single lens reflex (DSLR) camera—a digital camera that includes interchangeable lenses and more features than a consumer model camera.

Digital zoom—a zoom setting that crops a photo and then enlarges the image mathematically using interpolation.

Disk Cleanup—a Windows utility that removes unnecessary files, such as those in the Recycle Bin, so more disk space is available.

Disk Defragmenter—a Windows 7 utility that optimizes a disk so that files are not as fragmented.

Domain name—the address of an Internet site, composed of at least two parts, separated by a dot (as in www.nwscc.org).

Domain Name System (DNS)—the provision of domain names, which are used to identify one or more IP addresses.

Downloading—the transfer of electronic data from a Web server to a personal computer.

Draft view—a Word view in which margins, headers, footers, graphics, and other page features are not displayed.

Driver—a program that manages the functioning of a peripheral device, such as a printer or scanner.

DSL—a technology that increases the digital capacity of telephone lines, facilitating Internet communication as well as voice traffic.

DVD (digital video disc or digital versatile disc)—a common form of optical disc storage, capable of holding data, graphics, or music.

E-mail—an electronic message sent over the Internet or other network.

Encryption—encoding sensitive data that is being sent across a network so that a hacker cannot read the data without an encryption key.

Error Checking Utility—a Windows 7 utility that checks for disk errors, correcting any if possible.

EULA (end user license agreement)—a software license agreement spelling out terms of use.

Evil twin—a Wi-Fi hotspot that appears to be legitimate but that has been created by a hacker so that transmitted data can be compromised.

Facebook—a social network that enables users to connect with friends, posting comments and photographs.

Favorite—a URL stored for quick retrieval at a later date, sometimes called a bookmark.

Feed—a free online service that provides subscribers a short summary of a feed as soon as an update is available.

File compression software—utility software, such as WinZip, that compresses a file so it requires less storage software.

Fill handle—an Excel cell feature located in the lower-right corner of a cell or selection, which when dragged, causes cell or range data to be copied.

Firewall—software or hardware configured to prevent unauthorized access to or from a computer or computer network.

First Line Indent—a Word indent setting in which the first line of a paragraph is indented by a specified amount of space.

Flash drive—a small portable flash memory unit that plugs into a computer's USB port; also called a thumb drive or USB drive.

Flash memory—a form of storage that is neither magnetic nor optical and has no moving parts.

Folder—a holding area on a disk storage medium designed to organize files and other folders.

Follower—a person who reads the posts on Twitter of others.

Font—a particular typeface design.

Footer—text or graphic that appears in the bottom margin of every page of a document (unless you specify that it is to only occur on certain pages).

Formula—a combination of cell references and arithmetic operators that identifies how data in a specific cell is to be calculated.

Formula Bar—an area that displays the contents of the active cell in an Excel worksheet or the formula that produces results in the active cell.

Fragmented—a file that has been separated into parts as it was saved.

Frame—a still photo included in a series of multiple still pictures that, when combined and put into motion, creates a video.

Frame rate—the number of frames per second.

Freeware—software that is free for an unlimited period of time.

Friend—a person you choose to communicate with through a site such as Facebook.

FTP (File Transfer Protocol)—a method of communication for transferring data files from one computer to another on the Internet.

Full Screen Reading view—a Word view that displays a document as it would print but without the Ribbon, with multiple pages side by side, much as you would read a book.

Full Screen view—an Excel view that hides the Ribbon, Formula Bar, and Name Box features, as well as the status bar.

Function—a predefined formula that simplifies a lengthy or complicated formula.

Gadget—an on-screen item that provides information on data that changes, such as the weather or a calendar, or that provides access to a game or tool.

Gallery—a collection of items or formats that can be selected within an application.

Gateway—a device that connects any combination of LANS, WANS, and the Internet.

Gigahertz (GHz)—a measurement of processor speed, equating to one billion hertz (cycles per second).

Goal Seek—an Excel feature that enables you to set a goal and see how variables must be modified to achieve that goal.

Graphical user interface (GUI)—a visual environment in which you use a mouse to make selections and give commands.

Gridline—a horizontal or vertical border separating cells within an Excel worksheet or a table.

Hacker—a person who gains access to a computer or computer network without permission.

Handle—a small box or dot that appears on the outline of a selected graphic; by dragging a handle, you can resize an object.

Hanging indent—an indent setting in which the first line of a paragraph is not indented, but every other line within a paragraph is indented by a specific amount.

Hard drive—a form of magnetic disk storage with large capacity, often located within a computer, although external hard drives are also available.

Hard return—a forced return within a document that is initiated in Word when you press Enter.

Hardware—computer equipment that can be touched, such as the keyboard, monitor, and mouse.

Header—text or a graphic that appears in the top margin of every page of a document (unless you specify that it is to only occur on certain pages). A header typically includes identifying information such as a page number or author name.

History—a list of Web pages visited during a specified interval of time.

Home page—the first page displayed when accessing a website.

HTTP (Hypertext Transfer Protocol)—the method of communication used to connect to a server and then transfer HTML pages to a computer user's browser.

HTTPS (Hypertext Transfer Protocol over Secure Sockets Layer)—a secure version of HTTP; the protocol that should be in place before you transmit sensitive information online, such as a credit card or other personally identifying information.

Hub—an inexpensive device, with little routing capability, that enables computers to transmit data along a network.

Hyperlink—text or a graphic on a Web page that, when clicked, transfers the view to another Web page or area.

Icon—a small on-screen picture representing an object, such as a document, program, folder, or system resource.

IEEE 802.11 standard—a wireless router standard that facilitates wireless data transfer.

Image editing software—software that enables you to modify pictures—cropping, brightening, or otherwise enhancing them.

iMovie '11—image editing software included in the iLife suite.

Indent—a set amount of space from the left or right margins of a document, applied to individual paragraphs.

Inkjet printer—the most common type of consumer printer, in which characters are formed by spraying very fine drops of ink on a sheet of paper.

InPrivate Browsing—an Internet Explorer feature that prevents your browsing history, form data, cookies, and user names and passwords from being retained by the browser.

Input—data that is communicated to the computer through a device such as a mouse or the keyboard.

Insertion point—a blinking vertical line that indicates the current position in a document.

Install—the process of placing program files on a computer, typically accomplished by inserting a program CD in a CD drive and then responding to a series of prompts.

Instant messaging (IM)—also known as online chat, a form of online real-time communication.

Integrated phone—a phone that combines features of a mobile phone, camera, e-mail, address book, task list, calendar, and Web browsing into one multifunction unit.

Internet—a large system of computer networks that provides access to commercial, academic, and government information.

Internet backbone—the physical network that provides a connection between other computers and networks on the Internet.

Internet Corporation for Assigned Names and Numbers (ICANN)—a non-profit international association that manages Internet address and domain names.

Internet Engineering Task Force (IETF)—an international organization composed of several working groups with the goal of maintaining the Internet's architecture and stability.

Internet Protocol (IP) address—a string of digits representing the unique address of a Web page.

Internet Service Provider (ISP)—an entity that provides routers and cable that make up the Internet backbone; an ISP serves as a gateway to the Internet for customers.

iPod—a portable media player produced by Apple.

Keyboard—the primary input device for a microcomputer, consisting of a grid of keys representing letters, numbers, and special characters.

Keyword—a term on which you can base an Internet search.

Landscape—the orientation of a document so that it is wider than it is tall.

Laptop computer—a portable computer that integrates a monitor, keyboard, memory, disk storage devices, and a pointing device into a battery-operated package.

Laser printer—a high-speed printer that uses a laser to electrostatically adhere an image on a rotating drum and then transfers the image to paper.

LCD—a monitor that uses liquid crystals to project an image; a typical laptop monitor is an example of an LCD.

Left Indent—a Word indent setting in which a paragraph is indented a specified distance from the left margin.

Library—a collection of folders and subfolders that share a common purpose.

Light-emitting diode (LED)—a semiconductor light source technology used to transmit mouse movement in a remote mouse, causing a corresponding shift of the on-screen pointer.

Line spacing—space between lines in a paragraph in a Word document or PowerPoint presentation.

Link—See hyperlink.

LinkedIn—a social networking site aimed at building professional networks for career-related purposes.

Linux—an open-source operating system that can be installed on a microcomputer.

Live Preview—a feature applicable to certain formatting options in Office 2007 and Office 2010 that enables you to instantly see the effect of a potential formatting choice when you point to the choice without clicking.

Local Area Network (LAN)—computers and networked equipment located within a small geographic area, usually a home or building.

Mac OS—the operating system used for personal computers produced by Apple.

Mac OS X—an operating system unique to Apple computers.

Mac OS X Lion—the newest version of Mac OS X.

Magnetic disk storage—storage in which data is represented as magnetic spots on one or more rotating disks or platters.

Mainframe—a powerful, expensive computer that can handle large amounts of data for businesses or sizable organizations.

Malvertisement—an online marketing ploy that actually delivers malicious content to visitors' systems through links on what appear to be legitimate websites.

Malware—programs, such as viruses, worms, Trojan horses, and spyware that are designed to cause damage to a computer or electronic device.

Margin—the space left at the top, bottom, right, and left side of a document.

Maximize—to cause a window to fill the screen.

Megahertz (MHz)—a measurement of processor speed, equating to one million hertz (cycles per second).

Megapixel—the equivalent of one million pixels; a measurement of the clarity of images captured by a digital camera.

Memory—also called RAM (random access memory), a temporary holding area for data and programs currently in use.

Microblog—a short blog usually containing a post about what is happening in the blogger's life at that moment.

Microprocessor—the hardware unit that houses the CPU.

Microsoft Excel 2010—the version of Excel included in Microsoft Office 2010.

Microsoft Office 2010—the newest version of Microsoft Office.

Microsoft PowerPoint 2010—the version of PowerPoint included in Microsoft 2010.

Microsoft Web Apps—a feature that not only lets you store Office 2010 files online, but also enables you to open those files in a Web version of PowerPoint, Word, or Excel.

Microsoft Windows—an operating system produced by Microsoft.

Microsoft Word 2010—the version of Word included in Microsoft Office 2010.

Microsoft Works—a product that includes word processing functionality, along with other components that address specific categories of tasks, such as keeping a calendar and building worksheets.

Mini toolbar—a semi-transparent toolbar containing formatting options that can be applied to selected text.

Minimize—to reduce the window to a button on the taskbar without actually closing the window.

Mixed reference—an Excel formula in which either the cell or row reference is absolute, while other components remain relative.

Mobile phone—a phone that connects wirelessly to a communications network through radio wave or satellite transmission.

Monitor—the television-like component of a microcomputer that is a primary output device.

Mouse—a common input device that works by rolling across a surface, with corresponding movement of a pointer on-screen.

Multifunction device—a device with the ability to scan, print, and sometimes fax, often found in home offices.

Name Box—a feature that indicates the position of the active cell in Excel; it is located just above the workspace in an Excel worksheet.

Navigation Pane—the area on the left side of a Windows Explorer window that contains a list of folders and drives.

Netbook—a small, lightweight, inexpensive computer whose primary purpose is to connect to the Internet and use e-mail; a netbook does not have the computing power or all of the features of a laptop or desktop.

Network architecture—the configuration of a communication network.

Network interface card (NIC)—a hardware device that enables a computer to access the Internet wirelessly.

Network service set identifier (SSID)—the name assigned to a wireless network.

Networking—a configuration of equipment that facilitates communication and the exchange of information by linking one or more computers and peripheral devices.

Normal view—a PowerPoint view in which the current slide is displayed in a large format.

Notebook computer—See laptop computer.

Notes Page view—a view that displays not only individual slides but also accompanying notes in Microsoft PowerPoint.

Notes pane—an area in the PowerPoint Notes Page view and Normal view, at the bottom of the current pane, where the user can type notes that he or she can refer to when making presentation.

Object—an item, such as a picture, table, or chart that is included in a document, worksheet, presentation slide show, or other data file.

One Box—an Internet Explorer feature that integrates addresses and searches into one area.

Online—connected to the Internet.

Operating system—system software that coordinates system activities, including communication between the user and application software, or computer programs.

Optical disc storage—storage, such as a CD or DVD, in which a laser beam is used to read and write data.

Optical resolution—the measurement of resolution that can be captured by a digital camera.

Optical zoom—the magnification of an image using the optics (curvature) of a camera's lens, giving a true reproduction.

Order of operations (order of precedence)—the order in which mathematical operations are evaluated when more than one operator is present within a formula in an Excel worksheet cell.

Output—information that is produced by a computer and shown by a device such as a monitor or printer.

Outline view—a Word view that provides a hierarchical view of a document, with all headings and levels of detail.

Page border—a line or graphic that surrounds a page.

Page Break Preview—an Excel view that displays page breaks as blue lines.

Page Layout view—an Excel view that shows a worksheet as it will appear when printed.

Paragraph spacing—the amount of space between paragraphs.

Paste—to place a selection that was previously cut or copied into a document, worksheet, or presentation.

Peer-to-peer network (P2P)—a network that links two or more computers without going through a central server.

Peripheral—a device, such as a printer or mouse, that can be connected to your computer.

Personal Computer (PC)—a computer designed for individual use, providing access to the Internet and enabling a user to work with application software.

Phishing—sending an e-mail to someone falsely, usually claiming to be a legitimate financial institution, in an effort to obtain private information for the purpose of identity theft.

Photo sharing site—a website that makes it easy to share photos with friends and family and to create photo projects, such as calendars and cards.

Photoshop—full-featured image editing software favored by professional photographers and graphic design artists.

Photoshop Elements—similar to Photoshop image editing software, but less full-featured and more affordable for a consumer photo enthusiast.

Picture—a photograph or clip art image stored on a disk.

Picasa—free image editing software provided by Google.

Pixel—a single dot on a graphic display, which when combined with other pixels, creates an image or screen display.

Placeholder—an area on a PowerPoint slide that provides space for and determines the position and format of slide content.

Plugin—an add-on program that adds functionality, such as enhanced audio or video.

Podcast—audio or video files that can be downloaded from the Internet or otherwise copied and then played on a computer or portable media player.

Point-and-shoot camera—a simple-to-use lightweight digital camera that is appropriate for the typical consumer, as opposed to a professional photographer.

Portable media player (PMP)—a small handheld device that plays audio (and sometimes video) files.

Portrait—the orientation of a document so that it is taller than it is wide.

Presentation software—software used to prepare computer slide shows, which are consecutively displayed screens of information.

Preview pane—a Windows Explorer pane that shows a preview of a selected file.

Print Layout view—a Word view that shows how a document will print, with margins, headers, footers, and graphics displayed.

Printer—a peripheral device that prints documents and other files.

Processor—the hardware unit that controls all activity of a computer system.

Profile—information, such as your hometown, profession, and birth date, that you make available on your personal social networking account.

Program file—a file that contains program instructions that cause tasks to run on a computer.

Protocol—a hardware or software standard that coordinates data transmission between computers.

Quick Access Toolbar—a toolbar containing commonly accessed commands such as Save and Undo, located on the left end of the Title bar of a Microsoft Office application.

RAM (random access memory)—See memory.

Range—one or more cells in an Excel worksheet arranged in a rectangular fashion that can be referred to as a group.

Reader—See aggregator.

Reading view—a PowerPoint view in which a slide occupies the entire screen but still displays the Title bar, status bar, and Windows taskbar.

Real-time—communication that occurs synchronously online, like a face-to-face conversation, as opposed to an e-mail, which occurs asynchronously.

Resolution—the sharpness of an image on a printer, monitor, or digital camera—determined in part by the number of pixels in a grid.

Restore down—to return a window to its original, possibly less-than-full-size appearance.

Ribbon—the bar above an Office application window that displays grouped tabs including common commands.

Right Indent—a Word indent setting in which a paragraph is indented a specified distance from the right margin.

Rip—to copy music from a CD into another format, such as MP3.

ROM (read-only memory)—memory that can be read from, but not written to; its purpose is to perform basic system diagnostics and provide boot-up instructions.

Router—a network device that coordinates communication between networks.

RSS—Web technology in which news and other content is pushed out to a subscriber of a site.

Ruler—vertical and horizontal measures that can be displayed along a Word document to assist in setting tabs, indents, and vertical spacing.

Sampling rate—the number of samples per second that are used to convert from analog to digital sound.

Spam—unsolicited, and usually unwanted, e-mail.

Spyware—a form of malware that collects personal information about you and your surfing habits without your knowledge; it can also cause pop-up ads to appear and can change your browser settings.

Supercomputer—the fastest computer in existence, usually focusing on a single application such as weather forecasting or astrophysics.

Switch—a hardware device that sorts and distributes data packets between devices on a LAN(local area network).

System software—software, such as an operating system and utility software, that coordinates hardware and manages machine operations such as antivirus scanning and file compression.

System unit—the rectangular case that houses hardware components, such as the processor, memory, and disk drives.

Satellite—a form of Internet access that uses satellites to connect computers to the Internet.

Screen saver—a constantly moving image that appears when there has been no activity on a computer for a period of time.

ScreenTip—a short description of a screen item that appears when the mouse pointer is held steady over an option.

Search box—a text box located on the Start menu and in a Windows Explorer window, in which you can type any part of a file name, file contents, or tag to help locate a file or folder.

Search engine—software that searches the Internet for data based on search criteria specified by a user.

Secure Sockets Layer (SSL)—an industry standard protocol that encrypts (converts data into a coded form) the transfer of private or sensitive information, guarding against interception, and protecting data integrity.

Server—a computer that coordinates traffic between computers and provides essential network services, enabling linked computers to communicate and share data.

Shareware—software that is available to download so you can try the program for a limited time before you decide whether to purchase it.

Shortcut—a pointer on the desktop that provides access to a program or resource.

SkyDrive—a Microsoft file hosting service that provides up to 25 GB of free online storage space.

Slide—a single page of a PowerPoint presentation.

Slide layout—a PowerPoint slide format that is designed to contain specific content or objects.

Slide show—a progression of slides included in a PowerPoint presentation, often displayed for an audience.

Slide Sorter view—a PowerPoint view showing thumbnails of slides included in a presentation.

SmartArt—a feature that makes it easy to develop graphics that illustrate processes, lists, and relationships.

Smartphone—See integrated phone.

SmartScreen Filter—an Internet Explorer feature that helps detect phishing websites and protects you from downloading or installing malware.

Snap—a Windows 7 feature that enables you to position two windows (that are not already maximized) in an orderly arrangement on opposite sides of the desktop.

Social bookmarking—a site that enables users to share (or bookmark) online content they find interesting.

Social network—an online community of people with common interests, who connect with each other to share information and experiences.

Socially engineered malware—software, such as a virus or Trojan horse, that is designed to damage or disrupt a system.

Soft return—a code inserted into text by a word processor to mark the end of a line, where the word processor causes text to continue on the next line.

Software—a computer program used to direct the operation of equipment or to accomplish a task.

Software-as-a-service (SaaS)—software delivered through the Internet, usually at a much lower price than would be required for the purchase of a software license; SaaS is not installed on the recipient's computer or network—rather it is available for access online—and it is sometimes free.

Sparkline—new to Excel 2010, a small chart that fits inside a single cell.

Spider—a program that searches for information on the Internet based on search criteria specified by a computer user.

Spreadsheet—a grid, that may or may not be electronic, composed of a series of columns and rows.

Status bar—the horizontal bar that appears at the bottom of many software applications (such as Microsoft Office), giving information on document features and settings.

Subfolder—a folder located as a sublevel within another folder.

Subject directory—a searchable online directory that organizes websites by general subjects.

Subtitle—a heading shown as a sublevel of a major heading on a PowerPoint slide.

Surfing—aimlessly browsing the Web.

Syntax—rules related to the correct way to state or encode an item.

Tabbed browsing—having more than one Web page open at a time, with a tab representing each page.

Tab—a Ribbon group, such as the Insert tab, that includes related commands.

Table—data that is displayed in columns and rows.

Tablet PC—a wireless laptop computer model that enables a user to use either a finger or a stylus to communicate through a touch screen.

Tag—a custom file property that helps identify and categorize a file.

Taskbar—the horizontal bar, usually located at the bottom of the Windows 7 desktop, that includes the Start button, pinned programs, buttons for currently open programs, toolbars, and the Notification area.

TCP/IP (Transmission Control Protocol/ Internet Protocol)—a set of communication protocols used by the Internet, coordinating the transfer of data in units that are recognizable by both the sending and receiving device.

Tether—the process of connecting a camera to a computer's USB port through a cable, for the purpose of downloading pictures to the computer.

Text box—a rectangular area in which you can type text; a text box is treated as an object.

Theme—a collection of complementary colors, font, and alignment that can be applied to a PowerPoint slide or Word document.

Thumbnail—a miniature image of file or window contents.

Title—a major heading in a PowerPoint slide.

Title bar—the horizontal bar located at the top of a window, containing the name of the application and the file name.

Title slide—most often the first slide in a PowerPoint presentation, including a major title and an optional subtitle.

Toolbar—a bar that provides easy access to common tasks; various toolbars exist related to the particular application or operating system in which a toolbar is found.

Top-level domain—the characters of a domain name shown after the last period; they most often represent the purpose of the organization that sponsors the website.

Tracking Protection—an Internet Explorer feature that limits a browser's communication with certain websites, effectively blocking most malicious third-party links.

Transition—visual effects that appear between slides in a slide show, such as fading or dissolving.

Trojan horse—a form of malware that masquerades as a useful program when it is instead destructive.

Tweet—a post that a Twitter user creates, containing status updates or other comments.

Twitter—a microblogging and social networking site used by private individuals, celebrities, and even businesses.

Typeface—the design of a set of printed characters.

Uninstall—to remove software from a computer.

Uploading—the process of transferring a file from a personal computer to a Web server.

URL (Uniform Resource Locator)— a unique Internet address, comprising a string of characters; for example, http://www .whitehouse.gov.

User account—a set of permissions associated with a user name and password.

Utility software—a type of system software that addresses system tasks such as file compression and virus protection.

Video—images that are recorded in motion.

View—the way an application window appears, such as Print Layout or Draft.

Virus—a purposely written program designed to cause harm to a computer or its contents.

Vlog—short for video blog, a blog that displays video instead of text.

Voice over Internet Protocol (VoIP)— technology that enables you to make phone calls through a broadband Internet connection.

Watermark—a text or picture that appears behind document text.

Web authoring tool—software that enables Web pages to be created visually, producing underlying HTML code.

Web crawler—See spider.

Web Layout view—a Word view that displays a document as it would appear as a Web page.

Web page—a Web document that is identified by a particular URL.

Web scripting program—a programming language that is used to design and develop Web pages and to communicate with Internet resources.

Webcast—audio and video files broadcast over the Internet.

Webinar—a Web-based seminar or online lesson.

Website—a collection of one or more Web pages.

WEP—a wireless encryption standard that is not as secure as WPA or WPA2.

What-if analysis—an Excel feature that summarizes data in various scenarios to help you make the best decision.

Wide Area Network (WAN)—a geographically dispersed computer network.

Wi-Fi (wireless fidelity)—See IEEE 802.11 standard.

Wi-Fi hotspot—a location providing wireless Internet access to mobile computer users, sometimes free of charge.

Wildcard—a character used in a search that indicates anything; an asterisk represents any number of consecutive characters, while a question mark represents any one character.

Wiki—a collaborative website that enables users to share ideas and information with one another.

Window—a rectangular area that represents a computer application or resource.

Windowing environment—an operating system environment in which open applications, folders, and certain system resources are each shown in a boxed area called a window.

Windows 7—the Microsoft Windows operating system version that was released in 2009.

Windows 7 Home Premium—Windows 7 edition that focuses on the home computer market, including multimedia features.

Windows 7 Professional—Windows 7 edition that focuses on small business use and the interests of computer enthusiasts. It includes all of the features of Windows Home Premium in addition to basic networking and encryption capability.

Windows 7 Ultimate—Windows 7 edition designed to support large business applications, including advanced networking and multi-language features.

Windows Anytime Upgrade—a feature included with most versions of Windows 7 that enables you to acquire a more advanced Windows edition through a simple Internet download and purchase.

Windows Defender—software included with Windows 7 and Windows Vista that identifies and removes malware from a computer system.

Windows Live—a free collection of services and programs that coordinates to provide a complete package of entertainment and productivity software, communication, and file management.

Windows Live Movie Maker 2011—free video management software included with Windows Live Essentials.

Windows Live Photo Gallery 2011—free image editing software included with Windows Live Essentials.

Windows Starter—a limited Windows edition that is often preinstalled on netbooks.

Wireless—communication that occurs when electromagnetic waves carry a signal over part or all of a communication channel.

Wireless air card—a device that uses cell phone frequencies, providing Internet access wherever a cellular signal can be obtained.

Wireless Access Point (WAP)—a device that enables wireless devices, such as a laptop or e-reader, to connect to a wired network.

Wireless network adapter—a hardware device that connects a computer to a network wirelessly.

Wireless router—a device that coordinates signals from your Internet connection into a wireless broadcast, enabling multiple computers to use the same Internet connection.

Word processing—software that creates, edits, and prints documents.

Word wrap—a word processing feature that causes text to fit automatically between margins.

WordPerfect Office—a comprehensive productivity software suite marketed by Corel.

Workbook—an Excel file that can include multiple worksheets.

Workgroup—a collection of computers on a network that shares resources.

Worksheet—a table of items arranged in a grid of rows and columns.

World Wide Web—a subset of the Internet making broad use of hyperlinks so you can easily move among websites by clicking sites.

World Wide Web Consortium (W3C)—the leading organization that creates Web standards and develops specifications, guidelines, software, and tools for use on the Internet.

Worm—a form of malware that sends copies of itself to other computers without your awareness or involvement.

WPA—a secure encryption standard used in a Wi-Fi network.

WPA2—a secure encryption standard used in a Wi-Fi network; however, it may not work well with older network adapters.

YouTube—a popular video sharing site owned by Google.

Zoom Slider—an Office 2010 feature that enables you to slide a tab along a slider (located at the lower-right corner of the Office interface) to enlarge or reduce the view of text.

Index